This book offers new perspectives on the legal and intellectual develop-ments of the twelfth century. Gratian's collection of church law, the *Decretum*, was a key text in these developments. Compiled in around 1140, it remained a fundamental work on ecclesiastical law throughout and beyond the middle ages.

Until now, the many mysteries surrounding the creation of the *Decretum* have remained unsolved, thereby hampering exploration of the jurispru-dential renaissance of the twelfth century. Professor Winroth has now dis-covered the original version of the *Decretum*, which has long lain unnoticed among medieval manuscripts, and which is about half as long as the final text. It is also different from the final version in many respects – for example, with regard to the use of Roman law sources.

The resurgence of law in the twelfth century can now be reconsidered. For example, Gratian's efforts are placed in the context of contemporary explorations of Roman law, and the conclusion is drawn that the Law School at Bologna was not founded as early as had previously been thought.

ANDERS WINROTH is Assistant Professor of History, Yale University.

Cambridge Studies in Medieval Life and Thought
Fourth Series

General Editor:

D. E. LUSCOMBE
Leverhulme Personal Research Professor of Medieval History, University of Sheffield

Advisory Editors:

CHRISTINE CARPENTER
Reader in Medieval English History, University of Cambridge, and Fellow of New Hall

ROSAMOND McKITTERICK
*Professor of Medieval History, University of Cambridge,
and Fellow of Newnham College*

The series Cambridge Studies in Medieval Life and Thought was inaugurated by G. G. Coulton in 1921; Professor D. E. Luscombe now acts as General Editor of the Fourth Series, with Dr. Christine Carpenter and Professor Rosamond McKitterick as Advisory Editors. The series brings together outstanding work by medieval scholars over a wide range of human endeavour extending from political economy to the history of ideas.

For a list of titles in the series, see end of book.

THE MAKING OF
GRATIAN'S *DECRETUM*

ANDERS WINROTH

CAMBRIDGE
UNIVERSITY PRESS

PUBLISHED BY THE PRESS SYNDICATE OF THE UNIVERSITY OF CAMBRIDGE
The Pitt Building, Trumpington Street, Cambridge, United Kingdom

CAMBRIDGE UNIVERSITY PRESS
The Edinburgh Building, Cambridge CB2 2RU, UK   http://www.cup.cam.ac.uk
40 West 20th Street, New York, NY 10011-4211, USA   http://www.cup.org
10 Stamford Road, Oakleigh, Melbourne 3166, Australia
Ruiz de Alarcón 13, 28014 Madrid, Spain

© Cambridge University Press 2000

First published 2000

Printed in the United Kingdom at the University Press, Cambridge

Typeset in 11/12pt Monotype Bembo   [SE]

A catalogue record for this book is available from the British Library

Library of Congress Cataloguing in Publication data
Winroth, Anders.
The making of Gratian's Decretum / Anders Winroth.
p.   cm.
Includes bibliographical references and index.
ISBN 0 521 63264 1 (hb)
1. Gratian, 12th cent. Decretum.   2. Canon law – History.   I. Title.
LAW
262.9′22–dc21   00–025315   CIP

ISBN 0 521 63264 1 hardback

Till mormor och morfar

CONTENTS

ILLUSTRATIONS

TABLES

PREFACE

During the several years when I researched Gratian's *Decretum*, I incurred a number of scholarly and personal debts, which I am happy to acknowledge. In the first place, I want to thank my mentor, Robert Somerville, who supervised my dissertation at Columbia University and who continues to take great interest in my work. He has read the entire book in manuscript. His advice, support, and personal kindness over the years were and are invaluable and deeply appreciated. I owe him special thanks for putting his collection of microfilms of pre-Gratian canonical manuscripts at my disposal.

Rudolf Weigand of the University of Würzburg generously shared his enormous knowledge of the *Decretum* and the decretists, served on my dissertation committee, and continued to be a greatly valued discussion partner until shortly before his untimely death. I am particularly grateful to him for allowing me to use his large collection of microfilms of *Decretum* manuscripts. I am saddened that my thanks can no longer reach him.

Several fellow scholars very kindly put their unpublished materials at my disposal, and I want to thank them for their great generosity, and especially Martin Brett, Horst Fuhrmann, and Peter Landau. Many friends, colleagues, and teachers (most of whom would fit all three categories) helped me with intelligent criticism, valued information, stylistic advice, and encouragement. I want to thank Caroline Bynum, Raymond Clemens, Enrique De León, Gero Dolezalek, Carmela Franklin, Paul Freedman, Michael Galvin, Karen Green, Ingeborg Haazen, Jonas Hamilton, Bonnie Kent, Carlos Larrainzar, David Luscombe, R. I. Moore, Kenneth Pennington, José Miguel Viejo-Ximénez, and Jean Werckmeister.

I am also grateful to Jean Field for careful and efficient copy-editing.

I want to acknowledge financial support that made the research and writing of this book possible. Columbia University, the Fulbright

Commission in Stockholm, and the Centrala studiestödsnämnden of Sweden generously funded my dissertation work. The Sir James Knott Fellowship made possible two years of further research and writing at the University of Newcastle upon Tyne and the university additionally funded a research trip to Paris. The A. A. Heckman Fund financed research at the Hill Monastic Manuscript Library in Collegeville, Minnesota, and the A. Whitney Griswold Faculty Research Fund at Yale University contributed to some of the costs I had in finishing the manuscript. I am very grateful for the generosity of all of them, and also to three departments of history – in New York, Newcastle, and New Haven – for giving me institutional homes while I was working on this book

Pursuing a career in foreign countries has meant that I have been far away from my family and friends for long periods. They have all been missed, but I want to dedicate this book especially to my grandparents, Gun and Erik Winroth.

ABBREVIATIONS

AKKR	*Archiv für katholisches Kirchenrecht*
BAV	Biblioteca Apostolica Vaticana, Vatican City
BMCL	*Bulletin of Medieval Canon Law*, new series
BN	Bibliothèque Nationale de France
C.	*Causa*; subsection of Gratian's *Decretum*, part 2
c.	*canon* or *capitulum*
COD	Giuseppe Alberigo, ed., *Conciliorum oecumenicorum decreta*. 3rd edn. Bologna 1973
Cod.	The *Code* of Justinian
CSEL	Corpus scriptorum ecclesiasticorum latinorum
D.	*Distinctio*; subsection of Gratian's *Decretum*, part 1, and of *de penitentia* and *de consecratione*
d. a. c.	*dictum ante canonem*; for Gratian's commentary preceding a canon
d. init.	*dictum initiale*; for Gratian's case outline at the beginning of a *Causa*
d. p. c.	*dictum post canonem*; for Gratian's commentary following a canon
de cons.	*De consecratione*; Gratian's *Decretum*, part 3
de pen.	*De penitentia*; C. 33, q. 3 of Gratian's *Decretum*
JE, JK, JL	Philippus Jaffé, *Regesta pontificum Romanorum*. 2nd edn. [This edition was prepared under the auspices of Wilhelm Wattenbach, with the editorial assistance of Samuel Löwenfeld, Ferdinand Kaltenbrunner, and Paul Ewald. The work, thus, is cited as JK for letters up to 590, JE from 590 to 882, and JL from 883 to 1198, according to the reviser who worked on the section.]
MGH	Monumenta Germaniae Historica
MIC Subs.	Monumenta iuris canonici, series C: Subsidia

List of abbreviations

PL	J.-P. Migne, ed., *Patrologiae cursus completus, series latina*. Paris 1844–1855.
q.	*questio*; subsection of the *Causae* in Gratian's *Decretum*, part 2
RDC	*Revue de droit canonique*
ZRG KA	*Zeitschrift der Savigny-Stiftung für Rechtsgeschichte, Kanonistische Abteilung*
ZRG RA	*Zeitschrift der Savigny-Stiftung für Rechtsgeschichte, Romanistische Abteilung*

CONSPECTUS SIGLORUM

MANUSCRIPTS AND EDITIONS OF GRATIAN'S *DECRETUM*

Aa	Admont, Stiftsbibliothek 23 and 43. Austria, s. XII³ᐟ⁴.
Av	Abbeville, Bibliothèque municipale 33.
Bc	Barcelona, Arxiu de la Corona d'Aragó, Santa Maria de Ripoll 78. Italy, s. XII.
Bi	Biberach, Spitalsarchiv B 3515. Northern Italy, s. XII.
Br	Bremen, Staats- und Universitätsbibliothek a. 142. Written before 1168.
Cd	Cambridge, Mass., Harvard Law Library 64 (formerly *Phillippicus* 3625). S. XII².
Cg	Cambridge, Gonville and Caius College 6. France, s. XII.
Da	Darmstadt, Hessische Landesbibliothek 907.
Fd	Florence, Biblioteca Nazionale Centrale, Conventi Soppressi A 1.402. Southern Italy, s. XII³ᐟ⁴.
Fr.	Ae. Friedberg, ed., *Corpus iuris canonici*, 1 (Leipzig 1879). Fr.ABC etc. refers to variant readings found in Friedberg's manuscripts ABC, etc. Fr.A = Ka, Fr.B = Kb.
Gd	Gdańsk, Biblioteka Gdańska Polskiej Akademii Nauk, Mar. fol. 77.
Gg	Grenoble, Bibliothèque municipale 34 (475). France, s. XII.
Hk	Heiligenkreuz, Stiftsbibliothek 44. Southern Germany or Austria, s. XII.
In	Innsbruck, Universitätsbibliothek 90. France, s. XII.
Je	Jena, Thüringer Universitäts- und Landesbibliothek, El. fol. 56. S. XII/XIII.
Ka	Cologne, Erzbischöfliche Diözesan- und Dombibliothek 127. S. XII.
Kb	Cologne, Erzbischöfliche Diözesan- und Dombibliothek 128. Germany, s. XII.
Lenh.	Edition of C. 24, q. 1 in Lenherr, *Exkommunikationsgewalt*.
Mc	Munich, Bayerische Staatsbibliothek, clm 4505.
Me	Munich, Bayerische Staatsbibliothek, clm 13004. Salzburg, s. XII³ᐟ⁴.
Mk	Munich, Bayerische Staatsbibliothek, clm 28161. Italy, s. XII.
Mz	Mainz, Stadtbibliothek II 204. France, s. XIIᵐᵉᵈ.
P	Paris, BN, nouvelles acquisitions latines 1761. France, s. XII.
Pa	Paris, BN, 3888. S. XII².
Pf	Paris, BN, lat. 3884 I–II. France, s. XII.
Pfr	Fragmentum unius paginae in Pf (fo. 1) asservatum.

List of abbreviations

Pk	Paris, BN, lat. 3890. S. XII.
Pl	Paris, BN, lat. 11712. France, s. XII².
Pq	Paris, Bibliothèque de l'Arsenal 677. S. XII^{ex}.

Rom. The Roman edition, prepared by the *Correctores Romani* and first printed in Rome in 1582. The readings of the Roman edition are reproduced as reported in Friedberg, ed., *Decretum* and as found in *Decretum Gratiani . . . una cum glossis Gregorii XIII pont. max. iussu editum* (Venice 1600).

Sa	Salzburg, Stiftsbibliothek St. Peter a.XII.9. Southern Germany or Austria, s. XII.
Sb	Salzburg, Stiftsbibliothek St. Peter a.XI.9. Northern Italy, s. XII.
Tx	Trier, Stadtbibliothek 907 (2182a). S. XII.
Vd	Biblioteca Apostolica Vaticana, Vat. lat. 3529. S. XII.

MANUSCRIPTS AND EDITIONS OF OTHER WORKS

Alg. Edition of Alger of Liège's *De misericordia et iustitia* in Kretzschmar, *Alger von Lüttichs Traktat.*

Ans. *Anselmi episcopi Lucensis collectio canonum*, ed. Thaner.

Ans.G Anselm of Lucca's collection in Graz, Universitätsbibliothek 351.

Ans.p Transcription of book 13 from BAV, Vat. lat. 1363 in Pasztor, "Lotta."

orig. The material source. I have noted in each case which edition I used.

Pan.E The *Panormia* of Ivo of Chartres in St. Petersburg, Publichnaia Biblioteka, Erm., lat. 25.

Pan.F The *Panormia* in Florence, Biblioteca Nazionale Centrale, Magliabechiano XXXIV 73.

Pan.J The *Panormia* in Oxford, Jesus College 26.

Pan.L The *Panormia* in St. Petersburg, Publichnaia Biblioteka, lat. qu. II 4.

Pan.M The *Panormia* in Munich, Bayerische Staatsbibliothek, clm 4545.

Pan.m Edition of the *Panormia* of Ivo of Chartres in *PL* 161.

Pan.T The *Panormia* in Jena, Thüringer Staats- und Universitätsbibliothek El. q. 2.

Polyc.m Draft edition in typescript of the *Polycarpus* at the Monumenta Germaniae Historica, Munich. The edition was begun by Carl Erdmann and continued by Uwe Horst and Horst Fuhrmann. *Polyc.CKMR* refers to variant readings found in the manuscripts CKMR, cf. Horst, *Polycarpus* 11–13.

Polyc.P The *Polycarpus* in Paris, BN, lat. 3881.

Trip. Martin Brett's transcription of the text of the *Collectio Tripartita* in Paris, BN, lat. 3858B with collations of other manuscripts. *Trip.ABC*, etc. refers to variant readings found in Brett's manuscripts ABC.

Vulg. Robertus Weber, ed., *Biblia sacra iuxta vulgatam versionem*, tertia ed. (Stuttgart 1983).

3L The *Collection in Three Books.*

3LV The *Collection in Three Books* in BAV, Vat. lat. 3881.

OTHER ABBREVIATIONS

ac	ante correctionem
add	additio (in Aa Bc Fd)
add.	addidit
corr.	correxit
incl.	inclusit
om.	omisit
pc	post correctionem
sup. lin.	supra lineam
ut vid.	ut videtur

Chapter 1

GRATIAN AND THE *DECRETUM*

Gratian is the only lawyer authoritatively known to be in Paradise. Not that he is lonely there, surrounded as he is by theologians and philosophers, Albertus Magnus on one side and Peter Lombard on the other. How did Gratian earn this favored place? Given the scarcity of lawyers in heaven, one may justly query whether it really was his lawyerly qualifications that made Gratian deserve Paradise. After all, he was an expert on canon law, the law of the Church, which exists on the borders between law and theology. Dante, who reported on the inhabitants of the Afterworld, seems to acknowledge the ambiguity inherent in Gratian's vocation by praising his mastery of "both courts," i.e., the exterior, public court of justice and the interior, sacramental court of the confessional (*Paradiso* x 103–105). Perhaps it was as a theologian, not as a lawyer, that Gratian was admitted, and perhaps this is why he smiled, as Dante tells us he did. Or perhaps Dante thought of Gratian primarily as a pre-eminent teacher, since he awarded him a place between two other teachers. Albertus was the teacher of Thomas Aquinas, who was Dante's guide in this particular circle of Paradise. Medieval intellectuals knew also Gratian and the Lombard as eminent teachers through the textbooks which they had written and which were used in the basic teaching of canon law and theology throughout the middle ages and beyond. Thomas had early in his career lectured on Peter Lombard's *Sentences* and he often quoted from Gratian's *Decretum* in his works.

The pairing of Gratian and the Lombard is in fact common both in modern scholarly literature and in medieval writings. One of the more fanciful examples is the widespread medieval story that they were brothers, or even twins.[1] Credence is not given to this myth, and with good reason, but the pairing itself recognizes an important fact. Gratian and

---

[1] Joseph de Ghellinck, *Le mouvement théologique du XIIe siècle*, 2nd edn., Museum Lessianum: Section historique 10 (Bruges 1948), 285.

I

the Lombard were not twin brothers, but the twin pillars on which medieval education in theoretical and practical theology built. They had, each
in his discipline, produced the first successful compendium, comprehen-
sively summarizing the learning of that discipline using the scholastic
methods that were newly fashionable in their time, the middle of the
twelfth century. The continuing usefulness of their works is attested to
by the hundreds of medieval and early-modern commentaries that have
survived. Gratian's *Decretum* was in fact a valid law book, the oldest and
most voluminous part of the so-called *Corpus iuris canonici*, in Catholic
ecclesiastical courts until 1917.

It is obvious that books which were used so much for so long would
have been greatly influential. Gratian's *Decretum* was one of the corner-
stones of canon law. Its definitions of concepts and terminology as well
as its actual solutions to legal problems have in many cases been definitive and survive in the most recent compilation of the law of the Catholic
Church, the *Codex iuris canonici* of 1983. But the influence of Gratian's
Decretum is not restricted to the law of the Catholic Church. During the
middle ages, canon law regulated areas that would today be thought of as
thoroughly secular, such as business, warfare, and marriage. Together
with Roman law, canon law formed a coherent and autonomous legal
system, the so-called *ius commune* (European Common Law). This system
was the only legal system that was studied at the universities, and during
the middle ages (and in some countries also much later) it was in fact used
in local judicial practice and in producing local law codes.[2] This influence is still felt in modern legislation, for example in the rules concerning a third party's acquisition in good faith of stolen property. In such
cases, modern law tends to follow either Gratian in strongly protecting
the rights of the original possessor or Roman law in protecting acquisitions made in good faith.[3]

Against the background of the significance of Gratian's *Decretum*, it
comes as something of a surprise that practically nothing is known about
Gratian and not much more about how he created the *Decretum*.
Scholarship during the second half of the twentieth century attempted
to clarify Gratian's reasons for writing the *Decretum* and to explore the
political and other sympathies that he demonstrated in this, but these

---

[2] Historians have tended to undervalue the contribution of European Common Law to local practice and legislation, see Manlio Bellomo, *The Common Legal Past of Europe, 1000–1800*, Studies in
Medieval and Early Modern Canon Law 4 (Washington, D.C. 1995) and Kenneth Pennington,
"Learned law, droit savant, gelehrtes Recht: the tyranny of a concept," *Rivista internazionale di
diritto comune* 5 (1994), 197–209; reprinted with corrections in *Syracuse Journal of International Law
and Commerce* 20 (1994), 205–215.

[3] James Gordley and Ugo A. Mattei, "Protecting possession," *The American Journal of Comparative
Law* 44 (1996), 293–334.

attempts were misguided and unconvincing. On the contrary, an important article showed convincingly that the received account for Gratian's
biography is a myth constructed by scholars over the centuries and that
almost nothing remains when it has been carefully examined.[4] At the
same time, many scholars, particularly legal historians, religious historians, and social historians, do research on the basis of Gratian's *Decretum*
from different viewpoints. The publication of such research is often
accompanied by a reservation that the results are uncertain since the
circumstances surrounding the creation of their source text are so poorly
known.

This book will, I believe, remove the need for most such reservations.
A fresh consideration of the most important among the medieval manuscripts of Gratian's *Decretum* reveals that the creation of this work was an
even more complicated process than has been imagined. The text that
scholars have read, studied, and discussed for generations represents in
fact an elaboration of a considerably shorter text. This original *Decretum*
is not a hypothetical construction but actually a text which survives and
can be read in medieval manuscripts. It has, thus, become possible to
study Gratian's original book.

The discovery that Gratian's *Decretum* is not one book but two has
manifold implications. To begin with, it has become easier to read and
interpret the *Decretum*. Many have complained that Gratian's discussion
is rambling and that it fulfils but poorly the promise of the work's original title (see below) to harmonize the contradictions of canon law. In
comparison, Peter Lombard's slightly later *Sentences* seem better organized and better argued. The first version (or, as I call it, the first recension) is more succinct and to the point than the text previously known
(the second recension). This makes it less confusing for the reader, who
will be able to distinguish between Gratian's original argument and the
later additions of the second recension.

In the first recension, the nature of Gratian's project and his contribution to early scholastic methods is clearer. The ratio of commentary to
quoted text is higher, making the first recension a more analytical and less
discursive work than the second recension. Not every contradiction is
resolved even in the first recension, but it becomes easier to understand
why the *Decretum* was adopted as the primary text book of canon law.
Gratian deserved a place next to Peter Lombard in Paradise.

The first recension is not only shorter and more succinct, it is also
different from the second recension in many other respects, which allows

---

[4] John T. Noonan, "Gratian slept here: the changing identity of the father of the systematic study
of canon law," *Traditio* 35 (1979), 145–172.

the scholar to trace the surprisingly rapid legal and intellectual development during the interval between the two recensions. The first recension contains remarkably little Roman law and technical language. This reopens and redefines the long-standing debate about the role of Roman law in the *Decretum*. A comparison between the two recensions raises important new questions about the legal renaissance of the twelfth century, some of which will be addressed in this book. I shall argue that the lack of Roman law in the early version is not an expression of Gratian's distrust of or disgust for secular law. It simply shows that Gratian was not particularly well oriented in Roman law. This is in fact to be expected, since the teaching of Roman law was not as far advanced in his time as the foundation myth of the Roman law school in Bologna claims. I shall also suggest that the differences between the two recensions are so great that it becomes difficult to think of them as the products of a single author.

This book has six chapters. The first provides the historiographical background and a consideration of the printed editions and manuscripts that I have used. Chapters 2 and 3 constitute two test cases, in which I closely examine two selected sections in the *Decretum* (C. 24 and C. 11, q. 3, respectively). Chapter 4 will pull together the threads from the previous two chapters and demonstrate that the evidence presented there conclusively proves the existence of the first recension. I shall also consider some basic issues which now require re-evaluation, such as the place and date of the composition of each recension. The important problem of the incorporation of Roman law into the second recension of the *Decretum* is treated in chapter 5, where I also explore the development of Roman law teaching in Gratian's time. The authorship of the *Decretum* was already a vexed question before the discovery of the first recension. Some scholars believed that Gratian was responsible for the entire *Decretum*, while others preferred to think that his work was supplemented by others. The problem is even more acute after the discovery of the first recension. In chapter 6, I shall study the arguments for and against Gratian's authorship of both recensions.

In conclusion, I shall discuss the broader implications of this study. The realization that the received text of Gratian's *Decretum* is an uneasy composite of incongruous parts will, in the first place, change the ways in which scholars read this fundamental law book. To assist them, the Appendix lists the contents of the first recension. Even more importantly, this study has repercussions for our understanding of the intellectual and legal history of the twelfth century and opens up new possibilities for what promises to be fruitful further research in these areas.

The work usually known as Gratian's *Decretum* was originally entitled the *Concordia discordantium canonum* ("The Harmony of Discordant Canons").[5] This title illustrates the aims and methods of its author, who attempted to resolve the contradictions among the canons which were included in the work. The legislative texts with which he worked spanned the period from the early, pre-Constantine Church to the council celebrated in 1139 by Pope Innocent II, in addition to biblical quotations. The texts included papal decretals, conciliar canons, fragments from writings of the Church Fathers, and pieces of secular legislation. Gratian discussed the canons and contradictions among them in his commentaries, the so-called *dicta Gratiani*, which are interspersed among the canons.

The overall structure of the *Decretum* as presently known may appear peculiar and mystifying to modern scholars, particularly those who are used to the strictly logical structure of later scholastic texts. It consists of three parts. The first is divided into 101 *distinctiones*, which concern the sources of law, the ecclesiastical hierarchy, and the discipline of the clergy. The second part consists of thirty-six *causae*, each divided into *questiones*. This part discusses among many other things simony, judicial procedure, religious orders, heretics, and marriage. The third *questio* in *Causa* 33 is much longer than Gratian's *questiones* normally are. Its subject is penance and it is usually referred to as the *de penitentia*. This *questio* contains seven *distinctiones*. The third part consists of five *distinctiones*, is usually termed the *de consecratione*, and treats the remaining sacraments.[6]

GRATIAN

In 1979, John T. Noonan published an article which questioned the historical accuracy of the received opinion about Gratian's biography.

---

[5] Friedrich Heyer, "Der Titel der Kanonessammlung Gratians," *ZRG KA* 2 (1912), 336–342. See also below, chapter 6.

[6] When citing a text in the first part, I refer to *distinctio* and *canon*: "D. 1, c. 1." For the second part, I refer to *causa, questio*, and *canon*: "C. 1, q. 1, c. 1." The third part (the *de consecratione*) and C. 33, q. 3 (the *de penitentia*) are cited with an abbreviation for the name of the treatise, *distinctio* and *canon*: "de. cons. D. 1, c. 1" and "de pen. D. 1, c. 1," respectively. Gratian's *dicta* are cited as "C. 1, q. 1, d. a. c. 1" (*dictum ante . . .*) or "D. 1, d. p. c. 1" (*dictum post . . .*). The *dicta* introducing each *causa* are cited as "C. 1, d. init." At the head of each longer quotation from the *Decretum* or of each collation of variant readings, I indicate the relevant section in the *Decretum* with an abbreviated reference: "1.1.1" = C. 1, q. 1. c. 1. My citations consistently follow the divisions of the standard edition, Emil Friedberg, ed., *Corpus iuris canonici*, 1, *Decretum magistri Gratiani* (Leipzig 1879). When I refer to a line in Friedberg's edition, I number the line from the beginning of the text of the relevant canon or *dictum*, leaving the lines occupied by rubrics and inscriptions uncounted.

Until then, most scholars claimed that Gratian had been a Camaldolese monk who taught canon law, probably at the monastery of Saints Felix and Nabor in Bologna.[7] Noonan showed how layer after layer of Gratian's biography had piled up through the centuries. There is only one contemporary document which mentions a Gratian who might be identical with the author of the *Decretum*. When the papal legate Cardinal Goizo in 1143 judged a case in Venice, he consulted with three *prudentes: magister Walfredus, Gratianus,* and *Moysis.* The first and the third are usually identified with Bolognese lawyers, which makes it likely that the second expert was the author of the *Decretum.*[8] Very little else can be known with certainty about Gratian except that he wrote the *Decretum.* Even his religious status is open to question. The author of the *Summa Parisiensis,* a commentary on the *Decretum* probably written shortly before 1170, claims that Gratian was a monk.[9] Since Gratian treats questions of monasticism thoroughly in *Causae* 16 to 20, and in a manner that benefits monks, several modern scholars have remained convinced that he in fact was a monk, Noonan's doubts notwithstanding.[10] However, there is reason to query whether the author of *Summa Parisiensis,* who was commenting on passages which he thought beneficial to monks, communicated correct information or simply attempted to discredit Gratian's objectivity. Complicating the situation are statements that Gratian was a bishop. In a chronicle composed about 1180, the abbot of Mont Saint Michel, Robert of Torigny, claims that Gratian was bishop of Chiusi.[11] That Gratian was a bishop is also maintained by a gloss which appears in manuscripts from

---

[7] Noonan, "Gratian slept here." An uncritical summary of the traditional view is found in Carlo Mesini, "Postille sulla biografia del 'Magister Gratianus' padre del diritto canonico," *Apollinaris* 54 (1981), 509–537.

[8] Paul Kehr, *Regesta pontificum Romanorum: Italia pontificia* (Berlin 1906–1975), v 60. Cf. Stephan Kuttner, "The father of the science of canon law," *The Jurist* 1 (1941), 2, and Noonan, "Gratian slept here," 171.

[9] *Summa parisiensis* ad C. 2, q. 7, d. p. c. 52 et C. 16, q. 1, c. 61, in Terence McLaughlin, ed., *Summa Parisiensis on the "Decretum Gratiani"* (Toronto 1952), 115 and 181. For the date, about which there has been some controversy, see Kenneth Pennington, "Medieval canonists: a bio-bibliographical listing," to appear in Kenneth Pennington and Wilfried Hartmann, eds., *History of Medieval Canon Law* (Washington, D.C. 1999–) x, provisionally available on the web at http://www.maxwell.syr.edu/MAXPAGES/faculty/penningk/biobibl.htm.

[10] Most importantly Peter Landau, "Gratian," in *Theologische Realenzyklopädie* XIV (Berlin 1985), 124, Peter Landau, "Quellen und Bedeutung des gratianischen Dekrets," *Studia et documenta historiae et iuris* 52 (1986), 220, Stephan Kuttner, "Gratien," in *Dictionnaire d'histoire et de géographie ecclésiastiques* XXI (Paris 1986), 1236, and Stephan Kuttner, "Research on Gratian: acta and agenda," in *Proceedings of the Seventh International Congress of Medieval Canon Law,* MIC Subs. 8 (Vatican City 1988), 6; reprinted in Stephan Kuttner, *Studies in the History of Medieval Canon Law,* Collected Studies CS 325 (Aldershot 1990), no. v.

[11] Richard Howlett, ed., *The Chronicles of the Reigns of Stephen, Henry II, and Richard I,* IV, *The Chronicle of Robert of Torigni,* Memorials of Great Britain and Ireland during the Middle Ages ["Roll Series"] 82 (London 1889), 118.

the third quarter of the twelfth century.[12] In its oldest form, this gloss does not mention the *de consecratione* in its enumeration of the parts of the *Decretum*. The present book aims to show that the original version of the *Decretum* did not contain the *de consecratione*, which suggests that the gloss is very early and should be paid more attention than is usually the case. Unfortunately, it is impossible to check whether Robert of Torigny was correct in stating that Gratian was bishop of Chiusi, since extremely little is known about any bishops of Chiusi in the twelfth century.[13]

The evidence is, in other words, contradictory. To conclude that Gratian was both monk and bishop is not very satisfying and in any case methodologically questionable. Particularly striking is that what twelfth-century information there is derives from French sources, while the masters active in Bologna remain silent. Also, the oldest manuscripts of the *Decretum* do not even name its author (see chapter 6). This and the confusion about whether he was a monk or a bishop suggest that the canonists of the second half of the twelfth century, at least in Bologna, simply did not know who Gratian was, or that they did not care to investigate. They were, however, from the very beginning agreed about calling him *magister*, which suggests that he taught canon law. That this label was attached to his name could, however, be interpreted also in other ways. He could have been simply "the master of the *Decretum*" (which is the meaning the word has when Paucapalea refers to Gratian in the preface to his *summa*[14]), a judge, or even an abbot.[15] R. W. Southern has recently argued that Gratian in fact was a lawyer and not an academic teacher of law.[16] However, the form of the *Decretum* itself seems to contradict Southern's suggestion. The thirty-six fictitious cases that provide the layout of the second part are not, as Southern calls them, "imaginary lawsuits" or imaginary legal cases, as might be inferred from the term *causa*:

C. 32, d. init.
Since he did not have a wife, a man joined a prostitute to himself in marriage. She was infertile and the daughter of a serf and the granddaughter of a freeman.

---

[12] The gloss was edited on the basis of all known manuscripts in Rudolf Weigand, "Frühe Kanonisten und ihre Karriere in der Kirche," *ZRG KA* 76 (1990), 135–155.

[13] Noonan, "Gratian slept here," 153–154, Kehr, *Italia pontificia*, III 230, and Ferdinando Ughelli, *Italia sacra sive de episcopis Italiae . . . opus singulare* (Venice 1717–1722), III 631.

[14] Paucapalea, *Summa über das "Decretum Gratiani,"* ed. Johann Friedrich von Schulte (Giessen 1890), 3.

[15] Doubts were raised by Noonan, "Gratian slept here," 169–170, and also by Peter Classen, who was prevented by his untimely death from substantiating them, see Kuttner, "Research on Gratian," 7. For the possible meanings of *magister*, see also Johannes Fried, *Die Entstehung des Juristenstandes im 12. Jahrhundert*, Forschungen zur neueren Privatrechtsgeschichte 21 (Cologne 1974), 9–24, Franz Blatt, *Novum glossarium mediae latinitatis*, M–N (Copenhagen 1959–1969), 22–29, and J. F. Niermeyer, *Mediae latinitatis lexicon minus* (Leiden 1976), 625.

[16] Southern, *Scholastic Humanism and the Unification of Europe*, I: *Foundations* (Oxford 1995), 303–305.

Although the father wanted to give her to another, the grandfather joined her to this man, for the reason of incontinence only. Thereafter, the man, led by regret, began to attempt to conceive children with his own maid. Afterwards, when he had been convicted of adultery and punished, he asked a man to take his wife by violence, so that he would be able to divorce her. When this had been done, he married an infidel woman, but on the condition that she converted to the Christian religion. Now it is first asked if it is licit to take a prostitute as a wife? Second, if she who is taken [as a wife] for the reason of incontinence is to be called "wife"? Third, whose judgement would she follow, the free grandfather or the servile father? Fourth, if he is allowed to conceive children with a maid while his wife is alive? Fifth, if she who suffers violence is proven to have lost her virtue? Sixth, if an adulterous man can divorce his adulterous wife? Seventh, if a man may marry another while his divorced wife is alive? Eighth, if a Christian man may take in marriage an infidel under the aforementioned condition?[17]

This is not the description of a case in which all these questions had to be answered before judgement could be passed. Instead, it bears the hallmarks of a teacher who designs his examples in such a way that, however bizarre, they raise exactly those legal issues which he wants to discuss. Besides, every teacher knows the value of striking examples that stay in the memories of his students. Even as severe a critic as Noonan yields this point.[18]

Short of the unlikely event that some hitherto unnoticed source will throw light on Gratian's biography, the text of the *Decretum* is our most reliable source for knowing its author. Here, much work remains to be done. To mention only one detail, the rather sweeping assertions that Gratian favored monks deserve to be studied and substantiated in greater detail,[19] and to be contrasted with other twelfth-century canonical works. Such studies are, however, hampered by the fact that it is not entirely clear exactly what the text of Gratian's *Decretum* comprises.

---

[17] Friedberg, ed. *Decretum*, 1115: "Quidam, cum non haberet uxorem, quandam meretricem sibi coniugio copulauit, que erat sterilis, neptis ingenui, filia originarii; quam cum pater uellet alii tradere, auus huic eam copulauit, causa solius incontinentiae. Deinde hic, penitencia ductus, ex ancilla propria filios sibi querere cepit. Postea de adulterio conuictus et punitus quendam rogauit, ut ui uxorem suam opprimeret, ut sic eam dimittere posset, quo facto quandam infidelem sibi copulauit, ea tamen condicione, ut ad Christianam religionem transiret. Hic primum queritur, an licite meretrix ducatur in uxorem? Secundo, an ea, que causa incontinenciae ducitur, sit coniux appellanda? Tercio, cuius arbitrium aliqua sequatur, an liberi aui, an originarii patris? Quarto, si uiuente uxore liceat alicui ex ancilla filios querere? Quinto, si ea, que uim patitur, pudicitiam amittere conprobetur? Sexto, si adulter adulteram possit dimittere? Septimo, si uiuente dimissa aliam possit accipere? Octauo, si infidelem sub premissa condicione licet alicui fidelium in coniugem ducere?" [18] Noonan, "Gratian slept here," 169.

[19] Rudolf Weigand recently pointed to some details in D. 63, d. p. c. 34, where Gratian gives his interpretation a slant favorable to monks, see Rudolf Weigand, "Das kirchliche Wahlrecht im Dekret Gratians," in *Wirkungen europaischer Rechtskultur: Festschrift für Karl Kroeschell zum 70. Geburtstag*, ed. Gerhard Köbler and Hermann Niehlsen (Munich 1997), 1344.

Gratian and the "Decretum"

Despite the fundamental importance of Gratian's *Decretum* in the middle ages and beyond, it was never formally promulgated by the Church. It was, nonetheless, one of the texts which were subject to philological attention following the Council of Trent. A commission, commonly known as the *Correctores Romani*, was appointed in 1566 for the purpose of correcting and emending the *Corpus iuris canonici* (including the *Decretum* of Gratian, the *Liber extra* of Gregory IX, the *Liber sextus* of Boniface VIII, the *Clementinae* promulgated by John XXII, and the *Extravagantes*). The *Correctores'* efforts resulted in the so-called *editio Romana* published in 1582. Its impact on all later editions of the *Decretum* is so great that some acquaintance with the methods and aims of the *Correctores* is indispensable. For the scholar interested in Gratian's text, the most important drawback of the *editio Romana* is that the *Correctores* were less concerned with reproducing what Gratian actually wrote than with restoring the original text of his material sources. They would retrieve for each canon what seemed to be the most accurate text of the papal decree, conciliar decision, or patristic authority that Gratian was quoting, and then "correct" his text. As the most recent editor of the *Decretum* pointed out, the aims of the *Correctores* were "not to restore the *Decretum* as Gratian composed it, but as he ought to have composed it."[20]

The *editio Romana* was reprinted numerous times. The first editor after 1582 to go back to the manuscript tradition of Gratian was Just Henning Böhmer (Halle 1747), who, being a Protestant, did not feel bound by the official edition of the Catholic Church. The four manuscripts he used were late and unreliable, but he produced a better text than had earlier been available. The next editor, Emil Ludwig Richter (Leipzig 1839), returned to the *editio Romana*. However, he made and published collations of pre-1582 editions of the *Decretum*, of the editions of Gratian's material sources which were available at the time, and of other canonical collections. The most recent editor of the *Decretum*, Emil Friedberg,

---

[20] "Vides non id in animo habuisse correctores Romanos, ut restitueretur decretum, quale a Gratiano compositum esset, sed quale a Gratiano componi debuisset." Friedberg, ed., *Decretum*, LXXVIII. Columns LXXVII–XC give a convenient overview of the *Correctores'* activities including the texts of relevant sixteenth-century papal letters. The methods of the *Correctores* have serious implications for the usefulness of the recent translation into English of *distinctiones* 1–20, which unfortunately is based on the *editio Romana*: Gratian, *The Treatise on Laws (Decretum DD. 1–20)*, trans. Augustine Thompson and James Gordley, Studies in Medieval and Early Modern Canon Law 2 (Washington 1993). Katherine Christensen's statement in the introduction to this translation, p. xx, that "the Roman edition . . . remains the edition of choice for serious work on the *Decretum*" is incorrect. See also Rudolf Weigand's review of this translation, in *Theologische Revue* 92 (1996), 152–155.

used eight manuscripts for his edition (Leipzig 1879), and made substantial use of Richter's collations. The text he presented was based on the manuscripts, and the divergences from the *editio Romana* are signaled in a separate apparatus. A large and not always easily interpreted critical apparatus gives accounts of variant readings, sources, and parallels in other canonical collections.

Friedberg's edition remains an impressive monument to the great industry of an editor working alone,[21] but its shortcomings are, after more than a century of research, well known. Aside from formal inadequacies and a few purely typographical deficiencies,[22] one of the two fundamental problems is that Friedberg's manuscript basis is narrow, although in this he is typical of the editor of his time, understandably so given conditions of travel and technology.[23] Before re-editing C. 24, q. 1, Titus Lenherr studied the value of several old manuscripts and the edition of Friedberg by comparing their text of the canons that Gratian took from the canonical collection *Polycarpus* with a critical edition of this collection (available in typescript at the Monumenta Germaniae Historica in Munich).[24] Through this procedure, he determined which manuscripts of the *Decretum* have the highest number of readings in common with the *Polycarpus* and he assumed that these would best represent Gratian's text. He concluded that the two Cologne manuscripts (Ka and Kb[25]) which Friedberg used as the basis for

[21] Cf. Friedberg, ed., *Decretum*, CI.

[22] Every reader of Friedberg's edition is familiar with the eye-strain required to sort out the apparatus. In 1948 Stephan Kuttner pointed out that Friedberg's reports of the readings of manuscripts and sources are often ambiguous or even misleading and that his listing of other canonical collections' use of the same canons in many cases is inadequate, Stephan Kuttner, "De Gratiani opere noviter edendo," *Apollinaris* 21 (1948), 118–128. Titus Lenherr's research confirms that Friedberg does not always accurately report readings of his manuscripts, see Titus Lenherr, "Arbeiten mit Gratians Dekret," *AKKR* 151 (1982), 140–166.

[23] The least incomplete listing of *Decretum* manuscripts is found in Anthony Melnikas, *The Corpus of the Miniatures in the Manuscripts of "Decretum Gratiani,"* Studia Gratiana 18 (Rome 1975), 1261–1267, where 495 manuscripts are listed, unfortunately without date and origin. This listing is little more than an excerpt from Stephan Kuttner, *Repertorium der Kanonistik (1140–1234): Prodromus Corporis glossarum* I, Studi e testi 71 (Vatican City 1937) and fails to register many manuscripts mentioned in the literature since 1937. Cf. Carl Nordenfalk's review of Melnikas' work, in *Zeitschrift für Kunstgeschichte* 43 (1980), 318–337, and Hubert Mordek's review, in *ZRG KA* 72 (1986), 403–411 (with corrections and a list of fifty-nine additional manuscripts). For the oldest manuscripts, these works are superseded by Rudolf Weigand, *Die Glossen zum "Dekret" Gratians: Studien zu den frühen Glossen und Glossenkompositionen*, Studia Gratiana 26–27 (Rome 1991). I am preparing a new listing of *Decretum* manuscripts for the forthcoming Pennington and Hartmann, eds., *History of Medieval Canon Law* x.

[24] Lenherr, "Arbeiten," and Titus Lenherr, *Die Exkommunikations- und Depositionsgewalt der Häretiker bei Gratian und den Dekretisten bis zur "Glossa Ordinaria" des Johannes Teutonicus* (hereafter *Exkommunikationsgewalt*), Münchener theologische Studien, III, Kanonistische Abteilung 42 (Munich 1987), 12–17.

[25] In citing manuscripts of the *Decretum*, I use the *sigla* employed by Rudolf Weigand in various publications (fullest listing in Weigand, *Glossen zum "Dekret,"* xxi–xxiv). All the *sigla* I mention are listed in the Conspectus siglorum of the present book.

his edition represent an eccentric branch of the tradition. This branch is characterized by substitution of individual words and frequent transpositions of the word order. Among the twenty-one manuscripts thus examined he found a Munich manuscript (Mk) to contain the "best" text, i.e., the text which most closely corresponds to Gratian's source.

Within the limits imposed by his narrow manuscript basis, Friedberg's editorial skills were considerable. His sense of Latin style and of the content of the texts often allowed him to find the best reading where his basic manuscripts failed him. His edition of C. 24, q. 1 is, therefore, sometimes superior to that of Lenherr, who consistently follows a single manuscript. A striking example, indicated by Rudolf Weigand, is the beginning of C. 24, q. 1, c. 4, which in Lenherr's edition (p. 20) reads "Audiuimus quod hereticus Rauennas dictus archiepiscopus . . ." ["We have heard that the heretic who is called archbishop of Ravenna . . ."]. In Friedberg's edition (col. 967), the word *hereticus* is replaced by the correct *Henricus*, which is found in most *Decretum* manuscripts and in Gratian's source. The basic manuscripts of both Lenherr (Mk) and Friedberg (Ka) have *hereticus*, but Friedberg's sounder editorial methods allowed him to overcome this weakness.[26]

THE QUEST FOR THE ORIGINAL *DECRETUM*

The second major problem facing a scholar using Friedberg's edition is a consequence not so much of the shortcomings of the edition itself as of advances in scholarship on Gratian during the twentieth century. The edition presents the *Decretum* as a unified product of one author. The name *Gratianus*, for example, appears at the beginning of every *dictum* and every major division of the work, which is not the case in the manuscripts. Many old manuscripts do not contain Gratian's name at all except as added by later hands (see chapter 6). The genesis of the *Decretum* and the authorship of its different parts have attracted much scholarly attention over the last half century.[27]

(i) It has long been known that more than 150 canons present in the late medieval vulgate text were added by the masters of Bologna at various times after the work was completed. Already some medieval manuscripts label these *paleae*. They are also distinguished by their

[26] For criticism of this aspect of Lenherr's edition of C. 24, q, 1, see Rudolf Weigand's review of *Exkommunikationsgewalt*, by Lenherr, in *AKKR* 156 (1987), 649, and Rudolf Weigand, "Zur künftigen Edition des Dekrets Gratians," *ZRG KA* 83 (1997), 35–36.
[27] Surveys of this historiography are Jacqueline Rambaud, "Le legs de l'ancien droit: Gratien," in *L'âge classique 1140–1378*, by Gabriel Le Bras, Charles Lefebvre, and Jacqueline Rambaud, Histoire du droit et des institutions de l'Eglise en Occident 7 (Paris 1965), 47–129, Noonan, "Gratian slept here," and Kuttner, "Research on Gratian."

absence from some manuscripts and their varying location when present. Some of the *paleae* are, however, not additions by the school, but canons which had been cancelled in the schools, because they also appear elsewhere in the *Decretum*.[28]

(ii) One of the most significant advances in modern scholarship on Gratian's *Decretum* took place during enforced leisure at a Swiss military internment camp during the Second World War. The Polish historian Adam Vetulani, using little more than the critical apparatus of Friedberg's edition, postulated that over forty segments containing Roman law are also later additions, since they are not present in all manuscripts and their place in Gratian's argument is often awkward. This is true, however, only for the civilian chapters taken directly from Justinian's *Digest* and *Code*. The original compilation seems to have contained Roman law statements taken from earlier canonical collections.[29]

(iii) The third part of the *Decretum*, the *de consecratione*, abandons the dialectical method used in parts I and II and does not contain any *dicta*. Irregularities in the manuscript transmission of this section as well as indications in an early prefatory note to the *Decretum* that the work contained two parts suggested to Jacqueline Rambaud that it was not an original element of Gratian's composition.[30]

[28] Rudolf Weigand, "Versuch einer neuen, differenzierten Liste der Paleae und Dubletten im *Dekret Gratians*," in *Life, Law and Letters: Historical Studies in Honour of Antonio García y García*, Studia Gratiana 28–29 (Rome 1998), 883–899, Rambaud, "Le legs," 109, and Titus Lenherr, "Fehlende 'Paleae' als Zeichen eines überlieferungsgeschichtlich jüngeren Datums von *Dekret*-Handschriften," *AKKR* 151 (1982), 495–507. See also Walter Ullmann, "The paleae in Cambridge manuscripts of the *Decretum*," *Studia Gratiana* 1 (1953), 161–216; reprinted in Walter Ullmann, *Jurisprudence in the Middle Ages*, Collected Studies CS 120 (London 1980), no. IV, Hartmut Zapp, "Paleae-Listen des 14. und 15. Jahrhunderts," *ZRG KA* 59 (1973), 83–111, and Rudolf Weigand, "Fälschungen als Paleae im *Dekret* Gratians," in *Fälschungen im Mittelalter*, MGH Schriften, 33: 2 (Hanover 1988), 301–318.

[29] Adam Vetulani, "Gratien et le droit romain," *Revue historique de droit français et étranger*, ser. 4, 24/25 (1946/1947), 11–48; reprinted in Adam Vetulani, *Sur Gratien et les décrétales: Recueil d'études*, Collected Studies CS 308 (Aldershot 1990), no. III, and Adam Vetulani, "Encore un mot sur le droit romain dans le *Décret* de Gratien," *Apollinaris* 21 (1948), 129–134; reprinted in Vetulani, *Sur Gratien et les décrétales*, no. IV. This line of inquiry has also been pursued by Stephan Kuttner, "New studies on the Roman law in Gratian's *Decretum*," *Seminar* 11 (1953), 12–50; reprinted in Stephan Kuttner, *Gratian and the Schools of Law, 1140–1234*, Collected Studies CS 185 (London 1983), no. IV, Stephan Kuttner, "Additional notes on the Roman law in Gratian," *Seminar* 12 (1954), 68–74; reprinted in Kuttner, *Gratian and the Schools of Law*, no. V, Rambaud, "Le legs," 119–128, Jean Gaudemet, "Das römische Recht im *Dekret* Gratians," *Österreichisches Archiv für Kirchenrecht* 12 (1961), 177–191; reprinted in Jean Gaudemet, *La formation du droit canonique médiéval*, Collected Studies CS 111 (London 1980), no. IX.

[30] Jacqueline Rambaud-Buhot, "L'étude des manuscrits du *Décret* de Gratien conservés en France," *Studia Gratiana* 1 (1950), 129–130, and Rambaud, "Le legs," 90–99. The prefatory note which she mentions has since been edited in Rudolf Weigand, "Frühe Kanonisten," 152–155. An argument for Gratian's authorship of the *de consecratione* (ultimately unconvincing despite many valid points) is made in John Van Engen, "Observations on *De consecratione*," in *Proceedings of the Sixth International Congress of Medieval Canon Law*, MIC Subs. 7 (Vatican City 1985), 309–320.

(iv) The *de penitentia* (C. 33, q. 3) is a disproportionately long *questio* and its subject matter, penance, has little in common with the surrounding *Causae* 27 to 36, which treat marriage law. These facts have been taken to indicate that at least parts of the *de penitentia* were added after the completion of the *Decretum*. In 1914, Joseph de Ghellinck pointed out that the seventeenth-century theologian Stephan Bochenthaler had claimed that the *de penitentia* was not the work of Gratian but of his contemporary Ernest of Zwiefalten. It is unknown what basis, if any, Bochenthaler had for this assertion, which obviously could have served a polemical purpose and may not have been made in good faith. In 1952, Jacqueline Rambaud drew attention to some irregularities in the manuscript transmission of *de penitentia* and questioned whether the treatise was originally a part of Gratian's work. This issue was investigated by Karol Wojtyła (since 1978 Pope John Paul II), who suggested that distinctions 2 to 4 were not a part of Gratian's original composition. In 1965, Rambaud largely agreed with Wojtyła's results.[31]

(v) Finally, Gérard Fransen has observed that most canons from the Second Lateran Council, held in 1139, fit their context in the *Decretum* awkwardly. He assumed, therefore, that the *Decretum* was more or less finished when the Lateran canons reached the author.[32] In addition, Vetulani has suggested that the canons of the First Lateran Council of 1123 may likewise be later additions.[33]

When I survey this historiography, the contributions of Adam Vetulani and Jacqueline Rambaud stand out. While the latter's research and writings focused on examinations of manuscripts of the *Decretum*, the former used the evidence thus assembled as building blocks in a bold and imaginative interpretation of Gratian's work. Vetulani saw the original paucity of Roman law texts in the *Decretum* as an expression of Gratian's political objectives. Gratian rejected secular law because he was a supporter of Pope Paschal II (1099–1118), who attempted to solve the Investiture Contest by completely separating the Church from the secular sphere. Such a political orientation does not tally with a work supposedly written around 1140, and this explains Vetulani's insistence on putting the original composition of the *Decretum* earlier in the twelfth century. He

[31] Ghellinck, *Le mouvement théologique*, 512–513, Rambaud-Buhot, "L'étude des manuscrits," 130–131, Wojtyła, "Le traité De penitentia de Gratien dans l'abrégé de Gdańsk Mar. F. 75," *Studia Gratiana* 7 (Rome 1959), 355–390, and Rambaud, "Le legs," 82–90.
[32] Adam Vetulani, "Nouvelles vues sur le *Décret* de Gratien," in *La Pologne au Xe Congrès international des sciences historiques à Rome* (Warsaw 1955), 96; reprinted in Vetulani, *Sur Gratien et les décrétales*, no. v, Gérard Fransen, "La date du *Décret* de Gratien," *Revue d'histoire ecclésiastique* 51 (1956), 529, Rambaud, "Le legs," 57–58, and Titus Lenherr, "Die Summarien zu den Texten des 2. Laterankonzils von 1139 in Gratians *Dekret*," *AKKR* 150 (1981), 528–551.
[33] Vetulani, "Nouvelles vues," 96.

suggested that Gratian had begun his work by 1105, which is the year mentioned in a form letter in C. 2, q. 6, d. p. c. 31, and finished it before the Concordat of Worms of 1122. Vetulani attempted to undergird this argument with evidence garnered from an abbreviation of the *Decretum* in a manuscript in Gdańsk. Later research has revealed that this abbreviation is not as old as he thought and that his conclusions were often misguided. His reliance on this manuscript was an unfortunate effect of the political division of Europe during most of the second half of the twentieth century, which prevented him from frequent international travel for manuscript study. Vetulani's contribution is remarkable considering the personal circumstances under which he was forced to work.

Vetulani's interpretation of Gratian's work quickly became the target of criticism and is now generally rejected,[34] except for his basic work on the Roman law material in the *Decretum*, which is universally accepted. Gérard Fransen's observation that the canons of the Second Lateran Council were late additions to the text is also widely considered correct. The arguments of Rambaud, Vetulani, and Wojtyła that Gratian did not write most or any of the two treatises *de penitentia* and *de consecratione* have had a mixed reception. Some scholars accept them with reservations while others remain highly sceptical.[35] For a less important text, such problems may be thought minor, but any attempt at understanding the fundamental transformation of law that took place in the twelfth century is severely handicapped by the insecurity about what Gratian's work really contained. Indeed, in his article from 1988 about the "acta and agenda" of *Decretum* scholarship, Stephan Kuttner puts this problem first in his list of issues that need to be addressed:

1. The making of the *Concordia discordantium canonum*, its plan and structure: was it drafted and completed in one grandiose thrust, or did the original version go through successive redactions?[36]

Kuttner goes on to point out that this problem must be solved before the text can be accurately dated and the purpose of the book discussed in the context of historical developments (whether religious, political, intellectual, or legal). The signs that the *Decretum* outgrew Gratian's original plan and was revised are clearly visible in the text. The evidence for what Kuttner in a happy turn of phrase called "untidy seams"[37] extends well beyond the limits of the two treatises *de penitentia* and *de consecratione*, the Roman law material, and the canons of the Second Lateran Council.

---

[34] Among his earliest critics were Fransen, "La date du *Décret*," and René Metz, "A propos des travaux de M. Adam Vetulani," *RDC* 7 (1957), 62–85.

[35] For two authoritative but diverging recent accounts, see Landau, "Gratian," and Kuttner, "Gratien."   [36] Kuttner, "Research on Gratian," 10.   [37] *Ibid.* 13.

One may think of such passages as C. 1, q. 5, d. p. c. 2, where Gratian appears to refer to the two preceding canons in the singular (*hac auctoritate*) and C. 24, q. 3, c. 5, where the rubric *de eodem* ("about the same thing") makes little sense if it is taken to refer back to c. 4.

Recent scholarly advances make this the right time for a renewed consideration of the problems surrounding the composition of the *Decretum*. First, the manuscript transmission of the *Decretum* is infinitely better known now than ten years ago, thanks to Rudolf Weigand's research on the early decretists.[38] In order to study glosses pre-dating the *Glossa ordinaria* of 1215, Weigand examined and described practically every extant *Decretum* manuscript (more than 150) from the twelfth and the first half of the thirteenth century. His research greatly facilitates the selection of manuscripts to be used in a study of the text of the *Decretum*.

Second, recent scholarship has made important advances concerning Gratian's formal (i.e., immediate) sources. Because several centuries of scholarship concentrated on the material (i.e., original) sources,[39] the formal sources were traditionally given short shrift. Editors from the *Correctores Romani* to Friedberg habitually noted occurrences of Gratian's texts in other collections but without indicating from which of them he had extracted his text. While earlier scholars usually expected Gratian to have used a large number of sources, including papal registers, patristic manuscripts, and the Pseudo-Isidorian decretals, twentieth-century scholarship has more and more come to realize that he mainly used relatively few recent compilations. An important breakthrough came in 1984, when Peter Landau pointed out that a handful of sources account for most of the canons in the *Decretum*.[40] These sources are, in the first place, the following five collections.

(i) Anselm of Lucca's canonical collection, originally compiled around 1083. It is preserved in several recensions. Peter Landau has investigated the relationship between them and concluded that Gratian used a manuscript of recension A'.[41] For the text of this collection, I used Friedrich

---

[38] In addition to dozens of articles, the major result of this research is Weigand, *Glossen zum "Dekret."*

[39] This kind of research culminated in the four volumes of Carlo Sebastiano Berardi, *Gratiani canones genuini ab apocryphiis discreti* (Venice 1783).

[40] Peter Landau, "Neue Forschungen zu vorgratianischen Kanonessammlungen und den Quellen des gratianischen *Dekrets*," *Ius commune* 11 (1984), 1–29 and Landau, "Quellen und Bedeutung." Landau most recently summarized his work on Gratian's sources in Peter Landau, "Gratians Arbeitsplan," in *Iuri canonico promovendo: Festschrift für Heribert Schmitz zum 65. Geburtstag* (Regensburg 1994), 691–707.

[41] Peter Landau, "Die Rezension C der Sammlung des Anselm von Lucca," *BMCL* 16 (1986), 17–54, and Peter Landau, "Erweiterte Fassungen der Kanonessammlung des Anselm von Lucca aus dem 12. Jahrhundert," in *Sant'Anselmo, Mantova e la lotta per le investiture: Atti del Convegno Internazionale di Studi*, ed. Paolo Golinelli (Bologna 1987), 323–338.

Thaner's incomplete edition (*Ans.*), supplemented by the twelfth-century manuscript Graz, Universitätsbibliothek 351 (*Ans.G*), which belongs to recension A.[42]

(ii) The Pseudo-Ivonian *Collectio Tripartita*, usually thought to have been completed around 1095. Martin Brett has questioned this date and pointed out that the work could have been produced later. He also made a cogent case against attributing the collection to Ivo of Chartres, as is usually done.[43] This collection has never been printed. With Martin Brett's kind permission, I have used his transcription of BN France lat. 3858B, including his collations with other manuscripts (*Trip.*).

(iii) Ivo of Chartres' *Panormia*, usually dated to around 1095, but Martin Brett has questioned this dating, suggesting that the work could have been compiled at any point before Ivo's death in 1115.[44] I used the unreliable edition in Migne's *Patrologia Latina* (*PL* 161.1038–1343; *Pan.m*) supplemented by medieval manuscripts. This edition is a reprint ultimately based on the edition of 1557 by Melchior Vosmedian, who often changed the text so that it would correspond to a printed copy of Gratian's *Decretum*. In addition, Migne's (or his editor's) own editorial tampering with this text is even more detrimental than usual.[45]

(iv) Gregory of St. Grisogono's *Polycarpus*, which was completed after 1111. This collection has never been printed, although preparations for an edition have been made at the Monumenta Germaniae Historica, Munich, by Carl Erdmann, Uwe Horst, and Horst Fuhrmann. The latter kindly permitted me to use their draft edition (*Polyc.m*). I also used the twelfth-century manuscript BN, lat. 3881 (*Polyc.P*). Uwe Horst's book about the Polycarpus contains useful concordances and indices.[46]

---

[42] Anselm of Lucca, *Anselmi episcopi Lucensis collectio canonum una cum collectione minore*, ed. Friedrich Thaner (Innsbruck 1906–1915). A transcription of the thirteenth (last) book on the basis of two manuscripts is found in Edith Pásztor, "Lotta per le investiture e 'ius belli': la posizione di Anselmo di Lucca," in *Sant'Anselmo, Mantova e la lotta per le investiture: Atti del Convegno Internazionale di Studi*, ed. Paolo Golinelli (Bologna 1987), 403–421 (*Ans.p*). For Anselm's collection see now Kathleen G. Cushing, *Papacy and Law in the Gregorian Revolution: The Canonistic Work of Anselm of Lucca*, Oxford Historical Monographs (Oxford 1998).

[43] Martin Brett, "Urban II and the collections attributed to Ivo of Chartres," in *Proceedings of the Eighth International Congress of Medieval Canon Law*, MIC Subs. 9 (Vatican City 1992), 27–46.

[44] *Ibid.*, 46.

[45] Peter Landau, "Die Rubriken und Inskriptionen von Ivos *Panormie*: Die Ausgabe Sebastian Brants im Vergleich zur Löwener Edition des Melchior de Vosmédian und der Ausgabe von Migne," *BMCL* 12 (1982), 31–49, Jacqueline Rambaud-Buhot, "Les sommaires de la Panormie et l'édition de Melchior de Vosmédian," *Traditio* 23 (1967), 534–536. The manuscripts I used are listed in the *Conspectus siglorum*.

[46] Uwe Horst, *Die Kanonessammlung "Polycarpus" des Gregor von S. Grisogono: Quellen und Tendenzen*, MGH Hilfsmittel 5 (Munich 1980). For a critical appreciation of Horst's work, see John Gilchrist, "The *Polycarpus*," *ZRG KA* 68 (1982), 441–452.

(v) The *Collection in Three Books (3L)*. Several recensions of this collection were compiled between 1111 and 1140. It has never been printed, and I used the twelfth-century manuscript BAV, Vat., lat. 3881 (*3LV*).[47] Gratian also used other sources for specific sections of the *Decretum*. For the so-called *Treatise on Laws* (particularly for distinctions 1 to 9), he drew on Isidore of Seville's *Etymologiae*.[48] Important especially for C. 1 is Alger of Liège's *Liber de misericordia et iustitia*.[49] In the theologically oriented sections of the *Decretum*, particularly in the *de penitentia* and the *de consecratione*, many texts derive from the *Sententiae magistri A* and perhaps also from Peter Abelard's *Sic et non*.[50] While these sources contributed the great majority of the texts in the *Decretum*, a comparatively small number of canons remains unaccounted for. It appears that at least one source of some significance still remains to be discovered, which does not preclude Gratian having used some further sources only once or twice.[51]

Third, Titus Lenherr demonstrated in 1987 that it is possible to study Gratian's work in detail by combining evidence about his formal sources with a close reading of the text based on a fresh collation of selected

[47] A number of cases in which Gratian used this collection as his source are indicated in Erickson, "The *Collection in Three Books* and Gratian's *Decretum*," *BMCL* 2 (1972), 67–75. Some of the titles are analyzed in Paul Fournier, "Une collection canonique italienne du commencement du XIIe siècle," *Annales de l'enseignement supérieur de Grenoble* 6 (1894), 343–438. See also Giuseppe Motta, "Osservazioni intorno alla *Collezione Canonica in tre libri* (MSS C 135 Archivio Capitolare di Pistoia e Vat., lat. 3831)," in *Proceedings of the Fifth International Congress of Medieval Canon Law*, MIC Subs. 4 (Vatican City 1980), 51–65.

[48] Landau, "Neue Forschungen," 28, and Landau, "Quellen und Bedeutung," 227.

[49] Edition in Robert Kretzschmar, *Alger von Lüttichs Traktat "De misericordia et iustitia": Ein Kanonistischer Konkordanzversuch aus der Zeit des Investiturstreits*, Quellen und Forschungen zum Recht im Mittelalter 2 (Sigmaringen 1985), 187–375. Kretzschmar suggests a dating before 1101 but admits that the treatise might have been written later.

[50] Stephan Kuttner, "Zur Frage der theologischen Vorlagen Gratians," *ZRG KA* 23 (1934), 243–268; reprinted in Kuttner, *Gratian and the Schools of Law*, no. III, and Peter Landau, "Gratian und die *Sententiae Magistri A*," in *Aus Archiven und Bibliotheken: Festschrift für Raymund Kottje zum 65. Geburtstag*, Freiburger Beiträge zur mittelalterlichen Geschichte: Studien und Texte 3 (Frankfurt am Main 1992), 311–326.

[51] Peter Landau is currently investigating these issues. In a series of articles, he is exploring the possibility that Gratian made occasional use of some sources. He has shown that Gratian in three cases (all in the first recension) corrected the texts of other sources with the help of the collection of Dionysius Exiguus, see Peter Landau, "Gratian und Dionysius Exiguus: Ein Beitrag zur Kanonistischen Interpolationenkritik," in *De iure canonico Medii Aevi: Festschrift für Rudolf Weigand*, Studia Gratiana 27 (Rome 1996), 271–283. There is no evidence that Gratian used the register of Gregory I at first hand, as Landau showed in "Das *Register* Papst Gregorius I. im *Decretum Gratiani*," in *Mittelalterliche Texte: Überlieferung–Befunde–Deutungen*, ed. Rudolf Schieffer, MGH Schriften 42 (Hanover 1996), 125–140. He did, however, occasionally use the *Decretum* of Burchard of Worms, see Landau, "Burchard de Worms et Gratien: pour l'étude des sources directes du *Décret* de Gratien," *RDC* 48.2 (1998). For Gratian's possible use of Gregory I's *Register* and of Burchard's *Decretum*, see also Rudolf Weigand, "Mittelalterliche Texte: Gregor I., Burchard und Gratian," *ZRG KA* 84 (1998), 330–344 Additionally, Rudolf Weigand has pointed out that Gratian once (in D. 63, d. p. c. 34) refers to the *Breviatio canonum* of Fulgentius Ferrandus, see Weigand, "Kirchliche Wahlrecht," 1343.

manuscripts.[52] The result was an understanding of how Gratian compiled a *questio*, C. 24, q. 1, and in which order the different components of the text were inserted. Lenherr's analysis was based on the reasonable premise that Gratian did not use all of his sources at the same time; some sources would have been used in the beginning of his work and some later. His analysis proved this premise correct (and my investigations support it). Lenherr found that the formulation of the question at issue in C. 24, q. 1 is based solely on the three canons in this *questio* which derive from Ivo's *Panormia*. The discussion in the *dicta* draws on these and on canons which Gratian extracted from the *Polycarpus*. The canons coming from *3L* and the *Collectio Tripartita* do not seem to be reflected in the *dicta*. On the basis of these observations, Lenherr concluded that the *questio* grew around a kernel of the three *Panormia* canons, to which were first added the texts from the *Polycarpus* and then the canons deriving from *3L* and the *Tripartita*.

GOALS AND METHODS OF THIS BOOK

My work was originally conceived of as a study of Gratian's methods: his use of sources, his construction of (scholastic) arguments, his creation of a coherent system of law. In contemplating the stages in the composition of the *Decretum*, first explored by Lenherr, I became increasingly convinced that there were two separate main stages and that the result of the first of these is preserved in three manuscripts, now in libraries in Admont, Barcelona, and Florence (Aa Bc Fd). These manuscripts contain a text of the *Decretum* which is considerably shorter than the normal text – approximately half of the canons are left out – and their text has therefore been thought of as one of the many twelfth-century abbreviations of the *Decretum*. My work, therefore, focused on proving that the text of the three manuscripts is in fact an earlier version of Gratian's *Decretum*, a first recension. To that end, I made a detailed textual study of two selected sections of the text, C. 24 and C. 11, q. 3. A summary of this study is found in chapters 2 and 3. This study proved conclusively the existence of a first recension of Gratian's *Decretum* in the three manuscripts Aa Bc Fd, and I accounted for these findings at the Tenth International Congress of Medieval Canon Law in Syracuse, New York, in August of 1996 and at the defense of my doctoral dissertation at Columbia University four weeks later. Ironically, in the intervening period I discovered a fourth manuscript of the first recension, now in Paris (P). In July 1998, Professor Carlos Larrainzar informed me that he

[52] Lenherr, *Exkommunikationsgewalt*. Cf. Rudolf Weigand's review of this work.

18

had found a single-leaf fragment of a fifth manuscript containing the first recension (Pfr). It is likely that further research, especially among manuscript fragments, will unearth further manuscripts of the first recension. Each such discovery will be important, since all of the manuscripts so far discovered suffer from some form of deficiency: Aa is interpolated while Bc Fd P and Pfr are incomplete.

Since my defense, my work has concentrated on exploring the consequences the discovery of the first recension has for our understanding of Gratian's *Decretum* and the development of twelfth-century legal thinking and teaching. The results of these investigations are found in the last two chapters of this book, arguing for a novel understanding of the foundation of the law school in Bologna and for distinguishing two different authors of the two recensions of the *Decretum*. In selecting the sections of the *Decretum* to study closely, I chose C. 24, since Lenherr here provided a beginning with his analysis of q. 1, and C. 11, q. 3, because this *questio* has thematic similarities with C. 24. Both these sections treat formal aspects of excommunication: in which situations must a sentence of excommunication be obeyed? (C. 11, q. 3); is a sentence of excommunication given by a heretic valid? (C. 24, q. 1); is it possible to excommunicate a dead person? (C. 24, q. 2); may the members of a sinner's household be excommunicated even if they have not sinned? (C. 24, q. 3). These four *questiones* contain 188 canons in the second recension, which correspond to a little over 5 percent of its more than 3,800 canons. Although the selection may seem small compared to the enormous size of the *Decretum*, it is substantial enough to allow conclusive evidence to be assembled.

In the close readings of these two sections, I study the structure of Gratian's arguments and attempt to find out where he took each canon from. I first look at Gratian's "case description" in the beginning of the *causa* and then at the questions which he derived from this "case." For each *questio*, I trace how Gratian develops the answer to his question. The purpose is to prove that all the texts he needed to answer the questions were present in the first recension, and that the argument in the first recension is coherent and complete. Such a proof is a strong argument for the thesis that the text contained in the four manuscripts Aa Bc Fd P in fact constitutes a first recension of Gratian's *Decretum*.

Chapters 2 and 3 not only aim at showing the inner consistency of the first recension but attempt also to determine the source from which each of the canons was extracted. The (relative) consistency with which the two recensions used different sources is another strong argument for my thesis. This consistency proves that the shorter version of the *Decretum* found in the four manuscripts is not an abbreviation, since an abbreviator would have no practical possibility of excising only those texts deriving from a few particular sources. The treatment of each *questio* in chapters 2 and 3 is prefaced by a table which lists the occurrences of the canons in the collections known to be among Gratian's sources, with columns devoted, first, to Gratian's *Decretum*, and then to the *Panormia*, the *Collectio Tripartita*, the *Polycarpus*, the *Collection in Three Books*, Anselm of Lucca's collection, and, finally, Ivo of Chartres' *Decretum*. Although Ivo's *Decretum* is not, as far as is known, one of Gratian's formal sources, I have nonetheless included it, because it is one of the largest magazines of texts in the period immediately preceding Gratian's. A final column provides, in a few cases, additional information. The tables were drawn up on the basis of the information found in Friedberg's edition, and in the standard finding tools.[53]

After the tables, each canon is analyzed in order to determine which of the possible sources Gratian in fact used. My methods are based on the criteria which Stephan Kuttner outlined in 1948. John Erickson, Peter Landau, and Titus Lenherr have later employed and refined his methods.[54] Their criteria for establishing sources may be summarized as follows:

(i) Two or more canons are found in close sequence or juxtaposition only in Gratian and an earlier collection.
(ii) A canon's inscription (most frequently a misattribution) is common only to Gratian and an earlier collection.

---

[53] I have used the following: the concordances for the canons in the *Polycarpus* in Horst, *Polycarpus* and for Pseudo-Isidorian canons in Horst Fuhrmann, *Einfluß und Verbreitung der pseudo-isidorischen Fälschungen von ihrem Auftauchen bis in die neuere Zeit*, MGH Schriften 24 (Munich 1972–1974). Canons with *incipits* A–G were searched in M. Fornasari, *Initia canonum a primaevis collectionibus usque ad "Decretum Gratiani,"* Monumenta Italiae ecclesiastica, Subsidia 1 (Florence 1972), which is based on a broad survey of printed collections. For canons which also appear in the *Sentences* of Peter Lombard, I used the source apparatus in [Peter Lombard,] *Magistri Petri Lombardi Sententiae in IV libris distributae*, Spicilegium Bonaventurianum 4–5 (Grottaferrata 1971–1981). A nineteenth-century work containing still useful, albeit sometimes unreliable, tables of canons in Gratian and pre-Gratian collections is Augustin Theiner, *Disquisitiones criticae in praecipuas canonum et decretalium collectiones* (Rome 1836). Martin Brett of Cambridge University kindly made available to me his *incipit* indices to Anselm of Lucca's collection, the *Collectio Tripartita*, and the *Collectio Britannica*. Since the *Collection in Three Books* was one of Gratian's most important sources and I could not find any available index to it, I compiled a provisional *incipit* index to Vatican City, BAV, Vat., lat. 3831. This index is available on the internet at http://pantheon.yale.edu/~haw6/canonlaw/3l.htm. Electronic media have recently begun to provide a convenient and flexible means for retrieving information of this kind. I have made extensive use of the *Cetedoc Library of Christian Latin Texts: CLCLT* (Turnhout 1981–) and the *Patrologia Latina Full Text Database* (Alexandria, Va. 1992–) which contains the text of the *PL* editions of, e.g., Burchard's and Ivo's collections. Linda Fowler-Magerl, *Kanones: A Selection of Canon Law Collections Compiled Outside Italy between 1000 and 1140* (Piesenkofen 1998) was available to me only at a late stage of my work.

[54] Kuttner, "De Gratiani opere," 125–127, Erickson, "Three Books," 72–73, Landau, "Neue Forschungen," 14–15, Landau, "Quellen und Bedeutung," 220–221, and Lenherr, *Exkommunikationsgewalt*, 61.

Table 1 *Formal sources of C. 24, q. 3, canons 26–29*

Gratian	*Panormia*	*Tripartita*	*Polycarpus*	*3 Books*	Anselm	Other
24.3.26	—	—	7.5.5	3.3.1	12.48	Alger 3.2a
24.3.27	—	—	7.5.6	3.3.2	12.49	—
24.3.28	—	—	7.5.24	3.3.15	12.52	—
24.3.29	—	—	7.5.22	3.3.10	12.61	—

(iii) The length of the excerpt, the arrangement of textual fragments and/or textual variants are common only to Gratian and an earlier collection.

(iv) A canon appears in only one pre-Gratian collection (with the reservation that any number of these collections remain unstudied or even unknown).

Naturally, these criteria will have greater or lesser reliability in specific cases. Ideally, two or more will support each other. The criteria may seem clear enough in theory but are often difficult to apply in practice. An important reason is that the collections which Gratian used as sources are themselves related to each other. So are the *Panormia* and the third part of the *Collectio Tripartita*, both largely derived from Ivo of Chartres' *Decretum*, which in turn draws substantially on the first two parts of the *Tripartita*. The *Polycarpus* used Anselm's collection as a source,[55] and *3L* appears to have drawn on both these works.[56] The result is that the same canons often appear in close sequence in several collections.

Consider an example, canons 26 to 29 in C. 24, q. 3 (for the details, see below, pp. 75–76).

The order among the fragments is similar in three collections, so that criterion (i) cannot be used to determine which of them was Gratian's source. Furthermore, in all of the collections each text is the same length as in the *Decretum*. There is some variation in the wording of the inscriptions in Anselm's collection (for canons 26 and 28) and in Alger's work; this indicates that neither of these was Gratian's source. Otherwise, only a collation of textual variants provides a basis for singling out the work used by Gratian. Variants recorded below in chapter 2 show that *3L* exhibits readings significantly different from those of Gratian in canons 27, 28, and 29. Anselm shares one of *3L*'s readings in c. 27. I conclude,

[55] Horst, *Polycarpus*, 41–46.
[56] Paul Fournier and Gabriel Le Bras, *Histoire des collections canoniques en Occident depuis les Fausses Décrétales jusqu'au "Décret" de Gratien* (Paris 1931–1932), II 201–202.

Table 2 *Formal sources of C. 24, q. 1, canons 2–3*

Gratian	Panormia	Tripartita	Polycarpus	3 Books	Anselm
24.1.2	—	1.46.3	7.8.1	—	12.67
24.1.3	—	1.46.2	1.18.4	1.5.3	—

therefore, by elimination, that Gratian's source for canons 27 and 28 was the *Polycarpus*. The textual evidence points to the *Polycarpus* or the *3L* as the source for c. 26 and the *Polycarpus* or Anselm as the source for c. 29. Following criterion (i), one might conclude that the *Polycarpus* was the source of both of these canons. This conclusion should, however, be only tentative, since criterion (i) might lead the researcher astray. Canons 2 and 3 in C. 24, q. 1 provide an example of this.

Agreement in length and internal omissions indicates that the *Tripartita* was Gratian's source for c. 2 while the false inscription proves that *3L* provided c. 3 (see chapter 2 below). If it were not for the false inscription, however, criterion (i) would have pointed to the *Tripartita* as his source, since the text there is so close to the text of c. 2.

To avoid such mistakes, I have employed criterion (i) only when no other evidence is available. In general, I have relied on collations of textual variants more often than Erickson and Landau appear to have done. These collations are recorded below in chapters 2 and 3 whenever there have been significant variants. If a canon appears in only one relevant pre-Gratian collection, or if there is some other reason to single out one collection as Gratian's source, the collations are usually omitted. Even in these cases, however, the reader can be confident that I have collated Gratian's text against that of his source, without finding significant variants.

For such detailed textual work, Friedberg's edition alone does not provide a sufficiently reliable text of the second recension for this project. While it would be impossible to re-edit even parts of the *Decretum* within the framework of this book, I have as a rule checked Friedberg's text against the readings of a few representative manuscripts in those passages which are analyzed extensively in the book. In the *Conspectus siglorum*, the manuscripts to which I refer by *sigla* are listed and briefly described. The first recension remains unedited, so for its text I have used the manuscripts.

In collating the text of the second recension of the *Decretum*, I do not consistently use the same manuscripts nor do I consistently use the same number of manuscripts. The reason for this is that the textual value of the different manuscripts of the *Decretum* still remains to be established.[57] I have, therefore, deemed it desirable to take samples from as many manuscripts as possible, but without collating all available manuscripts for every variant. During the textual work, I gradually learnt which manuscripts were more likely than others to yield early readings. Those observations are discussed in chapter 4, and they are also reflected in the fact that some manuscripts appear more often than others in the collations. As to the number of manuscripts employed, I felt free to judge in each case what was needed to establish Gratian's text; thus problematic passages were checked in more manuscripts than were straightforward ones.[58] For the first recension, I always used every relevant manuscript.

MANUSCRIPT DESCRIPTIONS

The four manuscripts and one fragment of the first recension stand at the center of my attention for most of this book. I have, therefore, deemed it valuable to publish detailed descriptions of these manuscripts, while the reader is referred to Rudolf Weigand's *Die Glossen zum "Dekret" Gratians* for detailed descriptions of second-recension manuscripts.

Admont, Stiftsbibliothek 23 and 43 (Aa)

These manuscripts contain the *Decretum* in two volumes. Admont 23 ends after C. 14. They were written by a single scribe in the 1160s or the 1170s in the Benedictine monastery of Admont in Austrian Styria. In the twelfth century, Admont belonged to the diocese of Salzburg. Although briefly mentioned in Kuttner's *Repertorium*, 112, Aa was first described in print by A. Krause in 1951.[59] Fritz Eheim described the two volumes in 1959, not noticing that they form a set or that the text of the *Decretum* is shorter than

[57] A valuable examination of the relationship between eighteen well-chosen Gratian manuscripts is found in Regula Gujer, "Concordia discordantium codicum manuscriptorum? Eine Untersuchung zur D. 16 des *Decretum Gratiani* und zur Textentwicklung einiger ausgewählter Handschriften" (doctoral thesis, University of Zurich). Unfortunately, I was unable to study this unpublished thesis at length. A summary is found in Regula Gujer, "Zur Überlieferung des *Decretum Gratiani*," in *Proceedings of the Ninth International Congress of Medieval Canon Law*, MIC Subs. 10 (Vatican City 1997), 87–104.

[58] My collations are positive, i.e., nothing can be concluded from the absence of a manuscript *siglum*. The form of my collations corresponds to that used in classical philology, as codified in Martin L. West, *Textual Criticism and Editorial Technique* (Stuttgart 1973) and Jacques André, *Règles et recommendations pour les éditions critiques, série latine* (Paris 1972). I sometimes give the readings of the material source under the *siglum "orig."* Reference to the appropriate edition is given in each case. I identify and collate the material source only when I deem it useful. If, e.g., Gratian and the material source share a reading, while the *Panormia* has a significantly different variant, the latter was probably not Gratian's formal source. When I have perceived no advantage for my project in identifying the material source, I have not done so.

[59] A. Krause, "Die Handschriften des *Decretum Gratiani* in der Admonter Stiftsbibliothek," in *Jahresbericht des Stiftsgymnasium in Admont m. Ö. R. über das Schuljahr 1950/51* (1951). This work, referred to by Winfried Stelzer and Hubert Mordek (see below, nn. 63 and 68), was not available to me.

1 Admont, Stiftsbibliothek 23 (Aa), fo. 105r. The main text contains C. 1, q. 1, c. 110 – d. p. c. 113 including c. 110, which was added only in the second recension. The short, first-recension form of c. 113 in the text was augmented in the bottom margin. Reproduced with permission.

usual.[60] Stephan Kuttner clarified these issues in 1960.[61] Titus Lenherr used these manuscripts in his research on Gratian's *Decretum* during the 1980s,[62] and Winfried Stelzer carefully analyzed the manuscript, especially the so-called *Collectio Admontensis* found on fos. 198r–236v of Admont 43, which contains several interesting and unusual Roman law-texts.[63] In addition to examining the glosses in this manuscript, Rudolf Weigand determined in 1991 that the incomplete text is the same as that found in Bc and Fd.[64]

The content of Aa is as follows:

Admont 23 (296 fos.)

fos. 1v–8r: The beginning of the anonymous introduction to the *Decretum*, "In prima parte agitur."[65]

fo. 8 r–v: The beginning of the anonymous introduction to the *Decretum*, "Hoc opus inscribitur."[66]

fos. 9r–199v: Part 1 and *Causae* 1 to 14 in part 2 of the first recension of the *Decretum*.

fos. 200r–296v: Supplement containing the canons and *dicta* which were added in the second recension and are missing on fos. 9r–199v: "Exceptiones quorumdam capitulorum in corpore libri omissorum . . ."

Admont 43 (342 fos.)

fos. 1r–11r: Continuation of the anonymous introduction, "In prima parte agitur, omitting the *de consecratione.*"

fos. 11r–12v: Continuation of the anonymous introduction, "Hoc opus inscribitur."

fos. 13r–198r: *Causae* 15 to 36 in part 2 of the first recension of the *Decretum*.

fos. 198r–236v: The *Collectio Admontensis*,[67] including (fos. 198r–204r) the *De immunitate et sacrilegio et singulorum clericalium ordinum compositione*,[68] and an excerpt from the *Collectio Tripartita*.

---

[60] Fritz Eheim, "Die Handschriften des *Decretum Gratiani* in Österreich," *Studia Gratiana* 7 (1959), 129–130 and 132–133.

[61] [Stephan Kuttner], "Select bibliography 1959–1960," *Traditio* 16 (1960), 565, see also Stephan Kuttner, "Some Gratian manuscripts with early glosses," *Traditio* 19 (1963), 534, note 7. It seems to have escaped notice that the Benedictine Jacob Wichner correctly registered as early as 1887 or 1888 (for Admont 23, only) that the main text is incomplete, see his *Catalog of Manuscripts in Stift Admont, Austria* (Ann Arbor, Mich.: University Microfilms, 1982).

[62] Lenherr, "Summarien," 531, note 10.

[63] Winfried Stelzer, *Gelehrtes Recht in Österreich von den Anfängen bis zum frühen 14. Jahrhundert*, Mittelungen des Instituts für Österreichische Geschichtsforschung, Ergänzungsband 26 (Vienna 1982), 25–44.   [64] Weigand, *Glossen zum "Dekret,"* 662–663.

[65] This old introduction was printed in *Bibliotheca Casinensis seu codicum manuscriptorum qui in tabulario Casinensi asservantur* series II (Montecassino 1875), 171–196.

[66] This introduction is found only here and in Me, cf. Weigand, *Glossen zum "Dekret,"* 849.

[67] This legal collection was studied by Stelzer, *Gelehrtes Recht in Österreich*, 25–44.

[68] Studied by Hubert Mordek, "Auf der Suche nach einem verschollenen Manuskript . . .: Friedrich Maassen und der Traktat *De immunitate et sacrilegio et singulorum clericalium ordinum compositione*," in *Aus Kirche und Reich: Studien zu Theologie, Politik und Recht im Mittelalter: Festschrift für Friedrich Kempf* (Sigmaringen 1983), 187–200.

fos. 237r–279v: *De consecratione* (part 3 of the *Decretum*).

fos. 280r–340v: Supplement containing the canons and *dicta* which were added in the second recension and are missing on fos. 13–198r with the same rubric as in Admont 23.

fo. 341: Tables of Greek letters with their numerical values (these values are discussed in D. 73).

fo. 342r–v: D. 73 from the first part of the *Decretum* (this distinction is not found elsewhere in Aa).[69]

Barcelona, Arxiu de la Corona d'Aragó, Santa Maria de Ripoll 78 (Bc)

This manuscript, which breaks off after C. 12, belonged to the library of the monastery of Ripoll until this library was incorporated with the Archives of the Aragonese Crown in 1835. It was written in the twelfth century in Italy. The text is preceded by the anonymous introduction "In prima parte agitur," listing all thirty-six *causae*.

Bc was first mentioned in print in 1915 in a catalogue of patristic manuscripts in Spain.[70] Gérard Fransen was the first to point out, in 1954, that the original text omits many canons which a contemporary hand added in the margins.[71] Two years later, he characterized Bc as an abbreviation and indicated that most of the Roman law texts are missing from the original text.[72] Antonio García y García catalogued Bc in 1962 pointing out that the manuscript is very important for the study of Gratian's text.[73] In an article published in 1962, Pablo Pinedo argued that the *Decretum* originally contained only Gratian's *dicta,* while the canons were added later. He used the fact that canons had been added in the margins of Bc as evidence for this hypothesis.[74] Stephan Kuttner disagreed, stating that "it is out of the question that this MS could represent an early stage of the *Decretum*."[75] Rudolf Weigand examined the glosses of this manuscript in 1991.[76]

In an exhibition catalogue from 1992, Albert Torra pointed out that the volume contains several inserted leaves which were not originally part of the book. These leaves accommodate some of the additional texts that could not be written in the margins. According to Torra's collation, the

---

[69] About D. 73, which is a *palea*, see Rambaud, "Le legs," 106.

[70] Zacharias García, "Bibliotheca Patrum Latinorum Hispaniensis, 2," in *Sitzungsberichte der Kaiserlichen Akademie der Wissenschaften, philosophisch-historischen Klasse* 169: 2 (Vienna 1915), 45. Bc was included in Kuttner, *Repertorium*, 114, on the basis of this note.

[71] Gérard Fransen, "Manuscrits canonique conservés en Espagne (II)," *Revue d'histoire ecclésiastique* 49 (1954), 152.   [72] Fransen, "La date du *Décret*," 529.

[73] Antonio García y García, "Los manuscritos del *Decreto* de Graciano en las bibliotecas y archivos de España," *Studia Gratiana* 8 (1962), 165–166: *"Como se verá por el análisis completo, es éste un manuscrito muy importante para el estudio del texto de Graciano."* See also Antonio García y García, *Iglesia, Sociedad y Derecho*, Bibliotheca Salmanticensis, Estudios 74 (Salamanca 1985), 38 and 59.

[74] Pablo Pinedo, "Decretum Gratiani: dictum Gratiani," *Ius canonicum* 2 (Pamplona 1962), 149–166.

[75] Kuttner, "Some Gratian manuscripts with early glosses," 533, note 4.

[76] Weigand, *Glossen zum "Dekret,"* 686–687.

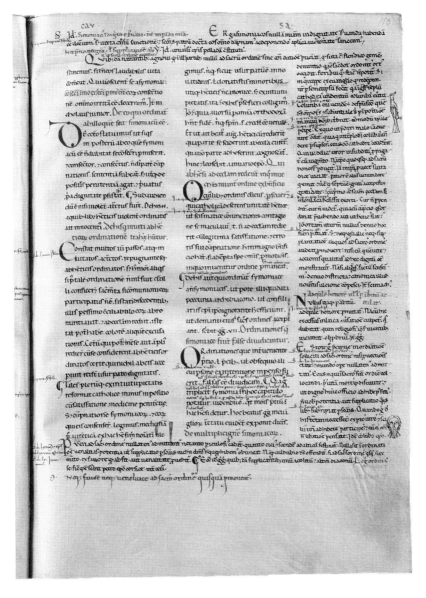

2 Barcelona, Arxiu de la Corona d'Aragó, Ripoll 78 (Bc), fo. 110r.
The main text contains the first recension of C. 1, q. 1, c. 108 – d. p. c. 113.
The margins contain additions made in the second recension, including
canons 110 and 117–120. The short first-recension text of c. 113 is augmented
between the lines. Reproduced with permission.

27

added leaves are folios 19, 23, 29, 30, 31, 36, 38, 63, 70–71 (bifolium), 77, 81, 82, 85, 88, 91, 98, and 106.[77] Judging from the quire signatures that are visible on the microfilm, the manuscript is otherwise composed of regular quires of eight leaves.

The content of Bc (180 fos.) is as follows:

fos. 1r–15v: The anonymous introduction to the *Decretum*, "In prima parte agitur," complete, but omitting the *de consecratione*.

fo. 16r–v: Blank.

fos. 17r–178v: The first recension of the *Decretum*, ending defectively with the end of C. 12. The manuscript once continued with C. 13 (and, probably, the rest of the *Decretum*), as is evident from the catchword at the bottom of fo. 178v: "<D>iocesi///". A later hand added, in the margins and on additional leaves, second-recension texts missing in the original text of the manuscript.

fos. 179r–180v: Fragment of a glossed Bible, Numbers 2: 27–3: 18.

Florence, Biblioteca Nazionale Centrale, Conv. Soppr. A. 1.402 (Fd)

Walther Holtzmann noticed this manuscript during his research for the *Kanonistische Ergänzungen zur Italia Pontificia*, because a marginal note contains the text of an otherwise unknown papal decretal, issued by Pope Adrian IV for Bishop Amandus of Bisceglie in Apulia. The bishop's letter to the pope is also present in the margins as well as two letters issued for the same bishop by a Cardinal John.[78] In 1957, Stephan Kuttner noted that Professor Peter Huizing of Nijmegen was studying Fd at Holtzmann's suggestion, and described the manuscript as "thus far considered an *Abbreviatio* but may turn out to be of especial value for tracing the stages of revision of the *Decretum* itself."[79] Holtzmann considered Fd a very old Gratian manuscript, but Jacqueline Rambaud objected that it was written in an archaizing hand around 1200, and she made little use of it.[80] In 1960, Francis Gossman noted that Fd "could well represent the work of the *magister* in a more pure form" than other manuscripts.[81] The manuscript was described in print in 1979.[82] Rudolf Weigand examined its glosses in 1991.[83]

The quire structure of Fd is complicated: 1^8 2^8 $(-1, 7^{th}$ leaf$)$ $3–5^8$ 6^4 $7–21^8$ 22^4 23^8 24^1 25^2 26^3 (singletons).

---

[77] *Catalunya Medieval: Del 20 de maig al 10 d'agost, Barcelona 1992* (Barcelona 1992), 204–205. I thank Alberto Torra for providing me with a photocopy of the description of Bc.

[78] Walther Holtzmann, "Kanonistische Ergänzungen zur Italia pontificia," *Quellen und Forschungen aus italienischen Archiven und Bibliotheken* 38 (1958; also published separately, Tübingen 1959), 145–149.   [79] Stephan Kuttner, "Annual report," *Traditio* 13 (1957), 466.

[80] Rambaud, "Le legs," 87. Holtzmann talks, *Kanonistische Ergänzungen*, 149, about "die . . . sehr alte Florentiner Gratianhs." and is reported by Rambaud to have said that it was "un des plus anciens."

[81] Francis Gossman, *Pope Urban II and Canon Law* (Washington, D.C. 1960), 128–129.

[82] M. Elena Magheri Cataluccio and A. Ugo Fossa, *Biblioteca e cultura a Camaldoli: Dal medioevi all'umanesimo*, Studia Anselmiana 75 (Rome 1979), 207–208.

[83] Weigand, *Glossen zum "Dekret"*, 748–752.

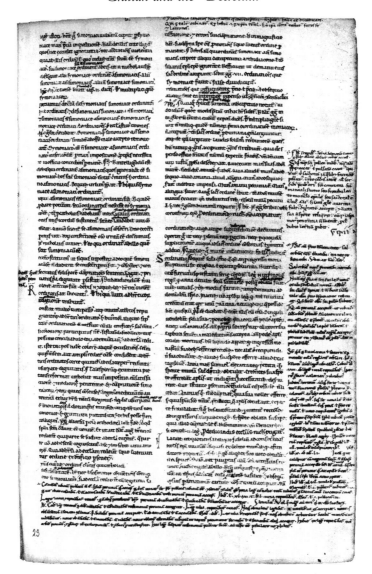

3 Florence, Biblioteca Nazionale Centrale, Conv. soppr. A. 1.402 (Fd),
fo. 23r. The main text contains the first recension of C. 1, q. 1,
canons 106 – d p. c. 123 and C. 1, q. 2, d. a. c. 1 and c. 1. The margins
contain texts added in the second recension, including the end of c. 113 at the
top of the page. The capital letters R and S refer the reader to further
additional texts in the supplement at the end of the volume. Reproduced with
permission.

The content of Fd (181 fos.) is as follows:

fos. 1r–104r: Parts 1 and 2 of the first recension of the *Decretum*, beginning defectively in D. 28, d. p. c. 13: "//stituti licite matrimonio . . ." (l. 5 in Friedberg's edition).

fos. 104r–164r: Supplement containing the canons and *dicta* which were added in the second recension and are missing on fos. 1r–104r. Before part 1 and each *causa* the appropriate section of the anonymous introduction to the *Decretum*, "In prima parte agitur," is reproduced.

fos. 164r–167: The *de consecratione* (incomplete).

fo. 167v: Canons 1 and 2 from the council of Reims of 1148.[84] Canon 2 ends defectively, ". . . quam ad desides neg//" suggesting that the text once continued on the next page.

fos. 168r–175v: Further texts from the *de consecratione*.

fo. 176r: *Compilatio quinta* 1.1.1–1.1.5, ending incompletely ". . . in quibus nostrum [!] monaste//."[85] Since 176v is blank, it would appear that 176r (which is fully written) originally was the verso side of the first leaf in a manuscript of the *Compilatio quinta*. It lacks Honorius III's bull of promulgation.

fo. 176v: blank.

fos. [177–181] in the end of the volume are five leaves containing fragments of liturgical books (four leaves from a breviary and one leaf from a missal) and three fragments of documents concerning the Camaldolese order.

In her unpublished dissertation, Adriana Di Domenico devoted a detailed study to the paleographical, codicological, and art-historical features of Fd.[86] The letters reproduced in the margins suggest that the manuscript was written in the second half of the twelfth century in Apulia, and Di Domenico finds the scripts on fos. 1–164 consistent with this date and origin. She identifies three, possibly four different hands on these folios. A first hand wrote fos. 1r–12v, a second fos. 12v–104r (with a possible change of hand at the beginning of fo. 44r), and a third fos. 104r–167v. I am inclined to think that fo. 44 (and following) in fact was written by a new scribe, which would explain why quire 6, ending with fo. 43, consists of only four leaves, while most other quires are made up of eight leaves. Folios 1–167 constitute, in Di Domenico's opinion, the original codex, to which the last nine folios (168–176) were added at a later point. I suggest that the original volume contained only fos. 1–107 (quires 1–14) with the text

[84] Iohannes Domenicus Mansi, *Sacrorum conciliorum nova et amplissima collectio* (Florence and Venice 1759–1798), XXI 713–714.

[85] Emil Friedberg, ed., *Quinque compilationes antiquae nec non Collectio canonum Lipsiensis* (Leipzig 1882), 151–152.

[86] Adriana Di Domenico, "Codici miniati romanici nel fondo Conventi soppressi della Biblioteca Nazionale Centrale di Firenze. Camaldoli – Vallombrosa – Santa Maria Novella" (doctoral dissertation, Università degli Studi di Firenze, 1989–1990). The dissertation is available in the manuscript department of the Biblioteca Nazionale Centrale, Florence. I thank Adriana Di Domenico, who is a librarian at this library, for drawing it to my attention and allowing me to quote it.

ending on fo. 104r. At a later point in the twelfth century, the supplement was added, first on the remaining blank pages (fos. 104r–107v), and then on new quires. These, making up fos. 108–176 (quires 15–22), are of coarser parchment than the earlier quires. Folios 168r–175v are written by a single hand in the second half of the thirteenth century and constitute a quire.

Di Domenico noted that the illuminated initials exhibit two distinct twelfth-century styles. Some of them appear to have been painted in Apulia while some are typical of the school of Arezzo. Di Domenico concluded that the manuscript came to Camaldoli in the twelfth century. It stayed there until Napoleon's army secularized that library in 1809. When the library of Camaldoli was catalogued in 1406, this manuscript is mentioned with a description that allows the conclusion that fo. 175 was its last leaf at that point, since fo. 175v ends with the words "voluntate accipitur perseverat" (*de cons.* D. 5, c. 27).

Clxviij Jtem decretum anticum quj incipit: statuti licite, et finit voluntate acquiritur, in cartis pecudinis et tabulis.[87]

In an article published in 1999, Carlos Larrainzar takes issue with many of Di Domenico's conclusions and argues that this manuscript belonged to Gratian himself and that he used it in composing the second recension.[88] Larrainzar's argument is complicated and I could not do justice to all its details here. A main component is his dating of fos. 1–167 earlier than other scholars. From the presence of two canons from the Council of Rheims in 1148 on fo. 167v (written by the scribe who also wrote fos. 104r–167v), Larrainzar concludes that what precedes must have been written *before* 1148.[89] There is, in my opinion, no reason to think that these conciliar canons were copied into Fd in 1148 or even soon after that year. Such texts continued to be of interest and could therefore be copied long after their promulgation. Their presence proves that the scribe who copied fos. 104r–167v worked *after* the time of the council, which in any case seems likely on paleographical grounds. Another important component in Larrainzar's argument is his identification of ten places in Fd where a correcting hand brings the text of Fd up to date with the second recension. Larrainzar argues that the perfect correspondence between these corrections and the second recension proves that only the author could have made them.[90] In my view, these corrections could have been made

---

[87] Magheri Cataluccio and Fossa, *Biblioteca e cultura a Camaldoli*, 153, n. 164. I reproduce the text of the manuscript in accordance with the notes to the editors' corrected text.

[88] Carlos Larrainzar, "El *Decreto* de Graciano del códice Fd (= Firenze, Biblioteca Nazionale Centrale, Conventi Soppressi A.I.402): in memoriam Rudolf Weigand," *Ius Ecclesiae* 10 (1998), 421–489.

[89] *Ibid.* 437–438: "Como se vió, esta 'colección' de 'Adiciones boloñesas' [fos. 104r–167v] es necesariamente anterior al año 1148, tal como sugiere la datación de los cánones que cierran la última hoja conservada del cuadernillo veintidós [fol. 167vb]."   [90] *Ibid.* 450–464.

by any interested reader who had a copy of the second recension at hand. There is, thus, no basis for Larrainzar's thesis that Fd was Gratian's original manuscript nor that any of the correcting hands belonged to him.

Paris, Bibliothèque Nationale de France, nouvelles acquisitions latines 1761 (P)

The Bibliothèque Nationale bought this manuscript on 24 November 1896 from the Parisian bookseller Th. Belin.[91] In 1952, Jacqueline Rambaud devoted an entire article to discussing the manuscript, which caught her interest, since it leaves out most of the excerpts from Roman law found in other Gratian manuscripts. Rambaud believed, however, that P was an abbreviation which allowed an indirect view of an early form of the *Decretum*, not that early form itself. Rudolf Weigand did not examine this manuscript for his *Glossen zum "Dekret,"* since Stephan Kuttner reported in the *Repertorium*, 108, that it lacks glosses. P does in fact contain at least two brief glosses (fos. 3r and 54v). Its quire structure is, with two small exceptions, regular: $1-12^8$ $13^{10}(-2,$ the 3rd and 5th leaves) $14-19^8$ $20^8(-2,$ 7th and 8th leaves).

The text of this manuscript ends suddenly in mid-sentence in the middle of C. 12, q. 2, c. 39 after only three lines have been written on the verso of fo. 158. It does not seem likely that P ever was a complete manuscript of the first recension. Unlike Aa, Bc, Fd, the additions of the second recension have not been added to this manuscript. The contents of P (158 fos.) are as follows:

fos 1r–158v: A text of the first recension of the *Decretum*, ending incompletely in C. 12, q. 2, c. 39: "episcopus absque ulla" (line 10 in Friedberg's edition).

Paris, Bibliothèque Nationale de France, latin 3884 I, fo. 1 (Pfr)

BN lat. 3884 I–II (Pf) is an important early manuscript of the second recension. Rudolf Weigand noted in 1991 that the first folio of the first volume is a fragment of another *Decretum* manuscript, containing C. 11, q. 3, d. p. c. 43–c. 69.[92] In 1998, Carlos Larrainzar observed that the leaf in fact comes from a manuscript of the first recension.[93]

---

[91] Henri Omont, "Nouvelles acquisitions du département des manuscrits de la Bibliothèque Nationale pendant les années 1896–1897," *Bibliothèque de l'Ecole des Chartes* 59 (1898), 96. I thank the staff of the Manuscript department of the Bibliothèque Nationale de France for informing me about the provenance.   [92] Weigand, *Glossen zum "Dekret,"* 881.
[93] Larrainzar, "El *decreto* de Graciano del códice Fd," 449.

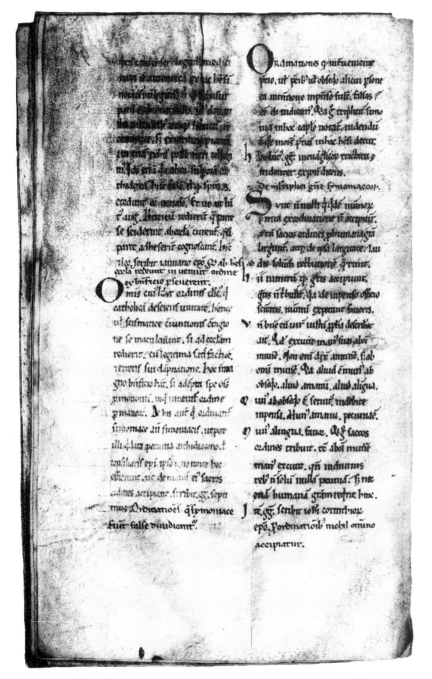

4   Paris, Bibliothèque Nationale de France, nouvelles acquisitions latines 1761
(P), fo. 95v. The text contains the first recension of C. 1, q. 1, c. 111 – c. 114.
Reproduced with permission.

Chapter 2

HERESY AND EXCOMMUNICATION: *CAUSA* 24

The first test case is *Causa* 24. The purpose of this chapter is to demonstrate that a close reading of this *causa* supports the thesis that the text of the manuscripts Aa and Fd is a first recension of Gratian's *Decretum* (the incomplete Bc P and Pfr do not contain C. 24). This demonstration follows two lines, showing that the text of Aa and Fd presents a coherent and complete argument, and that the two recensions used different sets of sources.

Causa 24 is the second of the *causae hereticorum*, so called since the author of the second recension at C. 7, q. 1, d. p. c. 48 refers to C. 23 with the words "in prima causa hereticorum."[1] Both *Causae* 23 and 24 are concerned with the treatment of heretics and the latter with the mechanics of excommunication (and reconciliation) in particular. In the second recension, C. 24 contains eighty-eight canons (and one *palea*), thirty-nine of which are (wholly or, in three cases, in part) present already in the first recension. The *causa* is, thus, of a reasonable size in the first recension and there are substantial additions in the second recension. Both circumstances make it a suitable test case.

Another reason for selecting C. 24 is that any examination of its first *questio* is greatly facilitated by Titus Lenherr's groundbreaking study from 1987, which contains an analysis and a new edition of this *questio*.[2] His work also allows the sceptical reader to compare my results to those of a scholar whose aim was not to prove the existence of a first recension. The following investigation of q. 1 draws on Lenherr's work, although I deemed it wise to test his results in each case.

As is his habit in the second part of the *Decretum*, Gratian begins *Causa* 24 by describing an imaginary situation, from which he derives the questions that he intends to answer in the following *questiones*:

---

[1] Cf. Johann Friedrich von Schulte, *Die Geschichte der Quellen und Literatur des canonischen Rechts* I (Stuttgart 1875), 49–50, note 9, for this and other self-quotations in the *Decretum*.

[2] Lenherr, *Exkommunikationsgewalt*.

A certain bishop, who had lapsed into heresy, deprived some of his priests of their offices and marked them with a sentence of excommunication. After his death he and his followers are accused of heresy and condemned together with all their families. Here it is first inquired whether a person who has lapsed into heresy may deprive others of their offices or mark them with a sentence. Second, whether a person may be excommunicated after his death. Third, whether for the sin of one person his entire household is to be excommunicated.[3]

Below, I shall follow Gratian's discussion of these questions and examine how he reaches his answers. His discussion and his conclusions are found in the *dicta*, which are supported by canons. All of the *dicta* in C. 24 were already present in the first recension. I will show that all three of Gratian's questions received a complete and coherent treatment already in the first recension. The canons added in the second recension are mostly less immediately relevant for the questions posed. Also, I will demonstrate the consistency with which the two recensions drew on separate groups of sources.

As a preliminary, table 3 documents occurrences of the texts of C. 24, q. 1 in the canonical collections which Gratian used when compiling the *Decretum*. Those canons wholly (or almost wholly) present in the first recension are indicated with bold face in the first column. Those only partially present appear in italics. In the table, I anticipate my conclusions by using bold face for Gratian's source. When Gratian used more than one source for a single canon, or when either of two works could have been the source, italics are used. Necessary detail is provided in the remainder of this chapter.[4]

CAN A HERETIC EXCOMMUNICATE?

In the first question of *Causa* 24, Gratian asks whether a heretical bishop's sentence of excommunication or deposition has legal validity. The beginning of d. a. c. 1 states that it is easy to prove that a heretic cannot depose or excommunicate. Initially, his argumentation follows two lines in accordance with a distinction which he immediately introduces: "For every heretic either follows an already condemned heresy or fashions a

---

[3] *Ibid.* 18 (cf. Friedberg, ed., *Decretum*, 965): "Quidam episcopus in heresim lapsus aliquot de sacerdotibus suis offitio priuauit et sententia excommunicationis notauit. Post mortem de heresi accusatus dampnatur et sequaces eius cum omni familia sua. Hic primum queritur, an lapsus in heresim possit alios offito priuare uel sententia notare. Secundo, an post mortem aliquis possit excommunicari. Tertio, an pro peccato alicuius tota familia sit excommunicanda."

[4] For a fuller treatment, see Anders Winroth, "The making of Gratian's *Decretum*" (Ph.D. dissertation, Columbia University 1996), 52–111.

Table 3 *Formal sources of C. 24, q. 1*

Gratian	Panormia	Tripartita	Polycarpus	3 Books	Anselm	Ivo, Decretum	Notes
24.1.1	—	—	—	—	—	—	Cf. 24.1.3
24.1.2	—	**1.46.3**	7.8.1	—	12.67	—	—
24.1.3	—	1.46.2	1.18.4	**1.5.3**	—	—	Alger 3.74
24.1.4	**5.133**	—	—	—	—	14.57	—
24.1.5	—	—	**7.2.1**	—	—	—	—
24.1.6	—	—	**7.2.2**	2.26.16	12.7	—	—
24.1.7	—	—	**7.3.1**	3.1.1	1.37	—	—
24.1.8	—	—	**7.3.2**	3.1.2	—	—	—
24.1.9	—	—	1.3.1	**1.2.1**	1.13 & 1.35	—	—
24.1.10	—	—	1.3.2	**1.2.2**	1.36	—	—
24.1.11	—	—	1.3.7	**1.2.6**	1.16	—	—
24.1.12	—	—	1.18.6	**1.5.5**	1.27 & 2.54	—	—
24.1.13	—	—	—	**1.5.8**	1.38	—	—
24.1.14	4.109	—	1.3.6 & 1.3.3	**1.2.3–4**	1.60	—	—
24.1.15	—	—	1.17.4	**1.1.11**	1.15	—	—
24.1.16	—	—	—	**1.3.6**	1.30	—	—
24.1.17	—	—	1.1.3	**1.3.2**	—	—	—
24.1.18	—	—	**7.3.3**	3.1.3	1.10 & 5.1	—	—
24.1.19	—	—	**7.3.4**	3.1.5	5.2	—	—
24.1.20	—	—	**7.3.5**	3.1.8	5.3	—	—
24.1.21	—	—	—	**2.34-39**	—	—	—
24.1.22	—	—	**7.3.6**	3.1.9	1.56	—	—
24.1.23	—	—	**7.4.1**	—	12.47	—	—
24.1.24	—	**2.50.13–14**	—	—	—	—	—
24.1.25	—	—	**7.4.2**	3.2.1	1.64	—	—

24.1.26	—	—	*3.30.3 & 7.4.3*	*3.2.2*	*5.20*	—	—
24.1.27	—	**2.50.17**	—	—	—	5.25	—
24.1.28	—	**3.2.22**	—	—	9.52	2.108	—
24.1.29	—	—	**7.5.1**	**3.3.32**	12.51	—	—
24.1.30	—	—	**7.5.7**	3.3.11	12.40	—	—
24.1.31	—	—	**6.15.19**	3.3.3	5.59	—	—
24.1.32	—	—	**7.5.8**	—	12.41	—	—
24.1.33	—	—	**7.5.9**	—	12.43	—	—
24.1.34	—	—	—	3.2.4	—	—	—
24.1.35	5.134	1.62.65	—	—	—	14.58	—
24.1.36	5.135	1.62.66	—	—	—	14.59	—
24.1.37	—	**1.62.67**	—	—	—	—	—
24.1.38	—	3.3.21	7.5.21	—	12.58	3.179	—
24.1.39	—	**3.10.25–26**	—	—	—	6.390–1	—
24.1.40	—	*3.1.8*	*7.3.8*	—	B 9.53 & C 9.61	—	1.170
24.1.41	—	—	**7.5.4**	3.3.12	11.117	15.117	—
24.1.42	—	—	**7.5.29**	3.3.13	—	—	—

new one."[5] The former group is discussed in canons 1–4 with the accompanying *dicta* (d. a. c. 1 and d. p. c. 3), while the latter is treated in d. p. c. 4 and in the following canons. This treatment is summarized in the first sentence of d. p. c. 37. At this point, the *questio* has, however, already shifted its focus away from the distinction between old and new heresies which is presented in d. a. c. 1. Many of canons 5–37 can certainly be taken to make statements about new heresies specifically, but it is hard to escape the impression that Gratian was more interested in what these canons say about heretics generally. The distinction plays no discernible role in the last section of the *questio*, i.e. in the *dicta* p. c. 37 and p. c. 39 and in canons 38 to 42. Here, Gratian is concerned with the possible objection stemming from patristic texts which affirm the validity of baptisms performed by heretics, if such baptisms are considered valid, why does not the same apply to excommunications performed by heretics?

OLD HERESIES

In regard to heretics following an old heresy, Gratian states in d. a. c. 1 that "he who follows an already condemned heresy takes part in the condemnation of that heresy."[6] Of the following three canons, only c. 1 is present in the first recension. This canon alone provides enough support for Gratian's statements about old heresies in d. a. c. 1. In fact, the *dictum* even contains verbal echoes of canon 1 (but not of canons 2 or 3). "Qui uero heresim iam dampnatam sequitur, eius dampnationis se participem facit" (d. a. c. 1) is obviously modelled on "Quicumque enim in heresim semel dampnatam labitur, eius dampnatione se ipsum inuoluit" (c. 1).

The two canons added only in the second recension were clearly drawn from the sources usually used in this recension, the *Collectio Tripartita* and the *Collection in Three Books* (*3L*). Canon 2 is found in three relevant collections, but only the *Tripartita* has a text of the same length and with the same omissions as the *Decretum*. This collection was in all likelihood the source.[7] Canon 3 appears in four of the usual sources, but only *3L* shares the misattribution to Pope Felix found in the *Decretum* and was therefore, most likely, the source.[8]

The provenance of c. 1 is more complicated and requires fuller treatment. Its text does not, to the best of my knowledge, appear before Gratian's *Decretum*. Gratian ascribes the canon to Pope Gelasius, who was

---

[5] Lenherr, *Exkommunicationsgewalt*, 18 (cf. Friedberg, ed., *Decretum*, 966, lines 2–3): "Omnis enim hereticus aut iam dampnatam heresim sequitur aut nouam confingit."

[6] Lenherr, *Exkommunicationsgewalt*, 18 (cf. Friedberg, ed., *Decretum*, 966, lines 3–5): "Qui uero heresim iam dampnatam sequitur, eius dampnationis se participem facit."

[7] Lenherr, *Exkommunikationsgewalt*, 63 and 85.   [8] *Ibid.* 85–86.

also the author of canons 2 and 3 (although the *Decretum* ascribes the latter to Pope Felix). Lenherr points out that c. 1 bears resemblances to parts of canons 2 and 3 as well as to a section of Gelasius' letter 10, which is the text from which c. 3 was excerpted. The relevant section of Gelasius' letter appears in Alger of Liège's *De misericordia et iustitia* 3.74.[9] Lenherr finds similarities between Alger's introductory sentence and Gratian's inscription to c. 1:

Vnde cum Achatius absque sinodali auctoritate ab Apostolico se dampnatum quereretur, contra Gelasius scribit dicens *Lenh. Fr.:* Quod vero dicebant eum, etiam si peccasset, non iuste tamen a Romana sede damnatum esse, . . . nec in generali concilio, sed sola Romana sede damnatus, hoc item Gelasius improbat hoc modo *Alg.*

Lenherr concluded that Gratian copied c. 1 from an as yet unidentified source, which is somehow related to Alger's work.[10] I cannot see, however, that there are any similarities so significant that they justify this conclusion. Gratian's source for this canon, thus, remains unidentified.

Having established that a heretic following an old, already condemned heresy automatically takes part of that condemnation, Gratian quotes a decretal issued by Pope Alexander II (c. 4). This decretal determines that an excommunicated person cannot excommunicate. In d. p. c. 3, Gratian combines this decretal with d. a. c. 1 and concludes that a person following an old heresy (and hence being "condemned with an old excommunication"[11]) cannot excommunicate someone else.

Obviously, c. 4 is necessary for the reasoning in d. p. c. 3, and it is, as could be expected, found in the first recension. The only relevant collection in which c. 4 appears is the *Panormia*, but the inscription there is, Lenherr points out, different from that of the *Decretum*.[12] While the *Decretum*, both in Friedberg's and in Lenherr's editions, reads the address as "Valeriano episcopo martiri," the manuscripts of the *Panormia* give the name of the addressee as William (*Willihelmo, Villermo, Guillelmo,* or other forms[13]) and his title as marquise (*marchioni* or *martioni*[14]).

The manuscripts of the *Decretum* show, as Lenherr clarifies, progressive corruption in the text of this inscription. A single manuscript, Aa, preserves the correct title *marchioni*, while a few old manuscripts give the

---

[9] Kretzschmar, *Alger von Lüttichs Traktat*, 366–367.
[10] Lenherr, *Exkommunikationsgewalt*, 62.
[11] *Ibid.* 20 (cf. Friedberg, ed., *Decretum*, 966, line 2): "antiqua excommunicatione dampnatus."
[12] Lenherr, *Exkommunikationsgewalt*, 86.
[13] I have noted the following variants: *Willermo* (*Pan.FJ*), *Villermo* (BN lat. 3868), *Willihelmo* (*Pan.M*), "*WiĦo*" (BN lat. 3864 and 13660), *Guillelmo* (BN lat. 14995), *Guilelmo* (BN lat. 3867), *Guilgelmo* (*Pan.E*) and even *W.* (*Pan.L*).
[14] The latter spelling is found in BN lat. 3864 and 3867; the former (as well as *marcioni*) is very common.

title as *martiri* only. Later, it developed into *episcopo martiri* and, finally, into *episcopo et martiri*. The name is, however, always *Valeriano*. It seems, therefore, that Gratian originally wrote *Valeriano marchioni*, and there is no reason to imagine that his source was not the *Panormia* (particularly if one assumes that his *Panormia* manuscript contained a name form such as *Villermo* that could have been misread as *Valeriano*). It is unlikely that Gratian used another source, since the canon was relatively recent, excerpted from a decretal issued by Pope Alexander II (1061–1073), and had not had any large canonical transmission in Gratian's time. It first appears in the *Collectio Britannica*, a collection compiled at the end of the eleventh century.[15] From there, it came into the collection of Paris, Bibliothèque de l'Arsenal 713 B, which was the source of Ivo of Chartres' *Decretum* and *Panormia*.[16]

It is, of course, significant that it is a first-recension manuscript, Aa, that is the only one to preserve what Gratian originally wrote.[17] The other first-recension manuscript available for C. 24, Fd, gives Valeriano's title as *marti.* which may be expanded either as *martioni* or as *martiri*. An awkward abbreviation such as this in an early *Decretum* manuscript may account for the erroneous *martiri* in second-recension manuscripts.

NEW HERESIES

In the lengthy d. p. c. 4, Gratian discusses those who fashion "a new heresy out of their heart."[18] In this complicated discussion, he draws on several canons in C. 24, q. 1, without referring to them explicitly. In the following analysis of this *dictum*, I aim at determining which canons Gratian actually used. The *dictum* was present in the first recension, and I will show that he used no canons which are not found in that recension.

Gratian begins the discussion by stating his conclusion or, as it were, the thesis which he strives to prove: "If someone fashions a new heresy out of his heart, he cannot condemn anyone from the moment when he begins

---

[15] London, British Library Add. 8873, fo. 51v, see Anders Winroth, ed., "Epistulae Alexandri papae secundi in *Collectione Britannica* asservatae" (unpublished edition), no. 85. Cf. Paul Ewald, "Die Papstbriefe der Brittischen Sammlung," *Neues Archiv der Gesellschaft für ältere deutsche Geschichtskunde* 5 (1880), 342.

[16] Fo. 148r. About this collection, see Robert Somerville, "Papal Excerpts in Arsenal MS 713B: Alexander II and Urban II," in *Proceedings of the Ninth International Congress of Medieval Canon Law*, MIC Subs. 10 (Vatican City 1997), and Robert Somerville with the collaboration of Stephan Kuttner, *Urban II, the "Collectio Britannica," and the Council of Melfi (1089)* (Oxford 1996), 16–21.

[17] Incidentally, it was the reading of Aa at this point, as reported by Lenherr, which first prompted me to speculate about a first recension.

[18] Lenherr, *Exkommunikationsgewalt*, 21 (cf. Friedberg, ed., *Decretum*, 967, lines 1–2): "ex corde suo nouam heresim."

to preach such things, since a person who already is thrown to the ground cannot overthrow anyone."[19] This sentence summarizes the contents of canons 35 and 36; it also contains two passages reproduced verbatim from these texts (which both derive from Pope Nicholas I's well-known letter to Emperor Michael III).[20] Gratian devotes the rest of the *dictum* to adducing evidence and arguments which support the thesis of the first sentence.

In the first part of the *dictum*, Gratian ties the power of binding and loosing to possession of the Holy Spirit, which can be received only in the Church. He first cites Christ's words to the apostles: "Those whose sins you forgive, are forgiven; those whose sins you retain, are retained" (John 20: 23).[21] Gratian points out that Christ immediately before this statement says: "Receive the Holy Spirit" (John 20: 22),[22] "in order that he might manifestly show to all that he who does not possess the Holy Spirit cannot retain or forgive sins."[23] He then adds that the Holy Spirit can be received only in the Church, "since it creates through grace also the unity itself."[24] He illustrates this statement by pointing out that it was only to the apostles gathered into one that Christ said "Receive the Holy Spirit" (John 20: 22) and that the Holy Spirit descended at Pentecost. He then concludes that if the Spirit cannot be received outside the Church, it cannot work there either (i.e., cause excommunication or reconciliation).

---

[19] Lenherr, *Exkommunikationsgewalt*, 21 (cf. Friedberg, ed., *Decretum*, 967, lines 1–3): "Si autem ex corde suo nouam heresim confinxit, ex quo talia predicare ceperit, neminem dampnare potuit, quia non potest deicere quemquam iam prostratus." Cf. Pope Nicholas I's words in c. 36 (Lenherr, *Exkommunikationsgewalt*, 49, lines 7–9; cf. Friedberg, ed., *Decretum*, 981, lines 9–12): "non potuisse . . . quemlibet remouere qui fuerant olim remoti, nec deicere quemquam iam ante prostrati." Nicholas is here, in turn, influenced by two statements made by Pope Celestine I. Celestine's statements are quoted in Nicholas' letter and present in canons 35 and 36: "non poterat quemquam eius remouere sententia, quia iam se prebuerat ipse remouendum" (c. 35, Lenherr, *Exkommunikationsgewalt*, 49, lines. 5–6; cf. Friedberg, ed., *Decretum*, 980, lines 6–8) and "neminem deicere uel remouere poterat qui predicans talia titubabat" (c. 36, Lenherr, *Exkommunikationsgewalt*, 49, lines 5–6; cf. Friedberg, ed., *Decretum*, 981, lines 7–8).

[20] Lenherr, *Exkommunikationsgewalt*, 104. The passages are "deicere quemquam iam prostratus," which appears in c. 36 (Lenherr, *Exkommunikationsgewalt*, 49, lines 8–9; cf. Friedberg, ed., *Decretum*, 981, lines 11–12), and "ex quo talia predicare ceperunt," which appears in both canons (Lenherr, *Exkommunikationsgewalt*, 48–49, lines 2–3, and p. 49, line 3; cf. Friedberg, ed., *Decretum*, 980, line 3, and 980–981, lines 3–4).

[21] Lenherr, *Exkommunikationsgewalt*, 21, lines 4–5 (cf. Friedberg, ed., *Decretum*, 967, lines 5–6): "'Quorum remiseritis peccata' etc." As was common during the middle ages, Gratian quotes only the first few words of scriptural passages. The argument clearly requires, however, that the reader keeps the entire passage in mind. Here, as elsewhere, I have, therefore, chosen to quote the entire passage in the English translation.

[22] Lenherr, *Exkommunikationsgewalt*, 21, line 5 (cf. Friedberg, ed., *Decretum*, 967, lines 6–7): "Accipe Spiritum sanctum."

[23] Lenherr, *Exkommunikationsgewalt*, 21, lines 5–7 (cf. Friedberg, ed., *Decretum*, 967, lines 7–8): "ut euidenter cunctis ostenderet, eum qui Spiritum sanctum non habeat peccata non posse tenere vel remittere."

[24] Lenherr, *Exkommunikationsgewalt*, 21, line 8 (cf. Friedberg, ed., *Decretum*, 967, lines 9–10): "quia et ipsam unitatem per gratiam facit."

Gratian here appears to be a proponent of an ecclesiology in which the Church is defined as a community united by participation in the grace of the Holy Spirit. Gratian's treatment is, apparently, based on some of the canons in the *questio* (particularly canons 18 and 19), but these texts are interpreted in the light of contemporary theology. Verbal similarities appear between Gratian's *dictum* and, e.g., the *Glossa ordinaria* to the Bible, although the similarities are such that they cannot be interpreted as proof of direct influence; it rather demonstrates Gratian's general familiarity with the language of contemporary theological discourse.[25]

Gratian continues to quote biblical passages, which he interprets as further support for his thesis. First, he adduces Romans 8: 26: "So when, as the Apostle says, 'the Spirit intercedes,' the Spirit accomplishes, it makes [us] neither intercede nor accomplish outside the Church."[26] Gratian's medieval readers would be familiar with the meaning of "the Spirit intercedes." The Pauline context of these words is: "Likewise the Spirit helps us in our weakness; for we do not know what to pray for, as we ought, but the Spirit himself asks for us with sighs too deep for words."[27] Gratian obviously interpreted this text in the light of the *Glossa ordinaria*, which states that it is not the Spirit which asks, but which "makes us ask."[28] The *Glossa* probably provided also the idea that "the Spirit achieves." An interlinear gloss, unearthed by Lenherr in two Munich manuscripts of the Pauline letters, interprets "the Spirit asks" with "it makes (us) ask and accomplishes."[29]

[25] Compare Gratian's words quoted in note 24 with the *Glossa ordinaria* ad Ephesians 4: 4: "unitatem ecclesiasticam quam facit spiritus sanctus" (quoted by Lenherr, *Exkommunikationsgewalt*, 131, note 88) and with Rupert of Deutz, *De glorificatione trinitatis* 6.15: "quam unitatem facit unus Spiritus et una fides" (quoted by Lenherr, *Exkommunikationsgewalt*, 132, note 92). For Gratian's interpretation of the first Pentecost, "nec nisi super congregatos in unum die pentecostes descendit Spiritus sanctus," (Lenherr, *Exkommunicationsgewalt*, 21, lines 10–11; cf. Friedberg, ed., *Decretum*, 967, lines 11–12) compare the *Glossa ordinaria* ad Act. 2: 2: **totam domum**. In una domo sedentibus infunditur spiritus ut ecclesie unitas commendetur . . . hic veniente spiritu congregatis erant in unum ex amore" (quoted by Lenherr, *Exkommunikationsgewalt*, 130, note 88).
[26] Lenherr, *Exkommunikationsgewalt*, 21, lines 12–13 (cf. Friedberg, ed., *Decretum*, 967, lines 14–16): "Cum ergo, sicut Apostolus ait, 'Spiritus postulet,' Spiritus impetret, extra ecclesiam nec postulare facit, nec impetrare." While it is not entirely clear in Gratian's Latin whom the Spirit makes to ask and to achieve, the context as well as the biblical gloss cited below indicate that the subject is "us faithful."
[27] Robertus Weber, ed., *Biblia sacra iuxta vulgatam versionem*, 3rd edn. (Stuttgart 1983), 1759.
[28] **Spiritus postulat gemitibus.** Non enim Spiritus sanctus postulat aut gemit, quasi indigeat aut angustias patiatur, sed quia ipse postulare nos facit, nobisque interpellandi et gemendi inspirat affectum. Adiutorium igitur hic spiritus sancti expressum est." *Biblia latina cum glossa ordinaria* (Strasburg c. 1480; repr. Turnhout 1992) ad Romans 8: 26.
[29] "Facit postulare et impetrat," quoted by Lenherr, *Exkommunikationsgewalt*, 131, note 88 from Munich, Bayerische Staatsbibliothek clm 3743 and 18532. The *Correctores* quotes an interlinear gloss "Spiritus impetret" in their note ★★★.

Gratian appears to connect Paul's just quoted words to the Romans with Christ's words to the apostles: "Whatever you ask for, will be done by my father, who is in heaven" (Matthew 18: 19).[30] The context of this statement makes it clear, Gratian says, that Christ is addressing only those who are members of the Church. For it is preceded by "if two of you agree on earth," and followed by "wherever two or three are gathered in my name, there am I in the midst of them."[31] Christ here clearly shows, Gratian says, that he does not live in the hearts of those who break with the Church. Gratian's treatment here is based on c. 19, which contains a similar argument and where the same passages from Matthew 18 are quoted.[32] And where Christ does not live, Gratian continues, there the Holy Spirit has no place. The conclusion he draws from these facts is:

Since it thus is the work of the Holy Spirit and the power of Christ to forgive or to retain sins, to excommunicate or to reconcile, it is clear that those who are outside the Church can neither bind nor loose, can neither through reconciliation restore ecclesiastical communion nor through excommunication deprive of its [i.e., the Church's] fellowship, which they, themselves stained by heresy or schism or marked by a sentence [i.e., of excommunication], are proven utterly to lack.[33]

This conclusion is followed by a short passage, the purpose of which seems to be to establish that it is the see of Rome which holds the right faith, although this is not explicitly stated. Gratian points out that, although all the apostles were given equal power to bind and to loose, this power was given to Peter "for all and above all," according to Christ's famous words: "I will give you the keys of the kingdom of heaven" (Matthew 16: 19).[34] A person who is estranged from the unity of the Church, "which is understood through Peter," cannot consecrate, only

---

[30] Lenherr, *Exkommunikationsgewalt*, 21, line 14 (cf. Friedberg, ed., *Decretum*, 967, lines 16–17): "Quecumque petieritis, etc."

[31] Lenherr, *Exkommunikationsgewalt*, 21, lines 14–16 (cf. Friedberg, ed., *Decretum*, 967, lines 17–19): "premisit: 'Si duo ex uobis consenserint super terram.' Et item: 'Vbicumque duo uel tres congregati fuerint in nomine meo, ibi et ego sum in medio eorum."

[32] Cf. Lenherr, *Exkommunikationsgewalt*, 129–130, note 88.

[33] *Ibid.* 22, lines 20–23 (cf. Friedberg, ed., *Decretum*, 967, lines 24–29): "Cum ergo dimittere peccata uel tenere, excommunicare uel reconciliare opus sit Spiritus sancti et uirtus Christi, apparet, quod hii qui extra ecclesiam sunt nec ligare possunt nec soluere, nec reconciliando ecclesiastice communioni reddere, nec excommunicando eius societate priuare, qua ipsi heresi uel scismate polluti siue sententia notati penitus carere probantur."

[34] Lenherr, *Exkommunikationsgewalt*, 22, lines 26–27 (cf. Friedberg, ed., *Decretum*, 967, lines 31–33): "Petro pro omnibus et pre omnibus claues regni celorum se daturum promisit dicens: 'Tibi dabo claues regni celorum.'" Gratian uses the phrase *pro omnibus et pre omnibus* in the same context in D. 21, d. a. c. 1. The words *pro omnibus* in the same context appear in the *Glossa ordinaria* ad John 19: 23 (see Lenherr, *Exkommunikationsgewalt*, 130, note 88).

execrate.[35] It is hard to imagine that Gratian's medieval readers would not equate Peter with the Roman Church. In this passage, Gratian draws on c. 6, which states that Peter symbolizes the Church,[36] and on c. 18, which contains the idea that, although all the apostles received equal power, Peter is foremost among them.

The section which follows serves both to undergird the earlier conclusion (that only orthodox priests can excommunicate) and as a transition to the next section. Gratian quotes I Corinthians 5: 3–5: "Though absent in body I am present in spirit, and as if present, I have already determined that, when you and my spirit are assembled with the power of our Lord Jesus Christ, the man who has so acted is to be delivered in the name of our Lord Jesus Christ to Satan for the destruction of the flesh."[37] Gratian comments that Paul in this passage teaches, by demonstrating the "formula for excommunication," that only the faithful are to be excommunicated, and only by the faithful.[38] He points out that only a true believer can accomplish anything "in the name of the Lord and with his power cooperating, since 'no one can say *"Jesus is Lord!"* except by the Holy Spirit.'"[39] In interpreting I Corinthians 5: 3–5, Gratian apparently draws on the *Glossa ordinaria*, which also uses the word "cooperate" for the power of Christ.[40]

The rest of the *dictum* is mainly concerned with establishing that only those who belong to the Church can be excommunicated. Heretics and schismatics have already removed themselves from the Church and need not be driven away. Gratian begins by explaining that the Lord, when he prohibited eating the lamb outside the church, does not drive away those

[35] Lenherr, *Exkommunikationsgewalt*, 22, lines 28–31 (cf. Friedberg, ed., *Decretum*, 967, lines 33–36): "Quicumque ergo ab unitate ecclesie, que per Petrum intelligitur, fuerit alienus, execrare potest, consecrare non ualet, excommunicationis uel reconciliationis potestatem non habet." Gratian probably found the idea here expressed, as well as the contrasting words *consecrare* and *execrare*, in c. 33 (Lenherr, *Exkommunikationsgewalt*, 45, lines 6–8; cf. Friedberg, ed., *Decretum*, 979, lines 8–10): "Iure ergo execratus tantum, non consecratus poterit dici, quem simul sacrare in unitate coniunctis membris non agnoscit ecclesia."

[36] Lenherr, *Exkommunikationsgewalt*, 24, lines 6–7 (cf. Friedberg, ed., *Decretum*, 968, lines 8–9): "Petrus quando claues acceperit, ecclesiam sanctam significauit."

[37] Lenherr, *Exkommunikationsgewalt*, 22, lines 32–35 (cf. Friedberg, ed., *Decretum*, 967, lines 37–41): "Ego quidem absens corpore, presens autem spiritu iam iudicaui ut presens eum qui sic operatus est, in nomine Domini nostri Iesu Christi congregatis uobis et meo spiritu cum uirtute Domini nostri Iesu Christi, tradere huiusmodi sathane in interitum carnis."

[38] Lenherr, *Exkommunikationsgewalt*, 22, lines 35–37 (cf. Friedberg, ed., *Decretum*, 967, lines 41–43): "In quo formam excommunicationis ostendens docuit, non nisi fidelem et a fideli notandum."

[39] Lenherr, *Exkommunikationsgewalt*, 22, lines 37–39 (cf. Friedberg, ed., *Decretum*, 967–968, lines 43–45): "In nomine namque Domini atque eius uirtute cooperante non nisi fidelis aliquid operari ualet, cum 'nemo possit dicere: "Dominus Iesus", nisi in spiritu sancto.'"

[40] **In nomine Domini**. Hoc modo iudicavi, ut vos congregati in unum sine aliqua dissensione, quibus mea auctoritas et virtus Christi cooperabitur" *(Biblia latina cum glossa ordinaria*, ad I Corinthians 5: 4).

who through their profession of faith voluntarily leave the Catholic Church. Instead, he allows them to leave. Gratian here alludes to Exodus 12: 46: "In one house shall it [i.e., the Paschal Lamb] be eaten; you shall not carry forth any of the flesh outside."[41] He follows an exegetical tradition, codified in the *Glossa ordinaria,* in taking "one house" to signify the Catholic Church and "outside" to refer to heretics.[42] This interpretation is also expressed in c. 25,[43] which in all likelihood inspired Gratian's words in this passage. He continues by comparing those who are outside the Church with those disciples of Christ, who in the Gospel of John reply "This is a hard saying; who can listen to it?" (6: 60) to Christ's words "Unless you eat the flesh of the Son of man and drink his blood" (6: 53). These disciples are, Gratian points out, not driven away but allowed to leave.[44]

Gratian further undergirds his thesis that only those in the Church can be excommunicated with yet another reference to the fifth chapter of I Corinthians. When Paul talks about those who are to be excommunicated, he begins with the words "if any brother," while when he talks about the unfaithful he says: "The Lord will judge those who are outside." Gratian concludes that "he entrusted judgement of those who are inside to us."[45] This conclusion appears to be based on an interlinear gloss to this biblical passage: "**The Lord will judge:** he did not entrust [them] to us, since you ought to judge about those who are inside."[46]

Gratian's following summation is couched in such complicated syntax that it needs to be quoted in full:

[41] Weber, ed., *Biblia sacra,* 93: "in una domo comedetur [scil. phasa] nec efferetis de carnibus eius foras."
[42] Cf. the following interlinear glosses found in *Biblia latina cum glossa ordinaria,* ad Exodus 12: 46: **una domo**: "Ecclesia catholica, non in conventiculis hereticorum"; **nec**: "quia nec iudei nec pagani nec heretici nec omnino qui extra ecclesiam sunt ad hanc communionem admittitur"; **foras**: "id est extra ecclesiam, ne impiis et peccatoribus communicent, quia catholica ecclesia privantur." The Paschal Lamb is, of course, a type for the Eucharist.
[43] Lenherr, *Exkommunikationsgewalt,* 38, lines 21–23 (cf. Friedberg, ed., *Decretum,* 976, lines 28–30): "Super illam petram fundatam ecclesiam scio. Quicumque extra hanc domum agnum comederit profanus est."
[44] Lenherr, *Exkommunikationsgewalt,* 23, lines 42–45 (cf. Friedberg, ed., *Decretum,* 968, lines 49–52): "Illi qui audientes: 'Nisi manducaueritis carnem filii hominis et biberitis eius sanguinem' etc., dixerunt: 'Durus est hic sermo, et quis potest eum audire?', atque ita abierunt retrorsum non repulsi, set abire permissi."
[45] Lenherr, *Exkommunikationsgewalt,* 23, lines 45–48 (cf. Friedberg, ed., *Decretum,* 968, lines 52–56): "Hinc etiam Apostolus, cum de excommunicandis ageret, premisit: 'Si quis frater'; de infidelibus autem supposuit dicens: 'Eos qui foris sunt Dominus iudicabit'; de his autem qui intus sunt nobis iudicium commisit."
[46] **Deus iudicabit**: non nobis commisit, cum debetis iudicare de his qui intus," quoted by Lenherr, *Exkommunikationsgewalt,* 132, note 88 from Munich, Bayerische Staatsbibliothek clm 14327.

Sicut autem ex eo quod Apostolus ait "frater," et ex his que de fidelibus et infidelibus supposuit, apparet non nisi fidelem excommunicandum, ita ex eo quod fidelibus tantum hoc scribitur, uel pocius, quia sicut ille qui benedicit maior est eo cui benedicitur, ita qui ex offitio maledicit maior est eo cui maledicitur, liquido constat eum qui ab integritate catholice fidei recedit maledicendi uel benedicendi potestatem minime habere.[47]

Lenherr understands the first part of this sentence as continuing the preceding discussion. This discussion is then interrupted at *uel pocius* by a new thought, which looks back to the beginning of the *dictum*. Lenherr finds the interruption so abrupt that he suggests that some words may have been lost.[48] However, Lenherr does not appear to have correctly understood the clause "ita ex eo quod fidelibus tantum hoc scribitur," which he takes to be a further argument for the conclusion that only the faithful can be excommunicated. Those words constitute, in my reading of the passage, an argument that only the faithful can excommunicate. The scriptural passage under discussion (to which Gratian refers with *hoc*) is I Corinthians 5: 11–13, where Paul writes to the congregation of Corinth not to associate with "brothers" who are guilty of sins. Hence, the conclusion which can be drawn "from the fact that this was written only to the faithful" is that Paul meant only the faithful not to associate with such members of the congregation, i.e., he meant only the faithful to excommunicate them. This, of course, is the conclusion Gratian draws a few lines further down.

Any attempt to translate literally Gratian's complicated syntax would probably be ill advised. In the following version, I have broken up the sentence and expressed the comparative construction by "similarly" introducing the second sentence (instead of "just as . . . so also").

From the fact that the apostle says "brother" and from what he adds about the faithful and about the infidel it is clear that none but the faithful is to be excommunicated. Similarly, that he who withdraws from the fullness of the catholic faith does not have the power to condemn or to bless is clearly established from the fact that this is written only to the faithful, or rather, since just as he who blesses is greater than he who is blessed, so is he who officially[49] condemns greater than he who is condemned.

In this summation, Gratian introduces a new element, which he continues to develop in his next sentence: "He (i.e., he who retires from the

---

[47] Lenherr, *Exkommunikationsgewalt*, 23, lines 48–54 (cf. Friedberg, ed., *Decretum*, 968, lines 56–63).

[48] Lenherr, *Exkommunikationsgewalt*, 121, note 51: "ist nämlich nach 'scribitur' ein Satzteil ungefähr folgenden Inhalts ausgefallen: 'constat non nisi fidelem excommunicare posse.'"

[49] Lenherr, *Exkommunikationsgewalt*, 121, note 52, points out that the words *ex officio* probably only serve the purpose of making the word *maledicere* refer to "formal condemnation" and not to "cursing" in general.

fullness of the catholic faith) is not capable of condemning a catholic, since that person is superior; he cannot pass judgement about someone who is alienated from the faith, as if about someone equal to him."[50] Lenherr points to several possible sources for this reasoning. Closest at hand is c. 37 in this *questio*: "For it is absurd that he who, according to the sacred rules, is not allowed to communicate even with the least (members of the Church) would be allowed to judge about those who are, as it were, greater than he."[51] Closer similarities appear in the section of the *Decretum* where Gratian discusses judicial process, i.e., in *causae* 2–6. Hierarchical considerations play a basic role in Gratian's discussion there about who can accuse whom and who can judge whom. This has already been made apparent from the manner in which he refers to C. 2: "in the *causa*, where lesser persons' accusations against greater persons are discussed."[52] Lenherr collected some quotations from C. 2 and C. 6 with direct bearing on the problem discussed in d. p. c. 4, as for example: "a heretic is inferior to a catholic"[53] and "in regard to accusation the equality of faith and conduct between the accusing and the accused has always to be considered, so that he who accuses is found either equal or superior."[54] Since the ideas expressed at the end of d. p. c. 4 turn out to be closely related to some of Gratian's fundamental legal principles, it seems well advised to refrain from attempting to pinpoint any specific texts as his sources.[55]

Gratian concludes d. p. c. 4 with a transitional sentence in which he highlights the main result of the preceding discussion and indicates that this result is proven by the following canons: "What has been said about

---

[50] Lenherr, *Exkommunicationsgewalt*, 23, lines 54–55 (cf. Friedberg, ed., *Decretum*, 968, lines 63–65): "Catholicum namque utpote superiorem se maledicere non ualet, in alienum a fide tanquam in sui equalem sententiam dare non potest."

[51] Lenherr, *Exkommunicationsgewalt*, 50, lines 3–5 (cf. Friedberg, ed., *Decretum*, 981, lines 3–5): "Absurdum enim est, ut cui non licet etiam cum minimis iuxta sacras regulas communicare liceat ei etiam de suis pene maioribus iudicare." The similarity with the presently discussed passage in d. p. c. 4 was noted by Lenherr, *Exkommunikationsgewalt*, 122. Lenherr's discussion, *ibid.*, of changes which Gratian made to this text needs to be revised, since the manuscripts of the *Tripartita* according to Martin Brett's collations show greater variation than was known to Lenherr. In my opinion, Gratian's changes were made in order to make sense of an already corrupted passage.

[52] C. 6, q. 1, d. p. c. 19 (Friedberg, ed., *Decretum*, 559, lines 4–5, supported by Bc Fd): "in ea causa, ubi de accusatione minorum aduersus maiores disputatum est."

[53] C. 6, q. 1, c. 20 (Friedberg, ed., *Decretum*, 559, lines 3–4, supported by Bc Fd): "cum hereticus catholico minor sit."

[54] C. 2, q. 7, d. p. c. 25 (Friedberg, ed., *Decretum*, 489, lines 9–12, supported by Bc Fd): "in accusatione equalitas fidei et conuersationis inter accusantem et accusatum semper consideranda est, ut is, qui accusat, uel par, uel superior inueniatur." Cf. Lenherr, *Exkommunikationsgewalt*, 122, note 56.

[55] In d. p. c. 37, Gratian refers, in fact, to these principles: "Non potest oris gladio ferire quem accusare uel in quem testficari non ualet" (Lenherr, *Exkommunikationsgewalt*, 51, lines 24–25; cf. Friedberg, ed., *Decretum*, 981, lines 27–28).

heretics and schismatics, namely that they do not have the power to bind or to loose, is proven by the authorities of many."[56] This is followed by a series of canons, which is not interrupted by a *dictum* until after c. 37, where the series is summarized as follows: "These authorities clearly demonstrate that from the moment when someone begins to teach something which is against the faith, he can neither overthrow nor condemn anyone."[57]

The previous analysis of d. p. c. 4 shows that Gratian here drew on several canons in C. 24, q. 1: canons 6, 18, 19, 25, 35, and 36. All of these were, like d. p. c. 4, included already in the first recension, which supports my thesis, as does Lenherr's analysis of canons 5–37. He shows how these canons were included in the *Decretum*, as it were, in installments. The kernel of this series consists of canons 35 and 36, both of which derive from Ivo of Chartres' *Panormia*. Lenherr indicates that the first group of canons to be added after canons 35 and 36 were canons 5–8, 18–20, 22–23, 25, 26 (partially), 30–31, and 33–34. Gratian found these canons in titles 2–5 of the seventh book of the *Polycarpus*. They appear in the *Decretum* in the same order as in the *Polycarpus*, although their sequence in Gratian's work is interrupted by other canons, which according to Lenherr's reconstruction were added later. These other canons derive (with one apparent exception, c. 32) from the *Tripartita* or *3L*.

As Lenherr notes, the series of canons derived from the *Polycarpus* repeat and develop the themes of d. p. c. 4:[58] the unity of the Church, which implies the power to bind and to loose, is symbolized by Peter (canons 5–8); those who leave the Church cannot partake of the Holy Spirit or of God's spiritual gifts, namely the ability to have God as a father (c. 19), the power to bind and loose (c. 20), the ability to perform a true sacrifice (c. 22), possession of true faith (c. 23), the perfection of the Holy Spirit (c. 30), the ability to celebrate divine office (canons 31 and 33), communion with the one Church (c. 34); he is profane who attempts to eat the Lamb outside the Church of Peter (c. 25); the company of heretics is to be avoided (c. 26).

Other canons were inserted at different points in this series. The largest insertion, canons 9–17, was drawn from *3L*. These nine have a common theme: all emphasize the orthodoxy of the Roman Church, thus defining Rome as the standard against which others are measured. In d. p. c.

---

[56] Lenherr, *Exkommunicationsgewalt*, 23, lines 57–59 (cf. Friedberg, ed., *Decretum*, 968, lines 65–67): "Hec autem que de hereticis atque scismaticis uel excommunicatis dicta sunt, uidelicet quod ligandi et soluendi potestatem non habeant, multorum auctoritatibus probatur."

[57] Lenherr, *Exkommunicationsgewalt*, 50, lines 1–2 (cf. Friedberg, ed., *Decretum*, 981, lines 1–3): "His auctoritatibus perspicue monstratur, quod, ex quo aliquis contra fidem ceperit aliqua docere nec deicere aliquem ualet nec dampnare." [58] Lenherr, *Exkommunikationsgewalt*, 150–151.

4 and in canons 5–7, Gratian had already established that Peter defines the unity of the Church. It must have been clear to medieval readers that Peter equals the Roman Church, but Gratian does not spell this out in the *dictum*.

The other insertions concern single canons, added at different points in the series derived from the *Polycarpus*: canons 21, 24, 27, 28, 29, and 32. These canons were found in *3L* and in the *Tripartita*. Canon 32 may derive either from the *Polycarpus* (as Lenherr posited) or from Anselm's collection. The inserted canons contribute further to some of the themes of the series derived from the *Polycarpus*: those who remove themselves from the Church should be avoided (c. 24) and are punished by God (c. 21); they also lose spiritual gifts, such as the remission of sins and entry to Heaven (c. 27), the ability to perform a true sacrifice (c. 28), the possession of true faith (c. 29), and they lose their position in the Church and in society (c. 32; cf. canons 31 and 33). It is hard to discern any system in the position of most of the additions. Lenherr's conclusions are consistent with the first recension, which contains canons 5–8, 18–20, 22–25, the second part of c. 26, canons 30–31, and 33–36, i.e., texts drawn from the *Panormia* or the *Polycarpus* plus c. 24, which Gratian probably extracted from the *Tripartita*.

In two cases, *Decretum* manuscripts contain textual details which further support the thesis that Aa and Fd contain a first recension. *Canon 23* appears in the *Polycarpus* and in Anselm's collection. Lenherr saw that Gratian's text must be a conflation of the texts in these two works. In most manuscripts of the *Decretum*, the canon is inscribed *Item Ambrosius*, while the text begins: "Aduocauit ad se Ciprianus episcopum Satyrum nec . . ."[59] The *Polycarpus* ascribes the text to Cyprian and begins it "Aduocauit ad se episcopum nec . . .,"[60] while Anselm of Lucca attributes it to Ambrose and begins it "Aduocauit ad se episcopum Satyrus nec . . ."[61] The reading of the *Decretum* can be explained as a combination of the texts in these two collections. Lenherr posited that Gratian first excerpted the text from the *Polycarpus*, because it appears there in close sequence to the text of c. 22 and because two of Lenherr's manuscripts (Br and Ka) have preserved the inscription *Item Ciprianus*.[62] My collations provide further evidence for Lenherr's suggestion: Je and Mz also ascribe the canon to Cyprian. More interesting is, however, the text of one of the manuscripts of the first recension, Fd, which originally contained the same text as the *Polycarpus*: "Item Ciprianus. <A>dvocavit

---

[59] *Ibid.* 35, 74 and 89.   [60] *Ibid.* Lenherr quotes the MGH's draft edition (cf. above, p. 16).

[61] Lenherr, *Exkommunikationsgewalt*, 35, 74 and 89, quoting BAV, Vat. lat. 1366, fo. 216 r.-v.

[62] Lenherr, *Exkommunikationsgewalt*, 89, cf. 35.

ad se episcopus nec . . ." This was later changed, through expunction, erasure and marginal addition, to "Item Ambrosius. <A>dvocavit ad se Ciprianus episcopum Saturum nec . . ." In the first recension, Gratian apparently reproduced the text of the *Polycarpus*, including the ascription to Cyprian. The author of the second recension discovered the text in Anselm's collection and changed the inscription inserting Cyprian's and Satyrus' names in the text.

The full text of *canon 26* is found in the *Polycarpus* (at 3.30.3) and in Anselm's collection. The second part of the text (from ed. Lenherr, line 9, ed. Friedberg, line 11: *Fides*) appears by itself in the *Polycarpus* (at 7.4.3) and in *3L*. It would seem reasonable to exclude the last two occurrences from a consideration of Gratian's sources, but Lenherr's work reveals a more complicated situation. Suspicion arises already from the fact that the second part of the canon in the third book of the *Polycarpus* and in Anselm contains a phrase which does not appear either in Gratian's work or in the other two sources.[63] There are, furthermore, irregularities in the textual transmission of this canon: it is in most manuscripts of the *Decretum* (correctly) inscribed *Item Ambrosius.*[64] Two of Lenherr's manuscripts have, however, the inscription *Unde Gregorius in moralibus libro vi.*[65] This is the inscription of the text at *Polycarpus* 7.4.3 and in *3L*. Also Aa has this inscription in the main body of the text (where only the second part of the canon appears), while the inscription to Ambrose appears in the supplement together with the first part of the text. The second part is here given a rubric of its own ("Sancta ecclesia nec deserenda nec mutanda est"), which in Me precedes the entire canon. The "normal" rubric ("Hereticorum consortia a catholicis sunt fugienda") appears in Me together with an *"Idem"* between the first and the second part of the text. Lenherr concludes that Gratian drew on two sources for his text of c. 26. He first took the second part of the text from the *Polycarpus* 7.4.3 (since the text there, but not in *3L*, follows immediately upon the texts of c. 23 and c. 25). The author of the second recension later added the first part of the canon, either from the *Polycarpus* 3.30.3 or from Anselm's collection.[66]

Lenherr's argumentation is sound. The text of Aa indicates that the first recension contained only the second part of c. 26, while the first was added only in the second recension. This is confirmed by Fd, whose

---

[63] Lenherr, *Exkommunikationsgewalt*, 40, see apparatus for line 16. The phrase was included in the Roman edition of the *Decretum* and is reproduced in Friedberg's note e.

[64] In addition to the manuscripts examined by Lenherr, I have found this reading in Cg Gg and Tx.

[65] Lenherr, *Exkommunikationsgewalt*, 39 and 88. The manuscripts are In and Sa; the latter manuscript does not contain the reference to book 6. Additionally, I have found this inscription also in Vd.

[66] Lenherr, *Exkommunikationsgewalt*, 89 and 90.

original text contains only the second part of the canon with the "normal" rubric (*Hereticorum* . . .). The first part of the text is added in the margin. The inscription *Ambrosius* is written over an erasure. The numeral *vi* is clearly visible at the end of the erased text, which probably contained the same attribution to the sixth book of Gregory's *Moralia* as found in the *Polycarpus* at 7.4.3.

HERETICS AND THE SACRAMENTS

D. p. c. 37 begins, as mentioned above, with a summary of the preceding series of canons and of the discussion in d. p. c. 4. Gratian now contrasts this conclusion with a text from Augustine, which is reproduced elsewhere in the first recension of the *Decretum* as C. 1, q. 1, c. 97: "But this statement by Augustine is opposed: 'Those who recede from faith lose neither baptism nor the power to baptize.'"[67] After this reference, containing a free summary rather than a literal quotation, Gratian explains how Augustine's statement is applicable to the issue being discussed in d. p. c. 37: since consecration as a priest gives both the power to baptize and the power to excommunicate, those who recede from faith should either lose both or neither of these powers.

Gratian's solution to this apparent contradiction is a distinction: "But the power of an office is one thing; its execution is another."[68] He goes on to explain that it is possible to have the power to do something without having the right to execute that power. Monks who have received sacerdotal ordination are a case in point, as are suspended priests who are prohibited from administration, although they retain their powers. Gratian points out that this is the basis for not renewing the sacraments of baptism or ordination for those who, having been baptized or ordained by heretics, return to the unity of catholic faith. He concludes that heretics retain the power to excommunicate as well as the power to baptize.[69] The question still remains whether they have the right to execute this power. Here, Gratian makes another distinction. If a heretic excommunicates with the purpose of bringing someone, catholic or heretic, into his heresy, then his sentence is iniquitous (*iniqua*) and lacks power. Gratian makes use of a distinction which he developed in C. 11, q. 3, the distinction between *sententia iniusta* and *sententia iniqua*. An

---

[67] *Ibid.* 50, lines 3–4 (cf. Friedberg, ed., *Decretum*, 981, lines 3–5): "Obicitur autem illud Augustini: 'Recedentes a fide nec baptisma nec baptizandi potestatem amittunt'."

[68] Lenherr, *Exkommunikationsgewalt*, 50, lines 6–7 (cf. Friedberg, ed., *Decretum*, 981, lines 7–8): "Set aliud est potestas offitii, aliud executio."

[69] Lenherr, *Exkommunikationsgewalt*, 51, lines 16–17 (cf. Friedberg, ed., *Decretum*, 981, line 19): "Cum ergo utraque potestas in hereticis remaneat . . ."

iniquitous sentence of excommunication attempts to force the excommunicated to do evil and should not be obeyed.[70]

In the case in which a heretic excommunicates for the purpose of correcting the sinful life of someone, Gratian makes a further distinction; if the subject of the excommunication is another heretic, he "seems to have power over him, just as the devil has power over the evil as if over his own cattle."[71] If, on the other hand, the excommunicated is a catholic, then "one can say that [he] is not bound by the sentence of a heretic."[72] The motivation given by Gratian is that a heretic could not even testify or bring an accusation against a catholic. These are legal principles which he discusses in C. 3, q. 4 and q. 5. The beginning of the next sentence is a verbatim but unacknowledged quotation from a text by Augustine, which appears as C. 23, q. 4, c. 24 (in the first recension).[73] Augustine says there that "those, whom divine testimonies do not follow, lose the claim to human testimony."[74] In d. p. c. 37, Gratian takes "those whom divine testimonies do not follow" to be those who are outside the Church and adds that they do not have "the claim to ecclesiastical authority."[75]

The thread of the discussion in d. p. c. 37 is taken up again in d. p. c. 39 after two intervening canons. Both of them are excerpts from letters of Augustine and state that someone who has been excommunicated by heretics on disciplinary grounds shall not be received into the Church without due penance. Canon 39 clearly derives from the *Tripartita*, which is the only relevant collection to contain the text.[76] The origin of c. 38 is more obscure, since it is found in three possible collections. None of them appears to have been the source, since they all lack the words *Donatiste et Rogatiste* found in the canon's inscription in the *Decretum*:

---

[70] Cf. C. 11, q. 3, d. p. c. 64: "Non ergo ab eius communione abstinendum est, nec ei ab offitio cessandum, in quem cognoscitur iniqua sententia prolata" (Friedberg, ed., *Decretum*, 661, lines 4–5). Cf. chapter 3 below.

[71] Lenherr, *Exkommunicationsgewalt*, 51, lines 29–30 (cf. Friedberg, ed., *Decretum*, 981, lines 33–35): "In hereticum autem potestatem habere uidetur hereticus, sicut et diabolus potest in malis tamquam in suo pecore."

[72] Lenherr, *Exkommunicationsgewalt*, 51, line 23 (cf. Friedberg, ed., *Decretum*, 981, lines 26–27): "Potest autem dici catholicum sententia heretici minime teneri."

[73] Lenherr, *Exkommunikationsgewalt*, 169.

[74] C. 23, q. 4, c. 24 (Friedberg, ed., *Decretum*, 909, lines 4–5): "Quos enim diuina testimonia non secuntur, pondus humani testimonii perdiderunt."

[75] Lenherr, *Exkommunicationsgewalt*, 51, lines 25–29 (cf. Friedberg, ed., *Decretum*, 981, lines 28–33): "Si enim quos diuina testimonia non secuntur, quia extra ecclesiam sunt, pondus humani testimonii perdiderunt aduersus eos qui in ecclesia esse uidentur, nec aduersus eosdem ecclesiastice auctoritatis pondus habere poterunt qui ab eius fide discessisse probati sunt atque ideo ab ecclesia sunt condempnati."   [76] Lenherr, *Exkommunikationsgewalt*, 92.

24.1.38

Inscr. Unde Agustinus scribit Vincentio Donatiste et Rogatiste *Lenh. Fr.:* Idem (sc. Augustinus) in epistola ad Vincentium *Trip.:* Augustinus *Ans. G Polyc.mP*

Searches among other canonical and theological works failed to turn up a potential source of c. 38. As Lenherr noted, the *Decretum* contains twelve other excerpts from Augustine's letter to Vincentius, but only one of them, C. 5, q. 5, c. 2 (a first recension text), calls him *Rogatista*.[77] I was unable to identify the source of this canon as well, which implies that Gratian may have taken both c. 38 and the canon in C. 5 from the same, unidentified source.

D. p. c. 39 begins with a reference to what has gone before: "But that statement by Augustine . . ."[78] The singular reference puzzled Lenherr,[79] but it is explained when one observes that c. 39 (deriving from the *Tripartita*) is missing from the first recension. Gratian is, thus, referring to c. 38.

In d. p. c. 39, Gratian appears to retract much of what he said in the second half of d. p. c. 37. He first states that Augustine's words (in c. 38) were written, not because the sentence of a heretic would be binding, but because sins should be hated and punished equally in heretics and in catholics. "For that statement of Augustine [i.e., 'Those who recede from faith lose neither baptism nor the power to baptize'] may be understood about the power to baptize [only], and not about the power to bind or to loose or to administer the other sacraments."[80] Gratian spells out a difference between baptism and the other sacraments: baptism can be validly administered by anyone, even a heretic or a layman, if only it is received within the catholic faith, while the other sacraments have no effect or even dangerous effect if administered by someone who is not a catholic priest. In other words, the objection summarized from Augustine in the beginning of d. p. c. 37 is not a valid objection, since it concerns only baptism, not the power to bind and to loose.

The last three canons (40–42) of the *questio* serve to support the statement made at the end of d. p. c. 39: one may not receive communion from a heretic. All three are found in the first recension, except for the second half of c. 40.

The rubric of *canon 40* states that a dying person may receive penance from a heretic. This rubric is peculiar in two ways: first, the rubric does not adequately represent the canon, which states that a dying person may receive *baptism* from a heretic. Second, the interpretation expressed in the rubric

---

[77] *Ibid.* 91–92 and 175.

[78] *Ibid.* 53, line 1 (cf. Friedberg, ed., *Decretum*, 982, line 1): "Set istud (variant reading: *illud*) Augustini . . ."   [79] Lenherr, *Exkommunikationsgewalt*, 177, note 275.

[80] *Ibid.* 53, lines 3–5 (cf. Friedberg, ed., *Decretum*, 982, lines 4–6): "Potest tamen illud Augustini de potestate baptizandi intelligi, non ligandi aut soluendi uel cetera sacramenta ministrandi."

does not suit Gratian's argument in the immediately preceding d. p. c. 39. Lenherr characterizes this rubric as an "oversight" by Gratian, who might have composed it before he decided to place the canon in this context.[81]

Canon 40 appears in different forms in the *Polycarpus*, in the *Tripartita*, and in the B and C recensions of Anselm's collection.[82] The text in the *Polycarpus* and Anselm's collection is shorter than in the *Decretum*; it ends at ". . . ubi unitatem seruabat" (ed. Lenherr, line 9; ed. Friedberg, line 11). Anselm's collection can be immediately excluded from consideration, since Gratian used recension A' of this work.[83] Only the *Tripartita* contains the entire canon, and this collection would, thus, seem to be Gratian's source. There are, however, several textual differences between this collection and Gratian's work:[84]

24.1.40

2(3) pacem catholicam custodiens *Lenh. Fr. Polyc.P:* pace catholica constituta (custodita *Rom.*) *Rom. Trip.*
9(11) credidit *Lenh. Fr. Polyc.P:* om. *Trip.*
11(14) ipsa *Lenh. Fr. Trip.R:* ipsa catholica *Rom. Trip.CWBNTA*
13(16) ecclesiam *Lenh. Fr.:* om. *Trip.*
13(16) certus *Lenh. Fr.CD:* certum *Fr.:* quia certus *Trip.*
15(18) perversus *Lenh. Fr.:* procul dubio perversus *Trip.*

Lenherr interpreted these findings as indications that Gratian may have taken a part of the canon from the *Polycarpus* and later added the rest of the text from an unknown source (rather than from the *Tripartita*).[85] He found support for this view in Gratian's rubric, which wrongly indicates that the canon concerns penance, not baptism. The first part of the canon, i.e., the part found in the *Polycarpus*, does not contain any references to baptism. Lenherr postulates that Gratian wrote the rubric before he added the second part of the canon.[86]

A problem with this reconstruction is, as Lenherr points out,[87] that the *Polycarpus* lacks the phrase "catholica unitate percepturus, si statim etiam de hac uita migrauerit, non eum nisi" (ed. Lenherr, lines 3–5; ed. Friedberg, lines 4–6), which is found in Gratian and in the *Tripartita*. Furthermore, the last word of the text in the *Polycarpus* is *servavit*, while Gratian and the *Tripartita* have *servabat*. Lenherr suggests either that

[81] Lenherr, *Exkommunikationsgewalt*, 182.
[82] Landau, "Rezension C," 43. The canon appears as 9.53 in recension B and as 9.61 in recension C.   [83] Landau, "Erweiterte Fassungen," 328.
[84] Lenherr's collations of the *Tripartita* were checked against Martin Brett's collations. The readings of *Polyc.P* may be assumed to be found also in *Polyc.m*, as implied by the silence of Lenherr's negative apparatus. Bold line numbers refer to lines in Lenherr's edition. Line numbers in Friedberg's edition follow within brackets.   [85] Lenherr, *Exkommunikationsgewalt*, 92–93.
[86] *Ibid.* 181–182.   [87] *Ibid.* 92.

Gratian used a manuscript of the *Polycarpus* without the variants here indicated, or that he later changed the text in accordance with his source for the second part of the canon.

The first-recension manuscript Fd throws light on these problems. This manuscript originally contained only the first part of canon 40, as it appears in the *Polycarpus*, i.e., without the phrase *catholica . . . nisi*. This phrase is added by a later hand in the left margin. The last letters of the word *servabat* are written over an erasure, allowing the assumption that the word originally was written *servavit* as in the *Polycarpus*. The second part of the canon is added in the right margin by the same hand that added the missing phrase in the left margin. In addition to the instances here mentioned, there are several other places in the first part of c. 40 where the original text of Fd agrees with the Polycarpus when most *Decretum* manuscripts agree with the *Tripartita*:

24.1.40
Inscr. unico *incl. Cg Gg Me Mk Mz Tx Vd Lenh. Fr. Trip.: om. Aa Fd Polyc.*
1(1) et *Aa Cg Me Mk Mz Tx Vd Fr.: om. Fd Rom. Polyc.m Trip. Ans.*
6(7) se *Cg Me Mk Mz^pc Tx Vd Lenh. Fr.: om. Aa Fd Polyc.m Ans.*
6(8) etiam *Cg Me Mk Tx Vd Lenh. Polyc.m Trip. Ans.: et Mz Fr.: om. Aa Fd*

These findings support both Lenherr's suggestion, that c. 40 in the second recension of the *Decretum* draws on two sources, and my thesis that Aa and Fd contain a first recension.

Canon 41 is found in the *Polycarpus*, in *3L,* and in Anselm's collection. In different manuscripts of the *Decretum*, the text is ascribed to different popes: Lucian, Julian, Lucius, or Julius, although almost the entire canonical tradition before Gratian identifies the pope as Eutychianus. None of these attributions is correct, since the text is an excerpt from the Irish penitential *Excarpsus Cummeani*.[88] One of the two main branches of the manuscript tradition of the *Polycarpus*, however, gives the pope's name as Lucian.[89] It appears, therefore, that Gratian's source for c. 41 was the *Polycarpus*. The confusion concerning the pope's name is understandable, especially if one imagines that some manuscripts might have lacked initials and hence the first letter of the name.

Canon 42 appears in the *Polycarpus* and in *3L*.[90] In Lenherr's and Friedberg's editions of the *Decretum*, the inscription correctly refers the

---

[88] Identification according to Hartmut Hoffmann and Rudolf Pokorny, *Das Dekret des Bischofs Burchard von Worms: Textstufen – Frühe Verbreitung – Vorlagen*, MGH Hilfsmittel 12 (Munich 1991), 237, at 19.105.

[89] Lenherr, *Exkommunikationsgewalt*, 83, note 147.

[90] A part of the text also appears in Alger of Liège's *De misericordia et iustitia* 3.21 (Kretzschmar, *Alger von Lüttichs Traktat*, 329), but the text there lacks the first sentence and cannot have been Gratian's source for c. 42.

text to Pope Gregory I. As far as is known, this inscription is found elsewhere only in manuscript C of the *Polycarpus*, which led Lenherr to conclude that this collection was Gratian's source. However, my collations show that Gratian in the first recension (as seen in Fd) of the *Decretum* ascribes the text to Augustine,[91] as do the other manuscripts of the *Polycarpus* and the Vatican manuscript of *3L*. It seems that Gratian first took the text from a collection ascribing it to Augustine and that the inscription was changed in the second recension. Lenherr's conclusion must, therefore, be tested anew.

A control of textual variants in the *Decretum* and in the two other collections shows, as Lenherr also points out, that Gratian's text is closer to the *Polycarpus* than to *3L*. While not decisive, the following instances seem most significant:

24.1.42
5(7) festivitatis *Lenh. Fr. Polyc.P*: festivitas *3LV*
5(7) intempeste *Lenh. Fr. Polyc.P*: intempesta *3LV*
9(12) dignis *Lenh. Fr. Polyc.P*: dignus *3LV*

Hence, Gratian's source for c. 42 was probably the *Polycarpus*.[92] The change in the inscription might have been prompted by a discovery that c. 42 is partially the same text as C. 1, q. 1, c. 72, which is (correctly) ascribed to Gregory.[93]

EXCOMMUNICATING THE DEAD

As the initial *dictum* of the *causa* indicated, the problem discussed in C. 24, q. 2, is whether a person can be excommunicated after his death. Gratian treats this question relatively briefly; the first recension contains five canons and two *dicta*. The second recension adds one canon and makes another canon longer. Table 4 documents occurrences of the texts of C. 24, q. 2 in the canonical collections which Gratian used when compiling the *Decretum*. I indicate by using bold face from which of the possible sources I think Gratian extracted each canon (for other conventions used in the table, see p. 35).

While Gratian at the beginning of the *causa* asked whether a person

---

[91] All other manuscripts collated by me contain the ascription to Gregory (Aa Cg Gg Me Mz Tx Vd); neither Friedberg nor Lenherr indicates that any of their manuscripts have a different inscription.

[92] But not the branch represented by the manuscript C, hence preventing the apparent anomaly that Gratian would have taken canons 41 and 42 from different branches of the manuscript transmission of the *Polycarpus*. Cf. Lenherr, *Exkommunikationsgewalt*, 93.

[93] The source of this canon, which already appears in the first recension, was probably Alger of Liège, *De misericordia et iustitia* 3.21 (Kretzschmar, *Alger von Lüttichs Traktat*, 329).

Table 4 *Formal sources of C. 24, q. 2*

Gratian	*Panormia*	*Tripartita*	*Polycarpus*	*3 Books*	Anselm	Ivo, *Decretum*
24.2.1	**5.118**	—	—	—	—	14.60
24.2.2	5.119	1.46.2a	7.1.30	2.25.11	11.5	14.61
24.2.3	**5.123**	—	—	—	—	14.68
24.2.4	—	—	7.1.8	2.26.12	12.29	—
24.2.5	—	—	—	S7.237 & S7.240	—	—
24.2.6	**5.115–117**	—	—	—	—	14.62–63

can be excommunicated after death, in the initial *dictum* of q. 2 he adds
the question whether an excommunicated person can be absolved after
death. In response, the *dictum* adduces Christ's famous words to Peter:
"Whatever you bind on earth shall be bound in heaven, and whatever
you loose on earth shall be loosed in heaven" (Matt 16: 19). Gratian points
out that Christ says "on earth" not "under earth" and draws the conclusion (which is restated in d. p. c. 5) that the priest's right to excommunicate and absolve concerns only living persons. Gratian took this line of
argument from canon 2. Canons 1, 3, and 4 undergird the conclusion of
d. a. c. 1, while c. 5 concerns a different problem, namely that a sentence
of excommunication cannot be relaxed if the culprit does not mend his
ways.

Canon 5 gives the impression of not belonging to the present context,
and it is not found in the first recension. Since it appears in no other relevant collection, this canon must have been extracted from the supplement of *3L*.

Canons 1 and 3 clearly derive from the *Panormia*, which is the only relevant collection to contain their texts. As could be expected, they are
found in the first recension. *Canon 4* is found in three collections, but the
Polycarpus can be excluded from consideration, since it contains a significant variant reading:

24.2.4
13 participare *Aa Cg Fd Gg Tx Vd Fr. 3LV Ans. G:* participatione *Polyc.mP*

I have found no variants revealing which of the two remaining collections was Gratian's source. The fact that c. 4 is found in the first recension indicates, however, that the source was Anselm of Lucca's collection
rather than *3L*.

Canon 2 is a complicated case which illuminates the relationship between
the two recensions of the *Decretum*. The final text of the canon was based
on at least two sources. In the manuscripts of the first recension (Aa and

Fd), the text begins with "Mortuos suscitasse" (line 13 in Friedberg's edition) and continues to the end of the canon. Aa contains an inscription different from that found in Friedberg: "Gregorius papa Fausto preposito milicie." Very likely, Fd once contained this (or a similar) inscription, which at some later point was changed into the usual one: "Gelasius papa Fausto magistro fungenti legationis officio Constantinopolim." The words *Gelasius* and *fungenti* are written by a later hand over erasures, and the three last words are awkwardly added between the lines.[94] The same hand has also supplemented the beginning of the text in the margin, while another hand added the same passage in the supplement at the end of the manuscript.[95] In Aa, the beginning of the canon is found only in the supplement, where it is accompanied by the longer inscription.[96]

Interestingly, the state of affairs in the first recension is reflected in several second-recension manuscripts. I have found that three such manuscripts divide c. 2 into two canons. Mz and Br let *Mortuos* begin with a new initial, although there is no new inscription or rubric. In Cg, which also divides the canon into two, its first half has the inscription found in Friedberg, while the second half is inscribed *G. Faustino magistro milicie*. G. should probably be expanded to *Gregorius*, since this name is so abbreviated in the inscription of C. 24, q. 1, c. 42 on the same page of the manuscript. It is easy to see that manuscripts such as Cg and Mz reflect first-recension manuscripts containing additions (such as Aa and Fd). Indeed, a scribe copying Aa and who attempted to insert the additions in the supplement in the correct places could very easily end up with the text of Cg.

It stands to reason that each of the two recensions would draw on a different source. The text of the canon is found in five of Gratian's usual sources, where its length varies greatly. The same excerpt as in the second recension is found in the *Polycarpus* and in *3L*, while the *Tripartita* contains a longer text. In the *Panormia*, the canon includes only the text from *Mortuos suscitasse* (line 13) to the end of Gratian's excerpt, i.e. the text of the first recension. Anselm of Lucca's text begins with Gratian's *incipit Legatur ex quo* and ends at line 7, *errore duremus*. Also the inscription varies considerably in different collections. The *Tripartita* and one manuscript of the *Polycarpus* has the same inscription as the second recension of the *Decretum*, while the *Panormia* gives the inscription of the first recension:[97]

---

[94] The longer inscription is the correct one, see JK 622, ed. Eduard Schwartz, *Publizistische Sammlungen zum Acacianischen Schisma*, Abhandlungen der Bayerischen Akademie der Wissenschaften, philosophisch-historische Abteilung, Neue Folge 10 (Munich 1934), 16–19 (this excerpt on p. 16 = *orig.*).

[95] Fd, fo. 151r. The inscription is here "Gregorius papa Fausto magistro militie."

[96] Admont, Stiftsbibliothek 43, fo. 309r.

[97] *Cg¹* and *Cg²* indicate the first and the second inscription, respectively, in the manuscript Cg.

24.2.2
Inscr. Gelasius papa (*om. Cg Mz*) Fausto magistro fungenti (*supra lin. add. Mz*) legationis offitio Constantinopolim *Aa^{add} Cg^1 Fd^{pc} Gg Me Mk Mz Tx Vd Fr.*: Gregorius (G. *Cg^2*) papa Fausto (Faustino *Pan.M*) magistro (preposito *Aa*) milicie (militum *Pan.M*) *Aa Cg^2 Fd^{add} Pan.EFJLM:* Gelasius Fausto magistro fungenti legationis officio Constantinopolim *Trip. Polyc.C:* Gelasius papa *Ans.:* Gelasius *Polyc.MPR 3LV: nulla inscriptio in Polyc.K.*

The *Polycarpus* is excluded on the basis of variant readings, so the *Tripartita* is most likely the source utilized for the second recension. Both the length of the text and the inscription indicate that Gratian used the *Panormia* for the first recension. These findings gain support from a collation of the text:

24.2.2
7 id quoque pariter *Aa Cg Gg Mk Tx Vd Fr.*: id quoque par esse *Trip.CKNB:* id quoque par est *Trip.Z2HQ:* id quoque parum est *Polyc.C orig.*: id quoque pars est *Trip.ZA:* id quoque est *Trip.GO: om. Polyc.mP 3LV*
15 tantum *Aa Cg Gg Fd Mk Tx Vd Fr. Pan.m:* tamen *Pan.M:* certam *Pan.EFJL Trip. Polyc.mP 3LV:* certe *orig.*
18 alligatione *Aa Cg Fd Mk Tx Fr.ABCD:* a ligatione *Gg:* in ligatione *Vd:* in alligatione *Pan.EFJLM:* in hac ligatione *Polyc.mP Trip. 3LV orig.*
19 esse absolvendum *Aa Cg Gg Fd Mk Tx Vd Fr.ABC Pan.EFJLM:* esse solvendum *Fr.DEGH:* absolvi *Trip. Polyc.mP 3LV orig.*

Canon 6 supports the statement in d. p. c. 5, that in fact there are some sins, such as heresy, for which condemnation can be made also after death. Gratian took this canon from the *Panormia*, which is the only relevant source to contain it. This collection is, in other words, the source of both the texts without which the two *dicta* of this *questio* could not have been written (second part of c. 2 and c. 6). Both of these texts are present in the first recension, which, thus, contains a coherent treatment of the question whether dead persons may be excommunicated.

EXCOMMUNICATING THE FAMILY

In his initial presentation of *Causa 24*, Gratian says that the third *questio* will ask whether the sin of one person causes the excommunication of his entire household.[98] This *questio* discusses, in fact, a whole range of issues connected with excommunication, most of which have only a superficial connection with the original problem. I discern six different general thematic units within the *questio*.

---

[98] Friedberg, ed., *Decretum*, 965, supported by Aa Fd Vd: "Tertio, an pro peccato alicuius tota familia sit excommunicanda."

(i) May the entire household be excommunicated due to one person's sins (d. a. c. 1–d. p. c. 1)?

(ii) Illicit excommunication damages only the one excommunicating; it is a person's life rather than the formal sentence of a priest which condemns or saves him (d. p. c. 1–d. p. c. 9).

(iii) A distinction must be made between rightful excommunication, which is made on account of love of justice, and unrightful communication, caused by lust for revenge (d. p. c. 9–c. 12).

(iv) Excommunication should be used by the Church (c. 13–c. 18).

(v) Some categories of persons who should be excommunicated (c. 19–c. 25).

(vi) Definitions of "heretic"; heretics should be avoided; excommunication is rightful; the different sects of heretics; why God allows heretics (d. p. c. 25–c. 40).

The exact problem formulated at the beginning of the *questio* is, in the main, solved already in the first canon and in the *dicta* surrounding it. The following section through c. 12 addresses some related problems concerning excommunication. The rest of the *questio* contains various texts about heretics and excommunication.

The first recension gives the same impression, although the contents of the *questio* are here less disparate. The entire middle section, canons 13 to 25, is missing. These canons lack accompanying *dicta* and they are the ones that stray the furthest from the theme of the *questio* and the *causa*. As could be expected, most of them derive from the *Tripartita* or from *3L*. The same is true for a few other canons which were also added in the second recension. Table 5 registers in which of Gratian's usual sources each canon appears. As always, I anticipate my conclusions by using bold face for Gratian's source (for other conventions used in the table, see p. 35).

MAY THE FAMILY OF A SINNER BE EXCOMMUNICATED?

The initial *dictum* in q. 3 discusses at some length, with arguments *pro et contra* extracted from the Bible, the question, whether an entire household can be excommunicated for one person's sins. In this *dictum*, Gratian touches on several issues which were much disputed among theologians of his time, and he seems to have been aware of their discussions, at least as reflected by the *Glossa ordinaria* to the Bible, which he apparently used.

Gratian begins by stating: "that the entire household should be excommunicated on account of one person's sin, is proven by the examples of many."[99] He then goes on to give such examples. The children of the Sodomites were killed by fire from heaven although they were too young to know their parents' misdeeds. When the Amalekites were punished, not only their children but also every one of their animals was killed. When Dathan and Abiron had provoked a schism against Moses and Aaron, they were devoured by hell together with all their property. And in the New Testament, one can read that pestilence which was caused by sins indiscriminately killed also those who did not commit any sins. Gratian summarizes: "If children are found to have been punished so severely for the sins of their parents, no one can doubt that they can be struck by the sentence of excommunication as well for the sins of the same" (i.e., their parents).[100]

At this point, Gratian introduces a distinction: "This is answered thus: it is clear from the words of the Gospel that children are bodily scourged for the sins of their parents . . . But spiritually, children are not bound by the sins of their parents from the moment they are purified from original sin through the sacrament of regeneration."[101] The Gospel passage to which Gratian refers is John 9: 2, where the apostles ask Christ about a blind man: "Rabbi, who sinned, this man or his parents, that he should have been born blind?" Gratian's use of this passage is noteworthy, since Christ's reply (not quoted by Gratian) states that the man's blindness was not caused by anyone's sin.[102] Also God's words to Moses on Sinai, that he visits "the iniquity of the fathers upon the children to the third and fourth generation" (Exodus 20: 5), are interpreted as concerning bodily, not spiritual punishment. To prove that children are not spiritually bound by their parents' sins, Gratian quotes Ezechiel 18: 20: "The soul that sins will die. The son will not bear the iniquity of the father, and the father does not bear the iniquity of the son; the righteousness of the righteous will be upon himself, and the wickedness of the wicked will be upon himself."[103] Augustine quotes a similar passage from the same chapter of

[99] Friedberg, ed., *Decretum*, 965–966, supported by Aa Tx: "Quod autem pro peccato alicuius tota familia excommunicanda sit multorum exemplis probatur."
[100] Friedberg, ed., *Decretum*, 988, supported by Aa Mk: "Si ergo tam severissime pro peccatis parentum inueniuntur paruuli puniti, nulli dubium est, quin pro peccatis eorundem sentencia excommunicationis pariter feriri ualeant."
[101] Friedberg, ed., *Decretum*, 988, supported by Aa Mk: "His ita respondetur: Pro peccatis parentum paruulos corporaliter flagellari (flag. corp. Aa) ex uerbis euangelii apparet . . . Spiritualiter (specialiter Aa) autem peccatis parentum paruuli (–is Aa) non tenentur, ex quo per sacramentum regenerationis ab originali peccato fuerint emundati."
[102] Also the *Glossa ordinaria* to the Bible interprets this passage out of context: "**Cecus** significat humanum genus in quo cecitas naturalis, quia peccante primo homine vicium propter naturam inoleuit, unde secundum mentem omnis homo cecus natus est" (*Biblia latina cum Glossa ordinaria*, ad loc.).
[103] Friedberg, ed., *Decretum*, 988, supported by Aa Mk: "Anima, que peccauerit, ipsa morietur; filius non portabit iniquitatem patris, et pater non portat iniquitatem filii; iustitia iusti super eum erit, et inpietas inpii erit super eum."

Table 5 *Formal sources of C. 24, q. 3*

Gratian	Panormia	Tripartita	Polycarpus	3 Books	Anselm	Ivo, Decretum	Notes
24.3.1	5.126	3.27.16	7.1.32	2.26.13	B 12.68 & C 12.67	—	14.44
24.3.2	**5.129**	—	1.24.1	2.26.20	—	14.17	—
24.3.3	—	—	—	**2.26.2**	—	—	—
24.3 4	—	—	—	**2.26.3**	—	—	—
24.3.5	5.132	—	—	—	—	14.20	—
24.3.6	5.124	3.27.13	—	—	—	14.21	—
24.3.7	—	—	—	—	—	—	**Gl. ord. ad Lev. 24: 10**
24.3.8	—	—	—	**3.3.17**	—	—	—
24.3.9	5.89	—	—	—	—	14.49	—
24.3.10	—	—	—	**2.25.16**	—	—	—
24.3.11	—	—	—	**2.25.17**	—	—	—
24.3.12	5.82	—	—	—	—	14.4–5	—
24.3.13	—	**1.54.26**	—	—	—	—	—
24.3.14	—	**1.2.24**	—	—	—	5.239, 250	—
24.3.15	—	**1.55.63**	—	—	—	—	—
24.3.16	—	—	—	**2.25.25**	—	—	—
24.3.17	—	—	—	**2.25.27**	—	—	—
24.3.18	—	—	—	**2.25.24**	—	—	—
24.3.19	—	**1.62.41**	—	—	—	8.227	—
24.3.20	—	**2.28.36**	—	—	—	10.38, 158	—
24.3.21	—	**2.35.5**	—	—	7.155	—	—
24.3.22	—	—	—	S 7.252	—	13.65	*Palea*
24.3.23	—	—	—	—	—	—	Lat. I
24.3.24	—	—	—	—	—	—	Lat. I
24.3.25	**5.114**	—	—	—	—	—	—

							Alger 3.2a
24.3.26	—	—	**7.5.5**	3.3.1	12.48	—	—
24.3.27	—	—	**7.5.6**	3.3.2	12.49	—	—
24.3.28	—	—	**7.5.24**	3.3.15	12.52	—	—
24.3.29	—	—	**7.5.22**	3.3.10	12.61	—	—
24.3.30	—	—	—	**2.34.7**	—	—	—
24.3.31	—	—	7.5.23	**3.3.14**	12.50	—	—
24.3.32	—	—	—	**2.9.33**	—	—	—
24.3.33	—	—	—	**2.34.18–20**	—	—	—
24.3.34	—	**1.43.2**	—	—	—	6.339	—
24.3.35	—	**2.18.69–71**	—	—	—	—	—
24.3.36	—	—	—	**1.11.8–9**	12.67	—	—
24.3.37	—	—	—	2.26.24	—	—	—
24.3.38	—	—	—	2.26.27	—	—	—
24.3.39	—	—	—	—	"13.ult."	—	—
24.3.40	—	—	—	3.3.18	—	—	—

Ezechiel in canon 1. That the two passages from Ezechiel seemingly contradict that from Exodus caused interpretative difficulties for both patristic and medieval theologians. Gratian's solution – the distinction between corporeal and spiritual punishment – is inspired by Augustine's words in canon 1 (lines 8–16).

Gratian adds the distinction that children are punished only for sins which were committed before their birth by their parents. This is the reason why the original sin of Adam, committed before he fathered children, affects everyone. The pedigree of this distinction is unclear. It appears also in C. 1, q. 4, c. 10 (a first-recension text), which according to its inscription comes from Augustine's letter to Bishop Auxilius, i.e. the letter from which C. 24, q. 3, c. 1 was extracted. The text of the former canon is not, however, found in this letter, and Augustine does not there make any statement implying such a distinction.[104] The distinction appears also in a theological sentence collection from the circle of Anselm of Laon, which uses the word *personaliter*, as Gratian does, to describe the manner in which a child is separated from its parents after birth.[105] Again, this shows Gratian being familiar with contemporary theological debates and terminology, although no direct influence can be demonstrated.

The rest of the *dictum* makes two related points, addressing the original question from a different perspective, namely by pointing out that a person must have sinned, and have been duly judged, to be rightly excommunicated. Neither of these requirements would apply to a family member excommunicated because of the sin of another family member. The first point, that God examines only the life of the accused, not the sentence of a priest, is in all likelihood inspired by canons 4 and/or 7. The second point is based on Paul's first letter to the Corinthians 5: 11: "If any brother is named a fornicator, or a miser or an idolater, you shall not eat with him."[106] Gratian interprets the expression "is named" (*nominatur*) to mean that a person has to be a sinner accused and convicted before a judge or a self-confessed sinner, before he can be excommunicated. His reading is no doubt based on Augustine's interpretation of this passage, which is quoted in the *Glossa ordinaria*.[107] Although

---

[104] Cf. the *Correctores'* note ★ to C. 1 q. 4 c. 10.

[105] Artur Michael Landgraf, *Dogmengeschichte der Frühscholastik* (Regensburg 1952–1956), IV: 1, 167.

[106] Friedberg, ed., *Decretum*, 988, supported by Aa, Fd Mk: "Si quis frater nominatur fornicator aut auarus aut (inmundus aut add. Aa) idolis seruiens, cum eiusmodi (huiusmodi Aa) nec cibum sumere debetis."

[107] *Biblia latina cum Glossa ordinaria*, ad I Corinthians 5: 11, quoting Augustine's sermon 351, n. 10 (*PL* 39.1547): "**Nominatur.** Aug. De penit. Eam nominationem voluit intelligi que in quemquam cum sententia et ordine iudiciario atque integritate profertur. Nam si quilibet nominatio sufficit, multi damnandi sunt innocentes, quia sepe falso in quoquam crimina nominantur."

Gratian had quoted Augustine's interpretation earlier (C. 2, q. 1, c. 18), it seems likely that he used the *Glossa* here.[108] His reading of I Corinthians 5: 11 should also be compared with canon 6, where it is stated (lines 3–4) that "no priest shall excommunicate anyone, before his case is proven."[109] At the end of the *dictum*, Gratian summarizes: "The whole family is thus not to be excommunicated for the sin of one person."[110] D. p. c. 1 restates this conclusion.

To summarize, d. a. c. 1 clearly draws on c. 1 and probably on one or both of canons 4 and 7. While c. 4 was added only in the second recension, canons 1 and 7 were present in the first recension (as was all of d. a. c. 1). Again, the first recension can be shown to be internally coherent.

Which was Gratian's source for c. 1? It appears in four relevant collections: the *Panormia*, the *Tripartita*, the *Polycarpus*, and *3L*. It also appears in recensions B and C of Anselm of Lucca's collection (as 12.68 and 12.67, respectively), but not in recension A', which Gratian used; this eliminates Anselm's collection as a possible source.[111] The three other collections reproduce excerpts of different length. The text is longest in the *Polycarpus*, where Augustine's letter is found in its entirety. In *3L*, it extends from the beginning of Augustine's letter to a point a few lines before its end.[112] The excerpts in the other two collections begin at the same point as Gratian's excerpt but are shorter than his text: in the *Tripartita*, the canon ends with ". . . grauissime commouerer" (Friedberg, ed., *Decretum*, line 24), and in the *Panormia* at ". . . uniuersae familiae" (line 37). It would thus appear that Gratian's source was either the *Polycarpus* or *3L*, since these are the only collections where all of his text is found. A collation of textual variants reveals, however, a more complicated relationship. I have noted the following significant variants:[113]

24.3.1
Inscr. Unde Augustinus scribit ad Auxilium (vel Auxentium *add. sup. lin. Mz*) episcopum *Aa Cg Fd Me Mk Mz Tx Vd Fr.:* Epistula (excepta *Pan.M*) Augustini

---

[108] C. 2, q. 1, c. 18 is found already in the first recension. The same passage is cited by the author of the second recension in C. 11, q. 3, d. p. c. 21. Cf. (for C. 24, q. 3, d. a. c. 1) John E. Rybolt, "The biblical hermeneutics of magister Gratian: an investigation of scripture and canon law in the twelfth century" (Ph.D. dissertation, St. Louis University, 1978), 295, who has not registered that Gratian here used the *Glossa*.

[109] Friedberg, ed., *Decretum*, 990, supported by Aa Mk: "ut nemo presbiter excommunicet aliquem ante, quam causa probetur."

[110] Friedberg, ed., *Decretum*, 988, supported by Aa Mk: "Non ergo pro alicuius peccato tota familia excommunicanda est."

[111] Landau, "Rezension C," 48 and 27. In Anselm's collection, the text is of the same length as in the *Polycarpus*. Cf. Landau, "Erweiterte Fassungen," 328.

[112] The excerpt in *3L* ends at ". . . homines sumus" on line 14 in *CSEL* LVII 597.

[113] *Orig.* = *CSEL* LVII 593–598.

ad Auxilium episcopum *Pan.EFLJM Trip.*: Augustinus ad Auxilium episc. *Pan.m:* Domino dilectissimo (*om. 3LV*) et venerabili fratri et sacerdoti (consacerdoti *Polyc.CPR 3LV*) Auxilio Augustinus in domino salutem *Polyc.Pm 3LV*

2 *post* nos *verbum* quoque *add. Polyc.m*

5 eo tempore *Aa Cg Fd In Me Mk Sa Vd Fr. Pan.EFJLMm Trip.*: eodem tempore *Polyc.Pm 3LV orig.*

6 nec *Gd Me Sa Vd Fr. Polyc.Pm 3LV orig.*: ne *Aa Bi Cg Fd Hk Mk Pf Pan.EFJLMm Trip.*

8 Hec enim (quippe *Aa*) fuit corporalis pena *Aa Bi Cd Cg Fd In Me Mk Sb Vd Fr.*: Hec enim corporalis est pena *Pan.EFJLMm:* Hec enim corporalis pena *Trip.*: Neque enim (hec *add. Polyc.CRP*) corporalis est pena *Polyc.Pm 3LV orig.*

10 *post* pariter *verbum* non *add. Polyc.m*

12 etiam *Aa Cg Fd Me Mk Vd Fr. Pan.EFJMm Trip.*: utique *Rom. Polyc.Pm 3LV orig.*

13 super terram *Aa Cg Fd Me Mk Vd Fr. Pan.EFJLMm Trip. Polyc.K:* in terra *Rom. Polyc.Pm 3LV orig.*

16 audistis *Aa In Pf Vd Fr. Pan.EFJLMm Trip. Polyc.C:* audistis *ex* auditis *corr. Mk:* auditis *Bi Cg Fd Me:* audisti *Gd Rom. Polyc.Pm 3LV orig.*

18–19 Sed forte – rationem *om. Pan.EFJLM, Trip.*: *incl. Aa Cg Fd Me Vd Fr. Pan.m Polyc.Pm 3LV orig.*

20 autem *Aa Cg Fd Me Mk Vd Fr. Pan.EFJLMm Trip.*: autem quoniam *Rom. Polyc.Pm 3LV orig.*

20 quesierit *Aa Cg Fd Gd Hk Me Mk Pf Vd Fr. Pan.EFJLMm Trip.*: querit *Polyc.Pm 3LV orig.*: querat *Rom.*

22–24 de (*om. Aa*) quorumdam facinoribus unanimiter adversus ecclesiam perpetratis nisi gravissime conmoverer (-eret *Pan.m*) *Aa Bi Cd Cg Fd In Me Mk Sb Vd Fr. Pan.EFJLm Trip.*: cum de quorundam facinoribus immaniter adversum (adversus *Polyc.m orig.*: adversum *Polyc.CPR*) ecclesiam perpetratis gravissime commoverer *Polyc.Pm 3LV orig.*

24 *post* conmoverer *explicit Trip.*

24–28 sed – doceri] item *Pan.EFJLMm.*

28 possim *Aa Bi Cg Fd Me Mk Sa Vd Fr. Polyc.Pm 3LV:* possumus *Rom. Pan.EFJLMm orig.*

30 ex *Cg Me Mk Vd Fr. Polyc.P 3LV:* sicut ex *Rom. Pan.EFJLMm*

31 spirituali *Aa Cg Fd Me Mk Vd Fr. Polyc.P 3LV:* originale peccatum spirituali *Rom. Pan.EFJLMm orig.*

32 patre *Aa Pf Fr. Pan.EFJLMm Polyc.m orig.*: parte *Cg Fd:* parente *Cd Hk In Me Mk Sa Sb Vd Fr.ABD:* parente *ex* parte *corr. Bi.*

37 universe familie *Aa Cg Fd Me Mk Vd Fr.*: in universa familia *Rom. Polyc.PC(post corr.), orig.*: in universali familia *Pan.m:* et universa familia *Pan.FJM:* vel universa familia *Pan.E^{pc}:* universa familia *Pan.LE^{ac}, Polyc.m 3LV; hic explicit Pan.*

The collation shows that Gratian sometimes follows one source, sometimes another. These observation may be systematized conveniently by dividing the text into three sections to be considered separately:

a. line 1 (*si habes*) – line 24 (*conmouerer*)
b. line 24 (*sed si tibi*) – line 37 (*uniuersae familiae*)
c. line 37 (*unde si*) – line 48 (*uideretur*)

Among the collections here under consideration, the text of section **c** appears only in the *Polycarpus* and in *3L*, and there are no significant variations between them and the *Decretum*. One of the two was, in all likelihood, Gratian's source. Section **b** appears in the *Polycarpus*, *3L* and in the *Panormia*. But since lines 24 to 28 are missing in the *Panormia*, and since Gratian and the other two collections share significant variants on lines 28, 30, and 31 (the *Panormia* contains different readings), it is reasonable to conclude that Gratian took section **b** also from either the *Polycarpus* or *3L*. Again, the collation provides no grounds for preferring one to the other.

The text of section **a** occurs in four collections. Here Gratian shares significant variants with the *Panormia* and the *Tripartita*, while the *Polycarpus* and *3L* have preserved the readings of Augustine's original text (lines 5, 12, 20 *quesierit*, and 22–24). It appears that Gratian found the text of section **a** either in the *Panormia* or in the *Tripartita*. One might be tempted to opt for the latter alternative, since the canon in the *Tripartita* ends exactly where section **a** ends, but all six manuscripts of the *Panormia* which I have checked have at this point *Item* (*Pan.EFJLMT*). This could have been a sufficient reason for Gratian to end his excerpt here, especially since the layout of at least one *Panormia* manuscript (*Pan.L*, fo. 139r) is such that the following text appears to be a new canon. The collation provides no basis for singling out either the *Panormia* or the *Tripartita* as Gratian's source. Since c. 1 appears close to canons deriving from the *Panormia* (canons 2, 5, 6), while there are no canons deriving from the *Tripartita* in the vicinity (the closest in this *questio* is c. 13), it is more likely that Gratian took section **a** from the *Panormia*.

The inscription in the *Decretum* differs from the inscriptions in the other three collections, but it is significantly closer to those of the *Panormia* (and the *Tripartita*) than to that of the *Polycarpus*. It would, therefore, appear that Gratian first included section **a**, perhaps from the *Panormia*, and that sections **b** and **c** were added later, when he found a longer text in the *Polycarpus* (or in the *3L*). This longer text was also used to fill out an omission in section **a** (lines 18–19). On line 6, the manuscripts of the *Decretum* are divided between the readings *nec* (which is the reading of the *Polycarpus* and the *3L*) and *ne* (the reading of the *Panormia* and the *Tripartita*). Gratian first might have written *ne* and later changed this to *nec*, or he might have furnished his manuscript with a variant reading. Otherwise, he does not appear to have "corrected" readings in this canon with the help of the longer text, but he seems to have made some editorial changes:

24.3.1

15 ut (ita *Fr.ABD)* anima patris, ita *(om Fr.)* et *(om. Aa Fd Me Mk Pf)* anima filii mea est *Aa Bi Cd Cg Fd Gd Hk In Me Mk Pf Sa Sb Vd Fr. Vulg.:* anima patris mea est et anima filii mea est *Rom. Pan.EFJLMm Trip. Polyc.Pm 3LV orig.*

20 a *Aa Cg Fd Hk Me Mk Vd Fr.:* ex *Pan.EFJMm Trip. Polyc.Pm 3LV orig.:* hec *Pan.L*

20 id *om. Rom. Pan.EFJLM Trip Polyc.Pm 3LV orig., add. sup. lin. Sb*

24 id *om. Rom. Polyc.Pm 3LV orig.*

34 post *Aa Bi Cd Cg Fd Hk In Me Mk Pf Vd Fr.:* postea *Rom. Polyc.Pm 3LV Pan.EFJLMm orig.*

46 hec] hoc *Polyc.m*

48 videretur] videtur *Polyc.m*

These readings either simplify the language or, on line 15, make a scriptural quotation adhere more closely to the text of the Latin Bible such as it circulated in the twelfth century.[114] Rather than postulating that Gratian used an unknown source, it is reasonable to assume that he made these purely editorial changes.

WRONGFUL EXCOMMUNICATION

The *dictum* p. c. 1 proceeds to point out that illicit excommunication damages only the one excommunicating. The series of canons which follows (canons 2–9) is summarized in d. p. c. 9: "It is clear from the foregoing, that illicit excommunication does not harm him who is condemned but him who condemns." The connection with d. a. c. 1 is apparent from what follows: "And because of this, those who are innocent cannot be condemned due to another's crime, as the households of powerful men used to be condemned by imprudent men for the sins of their masters."[115] But only three of the preceding canons in fact relate clearly to this exact issue. Canon 5 states that priests who judge incorrectly themselves commit sacrilege. Besides addressing several issues of due process, the lengthy canon 6 determines that if a priest illicitly

---

[114] As is often the case, Augustine's quotation of the Bible reflects a different translation than the versions of the Vulgate which circulated during the middle ages, see Petrus Sabatier, *Bibliorum sacrorum latinae versiones antiquae seu Vetus Italica* (Paris 1743–1749), ad Ez. 18: 4. Gratian's version is identical to the one found in the modern edition of the Vulgate: Weber, ed., *Biblia sacra*, 1289. For a convenient survey of the textual transmission of the different versions of the Latin Bible, see G. W. H. Lampe, ed., *The Cambridge History of the Bible* II (Cambridge 1969).

[115] Friedberg, ed., *Decretum*, 993, supported by Aa Mk: "Illicita ergo excommunicatio, ut ex premissis apparet, non ledit eum, qui notatur, sed a quo notatur, ac per hoc qui innocentes sunt ex alterius crimine condemnari non possunt, sicut ab imprudentibus familiae potentum pro peccatis dominorum consueuerunt notari."

excommunicates someone, he himself is to abstain from communion for a period determined by his superior. Canon 2 is an excerpt from a letter of Gregory I, where the pope tells the addressee that he can resume communion after having been excommunicated without cause by Laurentius, "formerly our brother and fellow bishop." Gratian's interpretation of the canon is clear from the rubric: "He who unlawfully excommunicates someone condemns himself and not the other."[116] Gratian may have taken Gregory's use of the word *quondam* ("formerly") to mean that the pope had excommunicated Laurentius, and then assumed a causal connection between this excommunication and Laurentius' illicit action.

Significantly, these three canons are all included in the first recension. Their source was the *Panormia*. This is the only relevant collection in which c. 5 appears. In the inscription of c. 2, Gratian and the *Panormia* mistakenly give the addressee, Magnus, the title of bishop, while the other two possible sources, the *Polycarpus* and *3L*, correctly call him priest.[117] Canon 6 appears in the *Panormia* and in the *Tripartita*. A collation of textual variants indicates that the former was Gratian's source:

24.3.6
28 vocatus *Cg Fd Mk Tx Vd Fr. Pan.EFJLM:* advocatus *Aa:* evocatus *Rom. Trip.*
34–35 et Ephesina sinodus de eodem decernens (discernens *Pan.J:* decernit *Cg*) *Aa Cg Fd Mk Tx Vd Fr. Pan.EFJLM: om. Trip.*
36 scribens *Aa Cg Fd Mk Tx Vd Fr. Pan.EFJLM: om. Trip.*

Also c. 7 is found in the first recension. The point which it makes is related to the point Gratian makes in d. a. c. 1, lines 31–33: it is not the sentence of excommunication that separates a sinner from the Church, but the very actions that made him deserve excommunication in the first place. Therefore, if someone is excommunicated without cause, he is still a part of the Church. The text of c. 7 is found in none of Gratian's usual sources, but it is present in the *Ordinary Gloss* to the Bible (at Leviticus 24: 10),[118] which Gratian sometimes used as a source.

Remaining canons before d. a. c. 9 (canons 3, 4, 8, and 9) were added only in the second recension. None of them contains anything which was used in the composition of the surrounding *dicta*. Their sources are easy to determine, since each of them appears only in one other collection. Canons 3, 4, and 8 are found only in the *3L*[119] and c. 9 only in the

---

[116] Friedberg, ed., *Decretum*, 990, supported by Mk Tx: "Illicite aliquem excommunicans, semet ipsum, condempnat non illum." Aa Cg Fd, and the Roman edition contain a differently worded rubric, which probably is the original: "Qui illicite (*qui il-* add. supra lin. Fd) aliquem exommunicat semet ipsum non illum condempnat (*dampnat* Aa)." The meaning remains the same.

[117] Cf. JE 1230.   [118] *Biblia latina cum glossa ordinaria*, ad Leviticus 24: 10.

[119] Cf., for canons 3 and 4, Guiseppe Motta, "A proposito dei testi di Origene nel *Decreto* di Graziano," *Revue bénédictine* 88 (1978), 318, nos. 9–10.

Panormia. Although they seem unnecessary for the *dicta*, the canons have some general affinities with their context. There are thematical similarities between c. 7, on one hand, and canons 4 and 8, on the other. Canon 3 states that "those who neglect to curtail the habit of a cursing mouth, incur (according to the word of Isaiah) unclean lips and a foul mouth, even though they do not curse in their heart."[120] The canon does not specifically deal with excommunication, but it could easily have been thought suitable in the context, since in *3L* it is found in the title *De excommunicantibus.* The short text of c. 9, finally, is difficult to interpret: "It is certain that he who is shown to be impious is entirely separated from God, just as he who is anathematized is separated on the ground of being impious, for anathema does not signify anything except separation from God."[121] In the context of Gratian's reading of I Corinthians 5: 11 in d. a. c. 1, lines 33–40, however, c. 9 can suitably be read with emphasis placed on the word "shown" (*demonstratus*). In this reading, c. 9 emphasizes that due judicial process is necessary for excommunicating someone; hence a member of an excommunicated person's family cannot be considered automatically condemned. One can also read the text in the light of canons 4, 7, and 8 as containing the idea that "visible" sin is as good for separation from God as the formal sanction of anathema.

The preceding analysis has shown that my hypothesis about a first recension causes no inconsistencies when applied to the nine first canons in C. 24, q. 3. In addition, this hypothesis explains a peculiarity among these canons, namely the rubric of c. 5, *De eodem.*[122] This canon states that when priests persecute sin (i.e., excommunicate) without discretion, they incur the crime of sacrilege and fall headlong themselves. The immediately preceding canon 4 makes a rather different point, namely that it is a person's way of life and not a formal sentence (of excommunication) which binds or frees him. To make sense of the rubric, one has to take it to refer to c. 2, the rubric of which could fit c. 5 as well ("He who unlawfully excommunicates someone condemns himself and not the other"). In the first recension, c. 2 indeed immediately precedes c. 5.

[120] Friedberg, ed., *Decretum*, 990, supported by Aa^add Mk: "Qui negligunt oris maledicti consuetudinem resecare, etiamsi non corde maledicant, tamen inmundiciam labiorum (secundum Ysaiae uerbum) et inquinamenta oris incurrunt."

[121] Friedberg, ed., *Decretum*, 993, supported by Aa^add Mk: "Certum est, quod qui inpius demonstratus est omnino separatus est a Deo, sicut etiam ille, qui anathematizatus est tamquam inpius separatus est. Nichil enim aliud significat anathema, nisi a Deo separationem."

[122] Friedberg, ed., *Decretum*, 990, supported by Aa Cg Fd Gg Me Mk Mz Tx Vd.

TURNING THE OTHER CHEEK

The next portion of the *questio* deals with the further objection that not even those who sin should be censured with the sentence of malediction, since Christ said: "Pray for those who persecute you and those who abuse you, do good to those who hate you"[123] (Matthew 5: 44). Gratian first furnishes the reader with this and two other scriptural quotations (in d. p. c. 9) and two patristic canons (canons 10–11). Subsequently (in d. p. c. 11), he gives a number of examples to the contrary, all taken from the Bible, pointing out, e.g., that God damned Adam, Eve, and Cain, that Peter damned Simon Magus, that Paul, who had said "bless and do not curse" (Romans 12: 14), also ordered that the fornicator in Corinth should be excommunicated (as Gratian had mentioned in d. a. c. 1). Gratian solves the problem by distinguishing between malediction based on hate or a wish for revenge and malediction based on love for justice. The former is prohibited, while the latter is permitted. Gratian did not invent this distinction; he took it from the passage in Gregory the Great's *Moralia*, which is quoted as c. 12. This canon also contains three of the scriptural references which Gratian used in the *dictum*. Obviously, this canon is necessary for his argument, and it is indeed included in the first recension.

On the other hand, canons 10 and 11 do not seem to contribute greatly to Gratian's discussion, which they rather seem to interrupt. It is particularly difficult to discern the purpose of c. 11 with its distinction between those who are driven to salvation by desire for benedictions and those driven by fear of maledictions. This distinction does not play any role in the *dicta*. Both canons are absent from the first recension where d. p. c. 12 follows immediately upon d. p. c. 9, forming a tighter argument. Their source seems to have been *3L*, which is the only one of the usual sources that contains either text.[124]

FURTHER ON EXCOMMUNICATION

Canons 13 to 18 are not accompanied by any *dicta*, and it is not entirely clear what point the author is attempting to make by adducing these rather disparate statements. Canon 13 states that the spirit both of those who err and of those who teach others to err should be handed over to

---

[123] Friedberg, ed., *Decretum*, 993, supported by Aa Mk: "Orate pro persequentibus et calumpniantibus uos, benefacite his, qui oderunt uos." Note that Gratian reproduces these two enjoinders in an order different from the normal. No such inversion is registered in the critical apparatus of Iohannes Wordsworth, H. I. White, and H. F. D. Sparks, eds., *Novum testamentum Domini nostri Iesu Christi latine secundum editionem S. Hieronymi* (Oxford 1889–1954), I 58.

[124] For c. 11, cf. Motta, "A proposito," 318, no. 5.

Satan. Canon 14 emphasizes that both priests and laity should see to it
that those who are perishing either mend their ways or, if they are incor-
rigible, are separated from the Church. According to Gratian's rubric, he
read c. 15 as stating that someone who had been admonished twice or
thrice (without result) should be excommunicated. Canon 16 under-
scores the importance of timely intervention against heresy by adducing
Arius as an example; if he had been excommunicated at once, his heresy
would not have spread all over the world. That different sins deserve
different punishment is stated in c. 17, and c. 18 points out that those who
do not wish to mend their ways should be cut away from the Church
with the sword of excommunication.

The most convenient explanation appears to be that these canons
underscore and exemplify the conclusion in d. p. c. 11, that excommunication indeed should be used by the Church. However, the canons are
not present in the first recension, which again shows itself more tightly
argued and succinct. It is easy to determine the sources of canons 13 to
18, since each of them appears in only one relevant collection: canons 13
to 15 in the *Tripartita*[125] and canons 16 to 18 in *3L*.

SOME SINS WORTHY OF EXCOMMUNICATION

Canons 19 to 25 specify some categories of sinners for whom excommunication is a suitable punishment: bigamists (c. 19), false witnesses and
homicides (c. 20), powerful men who despoil clerics, powerless men, or
monks and who refuse to come to the bishop for a trial (c. 21), those who
attack pilgrims and merchants (c. 23), those who injure churches and the
people who are in them (canons 24–25). (Canon 22 is a *palea*.[126]) There
are no *dicta* which tie these canons to the rest of the *questio*, and one may
legitimately wonder why this incomplete listing of sins meriting excommunication is found exactly here. They are indeed missing from the first
recension. The author of the second recension extracted them from
various sources. Canons 19 and 20 appear to derive from the *Tripartita*,
since this is the only one of the usual sources to contain either text.
Canons 23 and 24 contain legislation from the First Lateran Council.
Among the usual sources of the *Decretum*, c. 25 is found only in the
Panormia, which apparently was the source.

---

[125] For canon 14, cf. Fuhrmann, *Einfluß und Verbreitung*, 786–787.
[126] This *palea* is missing in Cg Fd Me Mk Mz Tx Vd, in all eight of Friedberg's manuscripts, and in
nine Cambridge manuscripts examined in Ullmann, "Paleae in Cambridge," 212. See also
Rambaud, "Le legs," 109 and 112. The source of this *palea* may well have been the supplement
of *3L*, since it shares the false inscription *Ex dictis Gregorii Papae* with this collection, while
Burchard's and Ivo's *Decreta* have another false inscription, *Ex concilio Tungrensi* (PL 140.853 and
161.815).

It is somewhat more complicated to determine the source for c. 21, which appears both in the *Tripartita* and in Anselm of Lucca's collection. In choosing between these, it is crucial to note that the author of the *Decretum* clearly knew that the canon derived from the First Council of Toledo.[127] Anselm apparently did not know the number of the council, while the chronological arrangement of the relevant section of the *Tripartita* makes this clear. The conclusion, that Gratian took this canon from the *Tripartita*, gains support from a collation of textual variants:

24.3.21
Inscr. Item ex concilio Toletano I (I *om. Cg) Aa Cg Fd Mk Tx Vd Fr.*: Ex concilio Toletano cap. XI *Ans.*
6 obediat *Aa Cg Fd Mk Tx Vd Fr. Trip:* audiatur *Ans. orig.*

The reading which Gratian and the *Tripartita* share on line 6 is significant.

DEFINITIONS OF HERESY

The first words of d. p. c. 25 look backward: "Since we are talking about heretics . . ."[128] This is a peculiar statement, since the *questio* so far has exclusively dealt with excommunication; heretics or heresies are hardly mentioned at all (with the exception of the reference to Arius in c. 16). I interpret this *dictum* as referring to the larger context of the entire C. 24 and probably also C. 23. The fictitious "cases" set up in each of these "*causae*" concern heretical bishops and the last part of C. 24, q. 3 (i.e., d. p. c. 25–c. 40) could perhaps be seen as a kind of epilogue to this "heresy-section" (the *causae hereticorum*) of the *Decretum* rather than as a continuation of the argument in the beginning of C. 24 q. 3.

In the rest of the *dictum*, Gratian poses three questions: what is the difference between schism and heresy? Who are heretics? How many sects of heretics are there? These questions are answered by canons 26 and 27, 28 and 29, and 39, respectively. C. 26 gives Jerome's distinction between perversion of dogma (heresy) and episcopal discord (schism), and c. 27 develops this definition with another quotation from Jerome, which gives the etymology of the word *heresis*. Preceded by a very short *dictum*, c. 28 states that a heretic is someone who follows false and novel opinions for the sake of worldly gain. But, c. 29 adds, he who is induced to heresy by someone else and does not stubbornly hold to his heresy is not a heretic. *Causa* 39, finally, reproduces Isidore of Seville's listing of various heresies.

---

[127] Gonzalo Martínez Díez and Felix Rodríguez, *La colección canónica Hispana*, Monumenta Hispaniae sacra, serie canonica (Madrid 1966–), IV 332–333 (= *orig.*).
[128] Friedberg, ed., *Decretum*, 998, supported by Aa Mk: "Quia uero de hereticis sermo habetur . . ."

The series of canons which relate to d. p. c. 25 is rather awkwardly interrupted by canons 30 to 38. Some of them could, to be sure, be seen as a continued development of the definition of "heretic." Canon 31 states that those who contumaciously defend improper views are heretics (the corollary of c. 29). According to c. 32, a defender of another's error is much more to blame than he who errs, and he is to be considered a heresiarch and not only a heretic. Canons 30 and 33 could also be taken as contributions to the definition of "heretic." The former canon condemns those who have recourse to their own mind rather than consulting scripture or those who are wiser and more learned. They become teachers of error rather than disciples of truth. Aside from derogating nocuous persons in biblical language, c. 33 states that it is manifestly known that heretics oppress churchmen with their sophistries and the art of dialectics. The connection between the questions of d. p. c. 25 and the other canons is here even more tenuous. In c. 34, Pope Leo I asks the addressee (the patriarch of Constantinople) to investigate and coerce those among his clerics who agree with the depravity of the enemies (*adversariorum*). Canons 35 and 36 contain disciplinary statutes concerning dealings with heretics: clerics should not discuss, pray, sing, or eat with heretics. Canon 37 discusses, at this point quite surprisingly, whether it is at all right to excommunicate, i.e., the question treated in d. p. c. 9–c. 12. Also c. 38 addresses this issue, explaining why Paul said "bless and do not curse" (Romans 12: 14). D. p. c. 9 quotes this passage, and c. 38 would have suited *that* context very well. At the end of the *questio* comes c. 40 almost as an afterthought, explaining why God allows heretics to err.

Some of canons 30 to 38 and 40 are clearly irrelevant to their immediate context, i.e., the questions put forth in d. p. c. 25 and answered in canons 26 to 29 and 39, while others help answering these questions. None of the latter is, however, necessary for Gratian's argument in the *dicta*. Canons 30 to 38 and 40 are not found in the first recension, where, again, Gratian's argument is more concise than in the second recension. These later inserted canons all derive from either *3L* or from the *Tripartita*. This is easy to discern for canons 30, 32,[129] 33, 37, 38,[130] and 40, which are found only in *3L* among the usual sources, and likewise for canons 34

---

[129] For c. 32, cf. Jörg Busch, *Der "Liber de Honore Ecclesiae" des Placidus von Nonantola: Eine Problemerörterung aus dem Jahre 1111: Die Arbeitsweise ihres Autors und seine Vorlagen*, Quellen und Forschungen zum Recht im Mittelalter 5 (Sigmaringen 1990), 55.

[130] Canons 37 and 38 both have incorrect inscriptions in the *Decretum*. "Item ex epistola Urbani papae" (c. 37; so in Aa Cg Fd Mk Tx Vd) for what is in fact a fragment from Placidus de Nonantola, cf. Stephan Kuttner, "Urban II and Gratian," *Traditio* 24 (1968), 504–505, and Busch, *Liber de Honore Ecclesiae*, 55. *Unde Augustinus in libro Numeri* (c. 38; so in Aa Fd Mk Tx Vd) for a fragment from Origen, cf. Motta, "A proposito," 319, no. 11. Both lack inscription in *3LV* and the context there does not explain Gratian's mistake. It is, nonetheless, likely that Gratian took these canons, as well as c. 40, from *3L* (cf. Erickson, *Three Books*, 71).

and 35, which are only found in the *Tripartita*. The provenance of c. 31, which is found in three relevant collections, is made clear by the false inscription in the *Decretum*: *Augustinus contra Manicheos* (so Aa^add Cg Fd^add Mk Tx Vd). The text derives in fact from *De civitate Dei*. The misattribution indicates that *3L* was the source, since the text lacks inscription there while the canon immediately preceding (= C. 24 q. 1 c. 42) is (incorrectly) inscribed *Augustinus contra Manicheos*.[131] Canon 36 is a composite of fragments from two different letters of Pope Gelasius (JK 664 and 622).[132] Among the usual sources, this composite is found only in *3L*, which must have furnished the author of the second recension with the text. The text from JK 664 appears also in Anselm of Lucca's collection, but JK 622 is missing there.

It remains to determine the sources of those canons which were included in the first recension, namely canons 26 to 29 and 39. The first four of these are best treated together, since it is reasonable to assume that Gratian took them all from one of his sources; this source is, however, difficult to pinpoint. All four canons appear in three earlier collections: Anselm of Lucca's collection, the *Polycarpus,* and *3L*. Canon 26 also appears in Alger of Liège's *De misericordia et iustitia*.[133] This collection cannot have been Gratian's source, since Alger omits the phrase "quod quidem in principio aliqua ex parte intelligi potest diversum" (Friedberg, ed., *Decretum*, lines 4–5). Furthermore, his inscription reports only that the text derives from one of Jerome's commentaries *"super epistolas,"* while Gratian mistakenly writes that it comes from the commentary on Galatians (as do the *Polycarpus* and *3L*). Likewise, Anselm inscribes c. 26 simply *Ieronimus*, and can hardly have been Gratian's source for this canon. Canon 28 is in Anselm's collection inscribed *Augustinus ex libro de utilitate credendi*. Since the *Decretum* does not specify from which of Augustine's works the text is excerpted it is unlikely that Anselm was Gratian's source for this canon.

The following variants help in distinguishing between the *Polycarpus* and *3L*:

24.3.27
4 a quo *Aa Cg Fd Mk Tx Fr. Polyc.P*: quo *Ans.G*: que *3LV*
5 recesserit *Aa Cg Fd Mk Tx Fr Polyc.P*: cesserit *3LV Ans.G*

24.3.28
1 temporalis commodi *Aa Cg Fd Mk Tx Vd Fr. Polyc.P Ans.G*: tempora vel communioni *3LV*

---

[131] In the *Polycarpus* and in Anselm's collection the canon is inscribed simply: *Augustinus.*

[132] The fragments reproduced by Gratian are found in Andreas Thiel, ed., *Epistolae Romanorum pontificum genuinae et quae ad eos scriptae sunt a S. Hilaro usque ad Pelagium II* (Braunsberg 1867–1868), 405 and 346, and (§ 1) in E. Schwartz, ed., *Publizistische Sammlungen*, 18, lines 7–8.

[133] Kretzschmar, *Alger von Lüttichs Traktat*, 314.

24.3.29
4 *post* qui *verbum* peccat *add. 3LV: om. Aa Cg Fd Mz Fr. Polyc.P Ans.G*

If Gratian extracted all four canons 26 to 29 from the same source, and that is likely, given the fact that they appear in close sequence in the possible sources, then it is clear that this source must have been the *Polycarpus.*

The lengthy canon 39 should, according to the *Correctores Romani* and Friedberg, be found as the last text in book 13 of Anselm of Lucca's collection. It is, however, missing from Edith Pásztór's edition of book 13,[134] and Peter Landau does not mention the text as one of the additions in recension C of Anselm's collection[135] (the recension which the *Correctores* and, indirectly, Friedberg normally used for book 13). Since this canon would be the very last in Anselm's collection, it is reasonable to assume that it, in fact, does not belong to the collection but was an addition at the end of the manuscript that the *Correctores* happened to use. The text appears to have circulated widely and Gratian could have found it in a number of places, for example at the end of a canonical manuscript or in some florilegium.

CONCLUSION

The preceding close reading of C. 24 has confirmed my thesis that the manuscripts Aa and Fd contain a first recension of this *causa*, not an abbreviation. The text in these manuscripts is more concise and contains less canons of marginal relevancy than the usual text. There is also a clear pattern in the utilization of sources. The first recension extracts its text predominantly from the *Panormia* and the *Polycarpus*, but never from *3L*. The second recension drew on *3L* and the *Tripartita* for most of the added canons.

---

[134] Pásztór, "Lotta," 421, and Cushing, *Papacy and Law in the Gregorian Revolution*, 200.
[135] Landau, "Rezension C," 27–28, 49.

Chapter 3

OBEDIENCE OR CONTEMPT: *CAUSA* 11,
QUESTIO 3

At the beginning of *Causa* 11, Gratian depicts the "case" which generates the questions that he intends to treat. Two clerics are litigating about estates (*de prediis*). The plaintiff wants to take the case to a civil court, while the defendant wishes the case heard by an ecclesiastical judge. The former manages to dispossess the latter and to take possession of the disputed property with the help of a civil judge. The bishop discovers this and suspends him from office. When the cleric in contempt continues to administer his office, the bishop deposes him without hope of restitution. Gratian now asks three questions: (1) Should a cleric be brought before a civil judge? (2) If he should not, is the crime of forcing him to appear before a civil judge punishable by suspension? (3) If it is not, should he who held his bishop's sentence in contempt be deposed without hope of restitution?

In this chapter, I shall examine the third question and how Gratian answers it. In the second recension, the *questio* contains 108 canons (plus two *paleae*), 56 of which are (wholly or, in three cases, in part) present already in the first recension. Gratian's discussion appears confusing and meandering in the second recension of C. 11, q. 3. He addresses the original question about the disobedient priest at the beginning of the *questio*, but then he discusses a different problem before returning to the main theme with c. 27 and d. p. c. 40. The rest of the *questio* is similarly organized. Most of the passages which break the continuity of Gratian's argument were added only in the second recension. The discussion is considerably easier to follow in the first recension. This *questio* presents, thus, a good illustration of how the character of the *Decretum* changed when the second recension was created, especially since a few *dicta* (most importantly d. p. c. 21 and d. p. c. 24) were added in this recension.

In regard to the use of sources in the two recensions, C. 11, q. 3 provides a less clear-cut case than does, e.g., C. 24. For several canons it proved impossible to identify positively Gratian's source. If a majority of these canons derived from a single, as yet unidentified source, as is likely, then Gratian may have extracted several other canons in this *questio* from the same source. There are, in fact, several canons for which my tentative determination of their sources may be questioned. I address these issues at the end of this chapter.

Table 6 documents occurrences of the texts of C. 11, q. 3 in the canonical collections which Gratian used when compiling the *Decretum*. As always, I account for my conclusions by bold-facing Gratian's source (for other conventions, see p. 35).[1]

FEAR AND CONTEMPT

Gratian's line of argument in the rather complicated first part of the *questio* emerges more clearly if one first examines d. p. c. 40. Here, Gratian summarizes some of the preceding canons and resolves the disagreements among them:

11.3.d.p.c. 40
To the preceding authorities, by which we are commanded to obey an unjust sentence until both sides have been examined, should be replied: Gregory does not say that an unjustly imposed sentence should be upheld, but that it should be feared. So also Urban. It should be held in fear, that is: it should not be held in contempt out of pride. The other authorities talk about persons who have been excommunicated, either since they were called to a synod and did not deign to come, or since, unable to defend themselves against the cunning of their enemies they received an unjust sentence from a judge, or since, in neglecting their lives, they allowed an unfavorable opinion to emerge about them and received a sentence.[2]

Gratian discusses the apparent contradiction between, on the one hand, Gregory (c. 1) and Urban (c. 27), who say that an unjust sentence should be feared, and on the other hand authorities, which state that one may appeal a sentence. His solution has two components. First, he explores the meaning of the term "to fear." To fear a bishop's unjust sentence

---

[1] Rambaud, "Le legs," 61, indicates, without discussing the evidence, the formal sources of most canons in this *questio*. But her work pre-dates some of the most significant work that has been done on Gratian's formal sources (particularly by Peter Landau and John H. Erickson), and her results are therefore flawed. Below, I have not referred to her conclusions.

[2] Friedberg, ed., *Decretum*, 655, supported by Aa Bc Mz: "Premissis auctoritatibus, quibus iniustae sententiae usque ad examinationem utriusque partis parere iubemur, ita respondetur: Gregorius non dicit sententiam iniuste latam esse seruandam, sed (esse add. Aa) timendam. Sic et Urbanus. Timenda ergo est (est ergo Bc Mz), id est non ex superbia contempnenda. Reliquae uero auctoritates de excommunicatis locuntur, qui uel uocati ad sinodum uenire contempserunt, uel calliditatibus aduersantium occurrere nescientes iniustam sententiam a iudice reportauerunt, uel qui (om. Mz), neglectu suae uitae sinistram de se opinionem nasci permittentes, sententiam in se (in se om. Aa) exceperunt." There follows a sentence which will be treated below.

means not to hold it in contempt out of pride. Such a sentence may, Gratian adds in d. p. c. 43, be ignored. He then points out that the cases in which an excommunicated person must obey until examined are the cases where he, to some degree, is to blame for the sentence, even if it is wrong; he may have failed to show up at a synod to which he was summoned, or defended himself poorly, or allowed himself to earn a bad reputation.

Gratian states that "the other authorities" (that is, other than Urban and Gregory) concern such cases. To which canons is he referring? It should first be noted that canons 5 and 9 use the words *superbia* ("pride") and *neglectu* ("neglect"), respectively, in a sense similar to Gratian's use of the words in d. p. c. 40. Both stipulate that excommunicated persons should not communicate before their cases are heard. Similar themes are found in canons 2 and 4, while canons 30, 34, 35, 36, and 37 state (or at least imply) that excommunications considered unjust may be appealed to a synod. What Gratian says about "the other authorities" clearly refers to some or all of these canons. His argument in d. p. c. 40 is based on these texts in addition to the fundamental canons 1 and 27, which he explicitly cites.

Gratian's treatment of these issues is, however, not sustained throughout the sequence of canons 1 to 40. It is interrupted, most obviously, by d. p. c. 20 and d. p. c. 26 with their accompanying canons, where a distinction is drawn between those excommunicated by a church authority and those who deserve such punishment on account of a sin, although they have not been formally sentenced. These texts are, not surprisingly, missing from the first recension, as are canons 10 to 20. The latter are certainly not irrelevant to the subject of the *questio*, but it is easy to see that Gratian's argument works equally well, if not better, with these canons removed. Some of them, such as canons 16, 18, and 19, are similar to, among others, canons 4 and 5, in that they prohibit an excommunicated person from communicating. In the latter canons, the prohibition is valid until the case has been reexamined, which implies that the sentence may be appealed. The former canons do not, however, mention anything about a possible reexamination, which makes them seem rather foreign to this *questio*, where Gratian discusses the possibility of appeal. Canons 16, 18, and 19 leave an impression of having been inserted here due to their general similarities with, e.g., canons 4 to 6 (i.e., their prohibiting excommunicants to communicate) and not because they would contribute directly to Gratian's argument. The same is true for canons 20 and 28, which also were added in the second recension. Again, the first recension reveals itself to be more succinctly argued.

A textual observation provides further evidence: canon 4 has the rubric

Table 6 Formal sources of C. 11, q. 3

Gratian	Panormia	Tripartita	Polycarpus	3 Books	Anselm	Ivo, Decretum	Notes
11.3.1	—	**2.6.4**	—	—	—	—	Cf. d. p. c. 77
11.3.2	5.101	—	—	—	—	14.27 & 14.101	—
11.3.3	—	—	—	—	**12.36**	—	—
11.3.4	5.127	2.5.10	7.1.33	2.26.7	**3.68**	14.15	—
11.3.5	—	2.16.5	7.1.22	2.25.13	**12.32**	6.239	—
11.3.6	—	2.6.2	7.1.18	2.25.8	**12.25**	5.362	—
11.3.7	—	**2.47.37**	—	S 7.12	—	—	—
11.3.8	5.128	**2.28.2**	—	—	—	14.16,81	—
11.3.9	—	3.9.11	7.1.19	2.25.9	**12.26**	5.314	—
11.3.10	—	**1.62.37 & 39**	—	—	—	8.226	—
11.3.11	—	—	5.1.53 & 4.14.2	**2.24.7**	—	—	—
11.3.12	—	1.1.1	1.18.3	**2.24.6**	2.35	5.47	—
11.3.13	—	—	—	**2.24.18**	—	—	—
11.3.14	—	—	—	**2.24.10**	—	—	—
11.3.15	—	1.18.2	1.18.2	—	1.6	14.22	D 93 c. 1
11.3.16	5.95	—	7.1.3	**2.25.1**	12.18	14.24	—
11.3.17	5.94	1.14.12	7.1.1 & (7.1.23)	**2.25.2**	12.13 & (12.19)	14.23 & 14.102	—
11.3.18	—	2.14.27–28	7.1.15	**2.25.3**	12.15	14.95–96	Cf. c. 28
11.3.19	5.99	2.18.72	7.1.17	**2.25.5**	12.17	14.28 & 14.108	—
11.3.20	—	**3.27.21**	7.1.11	2.26.19	12.31	14.65 & 14.113	—
11.3.21	—	—	—	**2.25.18**	—	—	—
11.3.22	—	—	—	**2.25.19–20**	—	—	—
11.3.23	—	—	—	**2.25.21**	—	—	—
11.3.24	—	—	—	**2.25.26**	—	—	—
11.3.25	—	—	—	**2.25.35**	—	—	—

II.3.26	—	**2.35.7**	6.1.3 & 7.1.22.26.10	—	6.139& **12.24**	14.30	—
II.3.27	—	(1.15.3)	(7.1.15)	(2.25.3)	(12.15)	14.74	—
II.3.28	5.98	**2.14.28**	7.1.24	—	—	14.96	Cf. c. 18
II.3.29	5.88	**2.16.4**	—	2.33.27	—	14.28 & 14.107	—
II.3.30	—	**2.18.65**	—	—	—	14.48	—
II.3.31	—	**3.27.18**	—	—	—	2.94 & 14.50	—
II.3.32	—	**3.27.19**	—	—	—	14.53	—
II.3.33	—	—	—	**2.26.23**	12.6	—	—
d.p.c. 33	—	2.22.10	—	**2.26.22**	—	—	—
II.3.34	—	**2.18.27** & 1.24.3	—	—	—	—	—
II.3.35	—	**2.19.12** & 3.10.14	7.1.27	—	—	6.232	—
II.3.36	5.136	**1.46.21**	7.1.5	2.25.6	—	14.111	—
II.3.37	—	—	7.1.5	—	12.27	14.112	*Palea*
II.3.38	—	**2.34.8**	—	—	12.28	—	—
II.3.39	5.121	3.27.22	—	S 7.9	—	14.114	—
II.3.40	5.93	—	—	**S 7.5**	—	14.80	—
II.3.41	—	—	—	**S 7.7**	—	—	—
II.3.42	5.112	3.27.4	—	**S 7.11**	—	14.122	—
II.3.43	5.86	—	7.1.34	—	7.115	14.7	*Palea*
II.3.44	—	3.27.5	7.2.3	—	—	14.8	—
II.3.45	—	3.27.6	—	—	—	14.9	—
II.3.46	5.83	3.27.2	—	2.26.30	—	14.5	—
II.3.47	—	3.27.7	—	—	—	14.10	—
II.3.48	—	3.27.8	7.1.14	—	—	14.11	—
II.3.49	—	3.27.9	—	—	—	14.12	—
II.3.50	—	**1.55.108**	—	—	—	—	—
II.3.51	—	—	—	—	—	14.13	—
II.3.52	—	**3.27.10**	—	—	—	—	—
II.3.53	—	—	—	—	—	—	—

Table 6 (cont.)

Gratian	Panormia	Tripartita	Polycarpus	3 Books	Anselm	Ivo, Decretum	Notes
11.3.54	—	**3.27.11**	14.14			—	
11.3.55	—	—	—	**2.32.114**	—	—	—
11.3.56	—	—	—	**3.19.123**	—	—	—
11.3.57	5.84	3.27.3	—	—	—	14.6	—
11.3.58	—	—	—	**S 2.1**	—	—	—
11.3.59	—	—	—	**3.19.130**	—	—	—
11.3.60	5.79	3.27.1	7.1.10	—	12.23	14.3	—
11.3.61	5.80	3.27.1	7.1.10	—	12.23	14.3	—
11.3.62	5.81	1.55.2 & (3.27.1)	—	—	—	14.3	—
11.3.63	—	1.45.2	2.33.1 & 3.15.23	2.28.6	4.3 & 6.58	5.140	—
11.3.64	—	—	—	2.33.58	—	—	—
11.3.65	3.80	2.37.8 & 3.10.16	2.36.1	—	8.24	5.367 & 6.237	—
d.p.c. 65							—
11.3.66	—	—	—	2.33.39	—	—	—
11.3.67	—	3.29.7	—	—	—	16.30	—
11.3.68	—	—	—	—	—	—	—
11.3.69	—	—	—	—	—	—	—
11.3.70	—	—	—	2.33.37	**13.25**	—	—
11.3.71	—	—	—	**2.33.44**	—	—	—
11.3.72	—	2.1.5	—	**2.25.29**	—	—	—
11.3.73	—	—	7.1.25	—	3.69	—	—
11.3.74	—	—	–.1.47	—	3.67	(14.100)	—
11.3.75	4.114	—	—	—	3.47	5.247	—
11.3.76	—	—	5.1.31	—		6.348	—

II.3.77	—	—	—	—	—	—	—
d.p.c. 77	—	**2.14.25**	**7.1.35**	—	—	—	—
II.3.78	—	—	—	2.33.39a	—	—	—
II.3.79	—	2.50.27	—	2.33.60	—	—	—
II.3.80	—	2.50.27	—	—	—	—	—
II.3.81	—	—	—	—	—	—	—
II.3.82	—	**2.50.19**	—	**2.5.32**	—	—	—
II.3.83	—	—	—	—	—	—	—
II.3.84	—	—	—	**3.14.23**	—	—	—
II.3.85	—	—	—	**3.14.24 & 3.14.51**	—	—	—
II.3.86	—	—	—	**3.14.38**	—	—	—
II.3.87	—	3.27.1 & (1.55.2)	7.1.13	2.26.18	12.66	14.3	Alger 1.66a
II.3.88	5.78–81	1.14.3	7.1.10	—	12.23	5.235	—
II.3.89	—	3.27.12	—	2.32.38	3.86	14.14	—
II.3.90	—	—	—	—	—	—	—
II.3.91	—	—	7.5.4	—	11.118	15.117	Alger 1.32
II.3.92	—	—	—	—	—	—	—
II.3.93	—	—	1.29.8	1.9.8	13.26	—	—
II.3.94	—	—	—	—	—	Cf. 5.7	—
II.3.95	—	1.18.7	—	—	—	6.322	—
II.3.96	—	**1.62.40**	—	—	—	8.227	—
II.3.97	—	—	1.29.3	**1.9.3**	—	—	—
II.3.98	—	—	1.29.5+7	**1.9.5+7**	—	5.7	—
II.3.99	—	—	—	**3.19.69**	—	—	—
II.3.100	—	**2.14.21**	—	S 7.220	12.5	14.110	—
II.3.101	—	**2.14.18–20**	—	—	—	—	—
II.3.102	5.106	1.62.34	—	—	—	14.46	—
II.3.103	5.125	3.27.15	—	2.26.26	—	14.43	—
II.3.104	—	**1.58.2 & 3.2.11**	—	—	—	—	2.95

Table 6 (cont.)

Gratian	Panormia	Tripartita	Polycarpus	3 Books	Anselm	Ivo, Decretum	Notes
11.3.105	—	**1.59.1**	—	—	—	—	—
3.2.12	—	—	—	2.96	—	—	—
11.3.106	—	—	—	**S7.1**	—	14.76	—
11.3.107	—	—	—	**S7.2**	—	14.79 & 3.126	—
11.3.108	—	—	—	**S7.3–4**	—	—	—
11.3.109	**5.104**	—	—	—	—	14.35	—
11.3.110	**5.107**	—	—	—	—	14.45	—

"About the same thing."[3] The rubric of the preceding c. 3, "He who communicates with excommunicants deserves a sentence of excommunication,"[4] contains a stipulation that cannot readily be found in c. 4. The rubric of c. 2 ("A person who has been excommunicated by his bishop is not to be received by another"[5]) does not suit their content well,[6] while the rubric of c. 1 is more suitable ("The sentence of the pastor is to be feared by the flock"[7]). This state of affairs is explained by the first recension, where c. 4 in fact follows directly upon c. 1.

My thesis about the first recension is supported also by the source analysis. Canons 2[8] and 7 must come from the *Tripartita*, and c. 3 from Anselm of Lucca's collection, since their texts are only found there among the usual sources. All of canons 10–26 probably derive either from the *Tripartita* or from *3L*, as do canons 28, 29, 33, 39, and the text found in d. p. c. 33. This is easily determined for canons 10, 13, 14, 21–26, 33, and 39, since each of them appears in only one of the usual sources.[9] That c. 16 derives from the *3L* is clear from the fact that it is the only relevant collection to contain the first sentence found in the Decretum.[10] To determine the sources of canons 11–12, 15–20, 28–29, and the text quoted in d. p. c. 33 is more complicated and each of them has to be treated separately.

Canon 11 is a short excerpt from a forged letter attributed to Pope Clement I (JK †12).[11] The same excerpt is found in the *3L*, which probably was the source. The *Polycarpus* contains this text twice, but with significant variants, indicating that this collection was not the source.

Canon 12 is a short excerpt from another forged letter ascribed to Pope

---

[3] Friedberg, ed., *Decretum*, 643 and 644, supported by Bc Fd Mz: *De eodem*.

[4] Friedberg, ed., *Decretum*, 642, supported by Cg Mk Mz: "Excommunicationis sententiam meretur (mer. sent. Cg Mk Mz) qui excommunicatis communicat."

[5] Friedberg, ed., *Decretum*, 642, supported by Cg Mk Mz: "A suo episcopo (om. Mz) excommunicatus non est ab alio recipiendus."

[6] Canon 4 prohibits, in its last sentence, communication with excommunicants, but it would be odd to take that as the main concern of the canon. Canon 5 does not contain any such prohibition.

[7] Friedberg, ed., *Decretum*, 642, supported by Cg Mk Sa: "Gregi timenda est sententia pastoris (past. sent. Sa)."

[8] Canon 2 consists of c. 6 from the Council of Antioch of 330 or 341 in the translation of the *Collectio Hispana*, see Martínez Díez and Rodríguez, *La colección canónica Hispana*, III 141 and Cuthbert Hamilton Turner, *Ecclesiae occidentalis monumenta iuris antiquissima: canonum et conciliorum Graecorum interpretationes Latinae* (Oxford 1899–1939), II 252, col. III. Among relevant collections, this translation of c. 6 appears only in the *Tripartita*, while the text in the *Panormia* is the second translation of Dionysius Exiguus, see Turner, *Ecclesiae occidentalis monumenta*, II 253, col. V. Gratian must, consequently, have taken his text from the *Tripartita*.

[9] For canons 21 to 25, cf. Erickson, "Three Books," 74.

[10] The inscription in *3L* is, furthermore, almost identical to that in the *Decretum*, while the other possible sources have differently formulated inscriptions: Item Fabianus episcopus *Bc Mz Tx Fr.*: Fabianus papa Romanus ecclesie comministris *Pan.EM*: Fabianus episcopus omnibus christianis *Polyc.m*: Fabianus episcopus *3LV.* [11] Cf. Fuhrmann, *Einfluß und Verbreitung*, 996–997, n. 439.

Clement (JK †10).[12] Several collections may have been the source used by the author of the second recension. A slightly longer excerpt from Clement's letter, including the text found in the *Decretum*, appears as the first canon in the *Tripartita* (1.1.1). A fragment of the same length as that in the *Decretum* is found in a forged letter ascribed to Pope Alexander I (JK †24).[13] Excerpts from Alexander's letter including the Clementine fragment appear in the *Polycarpus, 3L*, and in Anselm's collection. There are no variant readings that could be of help. The fact that the text in *3L* immediately precedes the text of c. 11 indicates that this collection is most likely to have been the source.

For *canon 15*, the author of the second recension quotes only the *incipit* of a canon, which was available *in extenso* at D. 93, c. 1 already in the first recension: "and so on as above in the treatise on those who are to be ordained, where the obedience of subordinates towards their superiors is discussed."[14] The reason for the duplication is probably that the author of the second recension added this reference when he realized that the text reproduced in D. 93 suited the context of C. 11, q. 3 as well.

The material source for both texts is a Pseudo-Isidorian decretal ascribed to Pope Fabian (JK †92), which quotes another false decretal ascribed to Pope Clement I (JK †10). This text, in turn, claims to quote Peter. That Gratian quotes JK †92 rather than JK †10 is obvious from the formulation of the inscription to D. 93, c. 1, which is a *verbatim* quote from JK †92: "Whence Blessed Peter, the prince of the apostles, when addressing the people at the ordination of Clement, said among other things."[15] The inscription of C. 11, q. 3, c. 15 (identical to the one used for c. 12) appears to be a condensed version of the same inscription: "Likewise, Peter at the ordination of Clement."[16] More significantly, Gratian's text (also at D. 93, c. 1) includes the name of Clement, as does JK †92 but not JK †10.[17]

---

[12] *Ibid.* 992–993, n. 434.

[13] Paul Hinschius, ed., *Decretales Pseudo-Isidorianae et Capitula Angilramni* (Leipzig 1863), 97. Cf. Fuhrmann, *Einfluß und Verbreitung*, 838–839, n. 107.

[14] Friedberg, ed., *Decretum*, 647, supported by Bc Mz Tx: "etc. ut supra in tractatu ordinandorum, ubi agitur de obedientia minorum erga maiores." *Minores* and *maiores* may refer to minor and major orders. Cf. Fuhrmann, *Einfluß und Verbreitung*, 784–785, n. 1.

[15] Friedberg, ed., *Decretum*, 320, supported by Aa Fd: "Unde B. Petrus princeps apostolorum in ordinatione Clementis populum alloquens, inter cetera ait." Cf. Hinschius, ed., *Decretales Pseudo-Isidorianae*, 159, and Fuhrmann, *Einfluß und Verbreitung*, 930–931, no. 319. Segments of this text appear also in forged letters ascribed to Pope Anacletus (JK †4; Hinschius, ed., *Decretales Pseudo-Isidorianae*, 86) and to Pope Alexander (JK †24; Hinschius, ed., *Decretales Pseudo-Isidorianae*, 97). These segments are, however, shorter than D. 93, c. 1, and are preceded by formulations different from the one in JK †92 and in the inscription to D. 93, c. 1.

[16] Friedberg, ed., *Decretum*, 647, supported by Bc Mz Tx: "Item Petrus in ordinatione Clementis."

[17] Ed. Friedberg, col. 647, supported by Bc Mz Tx: "Si inimicus est iste Clemens alicui." So also in Hinschius, ed., *Decretales Psuedo-Isidorianae*, 159 and in the *Tripartita* 1.18.2 (JK †92). Cf. Hinschius, ed., *Decretales Pseudo-Isidorianae*, 36: "Si inicimus est alicui," and the *Polycarpus* 1.18.2 and Anselm's collection 1.6: "Si inimicus ipse est alicui."

Among the usual sources, the *Polycarpus* and Anselm's collection contain a short excerpt from JK †10, while the *Tripartita* contains the same excerpt from JK †92 as D. 93, c. 1. It seems clear, therefore, that Gratian's source for D. 93, c. 1 was the *Tripartita*.

The text of *canon 17* appears in all five of the usual sources.[18] In the *Panormia*, at *Polycarpus* 7.1.1, in *3L*, and at Anselm 12.13 are excerpts of the same length as in the *Decretum*. Other occurrences in the *Polycarpus* and in Anselm's collection contain only a part of the last sentence and a subsequent sentence, not found in the *Decretum*. These can be excluded from consideration. The text in the *Tripartita* is much longer than in c. 17 and was probably not the source. The remaining four texts exhibit only few variants:

11.3.17
Inscr. Item Calixtus papa *Tx Fr.*: Item Calixtus *Bc^{add} Fd^{add} Mz Fr.ABC:* Calixtus episcopis Gallie *Pan.EFJLM:* Idem (*scil.* Calixtus) in secunda epistola. De conspiratione *Trip.*: Calixtus papa *Polyc.mP Ans.G:* Calixtus *3LV*
7 subiaceat *Fr. Pan.EFJLM Trip. Polyc.P Ans.G:* subiacebit *Bc^{add} Fd^{add} Mz Tx Rom. 3LV*

The manuscript evidence indicates that the inscription in the *Decretum* originally read *Item Calixtus*, which together with the variant recorded for line 7 points at *3L* as the source.

Canon 18 appears in four of the usual sources: the *Tripartita*, the *Polycarpus*, *3L*, and Anselm's collection. The text is of the same length as in the *Decretum* in all collections (although it is divided into two canons in the *Tripartita*). A collation of textual variants reveals that Gratian's source probably was the *3L*:

11.3.18
1–2 nisi (ea *add. Polyc.mP Ans.G*) que ad eandem excommunicationem pertinent *Bc^{add} Fd^{add} Mk Mz Tx Fr. Polyc.P 3LV Ans.G:* om. *Trip.*
3 *post* uesci *verbum* cuique *add. Trip.*: *om. Fd^{add} Mk Mz Tx Fr. Polyc.P 3LV Ans.G*
3 enim cum eo *Bc^{add} Fd^{add} Mk Mz Tx Fr. Polyc.P 3LV Ans.G:* frater *Trip.*
4 *post* absconse *verba* cum excommunicato *add. Trip.*: *om. Mk Mz Tx Fr. Polyc.P 3LV Ans.G*
4 communem *Cg Fd^{add} Sa Vd Fr. Ans.G: post* eo *locat Mk Mz Tx:* communionem *Bc^{add} 3LV:* aut iunctus communione *Trip.*: *om. Polyc.mP*

In all these cases, the *Tripartita* varies so greatly from the *Decretum* that it cannot have been the source. The addition of *ea* on line 1 suggests that neither the *Polycarpus* nor Anselm's collection was the source. In the case of the former collection, this indication is undergirded by the omission of *communem* on line 4. The *3L* has *communionem* instead, which does not

---

[18] Fuhrmann, *Einfluß und Verbreitung*, 842–843, n. 123.

make much sense in the context, and it could be expected that the author of the second recension would attempt to correct the text. The reading *communionem* in Bc[add] may be taken as evidence that the text in the *Decretum* at first shared the reading of *3L*. The fact that canons 2.25.1–2 and 2.25.5 in *3L* were the sources for Gratian's canons 16–17 and 19, respectively, strengthens the argument that his source for c. 18 was canon 2.25.3 of this work.

Before attempting to determine Gratian's source for *canon 19*, an error in Friedberg's edition should be noted. In the Roman edition of the *Decretum,* the text has the following *incipit: Qui communicaverit vel oraverit cum excommunicato.* Friedberg removed *vel oraverit*, claiming support from all the manuscripts and editions which he had collated.[19] These words are, however, present in the following manuscripts of the *Decretum*: Bc[add] Fd[add] Mk Mz Sa Tx Vd. Since they also appear in all five potential sources as well as in the material source,[20] it is clear that the text of the *Decretum* must have contained them:

11.3.19
Qui communicaverit vel oraverit cum excommunicato, si laicus est, excommunicetur, si clericus, deponatur.

This text is found in all five of the usual sources. The *Panormia* and the *Tripartita* can be excluded from consideration since their text contains significant variants:

Qui communicaverit vel oraverit cum excommunicato, sive clericus[21] siue laicus excommunicetur *Pan.ELM Trip.*

The *Polycarpus* contains the same text as the *Decretum*, except that the word *est* is added after *clericus. 3L* and Anselm's collection, finally, have the same text as the *Decretum*. There is no textual basis for preferring one of these to the other. The fact that c. 19 is surrounded by texts deriving from title 2.25 in *3L* (canons 16–18 and 20–25) indicates that this collection was also the source for c. 19.

Canon 20 is found in four of Gratian's usual sources: the *Tripartita*, the *Polycarpus, 3L*, and Anselm's collection. A collation of variants shows that the *Tripartita* probably was his source:

11.3.20
Inscr. Item ex decreto Honorii Papae *Bc[add] Fd[add] Mk Mz Tx Fr.:* Ex decretis Honorii pape, cp. xi *Trip:* Ex decretis Honorii pape *Polyc.m:* Honorius papa, kapitulo xi *Ans.G: nulla inscriptio Polyc.C 3LV*

[19] Friedberg, ed., *Decretum*, 648, note 203.
[20] Charles Munier, ed., *Concilia Africae, 345–525*, Corpus Christianorum: Series latina 149 (Turnhout 1974), 350.   [21] *Pan. E* adds the words *sit deponatur* after *clericus.*

2 suis *Fd^{add} Mk Tx Fr. Trip.: supra lin. add. Mz: om. Polyc.m 3LV Ans.G*
3 eaque *Fd^{add} Mk Tx Fr. Trip. Ans.G:* ea quo *Mz:* atque *Polyc.m: om. 3LV*
6 *post* causa *verbum* ab *add. 3LV Ans.G: om. Fd^{add} Mk Mz Fr. Trip.*

The variants registered for lines 2 and 3 point most clearly at the *Tripartita*, while the variant on line 6 tends to exclude Anselm and *3L*.

Canon 28 contains the same text, with some variant readings, as the second half of c. 18. These variants are identical to those which in the treatment of that canon allowed the conclusion that the *Tripartita* could not be its source. It is, therefore, likely that the *Tripartita* was Gratian's source for c. 28, which appears in three relevant collections. Additional variants support this conclusion:

11.3.28
1 frater *Bc^{add} Mk Mz Tx Fr. Trip.:* enim cum eo *Polyc.P 3LV Ans.G*
1–2 cum excommunicato *Bc^{add} Mk Mz Tx Fr. Trip.: om. Polyc.P 3LV Ans.G*
2 aut iunctus communione *Bc^{add} Mk Mz Tx Fr. Trip.:* communionem *3LV: om. Polyc.mP Ans.G*

A possible objection to this conclusion is that the *Decretum* mistakenly attributes the text to the Eighth Ecumenical Council. It derives, in fact, from Smaragdus' commentary to the rule of St. Benedict.[22] The text is not inscribed in the *Tripartita*, but follows a long series of excerpts from Isidore of Seville's writings in the title called *Sententia Grecorum doctorum* (2.14).[23] This title is, however, in the *Tripartita* immediately preceded by the canons of the Eighth Council. An investigation of the thirteen canons which in Gratian's *Decretum* are inscribed to the Eighth Council[24] shows that no less than ten are misattributed.[25] All ten are found in title 2.14 of the *Tripartita*. It seems safe to conclude that the author of the second recension had extracted all ten from this work without noticing that the canons of title 2.14 do not belong to the legislation of the Eighth Council, which is excerpted in title 2.13.

Canon 29, deriving from the Second Council of Carthage of 390, appears in three of the usual sources, none of which has a text of the same length as the *Decretum*. The *Panormia* lacks the last clause of Gratian's canon and cannot, therefore, have been his source. Both the *Tripartita* and the *Polycarpus* have longer texts than Gratian, although their additions

---

[22] *PL* 102.852.
[23] The canon is in the manuscripts of the "second version" of the *Tripartita* preceded by the heading *de eodem*, which probably refers back to the rubric *de excommunicatis* of the preceding canon, which is inscribed *cuius supra* (referring to Isidore).
[24] Most easily retrieved with reference to Timothy Reuter and Gabriel Silagi, eds., *Wortkonkordanz zum "Decretum Gratiani,"* MGH Hilfsmittel 10 (Munich 1990), 5039–5041.
[25] D. 54, c. 22; D. 81, c. 26; D. 90, c. 4; C. 5, q. 6, c. 7; C. 11, q. 3, c. 28; C. 11, q. 3, c. 77; C. 26, q. 7, c. 7; C. 27, q. 2, c. 22; de pen. D. 2, c. 1; de cons. D. 2, c. 25.

consist only of formulas which often appear in the canons of, e.g., the various councils of Carthage. These formulas, which name the bishop who suggested a decision and note that the council approved the proposal, often disappeared during the canonical transmission of a canon. It is certainly conceivable that the author of the second recension could have deleted these sentences,[26] so their presence in the *Tripartita* and in the *Polycarpus* does not preclude their being Gratian's source. A collation of textual variants helps to determine the source:

11.3.29

1 *ante* qui merito *verba* Geneclius episcopus dixit, Ergo recte suggerunt fratres et coepiscopi nostri ut *add. Trip.;* Augustinus episcopus legatus Numidie provintie dixit: Hoc statuere dignemini, ut si *add. Polyc.m*

1 qui merito *Bc^{add} Cg Fd^{add} Mk Mz Fr. Pan.EJM Trip.:* qui forte merito *Polyc.m*

1 *post* ecclesia *verbum* sua *add. Pan.EM Polyc.m: om. Bc^{add} Cg Fd^{add} Mk Mz Fr. Pan.J Trip.*

2–3 vel (aut *Cg*) clerico *Bc^{add} Cg Fd^{add} Mk Mz Fr. Pan.EJM Trip.: om. Polyc.m*

3–4 ipse . . . teneatur obnoxius *Bc^{add} Cg Fd^{add} Mk Fr. Trip. Polyc.P:* ipsi . . . teneantur obnoxii *Mz Fr.A Pan.EJM*

4–5 refugientes – iudicium *om. Pan.EJM: incl. Bc^{add} Cg Fd^{add} Mk Mz Fr. Trip. Polyc.mP*

4–5 refugientes *Bc^{add} Cg Fd^{add} Mk Mz Fr. Trip.:* refugientibus *Polyc.m*

5 *post* iudicium *verba* ab universis episcopis (*om. Trip.*) dictum est omnibus placet *add. Trip. Polyc.m*

While both the *Panormia* and the *Polycarpus* differ several times from the *Decretum*, the *Tripartita* generally agrees and seems to have been the source.

In editions of Gratian's work, the text in *d. p. c. 33* is printed as a *dictum*, although it contains only a text quoted verbatim from an authority preceded by the inscription *Item Ieronimus*. In most manuscripts that I have examined the text follows directly upon the text of c. 33, i.e., without either the initial which usually marks the beginning of a new canon or the paragraph mark which introduces a *dictum*.[27] Only *3L* contains an excerpt of the same length as the *Decretum*, but the text is here (correctly) attributed to Pope Eutyches rather than to Jerome.[28] Anselm of Lucca's collection contains a slightly longer excerpt (*incipit: Quibus regnum Dei*), which lacks inscription. There are no other significant variant readings in any relevant collection. In *3L*, the text immediately precedes the text

---

[26] Although neither he nor Gratian did do so consistently; cf. Reuter and Silagi, eds., *Wortkonkordanz*, 1662–1663.

[27] The following manuscripts were examined: Bc Cg Fd Mk Mz Tx. Cf. Friedberg's note 397.

[28] JK †146, Hinschius, ed., *Decretales Pseudo-Isidorianae*, 211. The attribution to Eutyches is, of course, only "correct" in the sense that the Pseudo-Isidorian forgers attributed the text to him.

of c. 33. The source was, therefore, most likely the *3L*, although it remains unclear why the text is ascribed to Jerome.

To summarize: among the first forty canons of C. 11, q. 3, twenty-five are missing from the four manuscripts Aa Bc Fd P, as are the *dicta* following after canons 20, 21, 24, 26, and 33. The analysis of the contents and the sources of these canons failed to produce any evidence inconsistent with my thesis that these manuscripts contain a first recension of Gratian's *Decretum*. The great majority of them derive from either the *Tripartita* or the *3L*. Their contents are never necessary for the *dicta* of the first recension and rarely contribute at all to the problems discussed by Gratian in d. a. c. 1 and d. p. c. 40. The text of the first recension presents, on the other hand, a more stringent and concise argument.

It remains to determine Gratian's sources for the canons which were included in the first recension. Almost all of these are texts that enjoyed widespread canonical circulation, which in many cases makes it difficult to determine which source Gratian might have used. A further complication is that I will argue below that Gratian used an as yet unidentified source when composing C. 11, q. 3. My conclusions below must, therefore, be considered provisional, since some or all of these canons may in fact derive from the unidentified source.

Canon 1, which Gratian attributes to Pope Gregory, cannot be found in any of his usual sources. The text is only a summary of Gregory's words, while d. p. c. 77 (where Gratian also refers back to c. 1) reproduces the actual wording of the canon as found in the *Polycarpus* 7.1.35. A text almost identical to that of c. 1 appears in some of the polemical works of the investiture contest, namely in Pseudo-Ulric's *Epistola de continentia clericorum* and in Gerhoch of Reichersberg's *Libelli de investigatione Antichristi*.[29] Neither of these works can have been Gratian's source. Gerhoch's work is excluded by its late date; Pseudo-Ulric's by the lack of attribution to Pope Gregory. They demonstrate, however, that Gratian copied an existing text and did not himself paraphrase Gregory's words. This excludes the possibility that his source for c. 1 was the *Polycarpus*. The identity of his source remains, thus, unknown.

Canon 4 appears in all five of Gratian's usual sources. It consists of canon 17 of the Council of Serdika,[30] and was quoted as such by Gratian. A part of this text was quoted in the *Epistula ad Bonifatium*, sent to Pope Boniface I by the council celebrated in 419 in Carthage.[31] It appears

---

[29] *Libelli de lite imperatorum et pontificum saeculis XI. et XII. conscripti*, MGH (Munich 1891–1897), I 255 and III 367. Pseudo-Ulric's work can be dated to the 1070s (see *ibid.* I 254) while Gerhoch's work postdates Gratian's *Decretum*, see Peter Classen, *Gerhoch von Reichersberg: Eine Biographie* (Wiesbaden 1960), 421–424.   [30] Turner, ed., *Ecclesiae occidentalis monumenta*, I 522–524.
[31] Munier, ed., *Concilia Africae*, 159.

attributed to that council in the *Polycarpus* and in *3L*; and since the African reincarnation is shorter than Gratian's text, neither of these can have been his source. The *Tripartita* contains the complete text of the canon, while both the *Panormia* and Anselm of Lucca's collection include an excerpt of the same length as in the *Decretum*. Decisive for determining Gratian's source are the following variant readings:

11.3.4
Inscr. Item ex concilio Sardicensi capitulo XVII *Aa Bc Fd Mz Tx Fr.*: Ex concilio Sardicensi capitulum XVII *Ans.*: Sardicense concilium cap. xvi *Pan.EFLMT*: De concilio Sardicense *et infra* cap. xvii *Trip.*: Ex concilio Africano VI *Polyc.mP*: Ex concilio Affricano *3LV*
3 *post* diaconum *verbum* suum *add. Trip. Polyc.m Ans.*: *om. Aa Bc Fd Mz Tx Fr. Pan.EFJLMT*
7 *post* tractetur *verba* quia non oportet ei negari audientiam roganti *add. Pan.EFJLMT Trip. Polyc.mP 3LV*: *om. Aa Bc Fd Mz Tx Fr. Ans.*
12 ante cognitionem *Aa Bc Fd Mz Tx Fr. Ans.*: *om. Pan.EFJLMT Trip.*

These soundings point clearly towards Anselm's collection as Gratian's source. The variant recorded on line 3 could seem to contradict this conclusion, but it is possible that Gratian independently decided to remove the *suum*.

Canon 5 appears in different forms in four of Gratian's usual sources. The text is an excerpt from c. 8 of the Second Council of Carthage, celebrated in 390.[32] The canons from this council appear in the Pseudo-Isidorian Decretals in a slightly altered form. Gratian's text seems to be a version of the unaltered text, while the *Tripartita* contains the Pseudo-Isidorian version. As indicated by the variants registered below, *3L* contains a form of the unaltered text which is different from the one in the *Decretum*. The text of the *Polycarpus* lacks the last sentence found in the *Decretum*, so this collection could not have been Gratian's source, which appears, hence, to have been Anselm of Lucca's collection.

11.3.5
Inscription: Item ex Concilio Cartaginensi *Aa Bc Fd Mz Tx Fr.*: Ex concilio Cartaginensi (cap. XI *add. Polyc.PR*) *Polyc.mP Ans.G:* De concilio Cartaginensi secundo *Trip.*: Ex concilio Affricano *3LV*
1 episcopo suo *Aa Bc Fd Mz Tx Fr. Polyc.P Ans.G:* a preposito suo excommunicatus vel *Trip. 3LV*
7 *post* obtulerit *verba* loco amisso *add. Trip. 3LV*: *om. Aa Bc Mz Tx Fr. Ans.G*
7 et nichilo minus *om. Polyc.P*
7–8 nichilo minus (et *add. Ans.G*) locum amittat at *Aa Bc Fd Mz Tx Fr Ans.G:* *om. 3LV*

8–9 At si – inquirendum est *Aa Bc Fd Mz Tx Fr. Ans. G: om. Polyc.mP*

Also *canon 6* (another canon from the Council of Antioch in 330 or 341) appears in four of Gratian's usual sources. The *Tripartita* can immediately be excluded from consideration, since it contains the translation of the *Collectio Hispana*, while the *Decretum* contains the second Dionysian translation.[33] The *Polycarpus, 3L,* and Anselm's collection also contain this version. A collation of textual variants yields two passages which help determine which of the three works was Gratian's source:

11.3.6

2 fuerint *Aa Bc Cg Fd Mz Fr. 3LV Ans. G:* precedente consuetudine *Polyc.mP*
5 liceat *Aa Bc Cg Fd Mz Fr. Polyc.P Ans. G:* precipiat *3LV*

While the evidence is too scant to allow certainty, this collation points to Anselm's collection as Gratian's probable source. Yet a few places where the text of the *Decretum* differs from earlier tradition should also be noted. These variants may reflect Gratian's changes of the text, but may also indicate that his source was not Anselm's collection.

11.3.6

1 dampnatur *Aa Bc Cg Fd Mz Fr.:* dampnatus *Polyc.mP 3LV Ans. G*
7 oportet *Aa Bc Cg Fd Mz Fr.:* om. *Polyc.mP 3LV Ans. G*
8 adversus *Aa Bc Cg Fd Mz Fr.:* adversum *Polyc.m 3LV Ans. G:* in *Polyc.P*

Canon 8 appears in three of Gratian's usual sources. The *Panormia* and the *3L* cannot have been his source, since the canon there lacks the last clause: lines 7–8, *ne forte . . . preueniantur.* This clause is present in the *Tripartita,* which also shares a couple of other variants with the *Decretum:*[34]

11.3.8

1 moderatione postposita *Aa Bc Fd Mz Fr. Trip. 3LV orig.:* moderamine postposito *Pan.EFJM:* ratione postposita *Tx*
3 baptismi *Aa Bc Fd Mz Tx Fr. Trip.CRNDB:* om. *Pan.EFJLM 3LV Trip.ZOGHA orig.*

Only some manuscripts of the *Tripartita* contain the word *baptismi.* These are manuscripts of the second version, while the manuscripts of the first version omit this word.[35] The second version of the *Tripartita* was probably Gratian's source.

The short *canon 9* is found in four of Gratian's usual sources, in the *Tripartita,* the *Polycarpus, 3L,* and in Anselm's collection. A collation of

---

[33] Turner, ed., *Ecclesiae occidentalis monumenta,* II 246–249.
[34] *orig.* = Munier, *Concilia Galliae, 314–506,* Corpus Christianorum: Series latina 148 (Turnholt 1963), 193–194.
[35] Communication by Martin Brett. For the two versions of the *Tripartita,* see Brett, "Urban and Ivo," 32.

variant readings excludes the possibility that the first mentioned work was the source:

11.3.9
1 fuerit *Aa Bc Cg Fd Mk Mz Fr. Polyc.P 3LV Ans.G:* fuit *Trip.*
3–4 communicare *Aa Bc Cg Fd Mk Fr. Polyc.P 3LV Ans.G:* communionem *Trip.*

Furthermore, the text lacks an inscription in the Vatican manuscript of *3L*, which makes this work a less likely candidate. The only basis for choosing between the two remaining collections is the fact that c. 9 in Anselm immediately follows upon what probably was Gratian's source for c. 6. It seems, therefore, most likely that Anselm's collection was the source also for c. 9.

Canon 27 appears in different forms in four of Gratian's usual sources, and in two of them it appears twice.[36] Only the *Polycarpus* (at 7.1.2), *3L*, and Anselm's collection (at 12.24) contain excerpts of the same length as Gratian's work, and his source is probably one of them. (A longer excerpt appears in the *Polycarpus* at 6.1.3 and in Anselm's work at 6.139. The text in the *Tripartita* begins with the last sentence of c. 27, *Valde timenda . . .*, and continues for several lines.) A collation produced no significant variants. The only remaining criterion is that the text in Anselm's collection is found immediately before the texts of canons 6 and 9 (which in the first recension immediately preceded c. 27), indicating that this was Gratian's source.

Canon 30, which contains c. 66 of the *Statuta ecclesiae antiqua* (although Gratian, as was usual during the middle ages, attributes it to a supposed Fourth Council of Carthage), appears both in the *Tripartita* and in *3L*. In the latter, the canon is joined with another excerpt from the same work (c. 29) into one canon. Since there are no other significant variant readings, the *Tripartita* probably was Gratian's source.

Canon 31 appears both in the *Tripartita* and in the *Panormia*. No variants help in determining which of these works was Gratian's source. Decisive, therefore, is the fact that c. 31 in the *Tripartita* immediately precedes the text of *canon 32*, which is found in no other relevant collection. Since Gratian in all likelihood took c. 32 from this work, it is likely that he found also c. 31 there.

Canon 34 is found only in the *Tripartita* among Gratian's usual sources. The text is one of the several duplicate canons in the *Decretum*: it appears also as C. 2, q. 6, c. 35, which is a canon added only in the second recension. The duplication of c. 34 raises several questions which can be addressed only in the context of an investigation of all the duplicate

---

[36] Fuhrmann, *Einfluß und Verbreitung*, 940–941, n. 343.

canons in the *Decretum*.[37] This book will attempt only to determine Gratian's source for the two versions of this text. The textual differences between the versions are small but potentially significant. Most important is the *incipit* itself. While the version in C. 2 begins *Placuit, ut presbiteri, diaconi*, the *incipit* in C. 11 is *Presbiteri, diaconi*. In the *Tripartita*, the text begins: *Item placuit, ut presbiteri, diaconi*. The words *placuit ut* are often found at the beginning of conciliar canons and it is not unusual that they disappear during the canonical transmission of such texts.

Another difference is the location of the particle *si* in the first sentence:

2.6.35: clerici in causis quas habuerint **si** de iudiciis
11.3.34: clerici **si** in causis quas habuerint de iudiciis
Trip.: clerici in causas quas habuerint **si** de iudiciis

It is a priori likely that, when a text is duplicated in the *Decretum* and there are textual differences between the two versions, they derive from different sources.[38] It is, therefore, tempting to suggest that the source for C. 2, q. 6, c. 35 was the *Tripartita*, while Gratian extracted C. 11, q. 3 c. 34 from another source. This source would be the unidentified work which, I will argue below, provided Gratian with many of the texts included in the first recension of C. 11, q. 3.

Canon 35 appears twice in the *Tripartita*. In the first part of this collection it is ascribed to Pope Felix I, while the second part attributes it to the Fourth Council of Carthage. The text derives in fact from the *Statuta ecclesiae antiquae*,[39] whose canons the *Collectio Hispana* already attributed to this fictitious African council. The Pseudo-Isidorian forgers used this text when producing the false decretal of Felix which is quoted in the *Tripartita*'s first part.[40] Since Gratian ascribes c. 35 to the Fourth Council of Carthage, his source was probably the second part of the *Tripartita*. Also, that text is slightly longer than in the *Decretum*.

Canon 36 is found in two of Gratian's usual sources: once in the *Polycarpus* and in both the second and the third part of the *Tripartita*. It is already clear from the inscription that Gratian's source was the *Tripartita* 2.19.12. While the *Tripartita* and Gratian's *Decretum* (correctly) attribute it to the Fifth Council of Carthage of 401, the *Tripartita* 3.10.14 ascribes the canon to an unspecified African council and the *Polycarpus* lacks inscription.

---

[37] Jean Gaudemet, "Les Doublets dans le *Décret* de Gratien," in *Atti del II Congresso internazionale della Società italiana di storia del diritto, Venezia 1967* (Florence 1972), 269–290; reprinted in Jean Gaudemet, *La formation du droit canonique médiéval*, no. XI, and Weigand, "Versuch einer Liste der Paleae." [38] Cf. Gaudemet, "Doublets," 281. [39] Munier, ed., *Concilia Africae*, 347.
[40] JK †142, see Hinschius, ed., *Decretales Pseudo-Isidorianae*, 198. Cf. Fuhrmann, *Einfluß und Verbreitung*, 924–925, n. 304. Excerpts from JK †142 including the text of c. 35 are found at C. 2, q. 1, c. 5 (the source of which apparently was Anselm's collection 3.65) and at C. 3, q. 6, c. 11 (which derives from the *Tripartita* 1.24.3).

Friedberg's edition apparently contains a typographical error in the text of c. 36:

4 insultationem *Fr.*: insolentem insultationem *Aa Bc Fd Mz Sa Tx Vd Rom. Trip.23 Polyc.m:* insolentiam *Cg:* insolentem exultationem *Mk:* exultationem *Fr.CD*

Canon 38 is a *palea* which provides the continuation of the text in c. 37.[41] All five of Gratian's usual sources contain the text of *canon 37*. A collation of variant readings helps determine which of them would have been his source:

11.3.37
1 ciuiliter siue publice *Bc Cg Fd Mk Mz P Tx Fr. Pan.EJM Trip.*: om. *Polyc.m 3LV Ans.G*
3 uideantur *Aa Bc Cg Fd Mk Mz P Tx Fr. Pan.EJM Trip.*: uidentur *Polyc.m 3LV Ans.G*
7 nec *Aa Bc Cg Mk Mz P Tx Fr. Trip.*: nec ex eis *corr. Fd:* om. *Pan.EJM Polyc.m 3LV Ans.G*
7 debemus *Aa Bc Cg Mk Mz P Tx Fr. Trip.*: non debemus *Fd:* non possumus *Pan.EJM Polyc.m 3LV Ans.G*

The variant registered for line 1 indicates that neither the *Polycarpus*, the *3L*, nor Anselm could have been Gratian's source, which must have been the *Panormia* or the *Tripartita*.

The short c. 40 is found in three of Gratian's usual sources: in Ivo's *Panormia*, in the *Tripartita*, and in *3L*. The two places where I have noted textual variants are not helpful for determining Gratian's source:

11.3.40
2 correctum *Aa Bc Cg Fd Mk Tx Fr. Pan.M:* correptum *Mz Pan.EFJL Trip. 3LV*
2 successori *Bc Cg Fd Mk Mz Fr. 3LV:* successorem *Aa Pan.EFJLM Trip.*

The two words *correctum* and *correptum* are often confused in canonical manuscripts,[42] so that variant is without value for my purposes. Likewise, the fact that the manuscript tradition of either recension of the *Decretum* does not unanimously support either of the variants *successori* or *successorem* does not help. The following three canons (41 to 43) all derive from title 7 in the supplement of *3L*, where also the text of c. 40 is found. Canons 41–43 were, however, added only in the second recension, so their provenance cannot contribute to determining the source of c. 40.

---

[41] Canon 38 is missing from the original text of all of Friedberg's manuscripts (see his note 440 in *Decretum*, 654), from nine Cambridge manuscripts examined in Ullmann, "Paleae in Cambridge," 211, and from the original text of Bc, Cg, Fd, Mk, Mz, Tx (in some of them, a later hand has added the *palea*).

[42] Other examples are C. 11, q. 3, c. 5, line 1 (cf. Friedberg, ed., 643, note 55) and C. 24, q. 3, c. 29, line 2 (where the following variants occur: correctionem *Fd Mk Tx Vd Fr. Polyc.P 3LV:* correptionem *Aa Cg Fr. Cd Rom.*)

A CONFUSING INTRUSION

In quoting d. p. c. 40 above, I left out the last sentence: "Only these may be struck with the sentence of excommunication."[43] Subsequently, three canons specify the cases in which excommunication may be used. Then follows d. p. c. 43:

> The preceding authorities speak about these persons and persons of that kind, not about persons unjustly suspended. But that an unjust sentence should not be obeyed is proven by many authorities, the first of which is that of Jerome on Matthew.[44]

It is hard to follow the argumentation here in the second recension. D. p. c. 40 says that certain excommunicated persons (namely those who, to some degree, are to blame for their excommunication, however incorrect) must strive for a new examination of their cases before they can be re-admitted to communion. The last sentence of d. p. c. 40 says something quite different, namely that the persons in question (I cannot see that *hos*, in this context, could refer to any other persons) "may be struck with the sentence of excommunication". The d. p. c. 43 then continues to refer to "these persons" (*his*) about whom the "preceding authorities" talk, and not about "those unjustly suspended." Again, "these persons" must refer to the three categories of excommunicated persons specified in d. p. c. 40, and the "preceding authorities" must refer to the canons that allow excommunicated persons to appeal their cases (but not to communicate in the meantime). In effect, the last sentence of d. p. c. 40 (only "these" may be excommunicated) contradicts the rest of d. p. c. 40 and d. p. c. 43 ("these" may appeal their cases).

These perceived inconsistencies are to be explained with reference to the first recension. Here, canons 41 to 43 are missing and so is the last sentence of d. p. c. 40. Before this addition, the text flowed directly, without contradictions, from the penultimate sentence of d. p. c. 40 to the beginning of d. p. c. 43.

For the second recension, the three canons 41 to 43 were given a short introductory sentence: "Only these may be struck with the sentence of excommunication." Considered only in the context of these three canons, which contain rules about who may be excommunicated, this is a suitable introduction. One may imagine that the author of the second

---

[43] Friedberg, ed., *Decretum*, 655, supported by Bc Fd Mz: "Hos siquidem solos excommunicationis sententia ferire licet."

[44] Friedberg, ed., *Decretum*, 656, supported by Aa Bc Mz Pfr: "De his, inquam, et huiusmodi premissae auctoritates (auct. prem. Pfr) locuntur, non de iniuste suspensis. Quod autem iniustae sententiae parendum (om. Pfr) non sit, multis auctoritatibus probatur. Quarum prima est illa Ieronimi super Matheum."

recension jotted it down before inserting the canons into the *Decretum*. It remains, however, difficult to fathom why he inserted them in the midst of a *dictum* where they, strictly, do not belong, thereby creating a contradiction and the possibility of misunderstandings.

The three canons derive from *3L*, which I argue was one of the two main sources used by the author of the second recension. For *canon 41*, which also appears in the *Panormia*, this is easily determined with the help of a collation of variants:

II.3.41

1 nemo Fd^{add} Mk Mz Fr. 3LV: ut nullus Pan.M: ut nemo Pan.EJ
4 *post* coepiscoporum *verbum* episcopus *add.* Pan.EJM: *om.* Fd^{add} Mk Mz Fr. 3LV
4 presumat ponere Fd^{add} Mk Mz Fr. 3LV: ponat Pan.EJM

The *Decretum* ascribes *canon 42* to a council of Clermont,[45] although it is in fact c. 2 from the Fifth Council of Orléans of 549.[46] *3L*, which is the only one of the usual sources containing this canon, has the same misattribution, and was probably the source.

Canon 43 appears in three of the usual sources. The *Panormia* contains a longer excerpt adding a few lines before the beginning of the excerpt. This and the variant readings registered below exclude the possibility that Ivo's work was the source. Both the *Polycarpus* and *3L* contain fragments of the same length as the *Decretum*. A collation of variant readings yields only one significant difference, registered below for lines 4–5. This variant indicates that the *3L* was the source.

II.3.43

1 certum Fd^{add} Mk Mz Fr. Polyc.m 3LV: decretum Pan.EM
1–2 aliquem excommunicari Fd^{add} Mk Mz Fr. Polyc.P 3LV: fieri Pan.EM
2 uocatus Fd^{add} Mk Mz Fr.: iussus Pan.EM Polyc.mP 3LV
3 si Fd^{add} Mk Fr.: supra lin. add. Mz: om. Pan.EM Polyc.mP 3LV
4 si Fd^{add} Mk Mz Fr.: om. Pan.EM Polyc.mP 3LV
4–5 finitam suae causae Fr.: finitam cause sue Fd^{add} Mk Mz Pan.EM 3LV: finite cause sue Polyc.mP
5 *post* sinodo *verbum* profugus *add.* Pan.EM: *om.* Fd^{add} Mk Mz Fr. Polyc.P 3LV

The variants listed for lines 2, 3, and 4 give the impression that the author of the second recension changed the text of his source.

---

[45] Friedberg, ed., *Decretum*, 655: "Item ex Concilio Aruernensi." The reference is to a Merovingian council (probably the one celebrated in 535, although Friedberg, note 470, says *hab. ca. 550*) rather than to Urban II's famous council of 1095. The canons of Clermont 535 are printed in Carolus de Clercq, ed., *Concilia Galliae, 511–695*, Corpus Christianorum: Series latina 148 A (Turnhout 1963), 104–112.   [46] Clercq, ed., *Concilia Galliae*, 149 (= *orig.*).

UNJUST AND INIQUITOUS SENTENCES

In the continuation of d. p. c. 43, Gratian shifts his focus to those affected by unjust sentences. He argues that such sentences should not be obeyed and proves this by adducing a string of authorities. The argument is summarized in d. p. c. 64:

> From these [authorities] one may understand that an unjust sentence does not bind anyone before God, nor is anyone burdened by an iniquitous (*iniqua*) sentence in his church, as is understood from the chapter of Gelasius. One should, thus, not abstain from communion with him, nor is he to cede his office, who is known to have been subject to an iniquitous sentence.[47]

Again, an intervening *dictum* with accompanying canons breaks the continuity between d. p. c. 43 and d. p. c. 64. *Dictum* p. c. 55 together with canons 55 and 56 emphasizes that a good conscience should be enough for each individual, regardless of what detractors may say. This point is certainly relevant in the greater context of C. 11, q. 3, but appears out of place here. Canons 55 and 56 must both derive from *3L*, which is the only relevant collection to contain them.

   At the beginning of d. p. c. 64, Gratian refers to "these authorities," which establish that an unjust sentence has no validity for God and his Church. On which canons is he drawing? Similar statements are found in canons 44, 46, 48, 50, 51, 53, and 54. At least some of these must have been present when Gratian wrote the *dictum*, which contains an explicit reference to c. 46. These observations are consistent with the contents of the first recension, which contains canons 44, 46, 48, 50, and 51. These texts provided Gratian with sufficient material to compose d. p. c. 64. On the other hand, canons 55 and 56 and d. p. c. 55 are missing. So are canons 52 to 54, which all derive from the *Tripartita*, and canons 58 and 59, which come from *3L*. It is simple to determine their sources, since none of these five canons appears in any other relevant collection. Canon 45 is a *palea*.[48]

---

[47] Friedberg, ed., *Decretum*, 661, supported by Bc Cg Fd Pfr: "Ex his datur intelligi, quod iniusta sententia nullum alligat apud Deum, nec apud ecclesiam eius aliquis grauatur iniqua sententia, sicut ex Gelasii capitulo habetur. Non ergo ab eius communione abstinendum est, nec ei ab offitio cessandum, in quem cognoscitur iniqua sententia prolata (prolata sententia Bc Cg Fd Pfr)."

[48] Canon 45 is missing in all of Friedberg's manuscripts (except for F where it was added in the margin), in nine of Walter Ullmann's Cambridge manuscripts (Ullmann, "Paleae in Cambridge," 210), and in Bc, Cg, Fd, Mk, Mz. It is found in the thirteenth-century manuscript Cambridge, Fitzwilliam Museum, no. 183 (Ullmann, "Paleae in Cambridge," 210). The text, which is attributed to Augustine, is a previously unidentified excerpt from a Latin translation of Origen's commentary on Matthew, see Anders Winroth, "Uncovering Gratian's original *Decretum* with the help of electronic resources," *Columbia Library Columns* 46: 1 (1997), 29.

It is, again, more complicated to identify the sources of the canons that were already included in the first recension, i.e. canons 44, 46 to 51, 57, and 60 to 64. Judging from table 6 at the beginning of this chapter, their source would appear to be the *Tripartita,* which contains most of them (in addition to canons 40, 53, and 54) in close sequence within title 27 of the third part. Detailed comparisons between Gratian's text and that found in the *Tripartita* reveal, however, several discrepancies. Since these discrepancies are not of a kind likely to be the result of Gratian's editorial tampering, the possibility that he used another source must be kept open. Further evidence for this possibility is that a few of the variants found in the *Decretum* but not in the *Tripartita* appear in other eleventh- and twelfth-century works (see canons 60, 61, and 63). This strongly suggests that Gratian, in these cases, probaby did not take his text from the *Tripartita.*

Canon 44 is a paraphrase of a passage in Jerome's commentary on the Gospel of Matthew, as the *Correctores* duly noted in their note *. Jerome's text in question is quoted by four of Gratian's usual sources: the *Panormia,* the *Tripartita,* the *Polycarpus,* and Anselm of Lucca's collection. Supposing that it was Gratian who did the paraphrasing, any of them could have been his source.[49]

Among Gratian's usual sources *canon 46* is found only in the *Tripartita,* which would, therefore, appear to have been his source. There are, however, two problems with this conclusion. Gratian's inscription is "Further, Pope Gelasius to the bishops of the east about the damnation of Dioscorus"[50] while the *Tripartita* inscribes the text "Gelasius to the bishops of the east about avoiding communion with Acacius."[51] The latter inscription is correct insofar as the text (which, in fact, was written by Gelasius' predecessor, Pope Felix III) concerns the Acacian schism and not Dioscorus. It is hard to imagine why Gratian would have changed the *Tripartita's* text, if this work indeed was his source. Furthermore, the *Decretum* shares the reading *illata* at the beginning of the canon only with the first version of the *Tripartita,* while the second version has *illa.*[52] Elsewhere, Gratian seems to have used a manuscript of the second recension for his excerpts from this work (cf. above p. 93). These two anom-

---

[49] Jerome's text appears also in the *Collectio Barberiniana* at 11.3, see Mario Fornasari, "Collectio canonum Barberiniana," *Apollinaris* 36 (1963), 238–239, and in Deusdedit's collection at 4.80, see Deusdedit, *Die Kanonessammlung des Kardinals Deusdedit,* ed. Victor Wolf von Glanvell (Paderborn 1905), 434.

[50] Friedberg, ed., *Decretum,* 656, supported by (with minor variants) Aa Bc Cg Fd Mk Mz Tx Vd: *Item Gelasius Papa Episcopis orientalibus de dampnatione Dioscori.*

[51] According to Martin Brett's collations: *Gelasius episcopis orientalibus de communione Achatii uitanda.*

[52] According to Martin Brett's collations. For the two versions of the *Tripartita,* see Brett, "Urban and Ivo," 32.

alies indicate that Gratian's source probably was a work other than the *Tripartita*.

Among Gratian's usual sources, *canon 47* is found only in the *Tripartita*, which therefore appears to have been his source. A couple of variant readings indicate, however, that this conclusion might be too rash:

11.3.47

1 *post* fidem *verba* sanamque doctrinam *add. Rom. Trip.: om. Aa Bc Cg Fd Mk Mz P Pfr Tx Vd Fr.*

3 potest *Mk Mz Tx Vd Fr.: om. Aa Bc Cg Fd P Pfr Rom. Trip.*

3 iniuste *Mk Mz Tx Vd Fr. Trip.:* iniuste *add. Bc:* iniuste *ex* vi *corr. Aa:* vi *Fd Pfr:* cuiquam *Cg: om. P*

3 patitur *ex* impatitur *corr. Bc*

It seems clear that the first recension of the *Decretum* lacked the word *potest* on line 3, as does the *Tripartita*. The word was probably added in the second recension in order to clarify the sentence. The confusion concerning the word *iniuste* on the same line is remarkable. The word was originally missing from Aa, Bc,[53] Cg, Fd, P, and Pfr. Since Aa, Fd, and Pfr on the one hand, and Cg on the other, have different words in its place, it is probable that P by simply omitting *iniuste* preserves the original appearance of the first recension. The addition of *vi* in the other first-recension manuscripts appears to reflect a wish somehow to qualify the somewhat peculiar, in the context, statement that no one is allowed to be harmed. In the second recension, comparisons with the text in the *Tripartita* clarified that the missing word was *iniuste*. This opens the possibility that Gratian's source for the first recension was not the *Tripartita*, which is an attractive conclusion also in light of the variant recorded for line 1. The text circulated widely, as is evidenced by its appearance in, e.g., the *Collectio Britannica*,[54] the *Liber canonum contra Heinricum quartum*,[55] Wenric of Trier's letter,[56] and Deusdedit's collection 4.76.[57] None of these works contains a text more similar to Gratian's than the *Tripartita*, and since there is no evidence that Gratian otherwise used any of them, there is no reason for suggesting that one of them was his source for c. 47.

Canon 48 is found in three of Gratian's usual sources. The text in *3L* lacks the last sentence of Gratian's canon (*quem solueris – in celo*) and cannot have been his source. The *Panormia* and the *Tripartita* contain this sentence but adds another before it: "Cum autem correxeris et

---

[53] I thank Robert Somerville for checking the reading of Bc for me from autopsy.

[54] Varia IC 99, attributed to Isidore, cf. Ewald, "Papstbriefe," 581.

[55] *Libelli de lite*, 1 483, line 41.   [56] *Libelli de lite*, 1 292, line 17.

[57] *Die Kanonessammlung des Kardinals Deusdedit*, 433–434.

concordaueris confratri tuo soluisti illum in terra."[58] It could have been Gratian who, using one of these collections (and probably the *Tripartita*), omitted this sentence.

Canon 49 is found only in the *Tripartita* among Gratian's usual sources. It would, therefore, seem that this was his source. The text appears also in several other canonical works, e.g., in the *Collectio Britannica*,[59] the *Liber canonum contra Heinricum quartum*,[60] Wenric of Trier's letter,[61] the *Collectio Barberiniana* 11.6,[62] and Deusdedit's collection 4.80.[63] None of these is likely to have been Gratian's source, but the wide circulation of the text calls for caution, particularly in light of my conclusions concerning the preceding canons.

Canon 50 is found in the *Tripartita* and in the *Polycarpus*. The text is longer in these works than in the *Decretum*. The *Tripartita* reproduces the preceding sentence, while the *Polycarpus* adds a sizeable block of text (corresponding to eleven lines in the MGH type-written edition). There are several interesting variant readings:

11.3.50

Inscr. Idem (*scil.* Augustinus) ad Clerum Yponiensem *Cg Mk Mz Tx Vd Fr.*: Idem (sc. Augustinus) ad clerum (Ypponiensium *add. supra lin. Aa Fd*) *Aa Bc Fd P Pfr*: Augustinus in epistola ad clerum Yponiensem *Trip.*: Idem ecclesie Ipponiensi *Polyc.m*: Idem (sc. Augustinus) ad clerum Iponensem *Alg.*
1 *post* tabula *verbum* non *add. Aa Bc P Trip. Polyc.m, exp. Fd: spatium erasum Cg*: om. *Mk Mz Pfr Tx Vd Fr. Alg.*
1–2 delere *Bi Cd Da Fd^pc Mc Mk Mz Pf^ac Pfr Pk Pq Tx Vd Fr.*: rapere *Alg.*: recitare *Aa Bc Fd^ac P Trip.*: recitari *Polyc.m: spatium erasum Cg*[64]
2 uiuentium *Aa Bc Cg Fd Mk Mz P Pfr Tx Vd Fr. Trip. Alg.*: vivorum *Polyc.m*
3 deleat *Aa Bc Cg Fd Mk Mz P Pfr Tx Vd Fr. Trip. Alg.*: delet *Polyc.m*

The variants registered for lines 2 and 3 and the inscription exclude the *Polycarpus* as a possible source. On lines 1 and 1–2, variant readings in Aa, Bc, Fd, and P show that the text in the first recension was the same as in the *Tripartita*, which is a strong candidate for Gratian's source. The author of the second recension seems to have changed the formulation from *non . . . recitare* to *delere*. In the first recension, the inscription read *Idem ad clerum*, which (together with the different length of the excerpt) might be taken as evidence, however weak, that Gratian's source was not the

---

[58] Text according to Martin Brett's collations of *Tripartita* manuscripts. The *Panormia* manuscripts have essentially the same text with a few variants.
[59] Varia IC 102, cf. Ewald, "Papstbriefe," 581.   [60] *Libelli de lite*, I 484, line 4.
[61] *Ibid.* I 292, line 22.   [62] Fornasari, "Collectio canonum Barberiniana," 239.
[63] *Die Kanonessammlung des Kardinals Deusdedit*, 434.
[64] The readings of Bi Da Cd Mc Pf Pk Pq were kindly communicated to me by Professor Carlos Larrainzar of the Universidad de la Laguna, Tenerife.

Tripartita. Among other collections in which this text is found are the *Collectio Britannica*,[65] and Wenric of Trier's letter.[66]

Among Gratian's usual sources, *canon 51* appears only in the *Tripartita*, which would seem to have been his source. But it also appears, as is the case with others in this *questio*, in several other canonical works, e.g., in the *Collectio Britannica*,[67] the *Liber canonum contra Heinricum quartum*,[68] and Wenric of Trier's letter.[69]

Canon 57 appears in both the *Panormia* and in the *Tripartita*. There are no variant readings that allow us to determine which work was Gratian's source.

Canons 60 to 62 are three short short excerpts from Gregory the Great's homily 26 on the Gospels. It is remarkable that C. 11, q. 3, c. 88 (also present in the first recension) contains a longer excerpt from the same homily, including the passages in canons 60 to 62. Gratian reproduces, however, only their *incipits* before interrupting them with *et cetera*. The text then continues after *et infra*. It seems unlikely that Gratian would have taken both canons 60 to 62 and 88 from one source and parcelled out the text in this manner. A more probable hypothesis is that he extracted canons 60 to 62 from one source, and then noticed the duplication when transcribing c. 88 from another. None of Gratian's usual sources contains exactly the excerpts found in canons 60 to 62 (except for the *Tripartita* 1.55.2, which corresponds to c. 62). Several polemical works from the time of the Investiture Contest, however, contain canons 60 and 61, alone or in combination (or c. 60 together with c. 63).[70] None of these works appears likely to have been Gratian's source (since they are not known to have been otherwise used by him), but the presence of the texts there proves that they circulated before Gratian's time. It is particularly interesting that they appear in combination, making it likely that Gratian's source was a collection containing all three fragments.

The very short *canon 63* is inscribed *Idem (sc. Gregorius) in Registro*[71] in the *Decretum* but derives in fact from a decretal of Pope Simplicius (JK 583). Gratian reproduces a longer excerpt from this letter, including the text of c. 63, at D. 74, c. 7 (already present in the first recension), where the attribution is correct. Among the instances of this text listed in table 6, three contain the same excerpt as c. 63 (the other collections have longer texts), namely the *Polycarpus* 3.15.23, *3L* 2.28.6, and Anselm's collection 4.3. In the latter, the text is uninscribed, and the preceding text

---

[65] Varia IC 103, cf. Ewald, "Papstbriefe," 581.   [66] *Libelli de lite*, I 292, line 24.
[67] Varia IC 104, cf. Ewald, "Papstbriefe," 581.   [68] *Libelli de lite*, I 484, line 6.
[69] *Ibid.*, I 292, line 27.   [70] Cf. *Libelli de lite*, I 483 553, II 37 47 192 395 463 407.
[71] Friedberg, ed., *Decretum*, 660, supported by Bc Pfr.

is attributed to Leo the Great. This might account for the inscription *Leo* found in the Carpentras manuscript of the *Polycarpus* (according to the draft edition of this collection); other *Polycarpus* manuscripts lack inscription. In that collection, the text follows upon some Roman law fragments. In the original text of the Vatican manuscript of *3L*, the text lacks inscription; the correct attribution was added in the margin by a medieval hand which also added numerous glosses to this manuscript. The preceding canon is inscribed *Gregorius Maximiano Siracusano episcopo.* None of these works seems a likely candidate for Gratian's source.

Canon 63 also appears several times among the polemical works of the Investiture Contest, but nowhere ascribed to Pope Gregory.[72] I have found only one pre-Gratian appearance of this text with such an attribution, in a letter ascribed to Fulbert of Chartres. The letter is probably composed in the twelfth century.[73] Here, a slightly different version of the text, following a text inscribed *Beatus quoque papa Gregorius dicit in Dialogo*, is introduced *Et alibi.*[74] Pseudo-Fulbert's letter proves that an attribution to Gregory is found in the tradition, although it is not certain that the letter pre-dates Gratian. Gratian's source remains unidentified, but it is likely that it was the same as the source of canons 60 to 62.

Among Gratian's usual sources, *canon 64* appears only in the *3L*, but he seems otherwise in the first recension never to have used this work. Perhaps his source was the same unidentified work as contributed canons 60 to 63. Canon 64 is found in the *Liber canonum contra Heinricum quartum*,[75] although this is not a likely source.

TYPES OF UNJUST SENTENCES

At the end of d. p. c. 64, Gratian points out that some texts appear to contradict the conclusion arrived at in the first half of the *dictum*. Gelasius states (c. 46) that an unjust and iniquitous sentence does not bind one with God or the Church. Why then, Gratian asks, do the canons of the councils of Carthage (probably referring to c. 5), "of Africa" (c. 9) and other councils (perhaps canons 2 and/or 4) prohibit those unjustly excommunicated from being received into communion before renewed examination? One may observe that the sentences which, according to Gelasius, can be ignored, are in the present *dictum* termed "unjust" (*iniusta*) and "iniquitous" (*iniqua*) while the conciliar canons discuss

---

[72] *Libelli de lite*, I 362 533 553, II 241 395 407, III 613.
[73] Frederick Behrends, "Two spurious letters in the Fulbert collection," *Revue bénédictine* 80 (1970), 253–275, and Frederick Behrends, *The Letters and Poems of Fulbert of Chartres*, Oxford Medieval Texts (Oxford 1976), lxi–lxii.   [74] Behrends, "Two spurious letters," 269, lines 238–241.
[75] *Libelli de lite*, I 501, line 32.

"unjust" sentences. Gratian does not discuss this terminological difference here, but he will pick up this thread in d. p. c. 90 and d. p. c. 101. Instead, he adds a conciliar canon, which stipulates that an unjustly deposed cleric who subsequently is found innocent must receive the insignia of his office from the hands of bishops in front of an altar. If not even bishops, Gratian then asks in the subsequent *dictum*, can restore an unjustly deposed cleric without going through this procedure, how can anyone, on his own authority, communicate with an unjustly excommunicated person, or, having been unjustly deposed, perform his duties without seeking absolution, as Gelasius (c. 46) seems to believe? Both *dicta* are present in the first recension and so are the canons to which they, apparently, refer (except for c. 2, but c. 4 alone warrants Gratian's statements), including c. 65 which is so closely woven into the argument of the *dicta*. The first recension proves, thus, to be internally coherent.

In d. p. c. 65, Gratian begins to reply to the question by distinguishing between different reasons for a sentence being unjust. It may be unjust *ex ordine* (due to procedural error), unjust *ex causa* (when either no sin has been committed or a sin other than that for which the sentence is imposed), or unjust *ex animo proferentis* (when the judge makes his decision not from love of justice, but due to hatred, bribes, or partiality). Gratian treats each case in order, beginning with sentences which are unjust *ex animo*. Canons 66 to 72 contains prohibitions against judgements based on wrath and bribes. Among these canons, only canons 68, 72, and the second half of c. 66 are missing from the first recension, which in no way impairs its coherence. After this series of authorities, Gratian adds in d. p. c. 72:

The sentence, therefore, which is imposed on someone not out of love for justice but for some other reason, is humbly to be obeyed.[76]

This is not supported by any of the preceding canons and must be Gratian's own opinion. He then turns his attention to procedural errors (d. p. c. 73):

Likewise, a sentence is unjust *ex ordine* when someone is damned for his sin without judicial order.[77]

Between these two *dicta*, a canon appears which does not address the issues of either of them (c. 73). Its text stipulates that other bishops cannot receive in communion a person excommunicated by his own bishop; this

---

[76] Friedberg, ed., *Decretum*, 663, supported by Bc Cg Fd: "Huic (hinc Cg) itaque sententiae, que non amore iustitiae, sed ex alia qualibet causa fertur in quemquam, humiliter obediendum est."

[77] Friedberg, ed., *Decretum*, 663, supported by Aa Cg Fd: "Item sententia est iniusta (iniusta est Fd) ex ordine, quando non seruato iudiciali ordine quilibet pro culpa sua (sua culpa Fd) dampnatur."

is a theme touched upon earlier in this *questio*, but it appears unsuitable at this place. It is therefore not surprising to discover that c. 73 was added only in the second recension.

The d. p. c. 73 is followed by three canons which specify different ways in which a sentence may be unjust *ex ordine*: a dubious case should not be determined through a certain judgement (c. 74); what is not proven by certain evidence should not be believed (c. 75); judgement may not be passed before proper examination (c. 76). A fourth canon (c. 77), which is missing from the first recension, seems less relevant in the context. It states that not only he who gives false testimony about another, but also anyone who believes him, are culprits.

These canons are followed by a substantial *dictum* (d. p. c. 77), in which Gratian discusses what should be done with sentences that are unjust *ex ordine*. Again, the discussion is not based on the preceding canons. He states that a sentence which is unjust *ex ordine* should be observed, because the sentenced person may already be excommunicated in God's eyes:

It happens sometimes that an adulterer receives a sentence for sacrilege, of which he is not guilty.[78]

This sentence is unjust, Gratian says, since it has been meted out on account of a sin of which the accused was not guilty, but he still received the sentence justly, since he was already excommunicated in the eyes of God on account of his adultery. This is, Gratian continues, how Gregory's words in c. 1 are to be understood. As I mentioned above, c. 1 reproduces a paraphrasing summary of Gregory's words, while Gratian now, in d. p. c. 77, quotes the pope's actual words. Here Gregory explains his statement that a pastor's sentence should be feared whether it is just or not: either the unjustly sentenced person deserved the sentence on account of some other crime, or, if he protests, he deserves the sentence even if he is not guilty of any crime, because, in protesting, he is now guilty of the sin of pride. Gratian draws on the former alternative for the beginning of d. p. c. 77. He draws on the latter in the end of the same *dictum* and in d. p. c. 90, reaching the conclusion that an innocent person should also obey an unjust sentence, lest he commit the sin of pride.

By the time Gratian reaches this conclusion, he has already strayed from the categories which he outlined in d. p. c. 64. This first happens in d. p. c. 77, when in the context of sentences which are unjust *ex ordine* he discusses the adulterer sentenced for sacrilege. In d. p. c. 65, Gratian seems to refer such cases to sentences which are unjust *ex causa*:

---

[78] Friedberg, ed., *Decretum*, 664, supported by Aa Bc Mk: "Contingit aliquando, ut adulter sententiam pro sacrilegio reportet, cuius reatum in conscientia non habet."

When it [the sentence] is unjust *ex causa*, sometimes there is no crime that is worthy of damnation in him [the sentenced person] at all; sometimes the crime, about which the sentence is passed is not in him, but he should be arraigned for another.[79]

Towards the end of d. p. c. 77, Gratian, apparently still discussing sentences that are unjust *ex ordine*, mentions the reasons why a sentence may be passed when there is no crime:

Sometimes there is no crime, and still he receives a sentence of damnation against himself, either due to the hatred of the judge, or due to the plotting of enemies.[80]

This, again, is all but identical with Gratian's definition in d. p. c. 65 of sentences which are unjust *ex animo proferentis*, namely judgements based on "the malice of hatred . . . or favor towards adversaries."[81] A modern reader may think that this section of the *Decretum* (also in the first recension) is poorly organized and that Gratian's definitions are not consistently applied, but it should be remembered that his was a pioneering effort. The distinction between the three possible reasons for an unjust sentence, for example, do not appear in earlier literature and seem to have been of Gratian's own invention. That he had not been able to polish some rough edges should not be surprising.

The source analysis for canons 66 to 77 gives a result similar to the analysis of canons 44 to 64: the texts added in the second recension derive from either the *3L* or from the *Tripartita*, while it proved difficult to identify the sources of the first-recension canons. This result further undergirds my hypothesis that Gratian's main source for C. 11, q. 3 has not yet been found.

To begin with the second-recension canons, it is easy to find the sources of canons 72 and 77. The former must come from the *3L,* which is the only relevant collection to contain the text. Canon 77 is an excerpt from Isidore of Seville's *Liber sententiarum* but is in the Decretum misattributed to the Eighth Council. As I clarified above in the examination of c. 28, this mistake indicates that Gratian's source was the *Tripartita,* where the text of c. 77 appears in the title immediately following upon the title devoted to the Eighth Council.

---

[79] Friedberg, ed., *Decretum,* 661, supported by Bc Cg Fd Pfr: "Cum autem ex causa iniusta fuerit, aliquando nullum in eo (in eo nullum Fd) omnino (omnino in eo Bc Cg Pfr) delictum (debitum Cg) est, quod sit dampnatione dignum: aliquando non est in eo illud, super (supra Pfr) quod (quod super Fd) fertur sententia (om. Bc Fd Pfr), sed ex alio nominandus est."

[80] Friedberg, ed., *Decretum,* 665, supported by Bc Fd Mz: "Aliquando nullum subest crimen (subest crimen nullum Mz), et tamen uel odio iudicis, uel factione inimicorum obpositam sibi sententiam dampnationis in se excipit."

[81] Friedberg, ed., *Decretum,* 661 supported by Bc Fd Mz: ". . . liuore odio . . . aut fauore aduersariorum."

I have not found the text of c. 68 in any canonical collection prior to the *Decretum*, so its source remains unidentified. Among relevant collections, c. 66 is found only in the *3L*, where the text is of the same length as in the second recension of the *Decretum*. The first recension includes only the text on the first three lines in Friedberg's edition. It seems highly unlikely that the *3L* is the source also of this shorter version. I have found no other relevant collection that could have been Gratian's source for the first recension.

Canon 73 is found in three of Gratian's usual sources. Among them, the *Tripartita* can be immediately excluded from consideration, since its text often differs from that in the *Decretum*:

11.3.73
3 ne *Fd^add Mk Mz Fr. Polyc.P 3LV*: si *Trip.*
3 quis *Fd^add Mk Mz Fr. Polyc.P 3LV*: om. *Trip.*
4 animi *Fd^add Mk Mz Fr. Polyc.P 3LV*: om. *Trip.*
4 tali *Fd^add Mk Mz Fr. Polyc.P 3LV*: om *Trip.*
5 stomachi episcopi sui abstenti (obstenti *Polyc.mP 3LV*) *Fd^add Mk Mz Fr. Polyc.mP 3LV*: episcopi sui excommunicati *Trip.*
5 *post* sint *verba multa add. Trip.*: om. *Fd^add Mk Mz Fr. Polyc.mP 3LV*
6 hi *Fd^add Mk Mz Fr. Polyc.P 3LV*: om. *Trip.*
9 *post* sententiam *verba multa add. Trip.*: om. *Fd^add Mk Mz Fr. Polyc.mP 3LV*

The texts in the *Polycarpus* and in the *3L* are almost identical and it is hard to judge which one was Gratian's source. I have found but one variant of interest:

11.3.73
9 circa *Cg Fd^add Mk Mz Fr. Trip. 3LV*: contra *Polyc.mP*

This variant indicates that *3L* was Gratian's source.

The source could be identified for only three of the texts found in the first recension. The quotation from Gregory I in d. p. c. 77 must come from the *Polycarpus*, which is the only relevant collection which contains it. Canon 65 is found in four of the usual sources, but only the *Tripartita* (at 3.10.16) shares Gratian's false attribution to a council of Mainz. Canon 70 appears in both the *3L* and in Anselm's collection. A collation shows that the latter was Gratian's source:

11.3.70
1–2 ecclesiae *Bc Fd Mz Sa Vd Fr. Ans.G*: ecclesiarum *3LV*
5 pleniter ad notitiam uenerit diuina tunc (tunc diuina *Bc Fd Mz Sa Vd Ans.Gp*) *Bc Fd Mz Sa Vd Fr. Ans.Gp*: om. *3LV*

For most of the canons found already in the first recension, no source could, however, be convincingly identified. In a couple of cases, namely the paraphrase of Bede at the end of d. p. c. 66[82] and c. 71, the texts do not appear at all in the canonical tradition pre-dating Gratian. Canon 69 is found only in Deusdedit's collection at 4.276,[83] but there is no evidence that Gratian used this collection otherwise, so its source remains unidentified.

Canons 72 to 74 are all found in close proximity to each other in Anselm of Lucca's collection. Canons 74 and 76[84] also appear in the *Polycarpus* and c. 75 is present in the *Panormia*. It is not likely, although it cannot be excluded, that any one of these collections was Gratian's source, since the excerpts there are much longer than in the *Decretum*. No variant readings provide any clues.

Among Gratian's usual sources, *canon 67* is found only in the *Tripartita*, where the text, however, is longer than in the *Decretum*. There are also two significant textual differences:

11.3.67
Inscr. Idem (*scilicet* Gregorius: item *Bc*) Mauricio inperatori *Aa Bc Cg Fd Mk Mz Pfr Sa Fr.*: Ex registro beati Gregorii pape ad Mauricium augustum cp. ccxiii *Trip.*
5 omne *Aa Bc Cg Mk Pfr Sa Fr.*: *supra lin. add. Fd Mz*: ira *Trip.*

The substance of Gratian's inscription could certainly be extracted from the inscription in the *Tripartita*, but Gratian seems usually to have followed the inscription of his source closely. The *Tripartita* may have been the source, but it is probable that it remains to be identified.

CORRUPTION OF JUDGEMENTS

Gratian's statement towards the end of d. p. c. 77, that a person may receive an unjust sentence because of the judge's hatred or the plotting of his enemies, is further elaborated in the following canons. Canon 78 specifies four ways in which judgement may be corrupted: through fear, avarice, hatred, and love. Four canons then follow which emphasize how serious it is to corrupt one's judgement or testimony. They are followed by a short *dictum*, which points out that to give false testimony for money amounts to denying or betraying God. This is also the substance of c. 83. Canon 84 states that we deny God every time we are defeated by vices and sins, while c. 85 declares that anyone who says that he is not a Christian denies Christ. Again the discussion has strayed from the main concerns of Gratian's argumentation. Canons 78 to 82 are immediately

---

[82] The text is a paraphrase of a passage in Bede's commentary on the letter of James (*PL* 93.16D-17A).   [83] *Die Kanonessammlung des Kardinals Deusdedit*, 547.
[84] Fuhrmann, *Einfluß und Verbreitung*, 946–947, n. 353.

relevant, and d. p. c. 82 and c. 83 introduce a new perspective. Canons 84 to 86 contain similar language ("denying God" or "betraying truth"), but their concerns are different from what preceded, and it is hard to see that they contribute to the discussion of how judgement may be corrupted. Are they found here only because of the similarities in language? The first recension brings greater clarity. Here, canons 82 to 86 are missing. Their sources are easy to determine, since they each appear in only one of the usual sources: c. 83 in the *Tripartita*, the others in the *3L*.

In d. p. c. 86, Gratian introduces the idea that an unjust sentence only harms the judge and not the judged. It is remarkable that he already in canons 56 to 64 reproduced texts making similar points. The statement of the present *dictum* is in its entirety supported by canons 87 and 88, while c. 89 concentrates on the subject of unjust judgements, and c. 90 refers to a just recipient of an unjust sentence. Such judgements have no validity, states c. 89, while c. 90 promises a reward for just persons who are unjustly condemned. The subject of d. p. c. 86–c. 90 (which is completely present in the first recension, except for § 1 of c. 89) is closely related to that of d. p. c. 78–c. 82, where Gratian emphasizes the gravity of corrupt judgement and testimony. Again, the addition of the intervening canons (particularly canons 84 and 85) in the second recension disturbs the course of Gratian's original discussion.

As earlier in this *questio*, the sources for many of the canons in the first recension are difficult to pinpoint. Each of them needs to be discussed in some detail. In several cases, I reach negative results, which indicate that Gratian's source may have been an as yet unidentified collection.

Canon 78 is found in *3L*, but a collation of variants suggests that this collection was not Gratian's source:

II.3.78

1 *post* peruertitur *verba* timore cupiditate odio amore *add. 3LV: om. Bc Cg Fd Mz Fr.*

3 animum *Bc Cg(supra rasuram?) Fd Mz Fr.:* muneris *3LV*

4–5 *post* molimur *verba* cuius hodio corrumpimur *add. 3LV: om. Bc Cg Fd Mz Fr.*

Canon 79 appears only in the *3L* among Gratian's usual sources. In the *Decretum*, the text, which is an excerpt from Jerome's commentary on the Book of Amos, is misattributed to Augustine. The text lacks inscription in *3L*, where it follows directly upon a canon ascribed to Augustine. It is, thus, tempting to see here the explanation of Gratian's mistake, but there are significant variant readings which seem to exclude *3L* as his source:

II.3.79

1 *post* vel *verba* contrario vel *add. 3LV: om. Bc Cg Fd Mz Fr.*

2 pervertit *Bc Cg Fd Mz Fr.*: pervertunt *3LV*

Canons 80 and 81 consist of four textual fragments which all appear in a single canon in the *Tripartita*. There are no significant variant readings, so it is plausible to assume that the *Tripartita* was Gratian's source. Since the sources of so many of the canons in the first recension of C. 11, q. 3 remain enigmatic, it is worth pointing out that the first fragment in c. 81 circulated quite widely; it appears, e.g., in Deusdedit's collection 4.61,[85] in his *Libellus contra invasores et symoniacos*,[86] in Placidus of Nonantola's *Liber de honore ecclesiae*, c. 125 to 126 (both fragments included in c. 81),[87] Anselm of Lucca's *Liber contra Wibertum*,[88] and Wido of Ferrara's *De schismate Hildebrandi*.[89]

The text of *canon 87* is an interesting cento of three different texts. The first few lines (*Illud plane* – *non agit perperam*) derives from Augustine's letter to Classicianus. What then follows (*Pax ecclesiae* – *columba dimittit*) is extracted from Augustine's *de baptismo*. The canon ends with a fragment which Gratian ascribes to Solomon and which resembles Proverbs 26: 2. The first two texts appear often in the canonical transmission before Gratian. Four of Gratian's usual sources contain parts of the first fragment, although none of them contains it fully. The excerpts in the *Polycarpus*, *3L*, and Anselm of Lucca's collections end with *penam* on line 5, while Alger's excerpt ends with *facit* on line 3. The second fragment is not to my knowledge found in any of Gratian's usual sources, but often elsewhere, e.g., in the *Collectio Britannica*, Varia IC 100,[90] in Deusdedit's collection at 4.77,[91] and in Wenric of Trier's letter.[92]

I have found the three fragments in c. 87 together only once, namely in the so-called *Collectio canonum Barberiniana* 11.4–7. This collection is preserved in a single manuscript in the Vatican library and was compiled at some point between 1071 and 1120.[93] In this work, the first fragment of c. 87 is followed by a short excerpt from Augustine's *de natura boni*, which is identical to the first sentence of C. 11, q. 3, c. 47. Then comes the second fragment of c. 87, followed by an excerpt from Augustine's *de sermone Domini in monte*, which appears in the *Decretum* as C. 11, q. 3, c. 49. Last appears the final fragment of c. 87, inscribed *in Salomone*, perhaps indicating that the text is from a commentary on Proverbs, which could explain why it departs from that of the Vulgate. Gratian's text is, however, not identical to that of the *Barberiniana*: Gratian's *incertum* is replaced by *contrarium*. The *Barberiniana* could have been Gratian's source for c. 87 (as

---

[85] *Die Kanonessammlung des Kardinals Deusdedit*, 428.   [86] *Libelli de lite*, II 335, line 35.
[87] Busch, *Liber de honore ecclesiae*, 106, 109, and 228, where further occurrences of the two texts in c. 80 are listed.   [88] *Libelli de lite*, I 527, line 7.   [89] *Ibid.* I 545, line 8.
[90] Ewald, "Papstbriefe," 581.   [91] *Die Kanonessammlung des Kardinals Deusdedit*, 434.
[92] *Libelli de lite*, I 292.   [93] Fornasari, "Collectio canonum Barberiniana."

well as canons 47 and 49), but its limited circulation makes this unlikely. The presence of the text of c. 87 therein proves that this cento circulated before Gratian and was not composed by him. His source remains unidentified.

Among Gratian's usual sources, *canon 88* is found in its entirety only in the *Panormia*. Since a collation reveals no significant variant readings, this collection was probably his source.

In the first recension, *canon 89* consisted only of the *principium* (to *acta non ualeat* on line 3 of Friedberg's edition). Paragraphs 1 and 2 were added in the second recension. It is clear that the source used by the author of the second recension was the *Tripartita*, which is the only one of the usual sources to contain a text of the same length as the second recension. The texts found in the *3L* and in Anselm of Lucca's collection are of the same length as the text in the first recension. Neither of them is, however, likely to have been Gratian's source, since their inscriptions differ from that of the *Decretum*:

Inscr. Item Calixtus Papa *Aa Bc Cg Fd Mz Fr.*: Calixtus *Trip.*: *nulla inscriptio 3LV*: Calixtus papa Benedicto episcopo *Ans.*

While the absence of an inscription in *3LV* rules out this collection (provided that this is not an idiosyncratic feature of the Vatican manuscript), the inscription in Anselm's collection contains all the information found in the *Decretum*. It would, however, be atypical of Gratian not to reproduce the information about the letter's addressee, had Anselm been his source. Again, one is tempted to suggest that an unknown source provided Gratian with the text of the first part of c. 89.

Among Gratian's usual sources, *canon 90* appears only in the *Tripartita*, which probably was his source.

SENTENCES FORCING TO EVIL

In the latter half of d. p. c. 90 (§ 1), Gratian raises the issue of sentences which are contrary to equity. Such sentences attempt to force subjects to do evil. This *dictum* is followed by a sequence of canons discussing such cases (canons 91–95 and 101) before Gratian summarizes in d. p. c. 101:

Thus, when subjects are excommunicated because they cannot be forced to do evil, the sentence is not to be obeyed, since in accordance with Gelasius' statement, "an iniquitous sentence does not burden a person, neither before God, nor in his Church."[94]

---

[94] Friedberg, ed., *Decretum*, 672, supported by Aa Cg Fd: "Cum ergo subditi excommunicantur, quia ad malum cogi non possunt, tunc sententiae non est obediendum, quia iuxta illud Gelasii. 'Nec apud Deum, nec apud ecclesiam eius, quemquam grauat iniqua sententia.'"

The text quoted from Pope Gelasius is extracted from c. 46, and Gratian explicitly refers to it also in d. p. c. 64. In that context, however, he does not make any explicit distinction between "unjust" and "iniquitous" sentences. He makes such a distinction only in d. p. c. 101, where Gratian answers the question posed in d. p. c. 64, as to why Gelasius appears to contradict certain conciliar canons. The solution entails a verbal distinction typical of Gratian: while all the variants of unjust sentences which he has discussed in this *questio* should be obeyed, if only to avoid the sin of pride, an iniquitous sentence should be ignored. He thus succeeds in drawing a relatively clear line (at least in theory) between condemnations which can be ignored and those which cannot, although the canons on which Gratian based his treatment make no such distinction.

While canons 91 to 95 and 101 directly support the main direction in which Gratian takes his discussion between d. p. c. 90 and d. p. c. 101, the intervening canons 96 to 100 address different issues. Canons 96 and 100 condemn those who consent to another's sin; in canons 97 and 98, Augustine, using hierarchical imagery, emphasizes that God is to be obeyed if his precepts conflict with those of secular rulers; and c. 99 states that obedience may sometimes interrupt something good but never induces evil. Canons 96 to 99, which undoubtedly break the train of thought sustained between d. p. c. 90 and d. p. c. 101, are missing from the first recension.

As is the case elsewhere in this *questio*, it is easy to find the sources used for the second recension, while the provenance of the canons in the first recension proved difficult to determine. In the second recension, canons 96 and 99 clearly derive from the *Tripartita* and the *3L*, respectively, since their text is found in no other relevant collection.

Canons 97 and 98 consist of three Augustinian fragments, which appear in two of Gratian's usual sources, the *Polycarpus* and the *3L*.[95] In the former, all three fragments continue beyond the point where Gratian's excerpt ends. This is the case also for c. 97 in *3L*, although the additional passage is shorter than in the *Polycarpus* (as indicated below). These findings indicate that *3L* was Gratian's source, a conclusion which is further supported by the variant readings registered below for c. 97, line 3, and for c. 98, lines 24–25.

11.3.97
3 *post* potestatem *verba* timendo potestatem *add. Polyc.m: om. Bc*[add] *Cg Fd*[add] *Mk Mz Fr. 3LV*

---

[95] The three fragments appear in close sequence in both collections: *Polycarpus* 1.29.3, 5, and 7; *3L* 1.9.3, 5, 7. The intermediate canons are the same in both collections: c. 4 = C. 23, q. 5, c. 4 and c. 6 = C. 23, q. 3, c. 2.

14 *post* extinguere *verba* sed insidiatur contra te potens et molitur contra te potens *add. Polyc.m: verba* sed insidiatur contra te potens *add. 3LV: om. Bc^{add} Cg Fd^{add} Mk Mz Fr.*

11.3.98

24–25 dicebat producite aciem *Bc^{add} Cg Fd^{add} Mk Mz Fr. 3LV:* producere aciem iubebat dicendo (dicente *Polyc.M) Polyc.m*

Among the first-recension texts (91–95 and 100–101) the least (apparent) problems are posed by canons 95, 100, and 101, which all seem to derive from the *Tripartita*. Canons 95 and 101 are found only there among the usual sources (although the former circulated widely[96]). Canon 100 appears in three relevant collections, but only the *Tripartita* has an excerpt of the same length and with the same misattribution to Isidore of Seville as the *Decretum*.

It is more complicated to find the source for the remaining canons. *Canon 91* appears in the midst of much longer excerpts both in the *Polycarpus* and in Anselm of Lucca's collection. An excerpt of the same length as in the *Decretum* circulated, however, and may be found in the *Collectio Britannica*[97] and in Manegold's *Liber ad Gebehardum*.[98] Gratian is not known to have used any of these works as a source otherwise, but the prior circulation of the shorter text makes it very unlikely that Gratian would happen to extract exactly the same fragment from the *Polycarpus* or from Anselm's collection.

Gratian ascribes *canon 92* to Augustine. As the *Correctores* noted, the first line is a quotation from Ambrose's *De paradiso* while the rest does not reproduce any known source. Alger of Liège has the same first line as Gratian, but the rest of his canon corresponds to Ambrose's words, to whom he also attributes the text. Alger's work could, therefore, not have been Gratian's source, which remains unidentified.

In the first recension, *canon 93* ends already with *obedire* on line 7 of Friedberg's edition. Among the usual sources, only Anselm of Lucca's collection contains an excerpt of exactly this length, and this work was probably Gratian's source. Excerpts including the end of the text in the second recension (but beginning only with *si bonum est* on line 7) are found in the *Polycarpus* and in the *3L*. The latter work was often used as a source in the second recension and was probably the source used also here.

---

[96] Canon 95 is found, e.g., in Deusdedit's collection, 4.64 (*Die Kanonessammlung des Kardinals Deusdedit*, 429), three times among the *Libelli de lite*, I 527 545, II 627, and in the *Collectio Barberiniana* 2.6 (Fornasari, "Collectio canonum Barberiniana"). See further Busch, *Liber de honore ecclesiae*, 228.   [97] Varia IC 56, cf. Ewald, "Papstbriefe," 579 (no. 57).
[98] *Libelli de lite*, I 428, line 5.

I have not found the text of *canon 94* anywhere in Gratian's usual sources, or in any of the works where canons 91 to 95 appear.

GRATIAN'S AFTERTHOUGHTS

The rest of C. 11, q. 3 forms, as it were, three afterthoughts to the themes of the *questio*. In the second part (§ 1) of d. p. c. 101, Gratian points out that when he stated "above" ("*supra*") that those who communicate with excommunicated persons should be expelled from the Church, he does not include every kind of communication. The reference is most likely to c. 6, whose language is echoed in the present *dictum*:

c. 6: communicantes ei (eis *Fd*) omnes abici de ecclesia oportet . . .[99]
d. p. c. 101: Quod autem supra (*om. Cg*) communicantes excommunicatis de ecclesia abici iubentur . . .[100]

The following canons, 102 to 105, serve to spell out the point that communicating with an excommunicated person of necessity or in ignorance is not sinful.

The very short d. p. c. 105 introduces three canons containing regulations for how an excommunication and a reconciliation should be carried out, including (in c. 107) a standard form for excommunication. Canons 109 and 110, finally, stipulate punishments for clerics who touch the sacraments while they are excommunicated and for those who communicate with excommunicated persons. Canon 110 allows for moderation in cases where ignorance, fear, or necessity play a role. This canon would thus fit the context of canons 102 to 105 excellently; it is oddly placed here.

Canons 102 to 110 are afterthoughts, loosely related to the general themes of the *questio*. It is therefore difficult to guess on the basis of their contents which canons belonged to the first recension and which were added later. The first recension included canons 102 to 105, while canons 106 to 110 were added in the second recension. It is easy to determine the sources for canons 106 to 110, since each of them appears only in one of the usual sources: 106 to 108 in the *3L*, and 109 to 110 in the *Panormia*.

It is slightly more complicated to determine the source for the remaining texts. Canons 103 to 104 are found in both the *Panormia* and the *Tripartita*. Canon 103 also appears in the *3L*, although a collation shows that this collection cannot have been the source:

11.3.103
1 *ante* quoniam *verbum et add. 3LV orig.: om. Bc Fd Mz Fr. Pan.EJMT Trip.*

---

[99] Friedberg, ed., *Decretum*, 644, supported by Bc Cg Fd Mz.
[100] *Ibid.* 672, supported by Bc Cg Fd Mz.

3 partim nimia *Bc Fd Mz Fr. Pan.EJMT Trip.*: partim etiam nimia *3LV orig.*
5 *post* possumus *verbum* oportune *add. 3LV orig.*: *om. Bc Fd Mz Fr. Pan.EJMT Trip.*
7 filios *Bc Fd Mz Fr.*: liberos filios *Pan.EJMT Trip.*: liberos *3LV orig.*

A single variant suggests that the *Panormia* rather than the *Tripartita* was Gratian's source:

13 orator *Bc Fd Mz Fr. Pan.EFJ 3LV orig.*: arator *Pan.LMT Trip.*

In collating many *Tripartita* manuscripts, Martin Brett has not found any text containing the word *orator*. As long as no manuscript of this collection can be shown to transmit this word, it remains more likely that the *Panormia* was Gratian's source for c. 103, and consequently also for c. 102.

Canons 105 to 106 are found only in the *Tripartita*, and they each appear twice in this collection. It is a reasonable assumption that these canons derived from this collection, except that there are textual differences: [101]

11.3.104
4 astrinxit *Aa Cg Mz Sa Fr.*: astrinxi *Bc Fd*: constrinxit *Trip.13*
11.3. 105
4 et *Bc Cg Fd Mz Sa Fr.*: *om. Aa Trip.13*
5 illam uoluit *Aa Bc Cg Fd Mz Sa Fr.*: uoluit *Trip.3CRWNB*: *om. Trip.1 Trip.3ZJTQA*
9 *post* pseudopresbiteros *verba* uel quocumque *add. Trip.1*: uel quosque *Trip.3*: *om. Aa Bc Cg Fd Mz Sa Fr.*

Again, these variants call into question whether Gratian's source for canons 104 and 105 might not have been another, unknown work.

GRATIAN'S UNKNOWN SOURCE

For several canons in C. 11, q. 3, I could not identify convincingly a source. In the treatment of specific canons, I have often suggested in passing that a source which has not yet been identified might have provided the author with the text. In the following, I shall evaluate the arguments that may be made for suggesting the existence of such a source.

That a source other than the usual sources, i.e., those listed by Peter Landau,[102] was used in compiling the *Decretum* is clear from the fact that several canons in C. 11, q. 3 are not found in any of the latter: canons 1, 68, 69, 71, 87, 92, 94, and the text quoted from Bede in d. p. c. 65. I was

---

[101] In the following collations *Trip.1* signifies the text in the first part of the *Tripartita*, and *Trip.3* the text in the third part. *Trip.13* indicates that both texts have the same reading.
[102] See above, ch. 1.

unable to find five of these at all in any work pre-dating Gratian. The remaining three appear in different places. Canon 1 is found in the polemical pamphlet *Epistola de continentia clericorum*, c. 69 in Deusdedit's canonical collection, and c. 87 in the *Collectio Barberiniana*.[103]

There are at least twenty canons which can be found in the usual sources, although in a form so different that it is unlikely that any of these was Gratian's source: canons 34, 44, 46, 47, 48, 50, 52, 60, 61, 63, 67, 74, 75, 76, 78, 79, 89, 91, 104, and 105. I have found only four of them in other pre-Gratian works in a form corresponding to that of the *Decretum*, namely canons 60, 61, 63, and 91. Interestingly, most of the canons for which the sources remain elusive belong to the first recension. A closer study of some of them serves to confirm that Gratian could not have found them in his usual sources, and to provide further insight into the nature of the source he used.

I have chosen canons 44 to 51 as a case study, since these texts yield the most interesting and least ambiguous results. When discussing them, I leave out c. 45, which is a *palea*. The separate examination above of each of these texts indicates that the most likely source for all of them (except for c. 44) is the *Tripartita*, which contains them in close sequence in title 27 of part 3. This conclusion is, however, marred by variations between the *Tripartita*'s version and that of the *Decretum* for several canons. Significantly different readings were registered for canons 44, 46, 47, 48, and 50 (see above, pp. 100–102). The text of the *Decretum* differs in most cases also from that of the material source. The theoretical possibilities that these differences are due to idiosyncrasies in the *Tripartita* manuscript used by Gratian or that they are the result of his editing, may be ruled out. The manuscript transmission of the *Tripartita* is comparatively well known, thanks to Martin Brett's substantial collations. Several of the textual variants are such that it is not likely that they are the result of Gratian's editing. The most reasonable explanation for the discrepancies is that he used another source. If that is true for these canons, it is also likely that canons 49 and 51, where the *Tripartita*'s text does not differ significantly from Gratian's, derive from this source.

Table 7 indicates some works from the late eleventh and early twelfth century which contain the texts under discussion.

It is notable that only three known collections contain all of the texts reproduced by Gratian in C. 11, q. 3, cc. 44–51, namely the *Tripartita*, Ivo of Chartres' *Decretum*, and the *Arsenal Collection*. The texts appear in the latter collection in the same order as in the two former. As is well known, the third part of the *Tripartita* is almost entirely based on Ivo's *Decretum*,[104]

---

[103] For references, see the treatment of each canon above.   [104] Fournier and Le Bras, *Histoire*, II 65.

Table 7 *Formal sources of C. 11, q. 3, canons 44–51*

Gratiani	Tripartita	Ivo, Decretum	Arsenal 713[a]	Deusdedit	Wenric of Trier[b]	Bernard[c]	Coll. Brit. Varia[d]	Caesaraugustana[e]
11.3.44	3.27.4	14.7	146v	4.74	—	—	—	—
11.3.46	3.27.5	14.8	146v	—	—	—	I B 1 § 6	14.37
11.3.47	3.27.6	14.9	146v	4.76	292.17	483.41	I C 99	14.38
11.3.48	3.27.2	14.5	146v	4.79	—	484.3	I C 102	5.15
11.3.49	3.27.7	14.10	146v	4.79	—	484.3	—	14.35
11.3.50	3.27.8	14.11	146v	—	292.24	—	I C 103	—
11.3.51	3.27.9	14.12	146v	—	292.27	484.6	I C 104	5.16

Notes:

[a] Refers to folios in the collection found in the second part of Paris, Bibliothèque de l'Arsenal 713. I thank Martin Brett for informing me where in this manuscript these texts appear. About this collection, which could not have been compiled earlier than in 1089, see Robert Somerville, "Papal Excerpts in Arsenal MS 713B," Somerville with Kuttner, *Urban II*, 16–21, and Martin Brett, "The sources and influence of Paris, Bibliothèque de l'Arsenal MS 713," in *Proceedings of the Ninth International Congress of Medieval Canon Law*, MIC Subs. 10 (Vatican City 1996), 149–167.

[b] Wenric was *scholasticus* in Trier and wrote his anti-papal letter in 1080 or 1081. It is edited in *Libelli de lite*, I 284–299; the numbers in the table refer to pages and lines in this edition. Cf. Carl Mirbt, *Die Publizistik im Zeitalter Gregors VII* (Leipzig 1894), 23–25, and Max Manitius, *Geschichte der lateinischen Literatur des Mittelalters* III, Handbuch der Altertumswissenschaft, Abt. 9, Teil 2, Band 3 (Munich 1931), 26–27.

[c] Bernard of Constance (sometimes called Bernard of Hildesheim) wrote his anti-imperial work *Liber canonum contra Heinricum quartum* in 1085. It is edited in *Libelli de lite* in 1085; the numbers in the table refer to pages and lines in this edition. Cf. Mirbt, *Publizistik*, 33–35, Manitius, *Geschichte*, III 30–31, and Detlev Jasper, "Bernhard von Hildesheim," in *Die deutsche Literatur des Mittelalters: Verfasserlexikon* I (Berlin 1978), 766–767.

[d] Calendared in Ewald, "Papstbriefe."

[e] Canons indexed in Theiner, *Disquisitiones criticae.*

which draws on the *Collectio Britannica*, usually through the intermediary of the *Arsenal Collection*.[105]

There is one particularly noteworthy text among the others in the table, namely the text of Gratian's c. 50 in Wenric of Trier's letter. In all examined works except this one, the text of this canon is longer than in the *Decretum*. Wenric's text is, however, the same length as Gratian's version, and it is attractive to assume that both authors, directly or indirectly, extracted the text from the same source. Ivo's *Decretum*, the *Tripartita*, or the *Arsenal Collection* could not, for chronological reasons, have been Wenric's source.

Another similar example is canons 60 to 62, all of which are excerpts from the same text. A longer fragment, which includes the texts of canons 60 to 62, is found in Ivo's *Panormia* and *Decretum* as well as in the *Arsenal Collection*. (Gratian included this excerpt, probably extracting it from the *Panormia*, as c. 88.) The text of c. 62 is found in the *Tripartita*, while canons 60 and 61 are missing there but appear in several polemical works connected with the conflict between the papacy and the German emperor, e.g., in Bernard of Constance's *Liber canonum*. It is reasonable to assume that Bernard and Gratian 1, directly or indirectly, drew on the same source, which would have extracted these fragments from the longer text.

It is attractive to suggest that canons 50, 60, and 61 all derive from one and the same source, which was used by Wenric, Bernard, and Gratian 1. Such a source must pre-date Wenric's and Bernard's works, compiled in the first half of the 1080s. It is likely that Gratian also extracted canons 44, 46, 47, 48, and 50 from this source, since variant readings indicate that he did not take them from the *Tripartita*. The source probably contained these canons (and, one may reasonably assume, canons 49 and 51) in the same or similar order as the *Tripartita*.

I suggest that most of the 24 canons in C. 11, q. 3 for which I could not identify a source derive from the source used by Gratian, Wenric, and Bernard. In studying the transmission of those texts, I have found no evidence against this hypothesis. A few further characteristics of this unknown source may tentatively be determined. Among the twenty-four texts, eighteen occupy six lines or less in Friedberg's edition. Also, several do not reproduce their material sources verbatim; at least canons 1, 44, 71, 92, 94, and the text in d. p. c. 65 contain paraphrases, while c. 87 is a cento of three different texts. Some of the canons are misinscribed, e.g., canons 63, 78, 91, and 92. Several are also found in the polemical literature of the eleventh century.

---

[105] Martin Brett, "Sources and influence."

Canon 92 suggests that Gratian's source also commented upon its texts:

It is not always bad not to obey a command; for when a lord commands what is contrary to God, then he is not to be obeyed.[106]

Only the first sentence (*non . . . precepto;* "It is . . . command") derives from the material source, Ambrose, while the rest of the text is neither a quotation nor a paraphrase of what follows there. It looks like a canonistic compiler's added explanation, of the kind one sometimes finds in Gratian's *dicta.* If this sentence were Gratian's addition, one would expect that at least some manuscripts would contain the sign that usually introduces his *dicta.* A possible explanation is that this is a *dictum* of the compiler of the unknown source, which Gratian unwittingly took as part of the canon. This might be a parallel case to the several instances in C. 1, q. 1, where Gratian extracted not only most of his canons from his main source, Alger of Liège's *De misericordia et iustitia,* but also several *dicta.* In doing so, he sometimes seems to have understood a *dictum* as part of a preceding canon.[107]

Judging from these indications taken together, we are dealing with a canonical collection containing short excerpts which sometimes have been tampered with, and which are accompanied by interpolations or even by *dicta.* As far as I know, there are no traces of substantial use of this collection elsewhere in the *Decretum.* It seems, hence, to have been a monographical treatment of the validity of clerical sentences in general and sentences of excommunication in particular. This description brings to mind works such as Alger of Liège's *De misericordia et iustitia,* Placidus of Nonantola's *De honore ecclesiae,* and Bernard of Constance's *Liber canonum contra Heinricum quartum.* The subject matter would undoubtedly have been relevant and even controversial during the late eleventh and early twelfth century.

The parallels with C. 1, q. 1 may be even more far-reaching. It seems clear that the unknown source contributed many of the canons that are central to the concerns of C. 11, q. 3, as did Alger's work for C. 1, q. 1. It is plausible that canons beyond the twenty-four with which this investigation began derive from the unknown source. After all, many of the canons which are central to Gratian's argument in C. 11, q. 3 share some of the characteristics of canons deriving from the unknown source.

---

[106] Friedberg, ed., *Decretum,* 669, supported by Bc Cg Mz: "Non semper malum est non obedire precepto; cum enim Dominus iubet ea (om. Bc Cg Mz), que Deo sunt contraria (contraria sunt Bc Mz), tunc ei obediendum non (om. Bc) est." The word *dominus* should be written with a lower-case d, since it clearly refers to an earthly lord, not to God.

[107] Kretzschmar, *Alger von Lüttichs Traktat,* 144–146.

Gratian might even have extracted some of his *dicta* from the unknown source. Until this source has been identified, my determination of sources for any number of the canons in C. 11, q. 3 must be considered provisional.[108]

---

[108] My attempts to identify the unknown source have been in vain. I have tested many of the canons deriving from it in the *Patrologia Latina Full Text Database*, in Fowler-Magerl, *Kanones*, and in the *Cetedoc* database as well as in, e.g., the indices of the *Libelli de lite*, in Fornasari, *Initia canonum*, and in Theiner, *Disquisitiones criticae*.

Chapter 4

THE TWO RECENSIONS OF THE *DECRETUM*

Many scholars have pointed out that it is not likely that Gratian wrote the *Decretum* in one giant sweep.[1] In this chapter, I want to demonstrate that the work was produced in two steps. A first effort produced a shorter text which I call the first recension. This text was later expanded to form the text that is generally known (from most medieval manuscripts and all modern editions), which I call the second recension. These terms are, admittedly, not always practical to use, particularly not when referring to the author of either recension. In the interests of simplicity and clarity, I have therefore chosen to call the author of the first recension Gratian 1 and the author of the second recension Gratian 2. These labels are not intended to suggest that Gratian 1 and Gratian 2 could not have been the same person.

The first recension is preserved in the original text of the three manuscripts Bc Fd P and in the fragment Pfr. Aa contains the same text with interpolations from the second recension in the main section of its two volumes. The second recension is known (in slightly varying forms) from some six hundred other manuscripts and in numerous modern editions.[2] The second recension contains 3,945 canons (including the *paleae*) in the editions. The first recension contains only 1,860 canons (47 percent).

The manuscripts containing the first recension have been known for some time, but scholars, not recognizing their significance, have generally thought that these manuscripts contain abbreviations of the *Decretum*. Gratian's work is bulky and hence expensive, so many different abridgements of it were composed, particularly during the twelfth century.[3] It

---

[1] Kuttner, "Research on Gratian," x.

[2] My listing of more than 600 manuscripts containing the *Decretum* will appear in Kenneth Pennington and Wilfried Hartmann, eds., *History of Medieval Canon Law*, 11.

[3] Kuttner, *Repertorium*, 257–271. Three abbreviations are edited and analyzed in Alfred Beyer, *Lokale Abbreviationen des "Decretum Gratiani": Analyse und Vergleich der Dekretabbreviationen "Omnes leges aut divine" (Bamberg), "Humanum genus duobus regitur" (Pommersfelden) und "De his qui intra claustra monasterii consistunt" (Lichtenthal, Baden-Baden)*, Bamberger theologische Studien 6 (Frankfurt am Main 1998).

is, however, possible to prove that the five manuscripts in question contain an earlier version of the *Decretum* and not a later abbreviation. I shall here provide such proof along three different lines. First, I shall give a few examples (among many possible) of passages where the text of the first-recension manuscripts is closer to the text of the source that Gratian used than is the text of the second recension. I shall then demonstrate that the two recensions draw on different sets of sources. This proof is based on Lenherr's finding that the author of the *Decretum* worked with different sets of sources in succession, not concurrently. Third, I shall show that the layout of the argument is more coherent in the first recension than in the second, where the additional material serves to break up and confuse the original discussion. This is a further indication that the second recension is derivative from the first (and not vice versa). After having thus established that the shorter version of the *Decretum* really is a first recension, I shall attempt to sketch an outline of how the two recensions were created. The chapter will conclude with a consideration of the place and the date of their composition.

TEXTUAL VARIANTS IN THE FIRST RECENSION

While attempting to determine Gratian's source for each of the canons in the sections of the *Decretum* I investigated in chapters 2 and 3, I remarked several times that Aa Bc Fd and/or P contain readings that are older than those in the usual text. This is the case for C. 11, q. 3, c. 47, c. 50, and c. 89; C. 24, q. 1, c. 4, c. 23, c. 26, c. 40, and c. 42; and C. 24, q. 2, c. 2. In earlier chapters, however, I omitted discussion of many further instances which do not contribute to identifying Gratian's sources. For example, the text of C. 24, q. 3, c. 6 provides several examples, where Aa and Fd appear to contain early readings (neither Bc, P nor Pfr contain C. 24):

24.3.6
37 demonstrans *Mk Tx Vd Fr.*: demonstrat *Aa Cg Fd Mz Fr.C*: monstrat *Pan.EFJLM Trip.*
39 iam *Aa Mk Mz Tx Vd Fr.*: add. *supra lin. post* protinus *Fd*: om. *Cg Pan.EFJL Trip.*
49 predicta *Cg Mk Tx Vd Fr.*: dicta *Fd Pan.EFJLM Trip.*: dicta *in* predicta *corr. Aa*

Gratian's source for this canon was the *Panormia*. In all three examples, the second recension contains a reading other than the source, while the first recension contains the reading of the source or a reading close to it. This is most clearly discernible for line 49, where the first recension retains the *dicta* of the *Panormia*, while the word has been changed into *predicta* in the second recension. On line 37, the text was changed in two steps, first from the *Panormia's monstrat* to *demonstrat* in the first recension and then to the participle *demonstrans* in the second recension. It is difficult to imagine how these findings could be explained if the text of the first-recension manuscripts in fact were a derivative abbreviation of the longer version. On line 37, not only Aa and Fd preserve the earlier form, but also the second-recension manuscripts Cg, Mz, and Friedberg's manuscript C. Cg distinguishes itself also on line 39, where Cg and the original text of Fd are the only ones to omit the word *iam*, obviously added by Gratian 2.

These apparent deviations from my thesis are easily explained. Aa is clearly a copy of an earlier manuscript where corrections and additions had already been made in order to bring the text up to date with the second recension (as will be discussed below). In this case, it seems clear that the word *iam* was added interlinearly in Aa's exemplar (as, incidentally, it is in Fd) and the scribe of Aa chose to include the word in his text. That Cg (alongside Mz and Friedberg's C on line 37) contains first-recension readings is a testimony that such readings survived in some second-recension manuscripts. I shall treat this phenomenon more fully below.

The most interesting examples discussed in the previous chapters are those in which two sources have been used for one canon, namely C. 24, q. 1, c. 23, c. 26, and c. 40; and C. 24, q. 2, c. 2. (C. 11, q. 3, c. 89 is a further but less certain example). In each of these cases, Gratian 1 first excerpted a text from either the *Panormia* or the *Polycarpus*. This is almost exactly the text found in Aa and Fd, as I have explained in chapters 2 and 3. When preparing the second recension, Gratian 2 discovered the same text in another source, either in Anselm of Lucca's collection or in the *Tripartita*.[4] This source provided either a longer text or a few variants, and Gratian 2 decided to change the text accordingly. The result can be seen in the second-recension manuscripts. In these cases, it is clear that the first-recension manuscripts contain the text in the shape it had when only one of the sources had been used. Again, it is very difficult to imagine that this would be the result of an abbreviator's efforts.

This discussion could be expanded at much greater length beyond the few examples deriving exclusively from C. 24. Indeed, other scholars, and particularly Rudolf Weigand, have directed attention to similar examples in other parts of the *Decretum*.[5] However, since I hope that my

[4] For C. 24, q. 1, c. 26 this other source may have been another occurrence of the same text in the *Polycarpus*.
[5] Rudolf Weigand, "Chancen und Probleme einer baldigen kritischen Edition der ersten Redaktion des *Dekrets* Gratians," *BMCL* 22 (1998), 53–75.

point has been made clear and further examples may become tedious, I have chosen to continue with the evidence that can be gleaned from what we know of the formal sources of the *Decretum*.

My analysis of *Causa* 24 showed that it grew around a kernel of canons excerpted from the *Panormia*. To this kernel was first added a number of texts extracted from the *Polycarpus*, and then texts deriving from the *Collectio Tripartita* and the *Collection in Three Books* (*3L*). The results concerning C. 11, q. 3 were less clear because of the existence of an unidentified source, but showed at least that the texts deriving from *3L* were among the last canons to be added to the text. Comparing these findings with the contents of the first-recension manuscripts, a remarkable state of affairs emerges. These manuscripts consistently omit the canons added last, i.e., those deriving from the *Tripartita* (in C. 24) and *3L*.

The situation is most clearly discernible for *Causa* 24, which contains eighty-eight canons. One of them (q. 3, c. 22) is a *palea* and will not be considered. Of the others, four (q. 1, canons 26 and 40; q. 2, c. 2; and q. 3, c. 1) are composites; for each of them, Gratian joined two texts from different formal sources. There are, therefore, 91 (87+4) textual fragments in C. 24. Among these 91 fragments, 16 derive from the *Tripartita* and 29 from *3L*. None of these fragments appears in the original text of Fd (nor in the main body of Aa). They can all be found among the added texts in the margins and in the supplements. Of the 14 fragments which derive from the *Panormia*, 12 were originally present in Fd (the interpolated manuscript Aa contains yet another of these canons). Twenty-three fragments come from the *Polycarpus*; twenty-two among them were originally present in Aa and Fd. Anselm of Lucca is represented in C. 24 by a sole fragment, which was not present in the original text of Fd. For the sake of completeness, I should mention that the single fragment deriving from the *Glossa ordinaria* to the Bible (C. 24, q. 3, c. 7) is present in the first recension, while the two canons from the First Lateran Council (C. 24, q. 3, canons 23 and 24) were absent (but were interpolated into Aa). I was not able to identify the source of the remaining five fragments (all of which are present in the first recension).

The remarkable correlation between source and presence/absence in the first recension can hardly be a coincidence. It is most unlikely that someone who already possessed the *Tripartita* and *Collection in Three Books* would make a copy of the *Decretum* and systematically exclude the canons present in these collections. Such a procedure is not only inherently implausible, but even if it did occur it would not produce the text of Aa

Bc Fd P Pfr, since these manuscripts contain many canons appearing in one or both of those collections although Gratian had found them elsewhere. The findings related here can be explained in one way only: the text of the first recension is an earlier version of Gratian's *Decretum*, not an abbreviation. I believe that examinations of other parts of the *Decretum* will lead to similar results; in each question or distinction, Gratian 1 and Gratian 2 used different sets of sources. However, one must not generalize the specifics of the results. I have demonstrated above that the *Panormia* provided the core texts of C. 24 but did not play that central role in C. 11, q. 3. Likewise, it seems clear that, while Gratian 1 did not use the *Tripartita* in compiling the first recension of C. 24, he used it elsewhere in the *Decretum*, e.g., in D. 63[6] and possibly even in C. 11, q. 3.

GRATIAN'S ARGUMENTS IN THE FIRST RECENSION

The discussion so far has concerned formal text-critical criteria. A scrutiny of the material contents reveals that the first recension is better organized, less contradictory, and more tightly argued than the usual text. It has often been noticed that the previously known text of the *Decretum* (i.e. the second recension) exhibits "deficient organization,"[7] which makes "the meaning and thrust of the arguments . . . seem difficult to follow the first time through."[8] Stephan Kuttner has perceptively commented about the *Decretum* that "in the course of its composition the material outgrew the original plan so that many untidy seams of the texture remain visible."[9] The discovery of the first recension allows us to study this original plan and the process through which the untidy seams came into being. Every section of the *Decretum* could be (and deserves to be) studied from this perspective, but I will here highlight, by way of example, only a couple of passages.

In my reading of C. 11, q. 3 in chapter 3, I attempted to follow Gratian's argument. I found that the main argument of the *questio*, which is defined in the beginning of the *causa* and developed throughout the *questio*, is interrupted several times – sometimes at rather inopportune moments – by subsidiary arguments. In the first recension, these disturbing elements are absent, making the main argument considerably easier to follow. Missing are, e.g., the last sentence of d. p. c. 40 and canons 41 to 43 (which contradict d. p. c. 43; see chapter 3), d. p. c. 55 and canons 55 to 56 (which appear out of place at this point in the *questio*), as well as c. 73 (see the discussion above in chapter 3). Most important among the omissions in the first

---

[6] Weigand, "Kirchliche Wahlrecht," 1333–1344.   [7] Kuttner, "Research on Gratian," 5.
[8] James Brundage, *Medieval Canon Law* (London and New York 1995), 47.
[9] Kuttner, "Research on Gratian," 13.

recension is the largest intrusion into the argument of the *questio*, namely
d. p. c. 20 – d. p. c. 26. As Elisabeth Vodola has pointed out, d. p. c. 24 is
the place where "Gratian used 'anathema' to designate the full social and
religious exclusion traditionally associated with excommunication, and
'excommunication' to mean mere exclusion from the Eucharist and the
other sacraments."[10] Gratian 1 did not employ this historically important
distinction in the first recension of the *Decretum*. Without doubt, his treatment of excommunication in C. 11 and elsewhere would have looked very
different if he had used it. It is clear that the distinction was introduced
only in the second recension, which explains the inconsistency which
readers may find between C. 11, q. 3, d. p. c. 24 and other sections of the
text.

Another feature of the text of C. 11, q. 3, which is explained as a result
of the additions in the second recension, are the rubrics *de eodem* of canons
4 and 5. These canons deal with a subject different from the one treated in
c. 3, despite the rubrics suggesting that they all treat the same subject. In
the first recension, these two canons follow directly upon c. 1. When they
are read as referring to c. 1 instead of c. 3, the rubrics make sense, since the
content of c. 1 is similar to that of canons 4 and 5. The same is true for the
identical rubric accompanying C. 24, q. 3, c. 5. Only by a substantial stretch
of the imagination can c. 5 be taken to treat the same issue as c. 4. Canons
3 and 4 are absent in the first recension, so the rubric there refers to c. 2,
which is more suitable. There are numerous similar examples elsewhere in
the *Decretum*; the rubric *de eodem* appears 398 times in Friedberg's edition.[11]

THE FIRST RECENSION

There is only one possible explanation for the findings outlined in the
previous sections: the text defined as the first recension is truly an earlier
version of the *Decretum*, earlier than the text that has been known previously. The examples that have been given in this chapter could easily be
multiplied. I have resisted doing this, particularly since other scholars
have found confirmation for my results in independent studies which
they have undertaken since I presented an outline of my results at the
Tenth International Congress of Medieval Canon Law in Syracuse, New
York, in August 1996.[12]

[10] Elisabeth Vodola, *Excommunication in the Middle Ages* (Berkeley 1986), 29.
[11] Winroth, "Uncovering Gratian's Original *Decretum*," 28.
[12] Anders Winroth, "The two recensions of Gratian's *Decretum*," *ZRG KA* 83 (1997), 22–31,
Weigand, "Zur künftigen Edition des *Dekret* Gratians," Weigand, "Das kirchliche Wahlrecht,"
Weigand, "Chancen und Probleme," J. M. Viejo-Ximénes, "La redacción original de C. 29 del
Decreto de Graciano," *Ius ecclesiae* 10 (1998), 149–185, Carlos Larrainzar, "El *Decreto* de Graciano
del Codice Fd," Jean Werckmeister, "Les études sur le *Décret* de Gratien: essai de bilan et perspective," *RDC* 48: 2 (1998).

The manuscripts of the first recension allow solutions to some long-standing discussions concerning the genesis of the *Decretum*. Two particularly controversial issues are the status of the *tractatus de penitentia* (C. 33, q. 3) and the *tractatus de consecratione* (see above, chapter 1). The latter treatise is missing from the original text of Fd. It was later added after the supplement containing second-recension texts by the scribe who wrote this supplement.[13] In Aa, the treatise does not follow directly upon C. 36, which ends in Admont 43 on fo. 198r. Instead it follows (fos. 198r–236v) the collection known as the *Collectio Admontensis*, before the *de consecratione* appears on fos. 237r–279v. Then comes (fos. 280r–340v) the supplement containing second-recension texts. The evidence of Fd alone allows the conclusion that the *de consecratione* was not included in the first recension, and the situation in Aa certainly points in the same direction. The *de penitentia*, on the other hand, is present in both Aa and Fd. The text is shorter than the text in Friedberg's edition, but all seven distinctions are represented.

SURVIVALS OF THE FIRST RECENSION IN SECOND-RECENSION MANUSCRIPTS

Since five manuscripts of the first recension are known to have survived, at least as fragments, it is clear that this text circulated but that the circulation remained limited. It is likely that it was relatively quickly supplanted by the second recension, which is found in hundreds of manuscripts. Some of these manuscripts contain, however, oddities which can be explained as survivals of the first recension. In the close reading in chapters 2 and 3, I pointed out such features in connection with determining the sources of C. 24, q. 1, c. 23 (for Br Je Mz), C. 24, q. 1, c. 26 (for In Me Sa Vd), C. 24, q. 2, c. 2 (for Br Cg Mz). Two further examples illustrate the point.

In at least seven second-recension manuscripts, canons 28 and 29 in C. 11, q. 3 are misplaced. In Mk and three other manuscripts, they follow after c. 30,[14] while in the original text of Mz and Br they are placed between c. 9 and c. 10.[15] In Pf, c. 30 appears twice, after c. 27 and after c. 29. The confusion is easy to understand when one considers the relation between the first and the second recension at this point. Canons 28

---

[13] Fd, fos. 168r–175v.

[14] Jacqueline Rambaud noted in her card file at the Bibliothèque Nationale de France that the canons appear in this order also in Evreux, Bibliothèque municipale 106, Paris, BN, lat. 3897 and Prague, Národní knihovna Ceské Republiky (formerly Universitní knihovna), L. I.

[15] Br is a copy of Mz, see Gero Dolezalek and Rudolf Weigand, "Das Geheimnis der roten Zeichen," *ZRG KA* 69 (1983), 181–186, Weigand, *Glossen zum "Dekret,"* 832, and Gujer, "Concordia," 302.

to 29 and 10 to 26 are missing in the first recension, where c. 9 is followed by c. 27, which immediately precedes c. 30. If a scribe incorporating canons 28 and 29 into the text placed them one canon too early, the resulting text would be that of Mz and Br. To place them one canon too late would result in the text of Mk. The scribe of Pf became sufficiently confused to transcribe c. 30 both after c. 27 (as in the first recension) and after c. 29 (as in the second recension).

A similar example is found in C. 1, q. 5, which in the second recension contains only three canons. The *questio* discusses whether a person who was simoniacally ordained may remain in sacred orders. Already the text of Friedberg's edition presents a peculiarity. The d. p. c. 2 begins by drawing the conclusion "from this authority,"[16] that ignorance of the fact may acquit a person for whom relatives simoniacally acquired an ecclesiastical office. The reference is in the singular and concerns clearly c. 1, which makes the distinction between those who do not know that they are guilty of simony and those who are not.[17] These circumstances by themselves make it tempting to suggest that c. 2 was added after the composition of d. p. c. 2. Further suspicion is aroused by Jacqueline Rambaud's report that c. 2 is placed before c. 1 in Paris, Bibliothèque Nationale, lat. 3888 (Pa).[18] The manuscripts of the first recension confirm that c. 2 was added only in the second recension.

The examples mentioned so far concern cases in which additions of entire canons or parts of canons are reflected in second-recension manuscripts because they have been misplaced. There are also many instances in which a few such manuscripts share a reading with the first-recension manuscripts and the formal source against the rest of the tradition. Several examples of this kind were mentioned earlier in this chapter.

In other instances, Gratian 2 cancelled a canon or a passage which appeared in the first recension, usually to avoid having the same text appear more than once.[19] Many second-recension manuscripts contain such canons. C. 2, q. 3 provides an example.[20] Canons 1 to 4 appear in both recensions but are in the first recension followed by a canon (I call it c. 4a) that was removed from the second recension. The reason for the removal was clearly that the canon contains the same text as c. 3. The inscriptions are, however, different: c. 3 is attributed to Pope Adrian I and

---

[16] Friedberg, ed., *Decretum*, 424: "Ex hac itaque auctoritate colligitur . . ."

[17] The d. p. c. 2 also echoes, on line 4, a phrase from c. 1, line 3: "postquam eas omnino dimiserint."

[18] Jacqueline Rambaud-Buhot, "Plan et méthode de travail pour la rédaction d'un catalogue des manuscrits du *Décret* de Gratien," *Revue d'histoire ecclésiastique* 48 (1953), 220.

[19] Several such places are mentioned by Rudolf Weigand, "Chancen und Probleme," 56–58.

[20] About the contents of this *questio*, see chapter 5.

c. 4a to Pope Fabian I. The true source for both was the *Lex Romana Visigothorum*, but the text in question was reproduced twice in the Pseudo-Isidorian forgeries and came to be attributed to Adrian and Fabian, respectively.

In preparing the second recension, Gratian 2 realized that it was not necessary to include this text twice, even if ascribed to different popes, so he cancelled one occurrence. Both texts can, however, be found in several second-recension manuscripts. I have found c. 4a in Gg Pa Pf Pk Pl. Friedberg found it in his manuscripts ADEGH. In her card file (at the Bibliothèque Nationale de France), Jacqueline Rambaud lists twelve further manuscripts containing c. 4a.

These survivals from the first recension suggest some important conclusions about the circulation of the texts of the two recensions of Gratian's *Decretum*, and about the creation of the second recension.

THE MAKING OF GRATIAN'S *DECRETUM*

The first recension of the *Decretum* was not a living text. It was a finished product which its author considered ready to be circulated. This is evident from its text, which is as much a finished and polished product as could be expected of any twelfth-century text. Further, it is also evident from the fact that the first recension survives in *one* version only; what differences there are among the manuscripts are all minor (the apparent exception of Aa will be discussed below). They are differences one would expect to find in any manuscript tradition, arising from scribal mistake or ingenuity. In other words, the manuscripts do not represent different stages in the development of the text, in the manner of "classically" living texts, such as the *Song of Roland*, where each different manuscript version has an equally valid claim to authenticity.

Four of the five manuscripts contain basically identical texts (except for the fact that none of these manuscripts preserves the complete text). The largest discrepancy between these four manuscripts that I have found concerns C. 1, q. 1, c. 105. The text of this canon and its rubric are missing in P while present in Aa Bc Fd. Its inscription (*Ex concilio Tiburicensi* P) is, however, present there, while instead the inscription of c. 106 is missing. If c. 105 in its entirety, including inscription, were missing, one might be inclined to suspect that P reflects an earlier stage in the composition of the first recension than do Bc and Fd (which both contain c. 105). However, the inscription is there, and the fact that the inscription of the following canon is missing suggests that the eye of the scribe had skipped. It is at first not obvious exactly how this happened (although eyeskips can happen for reasons that are far from obvious). If one takes into consideration that the rubrics are written by a scribe other than the one who wrote the text,[21] it becomes clear what the mistake of the latter was. When he had finished the inscription of c. 105, he left space for the rubric and continued with the canon itself. His exemplar would naturally have contained the rubrics, so when he looked for the text continuing after the rubric his eye skipped from the end of the rubric of c. 105 (. . . *aliquid exigi non debet*) to the end of the rubric of c. 106 (. . . *aliquid exigi debet*).

The Admont manuscript (Aa) may seem to contradict this, since its main text contains more canons than Bc Fd P Pfr. It could be argued that Aa represents the content the *Decretum* had in its author's workshop at a time somewhat later than that at which the text of Bc Fd P Pfr was circulated. However, such an argument would not take the unusual characteristics of Aa into account. The manuscript includes, in addition to several other legal texts, both a (longer than usual) text of the first recension and a supplement, containing the remaining canons and *dicta* which were added in the second recension. All these texts were written by the same hand (or at least by very similar hands using the characteristic writing of the Admont scriptorium) and clearly in one continuous effort. In Bc and Fd, the second-recension additions are written by hands different from the one that wrote the first recension (P and Pfr do not contain second-recension additions). This strongly suggests that what the original scribes had in front of them when copying out Bc and Fd was a manuscript of the first recension in which there were no additions (marginal or otherwise) of texts that are uniquely found in the second recension. The task of distinguishing between first- and second-recension readings in these manuscripts becomes, thus, a comparatively simple matter of distinguishing between different scribal hands. In the case of Aa, it is clear that the manuscript used by the original scribe already contained added second-recension texts. Hence, there is no paleographical basis for distinguishing texts belonging to different recensions in Aa. The only basis for such a distinction is the location of the text within the manuscript. It stands to reason that the texts found in the supplement belong only to the second recension, but it cannot be assumed that all texts in the main section of the manuscript belong to the first recension. Supposing that the exemplar of Aa, like Fd, contained second-recension texts in marginal additions as well as in the supplement, those additions would almost

---

[21] The hand writing the text is very similar to the one writing the rubrics (in red), so it is possible that they are in fact identical, which, however, does not affect the argument. It is obvious that text and rubrics were not written continuously, since the rubricator has often had to squeeze the rubric into the insufficient space left by the text-hand. The rubric of C. 1, q. 1, c. 106 is an example of this.

certainly, with what is known about the habits of medieval scribes, have been inserted into the text by a scribe transcribing the manuscript. It is likely that this explains why the first-recension text in Aa is longer than in the other manuscripts; Aa reflects a manuscript of the first recension which had been "updated" with additions in the margin and in a supplement to include all second-recension texts.

Another possible explanation is that the marginal additions in Aa's exemplar may reflect the first additions that Gratian made after having his text circulated in the form known from Bc Fd P Pfr. The text in the main section of Aa would then represent a recension that is intermediate between the first and the second recensions. A similar argument could be made about the marginal additions in Fd,[22] but not about both Aa and Fd, since the texts added in the margins of Fd are not the same as those added in the margins of Aa's exemplar. The hypothesis that the marginal additions in Aa's exemplar or in Fd reflect a distinct stage in the composition of the *Decretum* could only be true for one of those manuscripts, proving that the marginal additions in the other manuscript have nothing to do with the progress of the author's work. In this manuscript, the additions must simply bear witness to the needs of a user or owner of the manuscript. It is, in fact, not difficult to imagine why a user of a first-recension manuscript might have had some texts added in the margins and some in the supplement. If he, for example, was a student who arrived in Bologna with a copy of the first-recension *Decretum* owned by his home church,[23] he would quickly discover that his book contained a text that was incomplete in comparison with the second-recension text that his professor was lecturing from. To acquire a new and up-to-date copy of the *Decretum* would have been expensive, as would also the extra quires required to transcribe a supplement of the type found in Aa and Fd. It could make sense to add (or have a scribe add) the missing texts in the margin, as did an owner of Bc (occasionally supplying an extra leaf when the margins were not capacious enough). It could also make sense to transcribe provisionally in the margins a few texts in which the owner for some reason was particularly interested while waiting for the funds or time necessary to obtain a supplement containing all missing texts. It is also conceivable that the missing texts were added in the margins of the original manuscript after the inclusion of a deficient supplement. In other words, there are many possible reasons why a manuscript may have some additional texts in the margins and some in a supplement, even if

---

[22] Cf. Larrainzar, "El *decreto* de Graciano del códice Fd."

[23] About the wanderings of medieval law manuscripts, see Gero Dolezalek, *Repertorium manuscriptorum veterum Codicis Iustiniani*, Ius commune, Sonderhefte: Texte und Monographien 23: Repertorien zur Frühzeit der gelehrten Rechte (Frankfurt am Main 1985), 59.

we cannot expect to uncover the actual reason in most cases. We know with certainty that the additions in one of the two manuscripts Aa and Fd have nothing to do with the author's progress in his work, and we must query whether there is any reason to propose that the marginal additions in one of them in fact bear witness to a distinct stage in the composition of the *Decretum*. I have found no reason for such a proposition.

I know of no manuscript (beyond Aa) which contains a version of the *Decretum* that is longer than the first recension but shorter than the second and that could be an intermediate stage in the composition of the *Decretum*. There is, hence, no reason to imagine that the second recension came about in a piecemeal fashion. All second-recension manuscripts contain in general the same text, even though they can vary greatly and significantly in regard to textual details, as I have described above. These variations mainly concern dislocations of canons and additions of "extra" canons (and, later, the addition of *paleae*, but that topic is outside the scope of the present study). A closer study reveals that the variations are due to different interpretations of how the first recension should be expanded into the second recension. When extra canons (i.e. canons missing from Friedberg's edition) appear, those are canons which were present in the first recension but were cancelled in at least some second-recension manuscripts. These variations do not, therefore, testify to a living textual tradition in which new snippets of texts are gradually added; they are the result of different scribes and scholars making different choices when expanding first-recension texts into second-recension texts. In making those choices, however, they had a common pool of texts from which to choose. The subject is complicated and deserves to be treated in greater depth than I am able to do here, but the relationship between the manuscripts Aa and Me demonstrates my reasoning.

Aa and Me share many peculiarities, e.g. the introduction to the *Decretum* with the *incipit* "*Hoc opus inscribitur,*" which is found nowhere else, and a rare treatise on sacrilege.[24] A further peculiarity linking the two manuscripts together is the note written by the original scribe of Aa after C. 24, q. 3, c. 39: "Capitula que sic incipiunt, 'Firmissime tene,' require post primam causam et huic vicesime quarte cause in fine adiunge." This note instructs the scribe to move some chapters with the *incipit Firmissime tene* from their present place at the end of C. 1 to the end of C. 24. In Aa, C. 1 ends with a series of such chapters, so the scribe of Aa has not followed the instructions which he appears simply to have copied from his exemplar. In Me, on the other hand, C. 24 ends with

---

[24] Weigand, *Glossen zum "Dekret,"* 849, where further similarities are indicated, also in respect of the glosses found in the both manuscripts.

these chapters, which are not included in the normal text of the *Decretum* in either recension (nor, as far as I know, in any other manuscript of the *Decretum*). They are inscribed *Augustinus de fide ad Petrum*, and derive from a work by Fulgentius of Ruspe, which often was ascribed to Augustine.[25]

Rudolf Weigand rightly concluded that Aa and Me are probably copies of the same exemplar.[26] Aa was written in the 1160s or the 1170s in the monastery of Admont in Austrian Styria and in the diocese of Salzburg, while Me was produced in or close to Salzburg at approximately the same time. The scribe who copied out Aa followed the exemplar page by page, reproducing the arrangement with a main text and a supplement, and including the marginal instructions for how these texts should be joined together. The scribe of Me, on the other hand, followed these instructions and produced a second-recension text, although he was occasionally confused by his exemplar, as when, for instance, he divided C. 24, q. 1, c. 26 into two canons.[27] The evidence of Aa and Me clearly shows that a second-recension text was created in the diocese of Salzburg in the third quarter of the twelfth century by the scribe of Me copying out the original text and the additions of his exemplar as one continuous text. Similarly, the two different dislocations of C. 11, q. 3, canons 28 and 29 in Mz and in Mk, and the duplication of c. 30 in Pf strongly suggest that these three manuscripts testify to three independent occasions on which a continuous second-recension text was cobbled together on the basis of first-recension manuscripts with additions. Textual variants in other second-recension manuscripts (such as the dislocation of C. 1, q. 5, c. 2 in Pa) may attest to further separate occasions.

These observations allow a tentative understanding of the early history of the text of Gratian's *Decretum*. A number of first-recension manuscripts were in circulation when the second recension began to circulate. Owners of manuscripts containing the first recension encountering manuscripts of the second recension – or, perhaps, collections of only the additional material in this recension (the supplements in Aa and Fd might reflect such collections) – took care to incorporate the additional texts in their manuscripts. Bc and Fd represent two examples of how this may have been accomplished (by marginal additions and additional leaves). When copies were made of such manuscripts, the copyist was likely to insert the additions at what he thought was the appropriate place, thereby producing a continuous text of the second recension. It is only to be

---

[25] [Fulgentius of Ruspe], *Sancti Fulgentii episcopi Ruspensis opera*, ed. J. Fraipont and C. Lambot, Corpus Christianorum: Series latina 91A (Turnhout 1968), 744–760. These chapters are found, attributed to Augustine, in, e.g., Ivo's *Decretum* 1.4–44.

[26] Weigand, *Glossen zum "Dekret,"* 849.   [27] See above, chapter 2.

expected that different copyists would interpret their exemplars differently, creating the kind of variants that were described above. When these different versions of the second recension were copied, several different traditions of the text of the *Decretum* came into being, but these traditions soon intermingled, when manuscripts from one tradition were used to correct manuscripts from another. This explains why also the oldest textual tradition of the second recension is so confusingly rich in variants, a richness that for more than a century has haunted every attempt to improve on Emil Friedberg's edition of the *Decretum*.

This confusion does not, however, mean that there never was a single original of the second recension. The understanding of the complicated textual transmission that I outlined above sufficiently explains the variations among early second-recension manuscripts, which might otherwise be taken to suggest a tradition descending from multiple originals or a living text. It will be the unenviable and, I believe, frequently impossible task of the future editor of the second recension to reconstruct this original. The example of C. 11, q. 3, canons 28 and 29 illustrates the difficulty of this task. I pointed out above that these canons appear in different places in some twelfth-century manuscripts of the *Decretum*. Which place is the original one? These two canons state that anyone who communicates with an excommunicant is excommunicated. The same is stated in canons 3, 7, 10, 16, 17, 18, and 19 of C. 11, q. 3. While the context around canons 27 and 30 is far from inappropriate for canons 28 and 29, one could make a case that they would be as well if not better placed between canons 9 and 10, as they are in Mz and Br. The rationality of the arrangement of Mz and Br has to be weighed against the fact that most manuscripts contain the canons in their traditional order. Manuscripts are, however, to be weighed and not counted when judging the value of their texts. The number of manuscripts using the traditional order may simply reflect that this order by some accident of fate became the one used in the influential law schools of the twelfth century. On the other hand, it might be too much to ask of a medieval author to expect him to agree with the rationality that a modern scholar thinks he sees in a particular arrangement of the chapters.

The best approach for the future editor of the second recension might be to use manuscripts which were written in Bologna to reconstruct the earliest graspable Bolognese version of the text of Gratian 2. Supposing that Gratian 2 was actually active in Bologna, this text might be as close to his original text as it is possible to get. It was at any rate the textual tradition that came to dominate later in the middle ages and in modern editions, so this tradition is the historically most important one. I suspect that a future editor will find that the Bolognese text cancels most of the duplicate canons that appear in other manuscripts, and this seems a reasonably good indication that it descends directly from the original used by Gratian 2.[28]

DATE AND PLACE

The findings of this study re-open the debate about the date and place of the composition of the *Decretum*, which is currently believed to have been completed *circa* 1140 in Bologna. Below, I shall briefly outline the reasons why scholarship has arrived at this conclusion, before considering it anew in the context of the two recensions.[29] The earliest possible date of the text (as previously known) is 1139, since it contains legislation from the Second Lateran Council, which was celebrated in that year. The question of how long after 1139 Gratian completed his work was (temporarily) settled in 1956, when Gérard Fransen pointed out that the peculiar and sometimes awkward position in the *Decretum* of this legislation indicates that it was added at the last minute.[30] He took this to indicate that the work was finished shortly after 1139. Apart from these observations there is, as John Noonan has pointed out, no good evidence that it was finished before the early 1150s.[31] Further, in attempting to reconstruct the original form of the *Decretum*, Adam Vetulani argued a much earlier date for this version, which he thought was begun by 1105 (the year of the form letter in C. 2, q. 6, d. p. c. 31) and finished before the Concordat of Worms (1122).[32]

Scholars have seldom found reason to question the conventional wisdom that Gratian worked in Bologna, since the dominance of this city in the medieval teaching of law seems to exclude the possibility that he worked anywhere else.[33] The question will here be considered without prejudice, since arguments based on later developments easily mislead. Considering, for example, the dominance of Paris in the medieval teaching of theology, who would have guessed that essential groundwork was performed in Laon in the early twelfth century?[34]

My results come very close to confirming Vetulani's hypothesis about the date of the original form of the *Decretum*, since the first recension contains no text which may be confidently dated after 1119. In one of

---

[28] Differently Weigand, "Versuch einer Liste der Paleae."

[29] The seminal study on the date of the *Decretum* was Paul Fournier, "Deux controverses sur les origines du *Décret* de Gratien," *Revue d'histoire et de littérature religieuses* 3 (1898), 97–116 and 253–280, reprinted in Paul Fournier, *Mélanges de droit canonique*, ed. Theo Kölzer (Aalen 1983) I 751–797.

[30] Fransen, "La date du *Décret* de Gratien," 529.   [31] Noonan, "Gratian slept here," 159.

[32] Vetulani, "Nouvelles vues," 100.   [33] Noonan, "Gratian slept here," 161–162.

[34] Southern, *Scholastic Humanism*, 199–200, discusses the reasons for Laon's decline and for the ascendancy of Paris.

his *dicta* in the first recension (D. 63, d. p. c. 34), Gratian 1 refers, however, to a decision of the Second Lateran Council. This passage comes at the end of the discussion of episcopal elections by Gratian 1. He has established that the laity has no role in the elections and is in the process of investigating whether clerics other than the canons of the cathedral may participate. After citing two ancient conciliar canons prohibiting this, he continues:

> Nunc autem sicut electio summi pontificis non a cardinalibus tantum immo etiam ab aliis religiosis clericis auctoritate Nicholai pape est facienda, ita et episcoporum electio non a canonicis tantum set etiam ab aliis religiosis clericis, sicut in generali sinodo Innocentii pape Rome habita constitutum est. Nunc ergo queritur . . .[35]

> [And now, just as the election of the supreme pontiff is not to be performed by the cardinals alone but also by other religious clerics, by the authority of Pope Nicholas, so is the election of bishops not to be performed only by the canons, but also by religious clerics, as was determined in the general synod of Pope Innocent held in Rome.]

There can be no doubt that Gratian 1's reference concerns canon 28 of the council celebrated in 1139.[36] In the second recension, the legislative text in question was inserted after *constitutum est*.

No other canon from this council has left any discernible impact on the first recension,[37] and it is not certain that any of the important canons from the First Lateran Council of 1123 did so either.[38] Two texts deriving from decretals by Innocent II are likewise absent from the first recension: C. 2 q. 5 c. 17 and C. 35 q. 6 c. 8. This is odd if we assume that Gratian worked after 1139. Some of the canons from these councils would have substantially changed the direction of some of Gratian's arguments, had he taken them into account.[39] The possibility that the reference in D. 63, d. p. c. 34 was a later addition not found in his original work must, therefore, be tested.

It is, in fact, possible to argue, on the basis of interior criteria, that the passage was interpolated at some later point. The syntax would not suffer

---

[35] Edited on the basis of Aa Bc Fd P, and Friedberg's edition, following the spelling of Fd.

[36] *COD* 203.

[37] The following canons containing legislation from the Second Lateran Council are absent from the first recension: D. 28 c. 2; D. 60 c. 3; D. 63 c 35; D. 90 c. 11; C. 1 q. 3 c. 15; C. 8 q. 1 c. 7; C. 17 q. 4 c. 29; C. 18 q 2 c 25; C. 21 q. 2 c. 5; C. 21 q. 4 c. 5; C. 23 q. 8 c. 32; C. 27 q. 1 c. 40; de pen. D. 5 c. 8.

[38] The following canons containing legislation from the First Lateran Council are absent from the first recension: D. 62, c. 3; C. 1 q. 1 c. 10; C. 10 q. 1 c. 14; C. 12 q. 2 c. 4; C. 12 q. 2 c. 37; C. 16 q. 1 c. 10; C. 16 q. 7 c. 11; C. 16 q. 7 c. 25; C. 18 q. 2 c. 31; C. 24 q. 3 c. 23; C. 24 q. 3 c. 24. About the remaining three canons ascribed by Friedberg to this council, see below.

[39] See Noonan, "Gratian slept here," 160, for an example.

if the phrase *sicut . . . est* were absent, nor would the sense of the passage. Read without this phrase, the *dictum* establishes that the *religiosi clerici* should participate in an episcopal election in analogy with Nicholas II's statement about their role in a papal election.[40] The presence of the problematic passage in all four manuscripts of the first recension containing D. 63 is, however, strong evidence that the passage is authentic (although it remains possible that their archetype was interpolated).

In discussing the possibility that the reference to the Second Lateran Council is an interpolation, the exact meaning of such a statement should be considered. It is clear that the text of the first recension as it survives in the manuscripts cannot have been written before 1139. It is certainly possible to discern likely or at least possible stages in the composition of the text. Titus Lenherr has already pointed out that the composition of C. 24, q. 1 began with the canons extracted from the *Panormia* and then continued with those extracted from the *Polycarpus*. I have found no reason to contradict these conclusions, which I have shown are valid for the whole of C. 24. Likewise, few scholars are likely to dispute that the reference to the Second Lateran Council in D. 63, d. p. c. 34, has the appearance of being something that was included into the text at a late stage. The question whether or not it is interpolated hinges on whether the reference was added by Gratian 1 at a late stage of his work, or at a stage when the text had been completed, i.e., when it had begun to circulate. In the former case, the insertion would have been made by Gratian 1 himself; in the latter it might have been another person's gloss that has intruded into the text. The evidence about the circulation of a medieval text is to be found in the manuscripts, and in this case the manuscripts are unanimous: the reference is found in every manuscript that I have examined. In addition to four first-recension manuscripts, I have examined a large number of second-recension manuscripts, since it is possible that some of them may have left the reference out if it was not an original part of the text; as I have shown above, several second-recension manuscripts preserve details of the first recension. In other words, the evidence indicates that the reference to the Second Lateran Council was present in Gratian 1's completed text when it began to circulate.

It is certainly possible to argue that a hypothetical earlier version of the first recension excluded the reference to the Second Lateran Council. Such a version could have been composed as early as the 1120s. However, we can know very little about exactly what such a hypothetical version

---

[40] Weigand, "Das kirchliche Wahlrecht," 1343. Gratian's citation of Pope Nicholas does not refer to the famous papal election decree in D. 23, c. 1 (as Friedberg indicates in note 377), which does not mention the role of religious clerics, but to D. 79, c. 1.

would have contained, since any number of other passages could also have been later additions or interpolations. Hence, to say that an earlier version of the first recension was composed in the 1120s becomes pointless. The only text we know of the first recension is the one found in the manuscripts, and that text could not have been completed before 1139. The manuscript tradition strongly suggests that this was the first version to circulate. It is, therefore, likely that one and the same author (Gratian 1) was responsible for its text in its entirety, including all of D. 63, d. p. c. 34.

It remains to explain why Gratian 1 did not cite any other canon from the Second Lateran Council nor, indeed, any other text that can be safely dated after 1119.[41] The formulation of this problem reflects an approach which is common among historians of canon law, who tend to assume that a medieval canonist would, in general, be as interested in recent legislation as a modern lawyer is. Even without citing Fritz Kern's familiar *dictum* that "old law" was "good law" in the middle ages, there is much to contradict this assumption. The canonical collection known as the *Polycarpus* provides a relevant example. It was compiled at some point after 1111 by Gregory of St. Grisogono, who had been made cardinal by Pope Paschal II. Yet the *Polycarpus* includes only one letter issued by this pope, and one issued by his immediate predecessor Urban II.[42] The omission of most recent legislation by Gratian 1 is clearly not unprecedented and cannot be used as an argument against dating the first recension after 1139. It is, therefore, reasonable to conclude that he finished the work in 1139 or slightly later, possibly after having composed most of the text before becoming aware of the decisions of 1139.

The second most recent component in the first recension may seem to be three canons from the First Lateran Council of 1123 (D. 27, c. 8, D. 60, c. 2, and C. 16, q. 4, c. 1), but closer scrutiny reveals that none of them derives necessarily from the legislation of that council. Gratian 1 inscribed D. 27, c. 8 *Item Calixtus Papa*. A differently formulated canon with the same substance constitutes c. 7 of the First Lateran Council, which is identical to a canon found, as Friedberg notes, among the texts of the council celebrated by Calixtus II at Reims in October 1119.[43] It

---

[41] Cf. Werckmeister, "Les études sur le *Décret* de Gratien."

[42] Horst, *Polycarpus*, 222 and 226. J. T. Gilchrist pointed out that JL 6607 is not a letter of Paschal's, see J. T. Gilchrist, "Die *Epistola Widonis* oder Pseudo-Paschalis: Der erweiterte Text," *Deutsches Archiv für Erforschung des Mittelalters* 37 (1981), 581, note 17. Brett, "Urban and Ivo," 29–31, pursued a similar argument in discussing the date of the collections of Ivo of Chartres.

[43] *COD* 191. For the council of Rheims, see Robert Somerville, "The councils of Pope Calixtus II: Reims 1119," in *Proceedings of the Fifth International Congress of Medieval Canon Law*, MIC Subs. 6 (Vatican City 1980), 35–50, repr. in Robert Somerville, *Papacy, Councils, and Canon Law in the 11th–12th Centuries*, CS 312 (Aldershot 1990), no. XII, and Mansi, *Amplissima collectio*, XXI 235. Cf. JL, p. 787. It was common that subsequent councils issued identical canons.

is tempting to identify Gratian's text with this canon, despite the lack of correspondence in expression. The text of D. 27, c. 8 cannot, in any case, be securely dated later than 1119. Gratian 1 inscribed also D. 60, c. 2 *Item Calixtus Papa*[44] and Friedberg identifies it with canon 6 from the First Lateran Council of 1123. An identical canon survives also from the council of Toulouse celebrated by Calixtus in July of 1119.[45] The text cannot, hence, be securely dated later than 1119.

The third text which Friedberg attributes to the First Lateran Council is C. 16, q. 4, c. 1. Gratian, however, inscribes the canon *Quod Urbanus II. prohibuit, dicens.*[46] The text corresponds to the second sentence of c. 19 in the standard edition of the legislation of the First Lateran Council.[47] It is absent, however, from many manuscripts of this council's canons. The same is true for some other canons traditionally attributed to this council but ascribed to Urban II by Gratian. These canons may very well be Urban's and not Calixtus'.[48] In any case, the confusion surrounding these canons prevents us from unequivocally dating C. 16, q. 4, c. 1 to 1123. Thus D. 27, c. 8 and D. 60, c. 2 remain the most recent datable texts in the first recension. The other canons which Friedberg attributed to the First Lateran Council are missing in the first recension.

The earliest possible date for the completion of the first recension is, hence, 1139. Which is its latest possible date? There are no datable early references to the first recension, so we can only say that it pre-dated the second recension. When was the second recension compiled? It is no longer possible to argue that it must have been completed *shortly* after 1139. That argument was based on the fact that the legislation of 1139 is not intellectually absorbed into the arguments, but I have shown that this is the case for almost all the additions of the second recension. Instead, we must look for the earliest datable quotation of the *Decretum*.

Stephan Kuttner gave 1144 as the date before which the *Decretum* (i.e. the second recension) must have been completed.[49] This date is based on a manuscript of the *Collectio Caesaraugustana*, which under the heading *Excepcio ex decretis Graciani* contains the text of C. 16, q. 1, d. p. c. 41 § 1 – d. p. c. 45, written by the original scribe of the manuscript. This passage is already found in the first recension, so its appearance in this work cannot be used to date the second recension. More importantly, the dating of the manuscript to 1144 is questionable. It derives from a list of French kings

---

[44] Friedberg, ed., *Decretum*, 226, supported by Fd.

[45] *COD* 190. For the council at Toulouse, see Mansi, *Amplissima collectio*, XXI 226. Cf. JL, pp. 783–784.   [46] Friedberg, ed., *Decretum*, 796, supported by Aa (om. *dicens*) Fd Mz.

[47] *COD* 194.

[48] Cf. Gossman, *Pope Urban II and Canon Law*, and Martin Brett, "The canons of the First Lateran Council in English manuscripts," *Proceedings of the Sixth International Congress of Medieval Canon Law* (MIC Subs. 7; Vatican City 1985), 20–21.   [49] Kuttner, "Research on Gratian," 19.

included therein. Louis VII (king from 1137 to 1180) is said to have reigned for seven years. However, the same information is given in two other manuscripts of the *Caesaraugustana*. It is, as Linda Fowler-Magerl has pointed out, unlikely that all three manuscripts were transcribed in the same year.[50] They probably descend from a common archetype transcribed in 1144 but seem themselves to have been written after 1148, since at least the Paris and Vatican manuscripts contain the canons of the Council of Rheims, which was celebrated in this year.[51] The appearance of the excerpt from the *Decretum* is, hence, of no use for dating purposes.

The works of the early decretists may provide a date before which the second recension must have been completed. Unfortunately, they are difficult to date. They were long dated too early, due to the mistaken identification of the canonist Roland with another Roland, who in 1159 became Pope Alexander III.[52] Since the works of many decretists can only be relatively dated in comparison with other decretists' works, this mistake caused entire chains of authors to be misdated. The earliest *summa* is that written by Paucapalea, which contains references to texts added to the *Decretum* only in the second recension.[53] Paucapalea's work must have been written after 1146 and before the composition of Roland's *Stroma*, which in turn was composed before the *Summa* of Rufinus. For the latter work, there is a relatively safe date: 1164.[54] How much earlier Paucapalea's *Summa* was written is open for discussion. Rudolf Weigand suggested that Paucapalea probably worked at some point between 1146 and the early 1150s.[55] This is a reasonable assumption, but it remains possible that the date should be later.

The earliest abbreviation of the *Decretum* is probably the work with the *incipit Quoniam egestas*.[56] Rudolf Weigand suggested that this work, which

---

[50] Linda Fowler-Magerl, "Vier französische und spanische vorgratianische Kanonessammlungen," in *Aspekte europäischer Rechtsgeschichte: Festgabe für Helmut Coing zum 70. Geburtstag* (Frankfurt am Main 1982), 145–146.

[51] Martin Brett, "Sources and influence." Cf. Robert Somerville, "Baluziana," *Annuarium Historiae Conciliorum* 5 (1973), 428, repr. in Somerville, *Papacy, Councils, and Canon Law in the 11th–12th Centuries*, no. XIX (for the Paris manuscript).

[52] The mistake was discovered by John T. Noonan, "Who was Rolandus?," in *Law, Church, and Society: Essays in Honor of Stephan Kuttner*, ed. Kenneth Pennington and Robert Somerville (Philadelphia 1977), 21–48. Cf. Rudolf Weigand, "Magister Rolandus und Papst Alexander III," *AKKR* 149 (1980), 3–44.

[53] Paucapalea discusses, e.g., the following second-recension texts: C. 2, q. 6, c. 31; C. 24, q. 1, canons 10 and 21; C. 24, q. 3, c. 10. C. 29, q. 2, c. 2. See Paucapalea, *Summa über das "Decretum Gratiani."* A new edition of Paucapalea's commentary on C. 24, q. 1, based on two Munich manuscripts, is provided by Lenherr, *Exkommunikationsgewalt*, 264–266.

[54] Weigand, "Frühe Kanonisten," and Weigand, "Magister Rolandus," 10–11 and 20.

[55] Weigand, "Frühe Kanonisten," 136.

[56] Rudolf Weigand, "Die Dekretabbreviatio 'Quoniam egestas' und ihre Glossen," in *Fides et ius: Festschrift für Georg May zum 65. Geburtstag* (Regensburg 1991), 256.

draws on the second recension, was composed in 1150, since this date appears in the model letter in C. 2, q. 6, d. p. c. 31. However, there is no reason to presume that the unknown abbreviator would necessarily have written the year in which he was working (cf. below), so the date must be considered uncertain.

The earliest unassailable date before which the second recension must have been completed is when the Parisian theologian Peter Lombard quoted the second recension of the *Decretum* in his *Sentences*. This work can be securely dated to the period between 1155 and 1158. The latest editors thought that the Lombard compiled the work while lecturing on it during two academic years 1155 to 1157, completing one of the four books during each of the four semesters.[57] Since quotations from the *Decretum* only appear at the end of the third book and in the fourth book, this would mean that the second recension was known in Paris by the autumn of 1156. It was at any rate known there by 1158, which is the earliest absolutely certain date before which the second recension of Gratian's *Decretum* must have been completed.

In the context of dating the *Decretum*, several scholars have discussed C. 2, q. 6, d. p. c. 31, which contains standard forms for judicial appeals. It should be noted that the *dictum* is shorter in the first recension, where the first form letter is absent (*Forma apostolorum – apostolis dimitto*). Interestingly, the missing letter is the only one in this *dictum* which is attributed to the bishop of Bologna. Its presence in the *Decretum* is the only really good piece of internal evidence that points to Bologna as the place of composition.[58] Only one of the forms is dated: "pridie Kal. Magi A. incarnationis Domini MCV, feria quarta"[59] ("Wednesday, April 30, 1105"). Vetulani seized upon this date and explained that this was when Gratian began his work.[60] But Gratian could hardly be referring to an actual date, since April 30 in 1105 was not a Wednesday.[61] Moreover,

---

[57] [Peter Lombard], *Sententiae*, Tom. I, Pars I, 122*-129* and Tom. II 18*-19*.

[58] Bologna is perhaps referred to later in C. 2, q. 6, d. p. c. 31, where two persons are said to be *canonicorum S. B. E.* (so also in the first recension as evidenced by Bc, Fd, and P). The acronym is usually interpreted *sanctae Bononiensis ecclesiae*, but this is not necessarily the correct expansion. The only other mention of Bologna is in C. 16, q. 1, c. 9 (cf. Reuter and Silagi, *Wortkonkordanz*, 442), which reproduces a decretal sent by Pope Paschal II to the bishop of Bologna, but this canon is also absent from the first recension.

[59] This is clearly the original reading, since it is found in all four manuscripts of the first recensions (Aa Bc Fd P) as well as in most manuscripts of the second recension. Friedberg prints this date (col. 478), while the Roman edition gave the year as "MCLI". Among some 150 early manuscripts Rudolf Weigand found only eight with a different date, see his review of *Sur Gratien et les décrétales*, by Adam Vetulani.

[60] Vetulani, "Nouvelles vues," 95, and Adam Vetulani, "Le *Décret* de Gratien et les premier décrétistes à la lumière d'une source nouvelle," *Studia Gratiana* 8 (Bologna 1959), 332–333; reprinted in Vetulani, *Sur Gratien et les décretales*, no. VIII.

[61] Fournier, "Deux controverses," 783.

there is no particular reason to assume that he would choose the day (or the year) on which he was composing this form letter. Could Gratian 1 not have taken these standard forms, including the dates, from a collection of such texts? After all, Bologna was in the twelfth century the leading center for the teaching of the *ars dictaminis*.

In fact, the forms in C. 2, q. 6, d. p. c. 34 have interesting affinities with one product of the rhetorical school of Bologna. In the *Decretum*, Adelmus, bishop of Reggio Emilia, appeals against the sentence of Archbishop Walter of Ravenna. In a collection of model letters, apparently coming from Bologna, there is a letter from "A.," bishop of Reggio Emilia to Cardinal John of St. Grisogono, in which the bishop complains about the (unnamed) archbishop of Ravenna, who has imposed a sentence of excommunication on him.[62] The collection also contains the cardinal's reply. It is reasonable to assume that Gratian's standard forms and these two model letters refer to the same controversy. The collection of model letters is preserved in a thirteenth-century manuscript, but many of the letters contain names of persons active in the early twelfth century (including, e.g., the papal chancellor, Cardinal Haimeric), which suggests that the collection was composed at this time. Cardinal John signed papal documents from 1118 to January 1134,[63] which leads one to conclude that "A." really refers to Adelmus, who was bishop of Reggio Emilia at least between 1123 and 1150.[64] In the *Italia pontificia*, Paul Kehr furnishes the letter of Cardinal John (but not the appeal form of the *Decretum*) with a *crux*, indicating that it is fictitious.[65] He supports this by saying that the letters in this collection were composed for the use of students. However, collections of form letters usually contained actual letters, which have been more or less gutted of specifics such as dates and names,[66] so Kehr's verdict is not unassailable.

It seems clear that the school of *ars dictaminis* in Bologna used Adelmus' appeal to the pope against his metropolitan's sentence of excommunication as an example in the teaching of letter writing, whether or not this appeal was a historical fact. It does not seem to be a coincidence that Gratian used the same example. This may, on balance, be the best

---

[62] Wilhelm Wattenbach, "Iter Austriacum 1853," *Archiv für Kunde österreichischer Geschichts-Quellen* 14 (1855), 81–82.

[63] Rudolf Hüls, *Kardinäle, Klerus und Kirchen Roms 1049–1130*, Bibliothek des Deutschen Historischen Instituts in Rom 48 (Tübingen 1977), 176–178, and JL 7643 = Paul Kehr, *Italia pontificia*, VI 305. Cf. Gerhard Schwartz, *Die Besetzung der Bistümer Reichsitaliens unter den sächsischen und salischen Kaisern mit den Listen der Bischöfe 951–1122* (Leipzig and Berlin 1913), 199.

[64] Noonan, "Gratian slept here," 161, Ughelli, *Italia sacra*, II 288–291.

[65] Kehr, *Italia pontificia*, V 367.

[66] Olivier Guyotjeannin, Jacques Pycke, and Benoît-Michel Tock, *Diplomatique médiévale*, L'atelier du médiéviste 2 (Turnhout 1993), 230.

evidence for placing the composition of the first recension of the *Decretum* in Bologna. The composition of the second recension also took place, most probably, in Bologna. Already the added model letter in C. 2, q. 6, d. p. c. 31, issued by Henry, who was bishop of Bologna from 1130 to the 1140s,[67] suggests this location. The inclusion of a large number of extracts from the sources of Roman law also points to Bologna with its Roman law school.

The preceding paragraphs have strongly suggested that both recensions of the *Decretum* were completed in Bologna within the comparatively short timespan between 1139 and, at the very latest, 1158. These findings illuminate in interesting ways the beginnings of Bolognese teaching of canon law. Systematic teaching of canon law is barely imaginable before the composition of (the first recension of) the *Decretum*. No previous collection was particularly suitable for teaching canonistic doctrine, and there is no other evidence for any earlier teaching even approaching the level of sophistication reached by Gratian. This is dissimilar to the gradual growth of other scholastic disciplines in the twelfth century. In theology, for example, the *Sentences* of Gratian's younger contemporary Peter Lombard played a role similar to that of the *Decretum* in canon law. Unlike Gratian, the Lombard succeeded a long line of masters who had prepared the way for his synthesis. This is not to say that Gratian had no predecessors in reforming the hermeneutics of canon law. The names of Ivo of Chartres and Alger of Liège are often mentioned in this context, and rightly so, for their work clearly contributed to Gratian's methods. Ivo's contribution was, however, purely theoretical, and Alger's concerned a limited problem, so neither of them could serve as a model for creating a synthesis such as the *Decretum*. There is no evidence, and it is unlikely, that either of them was engaged in teaching canon law. It was Gratian who, by composing the *Decretum*, created the systematic study of canon law.

The first recension shows how he conceived of his subject. This original version is much more clearly a teaching text than the second recension. The ratio of commentary (*dicta*) to law text (canons) is substantially greater than in the second recension, demonstrating the didactic purpose of the work. There are also differences between the two recensions concerning the understanding of what constitutes the subject matter of canon law. In the first recension, Gratian did without the sacramental law later found in the *de consecratione*. Roman law had only a marginal place and some of the passages in which Gratian used romanistic concepts are

---

[67] Kehr, *Italia pontificia*, v 250, Noonan, "Gratian slept here," 161, and Ughelli, *Italia sacra*, II 18. Ughelli indicates that Henry died in 1145.

so amateurishly conceived that it was considered necessary to emend them for the second recension, which also bolstered or adjusted some of his arguments with the help of almost 200 extracts from Roman law. That this happened such a short time after the completion of Gratian's original work shows how fast the understanding of Roman law developed in the Bolognese canon law school of the middle of the twelfth century. The teaching of purely canonistic subjects also soon found the range of law texts provided by Gratian too small and many hundreds of new canonistic texts were added. A ten- or fifteen-year-old text book was already deemed so insufficient that the radical step was taken of doubling its size.

Everything points to a discipline in quick, almost revolutionary expansion, which in less than ten years outgrew the work that had formed it. Gratian's *Decretum* and the canon law schools obviously filled a deeply felt need for legal structure in a rapidly evolving society of increasing complexity. The continued growth during the second half of the twelfth century was no less impressive, but the scholars and teachers of canon law then found ways of incorporating new interpretative or legislative developments other than adding new texts to an existing text book. The margins of legal manuscripts became occupied with ever growing and ever more sophisticated commentaries, which absorbed the tenets of Roman law not by reproducing its texts but by constantly and specifically referring to its law books. Papal government became, particularly from the pontificate of Alexander III (1159–1181), more complex, ambitious, and bureaucratic, creating a new case law through the increasing number of legal cases decided in the pope's court. Canon law scholars collected this case law in so-called decretal collections forming, as it were, supplements to the *Decretum* of growing importance. These processes culminated in the definitive commentary on the *Decretum*, the *Glossa ordinaria* completed around 1215 by the Bolognese canonist Johannes Teutonicus, and in the definitive (for the time being) decretal collection promulgated by Pope Gregory IX in 1234, the so-called *Liber extra*. Within a century of its creation, the discipline of canon law had achieved a sophistication, a complexity and a level of technicality which would have seemed foreign to Gratian.

The first step in this fundamental transformation of canon law was the second recension of the *Decretum*. Was it Gratian himself who took this step or was it taken by others after the work had left his hands? In the following chapters, I shall argue that the second recension represents an attempt by Gratian's successors to bring their basic teaching text up to date with the developments in their discipline.

Chapter 5

GRATIAN AND ROMAN LAW

Gratian's use of Roman law has been much discussed in modern scholarship. The debate began in 1947 when Adam Vetulani argued that most texts in the *Decretum* deriving from Justinianic Roman law had been added after the completion of Gratian's work.[1] Only those romanistic texts that were available in earlier canonical collections would have been included in Gratian's original work. These conclusions were quickly accepted. In 1953, Stephan Kuttner retraced and expanded Vetulani's arguments and identified forty-six passages in the *Decretum* as late additions to the text.[2] His list was, with one or two exceptions, identical to Vetulani's.

This book confirms the general thrust of their work. All but three of the forty-six passages are absent from the first recension. One of the three exceptions is C. 2, q. 6, c. 28, which is the only Novel that the *Decretum* quotes directly from the *Authenticum*, rather than from the *authenticae* of Justinian's *Code*.[3] Vetulani suggested that this text was taken from some hypothetical intermediate collection, implying that it was part of Gratian's original composition.[4] Kuttner was not convinced by this reasoning; he included the text in his list of additions to the *Decretum*.[5] The presence of this text in the first recension indicates that Vetulani was right. The other two exceptions are C. 15, q. 3, canons 1 to 3 and canon

---

[1] Vetulani, "Gratien et le droit romain." A summary of the present chapter appears in Anders Winroth, "Les deux Gratiens et le droit romain," *RDC* 48: 2 (1998).

[2] Kuttner, "New studies on the Roman law."

[3] The *Authenticum* was a collection of Latin texts of imperial laws (*novellae*) collected after the publication of Justinian's *Code*. In the early twelfth century summaries of some of these laws were entered in the margins of manuscripts of the *Code*. These summaries are called *authenticae*.

[4] Adam Vetulani, "Une suite d'études pour servir à l'histoire du *Décret* de Gratien, II. Les *Nouvelles* de Justinien dans le *Décret de Gratien*," *Revue historique de droit français et étranger* 4: 16 (1937), 476–478, reprinted in Vetulani, *Sur Gratien et les décrétales*, no. II. Cf. Vetulani, "Gratien et le droit Romain," 19 and 42.   [5] Kuttner, "New studies on the Roman law," 33.

4, containing several fragments of Roman law, which appear to have been drawn directly from Justinian's *corpus*. I will analyze this *questio* in detail below.

While most scholars agree with Vetulani's findings as described above, there is no consensus about how to interpret them. Vetulani himself suggested that Gratian's motives for excluding Roman law from his original composition were ideological and political.[6] In his view, someone other than Gratian was responsible for eventually adding the romanistic material.[7] Most other scholars, however, remain unconvinced, although usually without offering an alternative interpretation.[8]

The discovery of the first recension provides an opportunity to reexamine this problem, particularly since it is now possible to study in detail the use of Roman law by Gratian 1 in the original *Decretum*. Such a study shows that he can by no means be said to have avoided this law, but that his grasp of its principles and technicalities was poor, at least as compared to the standards of the later twelfth century. Gratian 2 saw it necessary to reformulate a couple of the *dicta* of Gratian 1 which had romanistic content.

In order to explain why Gratian 1 had a poor grasp of Roman law and why he did not use Roman law wherever it would have been useful, I pose the question: how well versed in Roman law could a canonist in the time of Gratian 1 be expected to be? Vetulani and other scholars who have discussed this problem implicitly assume that the science of Roman law by Gratian's time was so advanced that the lack of such law in the original version of the *Decretum* must depend on a conscious choice on the part of its author. Such explanations fail, as Stephan Kuttner among others has pointed out, to account for the fact that the original composition contained numerous fragments of Roman law deriving from canonical collections.[9] I shall suggest that Gratian 1 used just as much Roman law in the first recension as he was capable of. His inexpert efforts when he employed romanistic doctrines and texts indicate that he simply was not familiar with this legal system. How is this possible if the study and teaching of Roman law flourished in Bologna when he wrote the *Decretum*? A scrutiny of the relevant historiography shows that the view that Roman law teaching flourished in Bologna in the first decades of the twelfth century is not supported by the sources. I argue that this teaching developed more slowly than was previously thought and that Gratian

---

[6] Vetulani, "Le *Décret* de Gratien," 337–339.
[7] Stanley Chodorow suggested a variant of this interpretation; see *Christian Political Theory and Church Politics in the Mid-Twelfth Century*, Publications of the Center for Medieval and Renaissance Studies, UCLA 5 (Berkeley 1972), 60–64.   [8] See, e.g., Kuttner, "Research on Gratian," 20–21.
[9] *Ibid.*, 20.

1's ignorance of Roman law is in fact to be expected. It should not be seen as an anomaly in need of explanation, but rather as evidence for the current state of legal teaching in Bologna, although the canonist Gratian 1 should, naturally, not be expected to be as well acquainted with Roman law as his colleagues who specialized in that law.

ROMAN LAW IN THE FIRST RECENSION

I have chosen to study the use of Roman law in three passages in the *Decretum*. In two of them, the author of the second recension changed the wording of *dicta* in which Gratian 1 had used romanistic concepts. In the third example, Gratian 1 did not employ any Justinianic texts or concepts in the first recension, while Gratian 2 introduced much material of this type, changing the force of the *questio* substantially.

Restitution to prior condition

In C. 3, q. 1, Gratian 1 discussed the case of a bishop who had been forced to leave his see, and he asked whether the bishop should be restored to the see before he could be tried for a crime. He answered the question affirmatively, supporting his case with Pseudo-Isidorian texts. The right of clerics to be reinstated in their prior condition before being subject to a trial (the so-called *exceptio spolii*) was one of the main points of law that the Pseudo-Isidorian forgers wanted to establish.[10] Their inspiration came from the *restitutio in integrum* of Roman law, which provided that a judge could order that a thing which a person had lost in an inequitable way should be restored to him.

Since in the first recension Gratian 1 treated this issue on the basis of Pseudo-Isidorian texts which depended on vulgar and pre-Justinianic Roman law, it is to be expected that a later generation, schooled in the doctrines of the Justinianic corpus, would find wanting the arguments put forward by Gratian 1. Already Gratian 2 seems to have done so, since he replaced two *dicta* of Gratian 1, in whole or in part, with new *dicta*. I shall here concentrate on the first of these, d. p. c. 2, which in the first recension reads as follows:[11]

Sed notandum est quod restitutio alia fit per presentiam*a* iudicis, veluti cum dicitur a iudice: "Censeo te in integrum restituendum", qua*b* restitutione*c* animo tantum, non corpore possessio recipitur. Alia fit per*d* executorem*d* iudicis quando

---

[10] Fuhrmann, *Einfluß und Verbreitung*, 42–44.
[11] For the changes in d. p. c. 6, which do not involve Roman law, see chapter 6.

restitutus corporalem recipit possessionem. Queritur*ᵉ* ergo que*ᶠ* harum*ᶠ* concedatur expoliatis, an illa tantum, que fit per sententiam*ᵍ* iudicis, an illa etiam que fit per executorem*ʰ* sentencie, qua expoliatis presentialiter omnia reciduntur*ⁱ*. Hec ultima expoliatis prestanda est.

a presentiam *Aa Bc Fd P*   *b* qua *Bc P:* quam *Aa:* quia *Fd*   *c* restitutione *Bc P:* restitutionem *Aa:* restitutione *ex* restitutionis *corr. Fd (ut vid.)*   *d* per executorem *Aa Bc P:* executione *Fd*   *e* queritur *Aa Bc:* quare *P:* qr *Fd*   *f* que harum *Aa Bc Fd:* quare *P*   *g* sentientiam *Aa Bc Fd:* presentiam *P*   *h* executorem *Aa Bc P:* in executionem *corr. Fd*   *i* reciduntur *Aa Bc P:* reconduntur *ex* reddi (*ex* recidi *corr.*) precipiuntur *corr. Fd*

[But it should be noted that restitution of one kind is achieved through the presence of a judge, as when he says: "I decree that you are to be restored to your prior condition." By this restitution, possession is received solely *animo* but not *corpore*. Another kind of restitution is through the executor of the judge, when the restored person receives corporal (*corporalem*) possession. It is thus inquired which of these is conceded to a despoiled person, if it is only that which is done through the sentence of the judge, or if it is also that which is done through the executor of the sentence, by which [procedure] everything is handed over *presentialiter* to the despoiled person.]

In the second recension this text was changed into:

But it should be noted that the sentence of restitution in itself does not suffice, unless everything is restored *presentialiter* through the office of the judge, in order that the ejected or despoiled person may receive also the actual (*naturalem*) possession, either *animo suo* and *corpore alieno*, for instance through a procurator, or *animo et corpore suo*. And everything, which had been taken away from him on any conditions, is to be returned to the place, from which it had been snatched away.[12]

Why was the *dictum* changed in the second recension? In relation to the question under consideration, both versions say essentially the same thing: the sentence that everything should be restored is not enough by itself; it has to be executed and the lost property (the episcopal see) actually restored before the beginning of the trial. The main difference between the versions is how this requirement is formulated, and this explains, I believe, why Gratian's original *dictum* was changed.

The terms *animo*, *corpore*, *naturalis* used in relation to possession are technical terms in Roman law, which is the reason they have been left

---

[12] Friedberg, ed., *Decretum*, 505, supported by Me Mz Vd: "Sed notandum est, quod restitutionis sententia sola non sufficit, nisi presentialiter omnia iudicis offitio restituantur, ut eiectus uel expoliatus etiam naturalem possessionem recipiat, siue animo suo et corpore alieno, ueluti per procuratorem, siue animo et corpore suo. Cuncta quoque, que sibi ablata fuerant quacumque conditione, in eodem loco, unde surrepta fuerant, sunt reuocanda."

untranslated above.[13] The exact meaning of terms describing ownership and possession developed significantly during antiquity. In the period of classical law, there was a strict distinction between ownership (*dominium*) and the mere factual possession (*possessio*) of a thing. An owner would not necessarily also have possession of the thing that belonged to him, and a possessor would not necessarily also be the owner. Possession was acquired *corpore et animo* by obtaining factual power over a thing while having the intention of possessing it. If the possessor lost his possession involuntarily (e.g., through theft), it was lost only *corpore*, while if he voluntarily abandoned it, the thing was lost *corpore et animo*.

The distinction between ownership and possession broke down during the so-called vulgar period of Roman law and the relevant terminology became vague. Justinian restored most of the classical doctrines concerning ownership and possession, but his great legislative work had very little immediate success in Western Europe. Instead, the laws of the vulgar period lived on in the various legal compilations employed in the "barbarian" successor states, the most influential of which was the *Lex Romana Visigothorum*. It was only with the rise of the law school of Bologna in the twelfth century that the full Justinianic *corpus* was received in Western European legal science.

I believe that the original *dictum* of Gratian 1 was replaced in the second recension because its formulations reflect those of the vulgar period, while the new *dictum* employs Justinianic terminology. The idea that a person could acquire possession *animo* through a judicial sentence that is not executed just does not make sense in the context of Justinianic law.[14] Further, Gratian 1 says that the restored person who actually reacquires the lost property receives *corpore* possession. In Justinianic law, someone who in fact holds the property of which he believes himself to be the owner (and this description fits the present case) would be described as a possessor with *animus domini*. It is only if the actual holder of the thing does not believe that he is its owner that he is said to hold *corporalis possessio*.[15] It is

[13] For the following, see Max Kaser, *Das Römische Privatrecht*, Handbuch der Altertumswissenschaft, Abt. 10, Teil 3, Band III (Munich 1954–1959), I 325–334, 340–343, II 177–196, Max Kaser, *Römisches Privatrecht: Studienbuch*, Kurzlehrbücher für das juristische Studium, 16th edn. (Munich 1992), §§ 19–22, Ernst Levy, *West Roman Vulgar Law: The Law of Property*, Memoirs of the American Philosophical Society 29 (Philadelphia 1951), and Adolf Berger, *Encyclopedic Dictionary of Roman Law*, Transactions of the American Philosophical Society, n. s., 43: 2 (Philadelphia 1953), s. vv. *dominium, possessio, possessio naturalis*.
[14] Cf. Dig. 41.2.3.3, see Theodor Mommsen and Paul Krüger, eds., "Digesta," *Corpus iuris civilis* I, 17th edn. (Berlin 1963), 698: "solo animo non posse nos adquirere possessionem, si non antecedat naturalis possessio" and Dig. 41.2.3.6 (Mommsen and Krüger, eds., "Digesta," 698): "amitti et animo solo potest, quamvis adquiri non potest."
[15] Kaser, *Römische Privatrecht*, II 181–182, Kaser, *Römisches Privatrecht: Studienbuch*, § 19 VI, and Berger, *Encyclopedic Dictionary*, s.v. *possessio*.

thus not surprising that Gratian 2, supposing that he was schooled in Justinianic law, was so disturbed by this *dictum* that he saw fit to reformulate it. The fact that he bothers to explain how the terms *animo* and *corpore* should be used "correctly" (even though it entailed discussing the role of procurators, which has very little relevance for the case at hand) supports this interpretation.

The terminology of the original *dictum* is comprehensible if one considers some of the relevant vulgar Roman law texts. The *interpretatio* of an excerpt from the *Pauli Sententiae* found in the *Lex Romana Visigothorum* could easily have been seen to justify Gratian's original words:

There are some things which we possess *animo et corpore*, some solely *animo*. We possess *animo et corpore* those things which we seem to hold and use at present. We possess *animo* those things which are situated far away and to which we have right, and which we are able to vindicate as our property.[16]

Against this background, it is easy to understand why Gratian 1 insisted that the lost property should be restored "also *corpore*" (*etiam corpore*).[17] This is, of course, not to say that Gratian 1 must have read this specific passage in the *Lex Romana Visigothorum*, although that could be the case. There are several other places where he could have acquired this terminology, but it seems clear that its intellectual pedigree is to be found in West Roman vulgar law.

When can women accuse?

The most substantial use of Roman law sources in the first recension is found in C. 15, q. 3, which discusses whether a woman is allowed to accuse a priest. In answering this question, Gratian 1 quoted three passages from Justinian's *Code* and four passages from the *Digest*, in addition to a Pseudo-Isidorian decretal. Of the Roman law quotations, only one appears (as far as is known) in earlier canonical collections.[18] It seems very likely that Gratian in this *questio* used the Justinianic *corpus* at first hand.[19]

---

[16] Gustav Haenel, ed., *Lex Romana Visigothorum* (Leipzig 1848), 414, interpretatio ad Pauli Sententias 5.2.1: "Aliqua sunt, quae animo et corpore possidemus: aliqua, quae tantum animo. Animo et corpore ea possidemus, quae in praesenti tenere videmur vel utimur: animo vero ea possidemus, quae in longinquo posita sunt et in nostro iure consistunt et ea proprietati nostrae possumus vindicare." Cf. Ernst Levy, *West Roman Vulgar Law*, 31.

[17] In the context, *etiam corpore* must be understood as *corpore et animo*.

[18] See Friedberg's note 15.

[19] The possibility that he reproduced some text written by a contemporary romanist cannot, however, be excluded. The subject was touched upon by Bulgarus in the work he sent to Chancellor Haimeric (see below) and also by a roughly contemporary treatise found in a Frankfurt manuscript, see Ludwig Wahrmund, *Quellen zur Geschichte des römisch-kanonischen Processes im Mittelalter* IV: 1 (Innsbruck 1925), 13–14.

How well did Gratian 1 use Roman law in this *questio*? The fact that he quotes no less than seven romanistic texts found in various places in two works indicates some proficiency in Roman law, although he could easily have been referred to the other six by a gloss on one of them. In his article about Roman law in the *Decretum*, Stephan Kuttner analyzes this *questio* and criticizes it for weakness of logic.[20] He singles out two passages for criticism. The first is in d. a. c. 1, where Gratian 1 uses a technical term incorrectly: he employs the verb *intercedere* where *intervenire* would have been appropriate.

The other passage which Kuttner criticized is in the beginning of d. p. c. 4. It turns out, however, that the offensive passage was added in the second recension, replacing a different (and inoffensive) formulation. In the first recension, the beginning of d. p. c. 4 reads as follows:

When the sacred canons dispense entirely with those [types of] accusations, which secular laws do not approve, then, on the contrary, it seems that those [accusations] which are not prohibited by secular laws are to be admitted [in canon law]. But this does not follow. **For all persons who are prohibited by human laws to marry are also prohibited by divine. The sacred canons do not permit the joining of everyone whose marriage is allowed by the laws of the emperors.** Even though the sacred canons remove those accusations, which secular laws do not approve, it does not therefore follow that whatever [accusations] the laws of princes admit are received [in canon law].[21]

In the second recension, the passage between the asterisks was replaced by a different text:

For every cleric is prohibited by the sacred canons and by the emperors' laws from contracting marriage. But the laws do not, consequently, permit this bond to all, whose union the sacred canons do not prohibit; for, according to the laws, only cantors and lectors are able to take a wife, but according to the canons also acolytes are able.[22]

---

[20] Kuttner, "New studies on the Roman law," 45–47.

[21] The original reading of the passage between the asterisks is preserved only in Aa, where the text of the second recension is followed by *Aliter* and the first-recension text: "Quecumque enim persone humanis legibus copulari prohibentur et divinis. Non omnium copula a sacris canonibus admittitur, quorum conventio legibus imperatorum indulgetur." In Fd, the text has been erased and replaced with the second-recension text. For the text of the rest of the passage, see the following note.

[22] Friedberg, ed., *Decretum*, 752, supported by Aa Fd[add] Me Mz Vd: "Cum autem sacris canonibus accusationes omnino (omnimodo Fd) submoueantur, quas leges seculi non asciscunt, e diuerso uidentur admittendae que legibus seculi non prohibentur. Verum hoc non infertur. **Quicumque enim clericorum nuptias sacris canonibus contrahere prohibentur, et legibus imperatorum. Non autem consequenter omnium copulam leges admittunt, quorum coniunctionem (coniunctiones Aa) sacri canones non prohibent; legibus enim soli cantores et lectores, canonibus autem etiam acoliti uxores ducere possunt.** Quamuis igitur sacris canonibus submoueantur accusationes, quas leges seculi non asciscunt, non ideo consequenter recipiuntur quascumque leges principum admittunt."

As the *Correctores* had already pointed out, this perceived discrepancy between the laws and the canons is not accurate. Acolytes did not exist as an order in the East, so it should not surprise us that Justinian's laws and, specifically, the novel which the *Correctores* identified as the probable (and misunderstood) source for this passage, do not mention them.[23] Such criticism of the passage does not, however, take into account that most twelfth-century canonists probably would have rather vague ideas about whether acolytes existed in the Eastern Church. The passage probably made good sense to them.[24]

But why replace the original reading of the passage, if its content is correct? It is certainly true that Roman law permits certain marriages which are prohibited in canon law, e.g. between persons related in the fifth to seventh (canonical) degree of consanguinity (as Gratian was well aware; cf. C. 35, q. 5, c. 2). Perhaps it was simply the vagueness of the original passage (which in any case is not easy to understand) that caused it to be exchanged for a more specific text, which happened to be inaccurate.

The first recension of C. 15, q. 3 reveals an author with good knowledge of a specific detail of Roman legal doctrine. Since this is the only such passage in the first recension of the *Decretum*, one should be careful not to base far-reaching conclusions on it. The fact remains that the first recension, with this single exception, contains no passages where Gratian 1 made substantial use of Justinian's *Corpus iuris civilis*.

False accusers and infamy

In addition to those places where Gratian 1 used Roman law in the first recension, there are numerous places where he would have reached significantly different conclusions had he used Roman law. In the second recension, relevant romanistic material was often added at such points. C. 2, q. 3 is one of many possible examples. In this *questio*, Gratian 1 discusses what the proper punishment is for an accuser who fails to prove his charges.[25] In the first recension, Gratian 1 apparently distinguished between three groups of failed accusers.[26] First, those who are not able

---

[23] The *Correctores'* note ★, Kuttner, "New studies on the Roman law," 46.

[24] Kuttner refers to two decretists' criticism of this passage ("New studies on the Roman law," 46). It is, however, uncertain exactly what Stephen of Tournai criticized in treating C. 15, q. 3, for the comment quoted by Kuttner ("unde Gratianum hic aut errare puto aut vagari") does not refer to a specific lemma. I cannot see that the *Summa Parisiensis* contains any criticism of Gratian at the point indicated by Kuttner. In other words, there seems to be no evidence that the decretists were disturbed by the discussion of acolytes.

[25] For the contents of the first recension of C. 2, q. 3, see the Appendix.

[26] Gratian's distinction is not entirely clear. Perhaps one should add a fourth group, namely those who realize that they have accused falsely and are forgiven by the accused (cf. d. p. c. 7, § 2 and c. 8).

to prove the crime of which they accuse someone are themselves to suffer the punishment prescribed for that crime, in addition to being declared infamous. Second, those who withdraw their accusation, because they have been deceived by some promise, are to be forgiven. Third, those who are bribed to abstain from completing their accusation are to be punished (although Gratian 1 did not specify what the punishment should be).

In making this threefold distinction, Gratian 1 proves himself unaware of the sophisticated legal doctrines available in Justinianic Roman law. The entire *questio* was, in fact, largely and ultimately based on pre-Justinianic Roman law. Gratian's treatment of his first group is based on five canons (canons 1–4b), four of which derive from Roman vulgar law as codified in the *Lex Romana Visigothorum* and transmitted (attributed to various popes) through the Pseudo-Isidorian Decretals. Canon 8, which provided the justification for the third group, derives from the same source although it was transmitted to Gratian 1 in another way, causing him to believe that the text came from a Carolingian capitulary.

His second group, those who withdraw an accusation because of a promise, is based on two excerpts from a letter of Gregory I (canons 6–7). This group caused commentators problems, because the difference between being "deceived by a promise" and being bribed is not self-evident. The *Glossa ordinaria* emphasizes that the promise could not concern money, while the *Summa Parisiensis* disagrees with Gratian's conclusion in pointing out that Pope Gregory said only that he forgave the culprit in question, not that he removed any infamy that had been incurred.[27] The problems experienced by commentators can be explained in part by their schooling in Roman law, which did not know of any special treatment for accusers who were deceived by a promise.

This is explicit in d. p. c. 7, which was added only in the second recension. The *dictum* discusses the problems raised by c. 6 and its interpretation by Gratian 1. There is a small, but significant shift in emphasis between the recensions: Gratian 1 distinguished (in d. p. c. 5) between those who simply cannot prove their accusations (and therefore incur infamy) and those who "being deceived by a promise" withdraw their accusation. He states that the latter are forgiven. In d. p. c. 7, Gratian 2 takes Gregory's text to mean that the infamy of clerics can be abolished by the pope. The non-technical approach ("forgiveness") of Gratian 1 is meaningless to him. Unlike Gratian 1, Gratian 2 thinks it self-evident that

---

[27] The *Glossa ordinaria* was studied in the manuscript Cg and in *Decretum Gratiani . . . una cum glossis Gregorii XIII pont. max. iussu editum* (Venice 1600), I 595. McLaughlin, ed., *Summa Parisiensis*, 104. Cf. the *Correctores*' note ⋆⋆ to c. 5.

Paulus – the deacon whose case is discussed by Gregory in c. 6 – incurred infamy when he withdrew his accusation without first going through the proper formalities, namely those prescribed by the *Senatusconsultum Turpilianum*. Gratian 2 concludes that Gregory abolished Paulus' infamy, but this conclusion clashes, he points out, with a statement by Pope Gelasius that popes cannot abolish infamy. Gratian 2 suggests the solution that not everyone who is declared infamous in secular law is also infamous according to canon law.

It is, in general, remarkable how the use of the concept of infamy develops between the two recensions.[28] In the first recension, Gratian 1 employed the concept (which canon law originally imported from Roman law) in the somewhat vague form that had been passed down through the Pseudo-Isidorian Decretals and other collections influenced by Roman law. It was not yet so technical a term that Gratian 1 could not replace it with the synonym *dispendium existimationis*, even when summarizing a canon using the term *infamia* (C. 2, q. 3, d. a. c. 1). In sharp contrast, Gratian 2 concerns himself with the technical, romanistic meaning of the term. He had already begun the process which by the early thirteenth century would transform the canonistic doctrine of infamy into a sophisticated system more complex than the one found in the Justinianic corpus.[29]

Also d. p. c. 8 (added only in the second recension[30]) can be considered an attempt to deal with the problems raised by c. 6. The second half of the dictum treats withdrawn accusations and the formalities that must be observed in such cases: the accuser must formally request dismissal (*abolitio*) from the presiding judge before he withdraws his accusations. This stands in stark contrast to the non-technical approach used by Gratian 1 in the first recension (d. p. c. 7, § 2), which allowed an accuser to withdraw his accusation if the accused forgives him. Otherwise, d. p. c. 8 introduces a new, threefold division of culpable accusers extracted from the *Digest* (48.16.1). There is no attempt to reconcile this division

---

[28] For the canonical use of infamy, see Georg May, "Die Infamie im *Decretum Gratiani*," *AKKR* 129 (1960), 389–408, Georg May, "Die Anfänge der Infamie im kanonischen Recht," *ZRG KA* 47 (1961), 77–94, Peter Landau, *Die Entstehung des kanonischen Infamiebegriffs von Gratian bis zur Glossa ordinaria*, Forschungen zur kirchlichen Rechtsgeschichte und zum Kirchenrecht 5 (Cologne 1966), E. Peters, "Wounded names: the medieval doctrine of infamy," in *Law in Mediaeval Life and Thought*, ed. Edward B. King and Susan J. Ridyard, Sewanee Mediaeval Studies 5 (Sewanee, 1990), Francesco Migliorino, *Fama e infamia: problemi della società medievale nel pensiero giuridico nei secoli xii e xiii* (Catania 1985).

[29] The observations here outlined are based on a survey of the words *infamia* and *infamis* in the *Decretum* which was performed with the help of Reuter and Silagi, *Wortkonkordanz*, 2263–2266.

[30] Note Friedberg's note 87, which mentions that d. p. c. 8 is missing in its entirety from his manuscript F.

with the one made in the first recension. The three new categories are those who accuse when there has been no crime (*calumniatores*), those who fail to accuse when there has been a crime (*prevaricatores*), and those who withdraw their accusation (*tergiversatores*).

This brief consideration of C. 2, q. 3 permits a few reflections. The first recension of this *questio* could only have been written by a man who knew nothing of the Roman law doctrines adduced by the author of the second recension. If he knew them, and wanted to construct a system of canon law that could provide a viable alternative (as Vetulani and others argued), then he succeeded very poorly. Even if he did not wish to adopt outright the system offered by Roman law, a conscious effort to create a (polemical) alternative would, one expects, have produced a more coherent and better-organized system.

ROMAN LAW IN THE ORIGINAL *DECRETUM*

This analysis of the role of Roman law in selected passages in the first recension of Gratian's *Decretum* suggests certain conclusions. First, it is clear that Gratian 1 by no means strove to avoid either secular law in general, or the *Corpus iuris civilis* in particular. C. 15, q. 3 shows that he had detailed knowledge of the treatment of a specific issue in Justinianic Roman law, and this was not an issue for which canon law lacked regulations. In fact, a large part of the *questio* is devoted to a discussion of the discrepancies between the two laws. Elsewhere, too, Gratian 1 introduced romanistic texts and doctrines into his *Decretum*. Some of these derived from the Justinianic *corpus* through the mediation of earlier canonical collections; some came from pre-Justinianic law. Although in numerous cases the provenance of such texts was hidden from Gratian through incorrect inscriptions, there are many cases in which he was aware of their imperial and secular pedigree. It is, therefore, all but impossible to argue on this basis that he represented an anti-imperial faction of the Church, and wanted to construct a purely canonical legal system in conscious opposition to a greatly successful system of imperial Roman law. It would also be difficult to maintain that in excluding Roman law Gratian 1 was following the prohibitions issued by Pope Innocent II at various councils between 1130 and 1139 against monks learning secular law.[31] The first recension of Gratian's *Decretum* simply contains so much secular law that such suggestions remain highly improbable.[32]

---

[31] Robert Somerville, "Pope Innocent II and the Study of Roman Law," *Revue des Etudes islamiques* 44 (1976), 105–114, repr. in Somerville, *Papacy, Councils and Canon Law in the 11th–12th Centuries.*

[32] Stephan Kuttner argued similarly, without knowing about the first recension, in "Research on Gratian," 20.

Instead, Gratian's insecurity in the technicalities of Roman law, his reliance on pre-Justinianic law, and his apparent ignorance of romanistic concepts which would have helped in his formulation of problems and solutions (even if he did not want to adopt wholesale the solutions offered by Roman law) indicate that he simply did not know very much about Roman law. If he had more than a passing acquaintance with the Justinianic law taught by Irnerius, Bulgarus, and others, it would be very difficult to explain how he could produce what appears in the first recension of the *Decretum*. But this conclusion raises an even more difficult problem: how is it possible that Gratian knew so little about Roman law?

THE TEACHING OF ROMAN LAW IN GRATIAN'S TIME

That Gratian used Roman law sparingly, and not altogether competently, in the first recension, can seem surprising, considering that he was, for all we know, active in Bologna, where the study of Roman law supposedly flourished during his lifetime. This is at least current scholarly opinion; but there might be reasons for submitting this view to closer scrutiny. The teaching of Roman law during the first half of the twelfth century is not an easily approached subject, since a fresh consideration of the topic on the basis of medieval sources is lacking in recent scholarship. The best available survey is still Friedrich Karl von Savigny's monumental *Geschichte des römischen Rechts im Mittelalter* (6 volumes; 2nd edition 1834–1851), particularly its fourth volume (1850). This work must be supplemented with later scholarship. Especially important are Hermann Kantorowicz's groundbreaking *Studies in the Glossators of Roman Law*,[33] the *Handbuch der Quellen und Literatur der neueren Europäischen Privatrechtsgeschichte*,[34] and the recent survey in Hermann Lange's *Römisches Recht im Mittelalter*.[35]

The lack of modern treatments is further aggravated by the scarcity of reliable and easily accessible editions of the romanistic writings of the early twelfth century.

The main points of the currently accepted account for the resurgence of Roman law in the early twelfth century are as follows.[36] The study of

---

[33] Hermann Kantorowicz with W. W. Buckland, *Studies in the Glossators of Roman Law: Newly Discovered Writings of the Twelfth Century* (Cambridge 1938); reprinted with "Addenda et corrigenda" by Peter Weimar (Aalen 1969).

[34] Helmuth Coing, ed., *Handbuch der Quellen und Literatur der neueren Europäischen Privatrechtsgeschichte*, 1 (Munich 1973).

[35] Hermann Lange, *Römisches Recht im Mittelalter*, 1, *Die Glossatoren* (Munich 1997).

[36] Similar accounts can be found in any number of places. See, e.g., Giorgio Cencetti, "Studium fuit Bononie: Note sulla storia dell'Università di Bologna nel primo mezzo secolo della sua esistenza," *Studi medievali*, ser. 3, vol. 7, fasc. 2 (Spoleto 1966), 781–833, Charles Donahue, "Law,

law in Bologna was founded by Pepo (active in the last quarter of the eleventh century) and Irnerius (mentioned in documents from 1112 to 1125). Not much is known about the former, but Irnerius is credited with having lectured on all (or almost all) parts of the *Corpus iuris civilis*. He was the teacher of the so-called Four Doctors (*Quattuor doctores*): Bulgarus (d. 1166?), Martinus Gosia (d. *c.* 1160), Ugo of Porta Ravennate (d. *c.* 1166/1171), and Jacobus de Porta Ravennate (d. 1178). The oldest of the Four Doctors was Bulgarus, and Kantorowicz assumes that his teaching had begun by 1115.[37]

The starting point for Savigny, Kantorowicz, and others who attempted to describe the beginnings of Roman law teaching in Bologna was the lectures of the law professor Odofredus (d. 1265).[38] He had a vivid interest in the history of his discipline and his university, and he enlivened his lectures with anecdotes about his predecessors. It is through these we learn, e.g., that Irnerius was called the "lamp of the law" (*lucerna iuris*) due to his great knowledge. Odofredus also told his students that Bulgarus grew so old that he became senile, and played with children in the sand. Kantorowicz uses this statement as the foundation for his guess that Bulgarus must have begun to teach by 1115.

Details in Odofredus' account have been questioned,[39] but his main outline of the early history of Bologna University has been allowed to inform recent treatments of the subject, even though he lived more than

---

footnote 36 (*cont.*)

    civil," in Joseph Strayer, ed., *Dictionary of the Middle Ages* (New York 1982–1989), Peter Weimar, "Irnerius," *Lexikon des Mittelalters* (Munich, 1977–), Bellomo, *The Common Legal Past of Europe*, 60–63, Ennio Cortese, *Il diritto nella storia medievale*, vol. II, *Il basso medioevo* (Rome 1995), 5–102, Ennio Cortese, *Il rinascimento giuridico medievale*, 2nd edn. (Rome 1996), Lange, *Römisches Recht im Mittelalter*, I 154–162.

[37] Kantorowicz, *Studies in the Glossators of Roman Law*, 69. Martinus wrote a gloss on the computation of degrees of consanguinity. This gloss appears to draw on pre-Gratian collections, but this does not prove that it was written before the *Decretum*. See Kantorowicz, *Studies in the Glossators*, 91–94 and Stephan Kuttner, "Zur neuesten Glossatorenforschung," *Studia et documenta historiae et iuris* 6 (1940), 289–294, reprinted with additions in Kuttner, *Studies in the History of Medieval Canon Law*, no. 1.

[38] His most interesting comments are found in Odofredus Bononiensis, *Lectura super Digesto veteri* (Lyon 1550); reprinted as Opera iuridica rariora 2: 1 (Bologna 1967–1968). He treated the beginning of the Bolognese law school in commenting upon *Digest* 1.1.6, and Hermann Kantorowicz has edited his comments in Hermann Kantorowicz and Beryl Smalley, "An English theologian's view of Roman law: Pepo, Irnerius, Ralph Niger," *Mediaeval and Renaissance Studies* 1 (1941–1943), 238; reprinted in Hermann Kantorowicz, *Rechtshistorische Schriften*, ed. Helmut Coing and Gerhard Immel, Freiburger Rechts- und Staatswissenschaftliche Abhandlungen 30 (Karlsruhe 1970). English translations are available in Donahue, "Law, civil," and in Charles M. Radding, *The Origins of Medieval Jurisprudence: Pavia and Bologna 850–1150* (New Haven 1988), 159.

[39] See, e.g., Fried, *Entstehung des Juristenstandes*, 104: "Nichts – nichts Konkretes wußte der glänzende Rhetoriker Odofred" about the beginning of legal teaching in Bologna. Charles M. Radding, "Vatican Latin 1406, Mommsen's Ms. S, and the Reception of the *Digest* in the Middle Ages," *ZRG KA* 110 (1993), 534, expressed reservations similar to mine.

a century after the events he describes. Odofredus may have drawn on tradition, but we do not have any guarantees about the quality of this tradition. An example of how quickly tradition could become corrupted is the Anglo-Norman canonist Honorius, who already in the 1180s or 1190s reported that he had heard that the canonist Rolandus and Pope Alexander III (died 1181) were the same person; they were not.[40] It seems, however, methodologically sounder to leave Odofredus' late testimony aside and explore this history with the help of contemporary documents and the writings of the early law teachers themselves. By the same token, the testimony of medieval chroniclers will be omitted. They begin to have interesting information about the beginning of the Bolognese law school only during the second half of the twelfth century.

A study of the contemporary source material shows that the reputation of the early Bolognese teaching of Roman law is exaggerated. The familiarity with romanistic texts and doctrines exhibited by Gratian in the first recension of the *Decretum* is on a level that could be expected from a canonist (being an interested outsider) working in the 1130s. Here I shall concentrate on Irnerius and Bulgarus, the two oldest Bolognese civilians from whom writings survive. I shall examine how far their knowledge of Roman law had advanced and how their methods and approach compare to Gratian's.

Bulgarus

Bulgarus' teaching is relatively well known through several works that can be safely identified as his through attributions in the manuscripts. They demonstrate a relatively high proficiency in Roman law, and his interpretative methods appear advanced in comparison with Gratian's. It is particularly fruitful to compare the *questiones* in the second part of the *Decretum* with the so-called *Stemma Bulgaricum*, a series of *questiones* which are reports of disputations among his students. Bulgarus' *questiones* are in the form of fictitious lawsuits in which different students argued the cases of the litigant and the defendant. The professor would in the end act the role of the judge and decide the case.[41] These *questiones* clearly testify to a specific teaching situation, while it remains less clear exactly what teaching function Gratian's *questiones* fulfilled. Bulgarus thus was active in a setting where the forms of teaching had reached greater stability and maturity than they had in Gratian's school. If the *Stemma* substantially pre-dated the *Decretum*, one would have to conclude that Gratian's

---

[40] Weigand, "Magister Rolandus," 24. Cf. Weigand, "Frühe Kanonisten," 147.
[41] For editions, see Lange, *Römisches Recht im Mittelalter*, I 168.

teaching methods were substantially more conservative than Bulgarus'. It seems more reasonable to suggest that the *Stemma* was written later than the *Decretum*.

The question of chronology is, therefore, of the utmost importance. When did Bulgarus teach and write his works? For Kantorowicz, it was self-evident that Gratian was Bulgarus' junior, since the *Decretum* (in C. 1, q. 4, d. p. c. 12) quotes a treatise written by Bulgarus, the *Summula de iuris et facti ignorantia*, which Kantorowicz discovered in a London manuscript.[42] However, the quotation is found only in the second recension of the *Decretum*, so it only proves that the *Summula* must have been written before 1158 (the *terminus ante quem* for the second recension), if Kantorowicz was correct in concluding that the *Decretum* borrowed from Bulgarus.[43] This conclusion is not, however, unassailable. Antonio Rota has argued that Bulgarus depended on Gratian, since he considered it more likely that a canonist rather than a civilist would say that ignorance of natural law is more serious than ignorance of civil law. An early romanistic gloss with the *siglum* "y" (and therefore ascribed to Irnerius) does in fact state that ignorance of natural law and ignorance of civil law are equally serious.[44] The statement that ignorance of natural law is the more serious offence already appears in the first recension of the *Decretum*, so perhaps this influenced Bulgarus' *Summula*, which in turn was copied in the second recension.

Furthermore, a gloss with Bulgarus' *siglum* "b." quotes three texts from Gratian's *Decretum*, one of which was added only in the second recension.[45] This gloss must have been written after the completion of the second recension of the *Decretum*.

Bulgarus appears in dated documents between 1151 and 1159.[46] The earliest datable testimony for his activities is his letter to the papal chancellor, Haimeric.[47] The chancellor died in 1141, so Bulgarus' treatise must

---

[42] Kantorowicz, *Studies in the Glossators*, 79–80, 244–246.

[43] *Ibid.*, 80, prints the relevant passages in both works in parallel columns. The first four lines (to *aliis non*) in the text extracted from the *Decretum* belong to the first recension, but there are no important similarities between the two texts here.

[44] Antonio Rota, "Il *Tractatus de equitate* come pars tertia delle *Quaestiones de iuris subtilitatibus* e il suo valore storico e politico," *Archivio giuridico* 146 (1954), 92–96.

[45] The gloss was printed in Friedrich Karl von Savigny, *Geschichte der römischen Rechts im Mittelalter* (Heidelberg 1834–1851), IV 475–476 on the basis of Paris, Bibliothèque Nationale, lat. 4523, which according to Dolezalek, *Repertorium*, 480, is a manuscript from the middle of the twelfth century. It cites C. 11, q. 3, canons 14 and 35 in addition to d. p. c. 47. Canon 14 was added only in the second recension. That Bulgarus read these texts in the *Decretum* is evident since he refers to the relevant *causa* and *questio*.

[46] Kantorowicz, *Studies in the Glossators*, 68, Lange, *Römisches Recht im Mittelalter* I 164–165.

[47] Edited in Wahrmund, *Quellen zur Geschichte des römisch-kanonischen Processes*, IV: 1 1–17, on the basis of two manuscripts and an early modern edition. Kantorowicz discovered a third manuscript (British Library, Royal II. B. XIV), which confirms that the addressee of the treatise is Haimeric:

have been finished by that year.[48] The work is "an elementary introduction . . . into the secrets of procedure and legal principles according to Roman law."[49] It presupposes that the study of Roman law had reached a certain maturity, since the Justinianic law books contain no special sections devoted to procedural law.[50] Such law is scattered almost everywhere in the *Corpus iuris civilis*, so it must have cost the medieval glossators much effort to produce a systematic account of procedure. It is, therefore, not surprising that Bulgarus' treatment is short (ten pages in print) and that it does not go into great detail. In the first recension of C. 15, q. 3, Gratian 1 (see above) discusses whether women can accuse in court in much greater detail than Bulgarus, who simply states that women cannot accuse.[51]

Scholars have argued that a papal bull from 1125 shows that Haimeric had already learnt enough Roman law to judge an intricate legal case and that Bulgarus' treatise must, therefore, have been written earlier.[52] The bull does not, however, prove this. Haimeric, being the pope's chancellor, wrote the bull, but the decision was left to the pope's judges.

"*Introductiones Bul. ad aimericum cancellarium rome incipiunt,*" see Kantorowicz, *Studies in the Glossators*, 71. The other manuscripts contain only his initial A. For further manuscripts and details, see Linda Fowler-Magerl, *Ordo iudiciorum vel ordo iudiciarius: Begriff und Literaturgattung,* Ius commune, Sonderhefte, Texte und Monographien 19 (Frankfurt am Main 1984), 35–40. A Parisian manuscript unknown to Fowler-Magerl was treated in Gunnar Teske, "Ein neuer Text des Bulgars-Briefes an den römischen Kanzler Haimerich," *Vinculum societatis: Joachim Wollasch zum 60. Geburtstag* (Sigmaringendorf 1991), 302–313. See also Teske, *Die Briefsammlungen des 12. Jahrhunderts in St. Viktor / Paris: Entstehung, Überlieferung und Bedeutung für die Geschichte der Abtei,* Studien und Dokumente zur Gallia Pontificia / Etudes et documents pour servir à une Gallia Pontificia 2 (Bonn 1993), 107–108.

[48] Johannes Matthias Brixius, *Die Mitglieder des Kardinalkollegiums von 1130–1181* (Berlin 1912), 32, and Rudolf Hüls, *Kardinäle, Klerus und Kirchen Romas,* 236 and 271.

[49] Kantorowicz, *Studies in the Glossators*, 71.

[50] See, e.g., Kaser, *Römisches Privatrecht: Studienbuch,* § 80 I 1, and Kantorowicz, *Studies in the Glossators*, 72.

[51] Wahrmund, *Quellen zur Geschichte des Römisch-kanonischen Processes im Mittelalter,* IV: 1, p. 4: "Accusare omnibus permissum est, his exceptis. Propter sexum prohibetur mulier." Cf. Gratian in C. 15, q. 3, d. a. c. 1 (Friedberg, ed., *Decretum,* 751, supported by Aa Fd Me Mz Vd): "quamquam passim et indifferenter ad accusationem mulier non admittatur, sunt tamen quedam crimina, quorum accusationem mulier subire non prohibetur."

[52] Kantorowicz, *Studies in the Glossators*, 71, Johannes Fried, "Die römische Kurie und die Anfänge der Prozeßliteratur," *ZRG KA* 59 (1973), 169, and Teske, "Ein neuer Text des Bulgars-Briefes," 307. The bull is JL 7210 = Kehr, *Italia Pontificia* III 154, no. 40, and cites several laws from Justinian's *Code* and *Digest.* Unsatisfactory editions without identifications of the romanistic passages are available in Julius von Pflugk-Harttung, ed., *Acta pontificum Romanorum inedita* (Tübingen 1880–1886), II 252–255, and in Ubaldo Pasqui, *Documenti per la storia della città di Arezzo nel medio evo,* I (Florence and Arezzo 1899), vol. 11, *Documenti di storia italiana,* 438–442. In the supplement to Savigny, *Geschichte,* VII 66–69, Johannes Merkel discussed a document which appears to be a legal memorial from the side of the bishop of Arezzo. The document quotes several Roman laws not mentioned in the bull. Savigny described this document in his *Geschichte,* II 226–227, believing it to have been written in 752.

Moreover, it was the parties in the case who cited Roman law, not the curia, and the passages quoted were not any of those which appear in Bulgarus' work. The bull testifies to the greater currency of Roman law in Italy at this time, but it does not tell us anything about the Bolognese law school or about Haimeric's or Bulgarus' knowledge of Roman law in 1125.

To summarize, there is no secure evidence that places any substantial part of Bulgarus' teaching before 1140. The dates at which his existence is ascertained (1141–1159) tally well with the impression that his methods were more advanced than Gratian's. These findings indicate that Bulgarus was a younger contemporary of Gratian.

Under such circumstances, chronological considerations make it very unlikely that he had studied with Irnerius, who appears in documents from 1112 to 1125.[53] It is, in fact, strange that so many modern scholars maintain that the Four Doctors were Irnerius' students, considering that Savigny thought this "not impossible, but unlikely."[54] Gustav Pescatore argued from analogy in the most detailed criticism of Savigny's position that I have been able to find. He pointed out that, in 1888 (when he was writing), there were still persons alive who had studied under Savigny, whose first printed work was published in 1803.[55] Pescatore's argument misses the point that there is a gap of some fifteen years between the last mention of Irnerius (1125) and the first testimony of Bulgarus' activity (before 1141). Surely many of Savigny's students had already made a name for themselves by the time the master finished his *Geschichte* in 1851. His perhaps most famous student, Karl Marx, published, for example, the *Communist Manifesto* in 1848.

Irnerius

There is no doubt that Irnerius was active before Gratian. He appears in documents from 1112 to 1125, at first as a *causidicus* and later as a *iudex*. In the subscriptions, he writes his name "Wernerius" while the notaries

---

[53] Enrico Spagnesi, *Wernerius Bononiensis iudex: La figura storica d'Irnerio.* Academica Toscana di scienze e lettere "La Columbaria," Studi 16. Florence 1969.

[54] Savigny, *Geschichte* IV 73: "Nach den sicheren und bekannten chronologischen Thatsachen ist jenes Verhältniß der vier Doctoren zu Irnerius, zwar nicht unmöglich, doch unwahrscheinlich." That the Four Doctors were Irnerius' students is first stated among the additions to the chronicle of Otto Morena, see *Das Geschichtswerk des Otto Morena und seiner Fortsetzer über die Taten Friedrichs I. in der Lombardei,* ed. Ferdinand Güterbock, MGH Scriptores rerum Germanicarum, Nova series 7 (Berlin 1930), 59. The editor believed these additions to have been made at the beginning of the 1220s in Milan, see Ferdinand Güterbock, "Zur Edition des Geschichtswerks Otto Morenas und seiner Fortsetzer," *Neues Archiv der Gesellschaft für ältere deutsche Geschichtskunde* 48 (1930), 116–147.   [55] Gustav Pescatore, *Die Glossen des Irnerius* (Greifswald 1888), 33–34.

writing the documents spelled it in several different ways, e.g. "Guarnerius." He is never called "Irnerius" in any contemporary document.[56]

In historical literature from the days of Odofredus to the present, Irnerius enjoys a reputation of being a profound and learned legal thinker. As a result, many anonymous legal works were attributed to him by scholars of the eighteenth century and the beginning of the nineteenth. These attributions were refuted by, among others, Hermann Kantorowicz, who considered authentic only two introductions to Justinian's *Code* and *Institutes* in addition to "his numerous and multiform glosses."[57] The two introductions were discovered and edited by Kantorowicz. The short introduction to the *Institutes*, which discusses definitions of justice and law, appears without attribution in the only manuscript that preserves it. Kantorowicz considered this introduction to be of a high intellectual level, and ascribed it, therefore, to Irnerius. The work uses Aristotelian terminology (*genus*, *species*), in which Kantorowicz recognized a former teacher of the liberal arts. The problem is that we have only Odofredus' word for Irnerius' having been a *magister artium*. Similarly, Irnerius' reputation for intellectual excellence is based on what Odofredus told his students more than a century later. The introduction edited by Kantorowicz is, in my view, not so remarkable that it could not have been written by anyone moderately well versed in Roman law.

Suspicion can, thus, be raised about Kantorowicz's attribution of the anonymous *Introductio Institutionum* to Irnerius. It is, therefore, advisable to approach Irnerius through writings attributed to him by the medieval manuscripts, which should give a better basis for evaluating his qualities than Odofredus' anecdotes. The *Materia Codicis secundum Irnerium* is attributed to "Guarnerius" in the manuscript. Kantorowicz judged this text harshly:

> The first impression is very disappointing, and makes one doubt whether the rubric is to be relied on . . . Instead of the perfect consistency which we found in the work of the pupil [the *Materia Codicis* of Bulgarus] and which we are entitled to expect in an even higher degree in the work of his master, the "lucerna iuris," we are faced with a quite disorderly set of eight observations.[58]

His reference to Irnerius being the *lucerna iuris* shows clearly how influenced Kantorowicz was by Odofredus' high opinion of the scholar he believed founded the law school of Bologna. Kantorowicz goes on to rearrange the eight observations according to the order of the corresponding sections in Bulgarus' *Materia*. He finds justification for doing so

---

[56] Spagnesi, *Wernerius Bononiensis iudex*, 109, note 1.
[57] Kantorowicz, *Studies in the Glossators*, 36–37.   [58] *Ibid.*, 46.

in the hypothesis that the components of the *Materia* originally were glosses, which a scribe copied in the wrong order when turning them into a small piece of continuous writing. It is easy to agree with the first part of this hypothesis, that the text is compiled from glosses. It remains uncertain, however, whether Irnerius ever envisaged any "correct" order in which the glosses were to be combined, if it occurred to him at all that they could be combined into a small treatise. It is at any rate inadmissible to read the arrangement of Bulgarus' *Materia* back into Irnerius' work to make it worthy of the *lucerna iuris*. Kantorowicz does something similar in editing the text: he "corrects" less suitable (but syntactically acceptable) readings of the manuscript with the help of works by later Bolognese masters. At one point he also posits a lacuna in the manuscript (and suggests a formulation of the missing passage), since its text does not treat the *utilitas propria* and the *pars philosophiae* of the *Code*. Kantorowicz could not imagine that the great Irnerius would fail to treat these aspects.[59] It seems safer to read the *Materia* as it appears in the manuscript (and as it can be reconstructed through Kantorowicz' critical apparatus). Naturally, the text of the manuscript gives a less positive impression than the text retouched by Kantorowicz. At any rate, Gratian's *Decretum* does not appear methodologically inferior to Irnerius' *Materia*. As to its contents, the *Materia* does not presuppose any particularly advanced understanding of the details of Roman law.

There remain the numerous glosses attributed to Irnerius.[60] Also here, there are problems concerning the attribution. Many (but not all) of the glosses found in the margins of manuscripts of the different parts of the *Corpus iuris civilis* are signed with *sigla*. Yet it is sometimes difficult to determine which teacher used which *siglum*. Earlier scholars believed wrongly that the *sigla* "Yr." and "J." referred to Irnerius, while it is now recognized that they refer to Henricus de Baylio[61] and Jacobus de Porta Ravennate, respectively.[62] Irnerius' *siglum* is now recognized to be "y."

---

[59] The fact that I feel obliged to criticize a few details in Kantorowicz's work does not detract from my admiration for his outstanding and groundbreaking achievements in clarifying the history of Roman law.

[60] Collections of glosses ascribed to Irnerius have been published in the following places: Pescatore, *Glossen des Irnerius* (Glosses on the *Code*), Enrico Besta, *L'opera d'Irnerio* II (Turin 1896) (Glosses on the *Digestum vetus*), Pietro Torelli, "Glosse preaccursiane alle Istituzioni: Nota prima: Glosse d'Irnerio," *Studi di storia e diritto in onore di Enrico Besta* (Milan 1939), 229–277, reprinted in Pietro Torelli, *Scritti di storia del diritto italiano* (Milan 1959), 43–94. For further editions, see Lange, *Römisches Recht im Mittelalter*, I 159.

[61] Henricus was a student of Martinus Gosia and appears in documents from 1169–1170, see Savigny, *Geschichte*, IV 286–288, Lange, *Römisches Recht im Mittelalter*, I 214–215. Savigny first showed that "Yr." was not Irnerius' *siglum*, see *Geschichte*, IV 34–35.

[62] One of those who mistook "J." for Irnerius' *siglum* was Gustav Pescatore, whose *Glossen des Irnerius*, therefore, contains many glosses that were in fact written by Jacobus. Pescatore realized his mistake in 1896, see Kantorowicz, *Studies in the Glossators*, 32.

Until quite recently, scholarship assumed that a gloss signed with a certain *siglum* was written by the law teacher, whose *siglum* it was. When the same gloss was found in other manuscripts accompanied by different *sigla*, it was usually explained as a scribal error or as plagiarism. In 1985, Gero Dolezalek published a systematic investigation of the glosses to two titles in the *Code*. The examination of a large number of manuscripts revealed that identical glosses are signed with different *sigla* so often that it cannot be the result of mere scribal errors.[63] Dolezalek developed a very attractive hypothesis, according to which the *siglum* indicated only that a specific gloss appeared in the copy of the relevant law book owned by the corresponding teacher (the *liber magistri*). The *siglum* does not indicate the author of the gloss, but a teacher who included the gloss in his copy of a law book, and thus, presumably, agreed with it. The glosses signed "y" might, therefore, not have been written by Irnerius. One may object that we know of no other teacher of Roman law contemporary with or earlier than Irnerius, so if a gloss was found in his book, he must have been the author. The objection presupposes, however, that Odofredus was right in singling out Irnerius as the only early teacher of any importance. When we find Wernerius in the contemporary charters, he is usually accompanied by other *iudices* and *causidici*, and several *legis doctores* appear in other charters of the time.[64] Could they have read and interpreted the sources of Roman law? One of them, Theuzo of Verona appears together with (and takes precedence over) Irnerius in three charters, and a treatise from the middle of the twelfth century preserves his interpretation of a legal issue.[65] It is entirely possible that he (and his colleagues) wrote other glosses which Irnerius inserted in his books and which therefore survive with Irnerius' *siglum*.[66] In fact, many of the glosses signed "y" contain references to the opinions of others.[67]

Doubts can, furthermore, be thrown on the long-standing belief that the *siglum* "y" refers to Irnerius. It is remarkable that this *siglum* is usually found at the beginning of glosses, while other *sigla* regularly appear at the

[63] Dolezalek, *Repertorium*, 49.

[64] Fried, *Die Entstehung des Juristenstandes*, 14. One should not from the title *doctor* conclude that the so-labelled person in fact was a teacher. The title indicates simply that he was well versed in the law (see above, chapter 1, and Fried, 18). See also Radding, *Origins of Medieval Jurisprudence*, 186–244 for a listing of "*iudices*" of Pavia from the ninth to the eleventh centuries. Radding's claims for the sophistication of the legal science pursued by these judges are exaggerated, but their existence suggests some level of legal culture.

[65] Gero Dolezalek, "Tractatus de diligentia et dolo et culpa et fortuito casu: Eine Abhandlung über die Haftung für Beschädigung oder den Untergang von Sachen aus dem zwölften Jahrhundert," in *Aspekte Europäischer Rechtsgeschichte: Festgabe für Helmut Coing zum 70. Geburtstag*, Ius commune, Sonderhefte: Texte und Monographien 17 (Frankfurt am Main 1982), 93–94 and 113.

[66] Dolezalek, *Repertorium*, 472, lists a few other *sigla* found in manuscripts from the early twelfth century.   [67] Pescatore, *Glossen des Irnerius*, 24–30.

end of glosses.[68] This formal difference warns against simply assuming that a *siglum* found at the beginning of a gloss filled the same function as those later appearing at the end of glosses.[69] Another detail points in the same direction: many glosses which in the oldest manuscripts lack *sigla* appear in later manuscripts with the *siglum* "y."[70]

Scholars ever since Savigny's day have tried to explain why a man who signed himself as "Wernerius" would chose the *siglum* "y." A related problem is the transformation of his name to Irnerius. In the twelfth century he was always referred to by a variant of "Wernerius" (e.g. "Guarnerius," "Garnerius") and some law teachers used this form as late as the early thirteenth century.[71]

Dolezalek has suggested, elaborating an idea proposed by Gustav Pescatore, that Irnerius put a paragraph mark in front of his glosses to distinguish them from marginal additions to the text.[72] A paragraph mark could look similar to a capital Y, and it is possible that later scribes misinterpreted the symbol as this letter. The *siglum* then influenced the way his name was written ("Yrnerius/Irnerius"). A Stuttgart manuscript of Justinian's *Code* from the middle of the twelfth century may bear witness to this development, since its glosses as a rule are preceded by either a "y" or a paragraph sign, although a few examples of the combinations "y §" and "§ y" appear as well.[73]

Dolezalek's explanation has much to recommend it. If it seems far-fetched, one need only consider the peculiar evolution that the abbreviation of the *Digest* underwent in the twelfth century, from a struck-through "Đ" to "ff".[74] If the "y," however, is a paragraph mark, there is no reason to attribute these glosses to Irnerius. Anyone could put a paragraph mark in front of his glosses, as is evident from the example of Gratian, who put such a symbol in front of his *dicta* (i.e., his commen-

---

[68] Dolezalek, *Repertorium*, 465–466. Glosses containing allegations always had the *siglum* at the beginning, probably because there otherwise was a risk that the *siglum* could be understood as part of the heavily abbreviated reference.

[69] Dolezalek, *Repertorium*, 472–473, discusses the developments in the use of *sigla*. Formal manuscript conventions in general became stable in Bologna only after the middle of the twelfth century. This is exemplified by the red signs (*Rote Zeichen*) which around the middle of the century were used for references before verbal references were used. See Dolezalek and Weigand, "Roten Zeichen," and Dolezalek, *Repertorium*, 476–480.

[70] Dolezalek, *Repertorium*, 474.   [71] *Ibid.* 465, note 11.

[72] Gero Dolezalek, review of Spagnesi, *Wernerius Bononiensis iudex*, in *ZRG RA* 88 (1971), 497. Cf. Gustav Pescatore, "Verzeichnis legistischen Distinktionen mit Angabe des Verfassers," *ZRG RA* 33 (1912), 495, note 1 and Cortese, *Il diritto nella storia medievale* II 76, note 39.

[73] Dolezalek, *Repertorium*, 472, note 24.

[74] Dolezalek, *Repertorium*, 483, dates this change to the middle of the twelfth century. Cf. Pierre Legendre, "Chronique de droit romain médiéval [C], I: Sur l'origine du sigle FF," *Revue d'histoire du droit* 4: 43 (1965), 309–310; reprinted in Pierre Legendre, *Ecrits juridiques du Moyen Age occidental*, Collected Studies CS 280 (London 1988), no. Vc.

taries on the texts of canon law), clearly with the purpose of distinguishing them from the texts which he quoted. In this interpretation, the "*y*"
preceding some glosses simply bears witness to the formal conventions of
early twelfth-century legal manuscripts, and has nothing in common
with the later convention of signing glosses with *sigla* indicating a teacher
who agreed with the content. There are glosses signed "y" which refer
to the opinions of *guar.* or *gar.* (Guarnerius/Irnerius).[75] In such cases it
can only with difficulty be maintained that the *siglum* meant that Irnerius
was the author of the gloss.

Taking this view, the glosses in Roman law books were initially anonymous. There is nothing remarkable about such an assertion, since glosses
were usually anonymous in non-legal disciplines.[76] I suggest that Roman
law teachers began to attach *sigla* to glosses at some point in the middle
of the twelfth century. Further research is needed to determine exactly
when the conventions in this respect changed. There are glosses beginning with "y" and ending with "b" or "m" (for Bulgarus and Martinus,
respectively),[77] which suggests that the paragraph mark later interpreted
as a "y" was still used when the Four Doctors had begun to teach. Since
this indicates that their generation also prefaced their glosses with a paragraph mark, some y-glosses without another *siglum* at the end may also
have been written by them. One cannot, therefore, be certain that a gloss
signed with "y" necessarily pre-dated Gratian's *Decretum*.

After some time, one may surmise, the teachers and students of
Roman law came to expect *sigla* to accompany most glosses, and they
began to read the paragraph marks preceding glosses in old manuscripts
as a *siglum* "y." The y-glosses outnumbered the glosses signed with any
other *siglum*,[78] which provided a fertile ground for the myths about
Irnerius. It remains uncertain exactly what reason twelfth-century law
teachers had initially for associating the y-glosses with Wernerius. One
may guess that he already had a reputation for being a skilled interpreter
of the law.

To summarize, it remains uncertain whether Irnerius really wrote all
or any of the glosses that are attributed to him. Some or even all of them
may have been written by other legal thinkers active in his time or later.
There is even less reason to attribute the old glosses found without *sigla*
in early manuscripts to him, as is often done.[79] There are reasons to think

---

[75] Pescatore, *Glossen des Irnerius*, 31 and 40–44, Besta, *L'opera d'Irnerio*, I 80, note I and II vi–vii.
[76] Beryl Smalley, *The Study of the Bible in the Middle Ages*, 2nd edn. (Oxford 1952), 62.
[77] Dolezalek, *Repertorium*, 484.
[78] Pescatore, *Glossen des Irnerius*, 41, estimated that the manuscript Munich, Bayerische
Staatsbibliothek clm 22 contained more than a thousand glosses signed "y."
[79] Dolezalek, *Repertorium*, 274, Lange, *Römisches Recht im Mittelalter*, I 160.

that several jurists were active before the Four Doctors, and that Irnerius simply was the most famous of them, which in itself could be sufficient to make his posthumous fame grow even larger and overshadow that of every other jurist.

For the purposes of this book, it does not really matter whether the glosses in question were written by Irnerius or by one of his contemporaries, as long as they were written before the completion of Gratian's *Decretum*. I hope I have shown that the fact that a gloss is signed "y" on its own does not necessarily mean that the gloss pre-dates the *Decretum*. I have dwelled on the issue of Irnerius' contribution, since I believe that the standard literature on the medieval study of Roman law, taking its cue from Odofredus, tends to exaggerate his importance. This exaggeration is one of the reasons why scholars have believed that Gratian's sparing use of Roman law in the original version of the *Decretum* is an anomaly that needs to be explained. The more sophisticated among the "Irnerian" glosses may in fact have been written after the publication of the *Decretum*. A scholar interested in the state of the teaching of Roman law during the period when Gratian was working on his *Decretum* must, therefore, leave the y-glosses aside and instead examine those glosses which, on paleographical grounds, can be dated to the early twelfth century.

Roman law in the early twelfth century

Dolezalek's thorough examination of glosses on two titles in Justinian's *Code* forms a firm basis on which a judgement can be formed. He clarifies that glosses of three types[80] survive from the early twelfth century. *Notabilia* direct the reader's attention to some particularly useful passage in the text. At first, such places were marked with ornate symbols in the margins, but the glossators soon began to repeat the interesting words in the margin. *Allegations* draw attention to parallel or contrary passages elsewhere in the *Corpus iuris civilis*. In the early twelfth century, these cross-references had not yet found the standard form which would be used for the rest of the middle ages and beyond. Most important for a scholar interested in the intellectual content of the early teaching of Roman law are the *explicatory* glosses. Dolezalek has characterized such glosses written in the first half of the twelfth century:

Anyone who hopes to read long, doctrinal expositions in the early glosses, will

---

[80] To these three types should be added the *authenticae*, which were summaries of some *novellae*, which the glossators added to the margins of the relevant places of the *Code*, see Dolezalek, *Repertorium*, 469–470.

be disappointed. In fact, one finds there a few distinctions and many summarizing transitions from one title to the next. But most explicatory glosses by far are only from one to four words long. Measured according to the number of *leges* that are accompanied by glosses of this type, the explicatory glosses stand far behind the allegations, the *notabilia*, and the signs.[81]

Dolezalek's conclusions are borne out by even a brief survey of the glosses which he edited. I concentrate on the explicatory glosses, which produce the clearest picture of the abilities of the men who wrote them. Typical for the explicatory glosses of the early twelfth century are those explaining a word (*transactum: id est pactum*[82]) or explaining a phrase that is not immediately intelligible (*nihil fraudis ei sit* in *Cod.* 5.1.2 is glossed *Vt uel accusetur uel arras reddat*[83]). There are also a few glosses which summarize the content of a passage, such as the one found at the beginning of *Cod.* 5.1.5.5: "Penam que olim lege constituta erat, pacto nunc constitui permissum est"[84] ("The punishment [for breaking an engagement] was earlier determined through law, now it is permitted to determine it through contract").

The character of the glosses which are found in early twelfth-century romanistic manuscripts suggests some conclusions about their authors. Explicatory glosses facilitate reading the text, greatly so when the text is full of technical terms, as Roman law texts often are. The summarizing transitions standing at the beginning of titles are suitable for a reader who is working his way through the text from beginning to end, or who wants to be able to find any specific topic quickly. The order of the text is, however not yet abandoned in favor of a more systematic treatment in, e.g., *questiones*. All this would be useful for a student studying at a law school, but also for a lawyer or a judge. In other words, the formulation of the glosses from the early twelfth

---

[81] Dolezalek, *Repertorium*, 471: "Wer hofft, in den frühen Glossierungen lange dogmatische Ausführungen zu lesen, wird enttäuscht. Zwar findet man darin einige wenige Distinktionen und zahlreiche summierende Überleitungen von einem Titel zum nächsten. Aber weitaus die meisten sinnerklärenden Glossen sind nur ein bis vier Worte lang, und gemessen an der Zahl der Leges, bei denen Glossen dieses Typs erscheinen, stehen die sinnerklärenden Glossen weit hinter den Allegationen, Notabilien und Zeichen zurück."

[82] Dolezalek, *Repertorium*, 723, note 192. This gloss appears with the *siglum* "y" in three early manuscripts.

[83] *Ibid.* 710, n. 105. The law text says that a betrothed woman under certain circumstances can break her engagement without this being a "fraud" in the technical, legal sense (*nihil fraudis ei sit*). The gloss explains that this means she cannot be accused of such a crime and she does not need to give back the gift the prospective groom had given her (*arra*). Cf. Kaser, *Römisches Privatrecht: Studienbuch*, § 36 IV 1 and § 58 III 3, and Berger, *Encyclopedic Dictionary*, s.v. *sponsalia*. The gloss is found in many manuscripts; one of them gives the *siglum* "y," three the *siglum* "m." (for Martinus Gosia).

[84] Dolezalek, *Repertorium*, 758, n. 394. The gloss appears in many manuscripts, in five of which it has the *siglum* "y." One manuscript gives the *siglum* "yr."

century does not prove that they originated in the course of regular, academic teaching of the subject. Unlike Bulgarus' moot court exercises (in the *Stemma Bulgaricum*), which are so clearly designed for students, these glosses could have been written by a lawyer in the solitude of his study.

In other words, the glosses from the early twelfth century do not prove that Irnerius or any of his contemporaries were teachers of Roman law. R. W. Southern has recently argued similarly on the basis of contemporary documents which show Irnerius in the role of a practicing lawyer and a politician working on behalf of Emperor Henry V.[85] Southern did not study his glosses (assuming that at least some of the glosses surviving from this period are his), but as I have just pointed out, they do not prove that their author was engaged in regular teaching of law. This does not mean, as Southern also states, that he could not have been accompanied by young men who learnt the craft of a lawyer from him, while he was practicing his profession. However, Southern is clearly correct in emphasizing that there is no good evidence for Irnerius being involved in systematic and academic teaching of Roman law, nor for the existence of a Bolognese law school at this time. Both phenomena are clearly attested only in the time of the Four Doctors. The foundation of their work was laid in the preceding period by persons like Irnerius, but there is no reason to assume that he did it alone.

When thirteenth-century chroniclers and law teachers with an interest in history (such as Odofredus) searched for the origins of medieval Roman law studies, Irnerius' political activities and his career in the courts were forgotten, but a large number of glosses signed "y" survived. Since they were accustomed to seeing glosses signed with the *siglum* of their author (or at least the *siglum* of a law teacher who agreed with their content), they assumed that an early and prolific legal thinker used the *siglum* "y." Somehow the name of Wernerius became associated with this man, which caused the name to be changed into Yrnerius/Irnerius. To these thirteenth-century scholars, glosses represented the teaching method *par excellence*,[86] and it was natural that they would jump to the conclusion that Irnerius was an academic teacher and the founder of the Bolognese law school.

---

[85] Southern, *Scholastic Humanism*, 274–282.

[86] For the teaching methods of the glossators, see Peter Weimar, "Die Legistische Literatur und die Methode des Rechtsunterrichts der Glossatorenzeit," *Ius commune* 2 (1969), 43–83, and Gero R. Dolezalek, "Les gloses des manuscrits de droit: reflet des méthodes d'enseignement," in *Manuel, programmes de cours et techniques d'enseignement dans les universités médiévales* (Louvain-la-Neuve 1994), 235–255.

Medieval jurisprudence and Gratian

The observations here outlined suggest a new understanding of the intellectual and jurisprudential climate in which Gratian compiled the *Decretum*. The medieval rebirth of jurisprudence appears to have happened later and more slowly than is usually assumed.

During the eleventh and early twelfth centuries, the legal profession in Northern Italy became slowly but steadily more sophisticated, as one can see in, e.g., the re-arrangement of the sources of Lombard law into the *Liber legis Langobardorum*,[87] the increasing use of law and legal arguments in the papal curia, and the fact that some lawyers began to quote Justinian's *Digest*. One should, however, be careful not to exaggerate the extent and sophistication of these activities, particularly with reference to Roman law. They do not necessarily prove the existence of a law school in Bologna or anywhere else. The jurists of this time worked closely with Roman law texts, laboriously striving to understand them word by word; but they did not build systems. Their purpose was practical rather than academic; their work served the needs of the courts, not the lecture rooms. This can be clearly seen in the juridical documents of the time, which generally quote terse rules, when they quote Roman law at all.[88] The first sizeable collection of excerpts from the *Digest*, in the *Collectio Britannica*, contains terse rules of exactly this kind.[89] The contemporary glosses are such that they would help the lawyer to find and understand such rules.

In such a slow continuous growth of legal culture it is difficult to identify any particular point in time as the point when medieval jurisprudence began. Traditionally, Irnerius has been identified as its originator, but there are also voices supporting his supposed teacher, the shadowy figure of Pepo.[90] In a controversial book, Charles M. Radding argued that medieval jurisprudence originated even earlier, in the first half of the eleventh century among the Lombard *iudices* of Pavia and that Pepo and Irnerius came out of this tradition.[91] His conclusions are flawed, since they are

---

[87] Radding, *Origins of Medieval Jurisprudence*, 78–84.

[88] See, e.g., the often cited judgement of Marturi from 1076 in Cesare Manaresi, ed., *I placiti del "Regnum Italiae,"* Fonti per la storia d'Italia 97 (Rome 1960), 333–335, and the papal judgement of 1125 (JL 7210; see above, note 52).

[89] See the edition in Carlo Guido Mor, "Il *Digesto* nell'età preirneriana e la formazione della 'vulgata,'" in Carlo Guido Mor, *Scritti di storia giuridica altomedievale* (Pisa 1977), 215–232.

[90] Carlo Dolcini, *"Velut aurora surgente": Pepo, il vescovo Pietro e l'origine dello studium Bolognese*, Istituto storico Italiano per il medio evo: Studi storici 180 (Rome 1987) and Cortese, *Il diritto nella storia medievale*, II 33–55.

[91] Radding, *Origins of Medieval Jurisprudence*. Radding expanded on some of his arguments in "Legal science 1000–1200: the invention of a discipline," *Rivista di storia di diritto italiano* 63 (1990), 409–432, and in "Vatican Latin 1406."

based on evidence which has been wrongly dated.[92] Some of his arguments and his questions are, however, noteworthy, particularly his insistence that the traditional view that Irnerius singlehandedly revived
Roman law and brought its study to a high level of sophistication cannot
be correct. Radding's conclusion was that Irnerius must have had predecessors, and he argued that the jurists of Pavia had prepared the way for
his achievements. In my view, Irnerius' achievements have been exaggerated; he did not singlehandedly create the medieval study of Roman law,
so there is no necessity to posit a previous period of preparation. His and
his contemporaries' efforts provide, instead, the background of the breakthrough in medieval jurisprudence achieved by the generation of the
Four Doctors, who brought the study of Roman law to the high level
formerly ascribed to Irnerius.

The reasons for the confusion in regard to the beginning of jurisprudence are not all related to problematic evidence. A large part of the
problem is that it has seldom been made really clear what is meant by
"jurisprudence." Is it evidence for jurisprudence that a lawyer is able to
quote the *Digest* in court proceedings (as was done in Marturi in 1076)?
Or does it require regular, academic teaching in a law school? Perhaps the
best approach is to avoid the abstract term jurisprudence and instead be
specific. In the present study, the pertinent question is whether the
science of Roman law in the time of Gratian 1 was so advanced that his
near-avoidance (in the first recension) of Justinianic texts and concepts
requires explanation. One would, ideally, like to compare the treatment
by Gratian 1 of specific legal issues with contemporary romanistic treatments of the same issues. I was able to do this above in connection with
women's right to accuse, since this issue is also treated in Bulgarus'
roughly contemporary letter to Chancellor Haimeric. Beyond that work,
there is very little with which to compare the efforts of Gratian 1. There
are no systematic romanistic treatises that can be confidently dated to his
time or earlier. The glosses printed as Irnerius' have been so identified
solely on the basis of *sigla*, which do not, I hope to have shown, form a
reliable basis for attributing or dating glosses. Comparative material
would, thus, have to be culled from manuscripts with glosses which can,
on paleographical grounds, be dated to the early twelfth century.
Without investigating specific issues, a survey of glosses from this period
suggests, as pointed out above, that legal science had not then advanced

---

[92] Bruce C. Brasington, review of *Origins of Medieval Jurisprudence*, by Charles M. Radding, in
Comitatus: A Journal of Medieval and Renaissance Studies 20 (1989), 97–100, James Brundage, review
of *Origins of Medieval Jurisprudence*, by Charles M. Radding, in *Journal of the History of the Behavioral
Sciences* 26 (1990), 400–402, and Stanley Chodorow, review of *Origins of Medieval Jurisprudence*, by
Charles M. Radding, in *Speculum* 65 (1990), 743–745.

as far as is generally thought. Towards the middle of the twelfth century this changes. Systematic treatises become increasingly common and the glosses more sophisticated.

The manuscripts of law books from around the middle of the twelfth century begin to show signs of a technical security and professionalism not found in earlier manuscripts, which is exactly what could be expected from manuscripts produced in an academic setting. After experimentation with various reference systems, including the peculiar "red signs,"[93] the forms of reference to passages in Roman and canon law were standardized in the middle of the century, and so were the formulations of glosses of several kinds (allegations, *notabilia*, etc.). I have argued that the custom of signing glosses with *sigla* also began at this time. The stylistic and formal differences between the two recensions of Gratian's *Decretum* show that legal culture changed considerably in the direction of professionalism between the end of the 1130s and the beginning of the 1150s. A comparison between the content of the glosses of Irnerius' time with the *Stemma Bulgaricum* or any other works written by the Four Doctors reveals a similar development.

These changes and their causes are interesting in themselves. What brought about these changes? I suggest that the law school of Bologna originated in the 1130s and that this caused the developments outlined above. There is no doubt that the school existed by the middle of the twelfth century, but evidence is lacking for its existence before Gratian 1 and Bulgarus, i.e. before the late 1130s. It is to be expected that the introduction of academic teaching in a subject would have this effect on the subject.

Earlier scholarship has discussed much source material (such as glosses, chronicles, charters, papal judgements, etc.) which illuminates the legal culture of the period before the 1130s. The standard account of the beginnings of legal teaching has, however, been allowed to prejudice the interpretation of this material, so that it has been taken to demonstrate or illustrate the activities of the early Bolognese law school. Read without this prejudice, the sources demonstrate an increasing interest in law. To take this as an indication that there was a law school is to put the cart before the horse. Interest in law is a necessary precondition for the creation of a law school.

Against this background, the relationship of Gratian 1 to Roman law appears less problematic than was earlier thought. When he worked on the *Decretum* in the 1130s, the Roman law school in Bologna was still in its infancy. The lack of systematic works meant that as important a subject

---

[93] Dolezalek and Weigand, "Roten zeichen."

as procedural law was extremely difficult to approach, since no one place in Justinian's legislation treats it. It is, therefore, not surprising that Gratian 1's grasp of Roman procedural law was shaky, and that most of the Roman texts added by the author of the second recension concern procedure. Gratian 1 did not choose to exclude Roman law from the *Decretum*; it was simply not possible for him to do much more than he did without devoting his time to specialized study in a subject other than his own.

Chapter 6

THE MEN BEHIND THE *DECRETUM*

This book has endeavored to answer Stephan Kuttner's question: "Was it [the *Decretum*] drafted and completed in one grandiose thrust, or did the original version go through successive redactions?" I hope to have proved that the latter is true. Kuttner followed his question up with another: "And if the latter, was it Gratian himself, or Gratian with his disciples, or an early generation of canonists after him, who completed the final recension which from the mid-twelfth century on was used in the schools and in adjudging cases?"[1]

Kuttner's second question has become even more pertinent with the discovery that two distinct recensions of Gratian's *Decretum* are preserved. Did the two versions have the same author? There is no external evidence to throw light on the issue; in fact, nothing at all is known with certainty about Gratian, except that he wrote at least one recension of the *Decretum*.[2] Under these circumstances, almost the only available evidence is the style and content of the texts themselves. Internal evidence of this kind is, however, seldom conclusive; many long-standing debates about the authorship of texts have arisen when the evidence is of this kind, as with fragments of the ancient poet Gallus, the Pauline epistles, the Rule of St. Benedict, and several Shakespearean plays. It may ultimately turn out to be impossible to determine with certainty whether or not the same man wrote the two recensions of the *Decretum*.

THE EVIDENCE OF THE MANUSCRIPTS

In the first place, what the oldest manuscripts of each recension have to say about the authorship of the *Decretum* must be examined. The manuscripts of the first recension are remarkably uninformative about their author. He is not identified in any text written by the original scribe in

---

[1] Kuttner, "Research on Gratian," 10.   [2] See above, chapter 1.

any of the uninterpolated first-recension manuscripts. The Paris manuscript, which is defective at the end, does not even have a rubric at the beginning, while the Florence manuscript, defective at the beginning, lacks a colophon at the end. The Barcelona manuscript (defective at the end) does not name the author, but at least contains a rubric immediately before distinction 1:

Concordia discordantium canonum ac primum de iure nature et constitutionis. Bc
[The concord of discordant canons, and first about the law of nature and of ordinance.]

The Admont manuscript is a more problematic witness, since the text written by the original scribe is interpolated with second-recension readings. This manuscript does in fact identify the author as Gratian, but this identification was probably not found in the original (uninterpolated) text of its exemplar. Gratian is named as the author at the end of the first-recension text in the first of the two volumes making up this manuscript:

Explicit prima pars Graciani de concordia discordantium canonum. *Admont 23, fo. 199v.*
[The end of Gratian's first part about the concord of discordant canons.]

The text is prefaced by a brief rubric similar to the second half of the rubric in Bc:

Primum capitulum de iure nature et constitutionis. *Admont 23, fo. 9r.*
[The first chapter about the law of nature and of ordinance.]

The second volume, Admont 43, does not contain any notes of this kind. (Gratian is named elsewhere in the volumes, but that is in connection with prefaces and other material which are extraneous to the first recension, e.g. on fo. 1r of Admont 43.) To assess the explicit on fo. 199v of Admont 23, it is significant to point out that Gratian is here identified only at the end of the text in the first volume. The *de luxe* Admont manuscript distributes the text of the *Decretum* over two volumes, something which is very unusual among Gratian manuscripts. Paris, BN lat. 3884 (Pf) is the only other example known to me. Aa's exemplar was most likely a first-recension manuscript with some additions in the margins and a supplement added on new quires. Even a luxury copy of the first recension would probably not have been long enough to require two volumes. It is, therefore, very likely that the explicit after C. 14 in Admont 23 was composed by the scribe of that manuscript and not present in his exemplar. Only the rubric before D. 1 can be supposed to have been present in the original hand in the exemplar, and this rubric does not mention the author's name. The manuscripts of the first recension thus do not contain any reliable information about the name of its author.

Remarkably, the same holds true for the oldest second-recension manuscripts (and, in fact, also for many more recent manuscripts), some of which contain a rubric identical or similar to the one in Bc:

(Titulus decretorum *add. Vd:* Incipit *add. Av:* Concordia *add. Pf Pk*) Discordantium canonum (*om. Vd*) concordia (*om. Pf Pk*) ac primum de iure nature et constitutionis (const. et nat. *Pf Tx Vd:* constitutionum et nat. *Gg*) (R. *add Tx*). *Av³ Cg Gg Pa Pf Pk Tx Vd Friedb.AE*
[The concord of discordant canons, and first about the law of nature and of ordinance.]

It is likely that one variant of this rubric is the original one and that it already prefaced the first recension.[4] Its second half is echoed in the cross-reference found in the first recension of C. 11, q. 1, d. p. c. 26 (see below, p. 179). It is also likely that neither recension originally contained any indication of who the author was.

INTRODUCTIONS TO THE *DECRETUM*

Gratian's *Decretum* does not contain a preface or a prologue of some kind which might have clarified some of the issues discussed here, although several early commentators provided such introductory comments in their own prefaces.[5] The most common in the earliest manuscripts is the lengthy *In prima parte agitur*, which in detail describes the contents of the first part and the *causae*. In many manuscripts, this introduction fails to mention the *de consecratione*,[6] so it is safe to assume that the introduction was written before the completion of the second recension. It does not identify the author of the *Decretum*.

The introduction *Hoc opus inscribitur* appears, as far as is known, only in two manuscripts, one of which is the first-recension manuscript Aa.[7] Both manuscripts were written in the diocese of Salzburg, so it is possible that the introduction was also written there. This introduction also appears to have been written for the first recension, since it does not mention the *de consecratione*. The author is named in the first sentence:

[3] The readings from Av are reported by Jacqueline Rambaud in her cardfile at the Bibliothèque Nationale de France, Paris.
[4] Cf. Heyer, "Der Titel der Kanonessammlung Gratians," who concentrates (arbitrarily) on the first three words of the rubric. Mz Me Pl lack rubric, while the first page of the text in Mk is missing. Sa has a longer rubric which does not name the author.
[5] Robert Somerville and Bruce C. Brasington, *Prefaces to Canon Law Books in Latin Christianity: Selected Translations, 500–1245* (New Haven 1998), 172.   [6] Rambaud, "Le legs," 93.
[7] Weigand, *Glossen zum "Dekret,"* 663.

Hoc opus inscribitur de concordia discordantium canonum. Quod a quodam Gratiano compositum (et *add. Aa*) in libros xxxvii est distinctum. *Aa Me*
[This work is entitled the concord of discordant canons, which was composed by a certain Gratian and divided into thirty-seven books.]

Perhaps the *quodam* indicates that the author of this preface did not know any more about Gratian than his name. In any case, the author of the first recension is here identified, as Gratian.

This identification appears also in a short introductory gloss to the *Decretum* which in its orginal form (preserved in Pf) begins:

Concordia discordantium canonum iuxta determinationem Gratiani episcopi que in duas partes principaliter est diuisa.[8]
[The concord of discordant canons according to the determination of Bishop Gratian, which is principally divided into two parts.]

Since this gloss mentions only two parts of the *Decretum*, it clearly refers to the first recension, whose author again is identified as Gratian. Rudolf Weigand considered it likely that the gloss was composed in France, so the identification of Gratian as the author of the first recension appears in the early tradition in both France and Austria.

The oldest Italian witness allows the author of the *Decretum* to remain nameless. In the first *summa*, Paucapalea refers, not to Gratian, but to *magistri hoc opus condentis* ("the master who produced this work") when he is commenting on the text of the second recension.[9] The vague formulation may indicate that Paucapalea did not know the name of the author of the *Decretum*, or that he did not think the name was important. It would be difficult to argue that Gratian's name was so well known that it was unnecessary to include it, when so many *Decretum* manuscripts from this time lack the name. Later decretists, such as Rolandus, Rufinus, and Stephen of Tournai, give the author's name as Gratian.[10]

In conclusion, the evidence of the early commentators suggests that the author of the first recension was called Gratian. When witnesses, e.g. the author of the *Summa Parisiensis*, referring in general terms to the second recension of the *Decretum*, name Gratian as its author, this does not prove that Gratian was also responsible for the additions in this recension. More specific statements are required for such an assertion, particularly as the earliest commentators show themselves to be so poorly informed about the author of the *Decretum*.

---

[8] Text in Weigand, "Frühe Kanonisten," 153.
[9] Paucapalea, *Summa über das "Decretum Gratiani,"* 3; transl. in Somerville and Brasington, *Prefaces to Canon Law Books*, 184.   [10] Schulte, *Geschichte*, I 47, note 1.

INTERNAL EVIDENCE

Since the external evidence has proved so scanty, I shall here investigate some internal evidence that may help in answering the question whether one author was responsible for both recensions of Gratian's *Decretum*. The purpose is to find out how great the differences are between the two recensions.

INTERNAL REFERENCES

There are twenty-nine internal references in the final version of Gratian's *Decretum*.[11] Thirteen of them were present already in the first recension, while sixteen were added in the second.

The following edition of the internal references in the first recension was made on the basis of Aa Bc Fd P and with reference to Friedberg's edition. I have added, within square brackets, modern references to the passages intended.[12]

C. 1, q. 1, d. p. c. 96
Unde etiam ab ecclesia Romana repudiatur, et a Deo fuisse (*om. Aa*) percussus legitur in gestis Romanorum Pontificum hoc modo: "Anastasius secundus natione Romanus, etc." [D. 19, c 9] Require retro in tractatu decretalium epistolarum. *Aa Bc Fd P*

C. 1, q. 7, d. p. c. 6
Item: "Priscis igitur (*om. Aa*), etc." Require supra in tractatu ordinandorum. [D. 55, c. 1] *Aa Bc Fd P*

C. 6, q. 1, d. p. c. 19
Hereticos namque accusare infamibus non prohibetur, ut supra patuit in ea causa, ubi (*ex ut corr. Fd*) de accusatione minorum adversus maiores disputatum est. [C. 2, q. 7] *Aa Bc Fd P*

C. 11, q. 1, d. p. c. 26
Unde Augustinus ait super Iohannem: "Quo iure villas defendis? divino, an humano, etc.?" [D. 8, c. 1] Require in principio, ubi (*om. Bc*) differentia designatur (assignatur *Aa*) inter ius nature et ius constitutionis. *Aa Bc Fd P*

C. 13, q. 2, d. p. c. 1
Quomodo autem (*om. Friedb.*) distinguende sint he auctoritates, in causa monachorum invenietur. [C. 16, q. 4] *Aa Fd*

C. 14, q. 1, d. p. c. 1
Unde Prosper in lib. de vita contemplativa (cont. vita *Aa*): "Sacerdos, cui dispensationis cura conmissa est, etc." Require in causa eius, a quo pro ingressu monasterii pecunia exigebatur. [C. 2, q. 2, c. 9] *Aa Fd*

---

[11] *Ibid.*, I 49–50, note 9.
[12] Any translation of these references would prejudge the question of how they are to be understood, as I argue below. They have therefore been left in Latin.

C. 15, q. 1, d. p. c. 13
Sicut de (quodam *add. Friedb.*) episcopo Gregorius scribit in registro ad Eleuterium Episcopum: "Quamvis triste sit nobis, etc.," ut supra: "Longa invaletudine gravatus episcopus." [C. 7, q. 1, c. 14] *Aa Fd*

C. 15, q. 3, d. p. c. 4
Sed sicut circa huius operis initium [D. 10] premissum est, tociens legibus inperatorum in ecclesiasticis negociis utendum est, quociens sacris canonibus obviare non inveniuntur. *Aa Fd*

C. 16, q. 1, d. p. c. 16
Ubicumque facultas rerum et oportunitas temporum suppetit, etc., sicut in eodem capitulo (*Aa Fd Friedb.CEGH*; capite *Friedb.*) supra legitur in causa eorum, qui de diocesi ad diocesim transierunt. [C. 13, q. 2, c. 6] *Aa Fd*

C. 16, q. 1, d. p. c. 20
Gelasius tamen, sicut in tractatu de promotionibus clericorum invenitur, in capitulo illo: "Monachus novicius, etc.," permittit illos ex dispensatione defensores fieri. [D. 77, c. 9] *Aa Fd*

C. 25, q. 2, d. p. c .25
Hostiliatis quoque vel paupertatis necessitate episcopales sedes vel mutantur, vel due in unum rediguntur, sicut supra in titulo de mutationibus episcoporum B. Gregorius fecisse legitur. [*probably* C. 7, q. 1, c. 42; cf. c. 44 and C. 16, q. 1, c. 48] *Aa Fd*

C. 25, q. 2, d. p. c. 25
Sed obicitur illud Simaci Pape: "Possessiones, quas unusquisque ecclesie suo reliquit arbitrio, etc.," que supra in titulo de alienatione rerum ecclesiasticarum leguntur asscripta. [C. 16, q. 1, c. 61] *Aa Fd*

C. 27, q. 1, d. p. c. 43
Quod autem voventes premissis auctoritatibus iubentur ab invicem discedere, quorum vero coniugia auctoritate Augustini [D. 27, c. 2] et Theodori [D. 27, c. 3] solvenda non sunt, in capitulo de ordinatione clericorum evidenter ostenditur. *Aa Fd*

After the later twelfth century, canonical references became heavily abbreviated and formalized. A canonist who wanted to refer to a particular canon did not have much, if any, choice as to how to cite it.[13] Against this background, it is striking that the references in the first recension are not formulaic at all. In fact, one gets the impression that each reference could have been formulated in several different, equally acceptable ways.

This impression is borne out by a detailed examination of the formulations. In the first recension, Gratian uses various terms which seem to refer to subdivisions of his work: *tractatus, principium, initium, capitulum, causa,* and *titulus.* These terms may easily be taken to refer to divisions that were intended or planned by Gratian. However, the fact that he used

---

[13] The system is explained in Hermann Kantorowicz, "Die Allegationen im späteren Mittelalter," *Archiv für Urkundenforschung* 13 (1935), 15–29.

six different labels suggests that, beyond *causa*, they are non-technical, i.e., Gratian thus referred not to a formal division of his work but simply to the place or a text where a certain subject was discussed. Each of the terms he used is capable of non-technical meaning as well as of being a reference to a formal section of a book: "Tractatus de promotionibus clericorum" could, e.g., be translated technically, as "the treatise on the promotion of the clergy" as well as, non-technically, "the treatment of the promotion of the clergy." This interpretation is further supported by the informal way in which Gratian specifies which "section" he refers to: "in the *causa* [or 'case'?], in which there is a discussion about accusations of subordinates against their superiors" (C. 5, q. 1, d. p. c. 19), "in the beginning, where the difference between the law of nature and the law of ordinance is defined" (C. 11, q. 1, d. p. c. 26), "in the case of him, from whom money was demanded for entry into a monastery" (C. 14, q. 1, d. p. c. 1), "in the treatment of papal decretals" (C. 1, q. 1, d. p. c. 96).

In the second recension, the procedure for referring to texts elsewhere in the *Decretum* is more formalized:[14]

D. 32, d. p. c. 6, princ.
Verum principia harum auctoritatum contraire uidentur Ieronimo, Augustino et ceteris, qui Christi sacramenta neque in bono, neque in malo homine fugienda demonstrant, sicut subsequens causa simoniacorum plenius ostendit. [C. 1]
C. 3, q. 1, d. p. c. 6
Unde supra in tractatu ordinandorum: "Si quis pecunia uel gratia humana, seu populari uel militare tumultu, etc." [D. 79, c. 9]
C. 7, q. 1, d. p. c. 48
Hinc etiam Augustinus: "Tu bonus tollera malum etc." infr. de tollerandis malis, in prima causa hereticorum. [C. 23, q. 4, c. 2]
C. 11. q. 3, d. p. c. 21
Hinc etiam Urbanus Vilimundo episcopo: "Sane quod super Richardo" et cetera. Require infra causam: "Quidam episcopus in heresim lapsus." [C. 24, q. 2, c. 3]
C. 11, q. 3, d. p. c. 24
Item illud Prosperi: "Facilius sibi Deum placabunt etc.," require infra causa "Maleficiis inpeditus," quest. 1 de penitentia.) [de pen. D. 1, c. 32]
C. 11, q. 3, d. p. c. 24
de qua supra: "Cum excommunicato nolite communicare." [?]
C. 11, q. 3, d. p. c. 24
Hanc distinctionem cuique licet aduertere ex auctoritate Iohannis Papae: "Engiltrudam uxorem Bosonis etc." Require supra in causa: "Quidam episcopus a propria sede deiectus." [C. 3, q. 4, c. 12]

---

14 Texts according to Friedberg, ed., *Decretum*.

C. 11, q. 3, d. p. c. 24
Item ex auctoritate eiusdem: "Si quis domum Dei uiolauerit etc." Require infra causa "Quidam presbiter infirmitate grauatus." [C. 17, q. 4, c. 21]

C. 11, q. 3, d. p. c. 24
Item ex auctoritate Siluestri Papae: "Presenti decreto censemus etc." Require supra in causa: "In infamia cuiusdam episcopi." [C. 5, q. 2, c. 2]

C. 11, q. 3, d. p. c. 24
Iuxta hanc ergo distinctionem intelligenda est illa auctoritas Innocentii: "Si quis suadente diabolo, etc." ut infra causa: "Quidam presbiter." [C. 17, q. 4, c. 29]

C. 11, q. 3, d. p. c. 24
Illud autem Petri de Clemente: "Si inimicus est iste Clemens etc." [D. 93, c. 1 = C. 11, q. 3, c. 15] de sententia notatis intelligendum est, sicut et illud Urbani: "Quibus episcopi non communicant etc." ut infra in eadem causa. [C. 11, q. 3, c. 27]

C. 11, q. 3, d. p. c. 24
Ceterum falsum esset illud Varensis concilii II.: "Si tantum episcopus alieni sceleris se conscium nouit." [C. 6, q. 2, c. 2] Item et illud: "Placuit, ut si quando episcopus etc." require supra in causa: "Duo fornicatores et infamia notati." [C. 6, q. 2, c. 3]

C. 11, q. 3, d. p. c. 26
Unde infra Urbanus: "Sane quod super Richardo etc." Causa: "Quidam episcopus in heresim lapsus." [C. 24, q. 2, c. 3]

C. 11, q. 3, d. p. c. 26
Item Nicolaus Papa "Excellentissimus rex Karolus" infra circa finem huius causae. [C. 11, q. 3, c. 102]

de cons. D. 1, d. p. c. 50
Unde Leo episcopus: "Quod a patribus nostris." [D. 75, c. 4] Item Pelagius: "Dilectionis tuae rescripta." [D. 76, c. 12] Require in tractatu ordinandorum.

de cons. D. 4, d. p. c. 20
Unde Urbanus II.: "Super quibus consuluit etc.," ut supra in tractatu coniugii, ubi de conpatribus agitur. [C. 30, q. 3, c. 4]

Most references follow a set format, referring to *causae* by indicating their *incipits*: "[Require] supra/infra [in] causa '*incipit*.'" Only one reference in the first recension gives the *incipit* of the relevant *causa* (C. 15, q. 1, d. p. c. 13), and in that case, the word *causa* is not included.

The formulation of internal references, thus, developed interestingly between the two recensions. From having been expressed in fairly ordinary language, the references became more standardized and technical, albeit not yet as standardized as in most early glosses.[15] The standardization of the formulations suggests a setting where cross-referencing between different canons had become common, and it is reasonable to assume that this was in connection with teaching of canon law on the

---

[15] See many early glosses edited in Weigand, *Glossen zum "Dekret."*

basis of the first recension of the *Decretum*. In other words, the compiler
of the second recension was someone who had taught canon law on the
basis of the first recension.

This conclusion wins further support from an investigation of the glosses
to the first recension. The writing of glosses implies that the text was
subject to teaching and there is no doubt that already the first recension
was glossed, for three first-recension manuscripts carry glosses (Aa Bc
Fd). Rudolf Weigand has shown that the glosses in these three manuscripts are related to each other (and to glosses in a number of second-
recension manuscripts).[16] Weigand has identified in these manuscripts the
first apparatus of glosses to Gratian's *Decretum*. He points out that an early
variant of this apparatus was written before the first part of the *Decretum*
was divided into distinctions, since some manuscripts – including Aa Bc
Fd – preserve references to the first part, which do not mention the
number of the relevant distinction.[17]

The fact that three first-recension manuscripts contain an early apparatus of glosses does not, of course, mean that these glosses were written
before the composition of the second recension. In Bc and Fd, the glosses
are written by a hand later than the main hand of each manuscript and
they could have been added on the basis of the glosses in a second-recension manuscript. Aa is interpolated with second-recension readings, so
the testimony of its glosses is useless in this context. It is, however, important to determine if these glosses antedate the second recension, and on
this issue the following can be said.

First, two glosses (appearing as such in Aa Fd Gg) are interpolated into
the text of C. 2, q. 6, c. 28 in the first-recension manuscript P (and also
in the second-recension manuscript Pf). This strongly suggests that P's
exemplar was glossed, even though P itself lacks glosses. Since P shows
no influence from the second recension, the glosses of its exemplar could
also have been written without such influence.

Second, there is at least one gloss which concerns only the text of the
first recension and which seems to have influenced the text of the second
recension. The gloss in question comments on the first recension of C.
3, q. 1, d. p. c. 6. The text of this *dictum* changed between the two recensions. In the first it says the following:

C. 3, q. 1, d. p. c. 6
It is, thus, plain that those previously despoiled are to be restored presently before

[16] *Ibid.*, 751.   [17] *Ibid.* 424 and 751.

they are called to court. But it is objected that where there is no legitimate installation, there cannot be any restitution. For he is not proven destituted, who was not previously installed, and for this reason he cannot demand restitution. Those, whose elections are faulty, who either are not elected by the clergy or desired by the people, or who have invaded through simony, are not to be included among the bishops, and therefore if they are expelled from the sees which they appear to be occupying, they cannot request restitution before they are called to court.** To this it is replied: if the error in the election is known to the church and they therefore have been reproved and if they have invaded their sees with violence, having been ejected they cannot request restitution. But if the church wishes to tolerate them patiently and to concede the rank of office to them, even if their election was faulty, they are nevertheless to be restored after having been ejected, before they are called to a synod in a regular manner.[18]

In the second recension, the beginning of the text was left unchanged, while the response to the objection (from *his ita responditur* ["to this it is replied"], marked with ** above) was replaced with new text:

C. 3, q. 1, d. p. c. 6

Hence above in the treatise about those to be ordained: "Si quis pecunia uel gratia humana, seu populari uel militari tumultu, etc." But this is to be understood only in the case when the apostolic see is occupied through violence, in which case no judge can be found, through whose office that apostate can be excluded. For in other cases this text does not apply, since a violently acquired possession cannot be taken away from the violent occupier, except through the sentence of a judge. If the true owner ejects him with violence from the possession, through renewed, not through continuous war, he shall restore the possession to the robber through the authority of the judge. If bishops, thus, are ejected from sees which they in some way appear to hold, violently and not through a judge, they are to be restored after the ejection and before being called to a synod in a regular manner.[19]

---

[18] "Patet ergo quod exspoliati prius presentialiter restituendi, ante quam ad causam sint vocandi. Sed obicitur ubi non fuit legitima institutio, ibi nec potest esse restitutio. Non enim probatur destitutus qui prius fuerit institutus, ac per hoc nec restaurationem postulare potest. Illi ergo quorum electio viciosa est, vel qui a clero non sunt electi vel a populo expetiti vel qui per symoniam irrepserunt, non sunt habendi inter episcopos et ideo si a sedibus quas tenere videbantur expulsi fuerint non possunt restitutionem petere ante quam vocentur ad causam. ** His ita respondetur. Si vicium electionis ecclesie notum fuerit et ideo reprobati fuerint et si aliqua violentia in sedibus illis irrepserint eiecti restitutionem postulare non possunt. Si autem ecclesia eos per pacientiam tolerare voluerit et eis gradum honoris concesserit et si viciosa fuerit eorum electio, tamen post eiectionem restituendi sunt, ante regularem ad synodi vocationem." Aa Bc Fd P.

[19] Friedberg, ed., *Decretum*, 507: "Unde supra in tractatu ordinandorum: 'Si quis pecunia uel gratia humana, seu populari uel militari tumultu, etc.' Sed hoc in eo tantum casu intelligitur, quo apostolica sedes per uiolentiam occupatur, quo casu iudex non inuenitur, cuius offitio ille apostaticus possit excludi. In aliis autem locum non habet, cum uiolenta possessio, nisi per iudicis sententiam, uiolento detentori detrahi non possit. Si autem uerus dominus, bello non continuato, sed renouato, ui illum eiecerit de possessione, iudicis auctoritate predoni possessionem restituet. Si ergo episcopi a sedibus, quas quoquomodo tenere uidebantur, non per iudicem, sed uiolenter eiecti fuerint, post eiectionem restituendi sunt ante regularem ad sinodum uocationem."

The changes made in the second recension of this *dictum* are a further example of the author's proficiency in Roman law. The new text contains several romanistic technical terms[20] and it shows greater awareness than in the first recension of the function of the Roman law institute of *restitutio in integrum*. The text of the first recension is vague about when restitution should be applied and indicates several cases when it is not necessary. These exceptions would in practice, it is easy to imagine, be possible to adduce in almost any imaginable case, so they in effect invalidate the basic rule.

The author of the second recension allows only one exception to the rule: an invader of the papacy does not have the right to restitution if he is dethroned.[21] The jurisprudential reason for this is that the pope cannot be judged by anyone; since no trial could take place, the restitution (the purpose of which was to restore the original conditions before a definite judgement was made) was meaningless. The second recension thus explicated a canon from Nicholas II's Roman council of 1059, which is cited and which was present in the first recension, but quoted *in extenso* in another context (D. 79, c. 9). This canon is not influenced at all by any romanistic doctrines about restoration, but it becomes relevant for the discussion in C. 3, q. 1, d. p. c. 6, since it discusses the removal of a pope who has invaded his see in an unlawful way.

The canon, in fact, if generalized to speak of any bishop (the pope is by definition a bishop), supports the *dictum* in its first-recension form, although there is no particular reason to assume that Gratian 1 had it in mind here. The thematical similarities were, however, quickly noticed, and soon noted in a gloss that appears in two first-recension manuscripts and in at least two second-recension manuscripts.

Glossa ad C. 3, q. 1, d. p. c. 6
S. (p. i *add. Aa*) d. lxxviiii (lxxiv *Pa*), Si quis pecunia (pe. etc. *Pa*) *Aa Bc Gg Pa*

This gloss was probably present in the specific first-recension manuscript used by Gratian 2, since he incorporates the reference into the text of the *dictum*. This strongly suggests that the glossing of, and hence teaching on the basis of, the *Decretum* had begun before the second recension was finished. Three steps can be outlined in the process that led to the final version of this *dictum*: the writing of the original *dictum* by Gratian 1, the glossing by a glossator, and the writing of the final version of the *dictum* by Gratian 2. The usual problem of whether Gratian 1 and Gratian 2 are identical persons is even more acute here. If they are identical, then it

[20] Cf., e.g., Emil Seckel, *Heumanns Handlexikon zu den Quellen des römschen Rechts*, 9th edn. (Jena 1914), s.vv. *dominus, possessio, praedo, vi.* [21] Cf. Chodorow, *Christian Political Theory*, 218.

would be difficult (although not impossible) to imagine that the glossator could be someone else. Gratian 1 and the glossator seem to understand the legal problem in the same way, while Gratian 2's solution is different and more inspired by romanistic thinking. If all three were identical, one would have to accept that Gratian first changed style (commentaries and parallels in glosses instead of in *dicta*) and then opinion and legal orientation. It seems more likely that at least two different persons were involved.

There are also a few glosses which refer to Roman law-texts that were incorporated into the *Decretum* only in the second recension. These glosses would appear to have been written before these texts were added, i.e., commenting on the first recension, since it would not be necessary to refer the reader to Roman law-books when the relevant texts were found in the *Decretum*.

Glossa ad C. 3, q. 11
C. qui acu. non pos. Si quis. *Gg*
C. libro viiii. T. 1. Si quis enim *Fd* [= Cod. 9.1.20 = C. 3, q. 11, d. p. c. 4, § 3]
Glossa ad C. 3, q. 11, d. p. c. 4
C. qui acu. non pos. l. ult. [= Cod. 9.1.21 = C. 3, q. 11, d. p. c. 4, § 4] *Gg*
Glossa ad C. 5, q. 6, c. 4
C. de episcopis et clericis. Presbiteri citra in. [= Cod. 1.3.8 = C. 5, q. 6, c. 3, § 1] *Fd*

These glosses refer to three laws in Justinian's *Code*, all of which were incorporated into the second recension. It is particularly remarkable that the glosses in the margins of the second-recension manuscript Gg refer to texts which in fact are to be found in the adjacent text column. This suggests that these glosses had been written before the second recension was compiled.

At the present stage of research, it is difficult to isolate a specific set of glosses which with certainty pre-dates the second recension. The "first apparatus" which Rudolf Weigand identified comments also on canons found only in the second recension.[22] To characterize the glosses on the first recension one may, however, study the glosses of the first apparatus, since the differences are not likely to be large.[23] The first apparatus consists preponderantly of *notabilia*-glosses, i.e. glosses that direct the reader's attention to some particularly useful passage in the text. An example is the gloss to D. 4, c. 6: "The practice of fasting should be undertaken by clerics from Quinquagesima."[24] This kind of gloss is often,

---

[22] E.g. Weigand, *Glossen zum "Dekret,"* 418–419, nos. 54 and 57.
[23] Many glosses from the first apparatus are edited in Weigand, *Glossen zum "Dekret,"* 403–423 and 749–751 (glosses in Fd); see also the glosses enumerated on p. 402.
[24] "A quinquagesima propositum ieiunandi clericis esse sumendum", ed. in Weigand, *Glossen zum "Dekret,"* 406, on the basis of 46 manuscripts.

as Rudolf Weigand has noted, very similar to the rubric of the relevant canon(s).[25] The rubric of D. 4, c. 6 is, e.g., "Those whom the dignity of church office honors should undertake the practice of fasting from Quinquagesima."[26]

In addition to the large number of *notabilia*, the first apparatus also contains many allegations (references), but only a few explicatory glosses. The allegations, as preserved in the manuscripts, use more modern methods of reference than either of the two recensions, e.g.: *infra xii. q. iii. Quicumque* (referring to C. 12, q. 3, c. 2 "below").[27] Not even the second recension refers to *causae* by number, but uses instead the *incipit*.

THE DICTA IN THE TWO RECENSIONS

The *dicta* in Gratian's *Decretum* bring the reader closer to its author than any other part of the text. They contain his comments on the law texts which he quoted and his attempts to iron out the contradictions between them. This section analyzes the differences between the *dicta* of the two recensions.

The passages added in the second recension contain comparatively fewer *dicta* than the first recension. This is because the author of the second recension usually did not attempt to recast the arguments of the first recension in light of the newly added canons. Often, he simply added some canons without discussing them in *dicta* at all (e.g. C. 24, q. 3, cc. 13–25). In other cases, where additional canons are accompanied by *dicta*, they are not well integrated into the argument of the first recension. In fact, the addition often gives the impression of being a parenthetical aside that does not address the main argument but introduces some subsidiary issue.

C. 10, q. 1, d. p. c 10
If a bishop is prevented by sickness and cannot himself visit his parishes, he may entrust the duty of visitation to others.[28] [In the context of a bishop's rights over his diocese.]

C. 11, q. 3, d. p. c 105
The form and manner of excommunication and reconciliation is this.[29] [In the context of a discussion of the rightful use of excommunication.]

---

[25] Weigand, *Glossen zum "Dekret,"* 423.

[26] Friedberg, ed., *Decretum*, 6: "A quinquagesima ieiunandi propositum sumant, quos ecclesiasticos gradus dignitas exornat." Cf. the translation in Gratian, *The Treatise on Laws*, 14.

[27] Weigand, *Glossen zum "Dekret,"* 408, n. 19, 423 n. 72. Weigand has not edited those glosses that contain only an allegation. Many more examples may be found in the manuscripts.

[28] Friedberg, ed., *Decretum*, 615: "Si autem episcopus inualitudine inpeditus dioceses suas per se-metipsum uisitare non poterit, uisitationis offitium aliis conmittat."

[29] Friedberg, ed., *Decretum*, 674: "Excommunicationis autem forma et modus, atque reconciliationis hic est."

C. 35, q. 6, d. p. c 9
No one is allowed to divorce his wife under the pretext of consanguinity and then marry another, unless the case is tried first.[30] [In the context of a discussion of how consanguinity should be proven.]

The point is not that the subjects of these *dicta* (with their accompanying canons) would be irrelevant to the context; they are not. But it is striking that the *dicta* simply state matter-of-factly the contents of the following canon(s) without indicating why or how this is important for the argument that Gratian had outlined in the first recension. They are in many cases very similar to the rubric of a neighboring canon:

C. 10, q. 1, c 11
A bishop who is oppressed by sickness may entrust the duty of visitation to others.[31] [Cf. C. 10, q. 1, d. p. c. 10 above.]

As pointed out above, many glosses that summarize the content of one or several canons also resemble rubrics. The similarity between these glosses and the *dicta* here discussed are such that one may suspect that they were written in the same intellectual environment. This impression is strengthened if one also compares a less common type of second-recension *dictum* with another kind of gloss. Occasionally, the second recension contains a *dictum* discussing several texts which it either quotes or refers to. Many of these *dicta* concern Roman law; Stephan Kuttner called them *summulae* when discussing the Roman law in Gratian's *Decretum*.[32] There are, however, also similar texts using canonical material. One of the longest is C. 11, q. 3, d. p. c. 24, which quotes or refers to more than a dozen texts and discusses their agreements and disagreements. Other similar dicta are C. 5, q. 4, d. p. c. 2; C. 7, q. 1, d. p. c. 48; C. 11, q. 3, d. p. c. 21 and d. p. c. 26. It is easy to imagine that these *dicta* were elaborations of a series of allegations *pro et contra* contained in a gloss, just as C. 3, q. 1, d. p. c. 6 in the second recension probably is, partially, an elaboration of the gloss that was found at that place in the first recension. In fact, glosses containing allegations *pro et contra* sometimes also contain some indication of how to resolve disagreements:

Glossa ad D. 5, c. 4 (in the first apparatus)
Contrarily below [causa] 22, q. 2, *Cum humilitatis* [c. 9]. Solution: This is said of those things that we do not know that we have committed, about which we ought to grieve . . .[33]

---

[30] Friedberg, ed., *Decretum*, 1280: "Occasione uero consanguinitatis uxorem suam dimittere, et aliam ducere non licet alicui, nisi causa primum fuerit probata."

[31] Friedberg, ed., *Decretum*, 615: "Inualitudine grauatus episcopus uisitationis offitium aliis conmittat."   [32] Kuttner, "New studies on the Roman law," 19.

[33] Ed. Weigand, *Glossen zum "Dekret,"* 408, n. 19: "Infra xxii. Q. ii. contra Cum humilitatis. Solutio. Hic dicit(ur) de illis que ignoramus nos commisisse, de quibus dolere debemus . . ."

The similarities between this gloss and the *summulae* in the text of the *Decretum* may appear slight, but the point is that there is a unity of method between the earliest glosses and the second recension of Gratian's *Decretum*, and this unity is not shared by the first recension. The *dicta* that can be called *summulae* (romanistic as well as canonical) are typical of the second recension and do not appear in the first recension. The short *dicta* that merely summarize the contents of neighboring canons are not entirely absent from the first recension. They can be found particularly in the first part (the distinctions), which should perhaps not be surprising, since the character of this part is less dialectical and more expository than the second part. Such *dicta* are less common in the second part of the first recension, where the second recension added numerous canons accompanied by *dicta* of this sort.

The additional *dicta* in the second recension usually appear poorly integrated into the argument of the first recension. A particularly clear example of this is found in C. 9, q. 1, where an addition in effect presents a new answer to the question posed and answered by Gratian 1 without giving any indication of how the two answers should be reconciled. The question posed is whether an ordination made by an excommunicated bishop is valid. This question was of great importance in a time when the Church was repeatedly divided by schism. In the first recension, Gratian first refers to texts by Popes Gregory I and Damasus I (cc. 1–3) which state that excommunicated persons cannot ordain (cc. 2 and 3 are labelled *paleae* in Friedberg's edition, but they were present in the first recension). He contrasts these texts with an excerpt from a famous decretal by Urban II (c. 4), where the pope determines that an excommunicated person can perform ordinations unless his excommunication came about through his own ordination.[34] Urban talks specifically about the taint of simony, but Gratian 1 gives the decretal general validity.

In the second recension, two canons are added, each accompanied by a *dictum*. The first (d. p. c. 4 and c. 5) states that those who have been excommunicated by name (*nominatim*) and those who have invaded another's see, cannot ordain. This provides a solution different from the one proclaimed in d. p. c. 3 and c. 4 without the author giving any indication about how the contradiction should be resolved. (Canon 6, also added in the second recension, does not even concern ordination; it states that only catholics can participate in an election.) The contradiction was, of course, noticed by the decretists. The author of the *Summa Parisiensis*, e.g., comments about the first solution (d. p. c. 3) that "here Gratian

---

[34] For Urban's decretal (JL 5393), see Somerville, *Urban II*, 134–151.

resolves first and less competently. He will resolve it better later." When
he comes to the second solution he exclaims: "See, here is another solution."[35] The additions made to C. 9, q. 1 in the second recension are
simply not integrated well into the argument. Several similar examples
could be given, e.g. C. 11, q. 3, d. p. c. 20–d. p. c. 26, which was discussed above in chapter 3.

How is this kind of addition to be understood? Are they clumsy or
hurried or even mechanical attempts to add more material to the
Decretum? Who added them? A Gratian who no longer had the power or
the time to equal his earlier efforts, or an epigone without the master's
genius? I believe that these questions are wrongly framed. It seems strange
that the second recension should be less "scholastic" (meaning "present-
ing a systematic discussion of arguments *pro et contra*") than the first recension, when the middle years of the twelfth century were a time when
scholastic method rapidly won ground. From this perspective, the second
recension seems to be a backward step, towards the methodology of
Burchard of Worms and Ivo of Chartres' collections (as distinct from Ivo's
Prologue). However, this line of reasoning overlooks the fact that Gratian's
Decretum is (almost) unique among canonical collections in incorporating a running commentary. Collections of canon law produced after the
Decretum, i.e., the various decretal collections culminating in Gregory
IX's *Liber extra*, include no commentary. This does not mean, however,
that their authors failed to comment upon their texts, indicating, among
other things, how contradictions could be resolved. A good example is
the work of Bernard of Pavia, who taught in Bologna in the 1170s,
became provost of Pavia in 1187 and bishop of Faenza in 1191.[36] Around
1190, he compiled a large collection of papal decretals that were not
included in Gratian's *Decretum*. This *Breviarium extravagantium* was much
used in teaching canon law and is known as the first of the *Quinque compilationes antiquae*. The *Breviarium* contained solely law texts without any
commentary, but Bernard also composed glosses, and eventually a *summa*
interpreting the *Breviarium*. The *Breviarium* was the text that he had compiled in order to lecture on it, while the glosses and the *summa* reflect his
lectures. Gratian 1 also compiled his own text on which to lecture (the
law texts in the *Decretum*), but his lectures are reflected in the *dicta*. There
is no difference in principle between the efforts of Gratian 1 and of
Bernard; what is different is essentially the formal layout of the

[35] McLaughlin, ed., *Summa Parisiensis*, 141: "Sed excommunicati. Hoc modo primo determinat
Gratianus minus competenter, postea melius determinaturus. – Sed illud. Ecce alia determina-
tio."
[36] About Bernard, see Kuttner, *Repertorium*, 322–323, and Somerville and Brasington, *Prefaces to
Canon Law Books*, 218–220.

manuscript page: Bernard's comments are placed in the margins, while Gratian 1's comments are included in the main text. In this respect, the work effort of Gratian 2 resembles that of Bernard more than that of Gratian 1. In cases such as C. 9, q. 1, we can expect that whoever added d. p. c. 4 would in his lectures have resolved the contradiction between this *dictum* and d. p. c. 3, as indeed the author of the *Summa Parisiensis* later did.

This analysis has revealed yet another significant difference in methodology between the two recensions of the *Decretum*, showing again a development towards greater professionalism and standardization. In the first recension, Gratian 1 both collected authoritative texts and commented upon them, as did Peter Lombard in his roughly contemporary *Sentences*. Both texts were written to meet the need for a basic text-book in the teaching of their respective disciplines. Other fields, such as Roman law, medicine, and biblical studies, already possessed authoritative texts which could serve as the basis for the teacher's commentary and interpretation. Gratian 1 and the Lombard were in effect forced to create their own authoritative texts (their authority deriving from the fact that they consisted mainly of quotations) to be able effectively to teach their subjects. When they did this, they had no reason to separate text from commentary. They could not have suspected that their texts would become standard school-texts, nor did they know that it later would become common to keep text and commentary separate. Could they ever have guessed how great the growth of their subjects would be after their deaths? In their works, we can observe teachers creating tools for their own teaching when there were as yet no standard forms for academic texts in their subjects. The development of glosses, *summae*, *questiones*, *distinctiones*, etc., came later, as did the awareness of teachers like Bernard of Pavia that their compilations might become standard school-texts (and, hence, that comments were best relegated to the margins). These developments had begun when the second recension was created.

There is one way, finally, which may lead to more certain conclusions concerning the authorship of the two recensions. If Gratian was responsible for both recensions, it would be expected that the text which is common to both versions would be identical in both recensions. If instead the first-recension core of the second recension turns out to contain a text which has been corrupted through copying errors, this would be a strong argument against common authorship. Why would the author of the original text use an inferior copy of his own text when revising it? One such corruption, minor but revealing, is found in the inscription of C. 24, q. 1, c. 4. Every second-recension manuscript studied by me or Titus Lenherr contains the corruption *martiri*, while only the first recension preserves the correct reading *marchioni*. If such corruptions are common, my inference that the *Decretum* had at least two authors would gain greater strength. An investigation of such matters must, however, await the appearance of critical editions of both recensions.

Conclusion

MEDIEVAL LAW AND THE *DECRETUM*

Gratian's *Decretum* is not one book, but two. The *Decretum* that has been known until now was preceded by another, much shorter book, which was almost entirely subsumed into the later version. This explains many of the mysteries that have surrounded the *Decretum* and that have hampered study of this pivotal text. It also raises new questions, about the authorship of the *Decretum*, about the environment in which its author or authors worked, and about the development of legal science and scholasticism in the twelfth century. This book could only begin to address those questions.

Gratian's *Decretum* is often quoted, cited, and discussed in the scholarly literature treating various aspects of the middle ages. Authors of such studies are now invited to introduce another level of complexity into their work. The discovery of the first recension will, in the first place, facilitate study of the *Decretum* for those scholars who simply want to explore Gratian's standpoint on some specific issue. The *Decretum*, as known from Friedberg's edition, is not an easy book to approach or to understand. The second recension introduced much new material which was not synthesized into a coherent whole, although the additions, had their implications been worked out, would frequently invalidate or modify the synthesis achieved in the first recension. The result is that the more carefully a modern scholar reads the *Decretum*, the more confused and confusing it appears. With the help of the Appendix which follows and which contains a detailed listing of the contents of the first recension, readers will now be able to study Gratian's arguments in their original, undisturbed form. They may, if they so wish, continue to examine the additions of the second recension as evidence for the concerns of a slightly later period. Approaching the text in two steps, as it was composed, will make its interpretation considerably easier. In any case, the *Decretum* can no longer be read as a homogeneous product of one person, one time, and one place.

The discovery of the first recension creates a new area for research: comparing the two recensions of the *Decretum*. I have made a beginning in chapters 5 and 6 above, but much remains to be done. To mention but one example: all the statements in the *Decretum* about as central a doctrine in medieval canon law as the pope's judicial immunity, i.e., that the pope cannot be judged by anyone, belong to the additions made for the second recension.[1] The first recension does not mention whether or not the pope could be judged. This lacuna is interesting, as is the fact that Gratian 2 thought it necessary to insert repeated statements to the effect that the pope could not be judged. One should probably not draw the conclusion that Gratian 1 thought that the pope could be judged (this would not be consistent with his statements about who could judge whom in, e.g., D. 22), but rather that Gratian 1 did not find the issue as urgent as did Gratian 2.

The period between the two recensions of Gratian's *Decretum* was a time of activity and development within legal science. I have shown that glosses were composed during this time, which strongly suggests that canon law was taught on the basis of the first recension. This teaching has also left traces in the second recension, which in some respects is similar to glosses and which occasionally even seems to draw directly on glosses. Also the first recension reflects a teacher's efforts, but chapters 5 and 6 have shown that the teaching habits of Gratian 1 were different from those of the teacher behind the second recension. Considering that the first may be a record of the first "university course" in canon law ever taught, it is perhaps not surprising that its author was still struggling with form: the strange organization of the work, the non-technical language, the mixture of text and commentary. In this he reveals that he was a pioneer also in using scholastic methods. After all, the first recension of Gratian's *Decretum* is the first fully elaborated scholastic *summa* of an entire discipline. The author of the second recension is certainly far from representing scholastic canon law fully developed, but he has taken several steps in that direction.

The question remains: could one person have undergone the intellectual development that is reflected in the differences between the two recensions? That person would also have studied the Roman law of Justinian and acquired a technical grasp of that law in the interval between the two recensions. It is impossible to draw any certain conclusions, but the evidence presented in the two last chapters supports the

---

[1] D. 17, d. p. c. 6; D. 40, c. 6; C. 3, q. 1, d. p. c. 6; C. 9, q. 3, d. p. c. 9; C. 17, q. 4, c. 30. About this doctrine, see Brian Tierney, *Foundations of Conciliar Theory: The Contribution of the Medieval Canonists from Gratian to the Great Schism* (Cambridge 1955), esp. p. 57, and Chodorow, *Christian Political Theory*, 178–186.

view that the two recensions had different authors. It is difficult to imagine that one man's attitudes, orientation, and style would change so much.

What scanty evidence there is from the earliest introductions to the *Decretum* suggests that it was the author of the first recension who was called Gratian. I have no name, other than Gratian 2, for his successor. We cannot even be certain that more than one law teacher did not contribute to the work on the second recension. But we can infer something about his (or their) background: before teaching canon law in Bologna, he had studied the subject with Gratian, and also studied Roman law with a contemporary, e.g., Bulgarus or Martinus.

In chapters 5 and 6, I mapped the development of legal thinking and teaching in the middle of the twelfth century. These developments are interesting in themselves, whether one imagines that they illustrate the differences between two generations (Gratian and his students), or between the young and the mature Gratian. They raise further complex questions about the legal and scholastic developments of the twelfth century. To work out fully the meaning of the changes imposed by the author of the second recension will take much time and research, but the effort is worthwhile, since it promises to yield important insights. It is already clear that Gratian 1 and his successor lived in different worlds. The author of the second recension was a professional jurist with a lawyer's appreciation for precise definitions, technicalities, and correct procedure, a man who was always ready to cite parallel and contrary passages from canon as well as Roman law. Gratian 1 worked with cruder tools, drew on another and partially different set of sources, and had barely begun to explore the *Corpus iuris civilis*. That he possessed a legal mind is clear from the way in which he always extracted the legally relevant aspects of the problems at issue. His discussion of these problems was, however, sometimes strikingly non-technical and imprecise, simply because he was not operating within an established and well-defined system. He was, as it were, making the system up as he wrote. In doing so, Gratian 1 created the necessary conditions for the emergence of canon law as an academic discipline and for the appearance of men such as the one responsible for the second recension.

I suggest that at about the same time, in and around the 1130s, other Bolognese teachers similarly created the academic discipline devoted to Roman law. My interpretation differs from the previously accepted view that Irnerius founded this discipline and the law school of Bologna already around 1100. I have tried to show that this view reflects a foundation myth which developed from the late twelfth century among Bolognese law professors. The myth was cherished by medieval law professors, such as Odofredus, who strove to make their lectures on the Justinianic *Corpus* more entertaining. Modern historians who are frustrated by the scanty contemporary sources illustrating the teaching of Roman law in the early twelfth century also have recourse to this myth. But it is the contemporary sources, not later myths, that contain accurate information.

In the early years of the Bologna law school, its professors began to compare the two legal systems which were taught there, canon law and Roman law. They found that their rules sometimes conflicted and sometimes agreed, but most often they found that the rules of one legal system could be used to illuminate, qualify, or refine the rules of the other system. They wrote down these observations in the margins of their law books. Later on, they began to write longer, continuous works of commentary or summary, drawing on both Roman law and canon law. Eventually, the two systems would become inextricably entangled with each other, in effect forming a new legal system. This is the *ius commune*, the European Common Law, which dominated European law for the rest of the middle ages and beyond. Such a system could only come about in an academic institution, where the theoretical problems created by the confrontation between the two laws could be addressed. Naturally, it had to be an institution where both Roman and canon law were studied. Therefore, the *ius commune* could not have developed before the 1130s, when law began to be taught in earnest in Bologna. Its development had begun when Gratian 2 struggled to incorporate Roman law into the *Decretum*. It had not yet begun when Gratian 1 wrote his text without using Justinianic law. On balance, the most significant result of the discovery of the first version of the *Decretum* might be that it allows the historian to study the very moment when the *ius commune* was born.

THE CONTENTS OF THE FIRST RECENSION
OF GRATIAN'S *DECRETUM*

This is a list of the contents of the first recension of Gratian's *Decretum*. I have used the divisions and numbering of Friedberg's edition. When the entire canon or *dictum* is included in the first recension, it is simply listed below. When only a part of the text appears there, its *incipit* and *explicit* are given with the line numbers of Friedberg's edition in bold type. The first recension sometimes contains a text very different from Friedberg's text. In those cases, the text of the first recension is reproduced. Additional phrases within canons or *dicta* which are otherwise the same as in Friedberg's edition are given within angle brackets <>. The list is based on a collation of *incipits* and *explicits* of every canon and *dictum* in the first recension. Differences within the texts may very well have been overlooked, and minor differences have not normally been registered.

D. 1

d. a. c. 1
c. 1
d. p. c. 1
c. 2
c. 3
c. 4
c. 5
d. p. c. 5
c. 6
c. 7
c. 8
c. 9
c. 10
c. 11
c. 12

D. 2

d. a. c. 1
c. 1
c. 2
c. 3
c. 4
c. 5
c. 6
c. 7
c. 8

D. 3

d. a. c. 1
c. 1
c. 2
d. p. c. 2
c. 3

d. p. c. 3
c. 4

D. 4

d. a. c. 1
c. 1
d. p. c. 1
c. 2
d. p. c. 2
c. 3
d. p. c. 3
d. p. c. 5
c. 6
d. p. c. 6

Appendix

D. 5

d. a. c. 1
c. 2 [with inscription of
c. 1]
c. 3
c. 4: **1** *Ad eius uero* − **2**
qui gignitur ablactetur. + **8**
Si autem filios − **35** *est ut
esuriamus.*

D. 6

d. p. c. 3

D. 7

d. a. c. 1
c. 1
c. 2

D. 8

d. a. c. 1
c. 1
d. p. c. 1
c. 2
c. 3
c. 4
c. 5
c. 6
c. 7
c. 8
d. p. c. 9

D. 9

d. a. c. 1
c. 1: **6** *Quicumque legibus
imperatorum* − **10** *acquirit
grande premium.*
c. 3
c. 4
c. 5
c. 7
c. 8
c. 9
c. 10

d. p. c. 11

D. 10

d. a. c. 1
c. 1: **1** *Lege imperatorum
non* − **6** *iura ecclesiastica
dissolui.* + **21** *Non
quod imperatorum* − **27**
*inferre preiudicium
asseramus.*
c. 2
d. p. c. 6
c. 7
c. 9
c. 11
c. 12
c. 13

D. 11

d. a. c. 1
c. 1
c. 2
c. 4
d. p. c. 4
c. 5
c. 6
c. 7

D. 12

c. 3
c. 5
c. 6
c. 7
c. 8
c. 9
c. 11
d. p. c. 11
c. 12

D. 13

d. a. c. 1
c. 1
c. 2

D. 14

d. p. c. 1
c. 2

D. 15

d. a. c. 1
c. 1
c. 2
c. 3: **1** *Sancta Romana
ecclesia* − **39** *uenerabiliter
suscipiendae sunt.*

D. 16

d. a. c. 1
c. 1
c. 2
c. 3
c. 4
d. p. c. 4
c. 5
d. p. c. 5
c. 6
d. p. c. 6
c. 7
c. 8
c. 9
c. 10
c. 11
c. 12
d. p. c. 12
c. 13

D. 17

d. a. c. 1
c. 1: **1** *Sinodum episcoporum absque* − **3** *potestis
regulariter facere.*
c. 6

D. 19

d. a. c. 1
c. 1: **1** *Si Romanorum
Pontificum* − **45** *sibi*

*obicitur illud Tripartitae
ystoriae.*
c. 12
c. 13
d. p. c. 13
c. 14
d. p. c. 14

D. 32

d. a. c. 1
c. 1
c. 3
c. 4
c. 6: **1** *Preter hoc autem –*
24 *ecclesiae communione
separentur.*
c. 7
c. 8
c. 9
c. 10
c. 11
c. 12
c. 13
c. 14
c. 15
c. 16
c. 18

D. 33

d. a. c. 1
c. 1
d. p. c. 1
c. 2
c. 6

D. 34

d. p. c. 3
c. 4
c. 5
d. p. c. 6
c. 7
d. p. c. 8
c. 9
c. 10
c. 11

d. p. c. 12
c. 13
d. p. c. 13
c. 14
d. p. c. 14
c. 15
d. p. c. 16
c. 17
d. p. c. 17
c. 18
d. p. c. 19
c. 20

D. 35

d. a. c. 1
c. 1

D. 36

d. a. c. 1
c. 1
c. 2
d. p. c. 2

D. 37

d. a. c. 1
c. 1
c. 2
c. 7
d. p. c. 7
c. 8
d. p. c. 8
c. 9
c. 10
c. 15
d. p. c. 15
c. 16

D. 38

d. a. c. 1
c. 1
c. 3
c. 4: **1** *Nulli sacerdotum
liceat –* **2** *Patrum regulis
obuiare.*

c. 5
c. 8
c. 9
c. 16

D. 39

d. a. c. 1
c. 1

D. 40

d. a. c. 1
c. 1
c. 2
c. 3
c. 4
c. 9
c. 12

D. 41

d. a. c. 1
c. 1
d. p. c. 8

D. 42

d. a. c. 1
c. 1
d. p. c. 1: **1** *Hinc etiam
Iohannes –* **3** *de ecclesia
eiciebat.*

D. 43

d. a. c. 1
c. 1
d. p. c. 5

D. 44

d. a. c. 1
c. 1
d. p. c. 12

D. 45

The contents of the first recension

201

c. 3
d. p. c. 3
c. 4
c. 6
d. p. c. 6
c. 7
c. 8
c. 9
c. 11
c. 12
d. p. c. 12
c. 13: **15** *Illi cui erutus –*
27 *sui perderet facultatem.*

D. 56

d. a. c. 1
c. 1: **1** *Presbiterorum filios*
a sacris ministeriis remoue-
mus.
d. p. c. 1
d. p. c. 2
c. 3
c. 4
c. 11
c. 12
d. p. c. 12
c. 13
d. p. c. 13
c. 14

D. 57

d. a. c. 1
c. 1

D. 58

d. a. c. 1
c. 1
c. 2

D. 59

d. a. c. 1
c. 1

D. 60

d. a. c. 1
c. 2
d. p. c. 3
c. 4
d. p. c. 4

D. 61

d. a. c. 1
c. 1
c. 3: **1** *Non negamus in –*
5 *prestare quam sumere.*
c. 5: **28** *Patrum beatorum*
uenerabiles – **36** *loci*
premium debetur.
d. p. c. 8
c. 10
d. p. c. 10
c. 11
d. p. c. 11
c. 12
c. 13
c. 16: **1** *Obitum Victoris*
Panormitanae – **14** *credi-*
mus poterit inueniri.

D. 62

d. a. c. 1
c. 1: **1** *Nulla ratio sinit –* **2**
a plebibus expetiti.
c. 2: **1** *Docendus est*
populus, non sequendus.

D. 63

c. 1
c. 2
c. 6
c. 7
c. 8
d. p. c. 8
c. 9
c. 11
c. 12
c. 13

c. 14
c. 15
c. 16
c. 18
c. 19
c. 20
c. 22
c. 23
d. p. c. 25
c. 26
c. 27
d. p. c. 27
c. 28
d. p. c. 28: **1** *Verum quia*
inperatores – **8** *anathematis*
uinculo innodaretur. + **18**
Postremo presentibus legatis
– **22** *ecclesiae Dei confe-*
rentes.
c. 29
c. 30
c. 32
c. 33
d. p. c. 34: **1** *Ex his con-*
stitutionibus – **17** *habita*
constitutum est.
d. p. c. 35
c. 36

D. 64

d. a. c. 1
c. 1
c. 2
c. 4
c. 5

D. 65

d. p. c. 8
c. 9

D. 66

d. a. c. 1
c. 1
d. p. c. 1
c. 2

The contents of the first recension

D. 86

d. a. c. 1
c. 1
c. 2
d. p. c. 4
c. 5
d. p. c. 5
c. 6
d. p. c. 22
c. 23
c. 24
d. p. c. 25
c. 26

D. 88

c. 1
c. 2
c. 8
c. 9
c. 14

D. 89

d. a. c. 1
c. 1
c. 2
c. 4
c. 5: **8** *cauendum est a –* **14** *amministrent quam accusent.*

D. 90

d. a. c. 1
c. 1
c. 2

D. 91

d. a. c. 1
c. 3

D. 92

d. p. c. 2
c. 3

d. p. c. 3
c. 4
d. p. c. 8
c. 9

D. 93

d. a. c. 1
c. 1
c. 3
d. p. c. 4
c. 5
c. 6
c. 7
c. 11
d. p. c. 12
c. 13: **1** *Diaconos propriam constituimus –* **9** *facere plerumque conceditur.*
c. 14: **7** *In sua diaconi –* **15** *ministerio cessare debebit.*
c. 15
c. 17
c. 18
c. 19: **1** *Diaconus sedeat iubente –* **3** *presbiterorum interrogatus loquatur.*
c. 23
d. p. c. 23
c. 24
d. p. c. 25
c. 26

D. 94

d. p. c. 2
c. 3

D. 95

d. a. c. 1
c. 1
c. 5
c. 6
c. 7

D. 96

d. a. c. 1
c. 1

D. 97

d. a. c. 1
c. 1
c. 2

D. 98

d. a. c. 1
c. 1
c. 2
c. 3

D. 99

d. a. c. 1
c. 1

D. 100

d. a. c. 1
c. 1

D. 101

d. p. c. 1

C. 1

d. init.

C. 1, q. 1

d. a. c. 1
c. 1
c. 2
c. 3
c. 4
c. 6
c. 7
c. 8
c. 11
c. 12

The contents of the first recension

Appendix

c. 7
d. p. c. 7
c. 8
d. p. c. 8
c. 9
d. p. c. 10

C. 1, q. 3

d. a. c. 1
c. 1
c. 2
c. 3
c. 7
c. 8
c. 9
d. p. c. 11
c. 12
d. p. c. 15

C. 1, q. 4

d. a. c. 1
c. 1
c. 2
c. 3
c. 4
d. p. c. 9: **14** *Cum ergo de baptizatis* – **21** *inpediat nomen erroris.*
c. 10
d. p. c. 10
c. 11
d. p. c. 11
c. 12
d. p. c. 12: **1** *Ignorabat autem Petrus* – **22** *permittitur ignorare, aliis non.*
d. p. c. 13

C. 1, q. 5

d. a. c. 1
c. 1
d. p. c. 2
c. 3

C. 1, q. 6

d. a. c. 1
c. 1

C. 1, q. 7

d. a. c. 1
c. 1
c. 2
c. 4
d. p. c. 4
d. p. c. 5
c. 6
d. p. c. 6
c. 7
d. p. c. 10
c. 11
d. p. c. 11
c. 12
d. p. c. 12
c. 13
c. 14
d. p. c. 16
c. 17
d. p. c. 17
c. 18
d. p. c. 22
c. 23
d. p. c. 23
c. 24
d. p. c. 27

C. 2

d. init.

C. 2, q. 1

d. a. c. 1
c. 1
c. 2
d. p. c. 2
c. 3
c. 4
c. 5
d. p. c. 5
c. 7: **43** *<Quod quidam*

frater> *de falsis se capitulis* – **60** *modis omnibus reuocetur.*
c. 11
c. 12
d. p. c. 14
c. 15
c. 16
d. p. c. 16
d. p. c. 17
c. 18
c. 19
d. p. c. 19
c. 20
d. p. c. 20

C. 2, q. 2

d. a. c. 1
c. 1
c. 2
c. 3
c. 5
c. 6

C. 2, q. 3

d. a. c. 1
c. 1
c. 2
c. 3
c. 4
c. 4a: *Item Fabianus papa. De eodem. Qui non probauerit quod obiecerit penam quam intulerit ipse patiatur.* Aa Bc Fd P
d. p. c. 5
c. 6: **1** *Paulum itaque diaconum* – **4** *ei culpam ignoscimus.*
c. 7
d. p. c. 7, § 2
c. 8

C. 2, q. 5

d. a. c. 1

206

207

c. 54

d. p. c. 54

c. 55

c. 56

c. 57

c. 58

d. p. c. 60

C. 2, q. 8

d. a. c. 1

c. 1

c. 3

c. 4

c. 5

d. p. c. 5: **1** *Sed Calixtus Papa* – **4** *per epistolam accusare audeat.*

C. 3

d. init.

C. 3, q. 1

d. a. c. 1

c. 1

c. 2

d. p. c. 2: *Sed notandum est quod restitutio alia fit per presentiam iudicis, veluti cum dicitur a iudice: "Censeo te in integrum restituendum", qua (quam Aa Bc, ut vid.; quia Fd) restitutione (-ionem Aa) animo tantum, non corpore possessio recipitur. Alia fit per executorem (per ex. Aa Bc P: executione Fd) iudicis quando restitutus corporalem recipit possessionem. Queritur (quare P) ergo que harum concedatur expoliatis, an illa tantum, que fit per sententiam (presentiam P) iudicis, an illa etiam que fit per executorem sententie,*

qua expoliatis presentialiter omnia reciduntur (recidi precipiuntur Fd[ac]). Hec ultima expoliatis prestanda est. Aa Bc Fd P

c. 3

c. 4

d. p. c. 6: **1** *Patet ergo quod* – **10** *quam vocentur ad causam.* <*His ita respondetur. Si vicium electionis ecclesie notum fuerit et ideo reprobati fuerint et si aliqua violentia in sedibus illis irrepserit eiecti restitutionem postulare non possunt. Si autem ecclesia eos per pacientiam tolerare voluerit et eis gradum honoris concesserit et si viciosa fuerit eorum electio, tamen post eiectionem restituendi sunt, ante regularem ad synodi vocationem.*> *Aa Bc Fd P*

C. 3, q. 2

d. a. c. 1

c. 1

c. 5

c. 6

c. 7

c. 8

C. 3, q. 3

d. a. c. 1

c. 1

c. 2

c. 3

C. 3, q. 4

d. a. c. 1

c. 1

c. 3: **1** *Si quis vero* – **4** *fide suspecti sunt.*

c. 4: **1** *Consanguineorum coniunctiones* – **9** *omnes eis consentientes.*

c. 5

c. 6

c. 7

c. 8

c. 11

d. p. c. 11

c. 12

d. p. c. 12

C. 3, q. 5

d. a. c. 1

c. 1

c. 2

c. 4: **1** *Suspectos aut inimicos aut facile litigantes* + **4** *accusatores esse et* – **6** *temporibus futuris excludimus.*

d. p. c. 14

c. 15: **15** *Athanasius a patriarcha suo* – **18** *suae ecclesiae reddi precipitur.*

C. 3, q. 6

d. a. c. 1

c. 1

c. 2

c. 3

d. p. c. 3

c. 4

c. 5

c. 7

d. p. c. 10

c. 11

d. p. c. 11

c. 12

c. 14

d. p. c. 14

c. 15

c. 16

c. 17

c. 18

The contents of the first recension

C. 3, q. 7

d. a. c. 1
c. 1
d. p. c. 2
c. 3: **1** *Qui sine peccato* – **2** *illa lapidem mittat.* + **14** *Prius ipsi purgandi* – **16** *uicia corrigere festinant?*
c. 4: **1** *Iudicet ille de alterius* – **5** *nulla leuitate ducatur.*
c. 5
d. p. c. 7

C. 3, q. 8

d. a. c. 1
c. 1
c. 2

C. 3, q. 9

d. a. c. 1
c. 1
c. 2
c. 3
c. 4
c. 5
c. 6
c. 8
c. 9
c. 10: **1** *Decreuimus uestram debere* – **7** *occasione non utitur.*
c. 11
c. 14
c. 15
c. 18
c. 19
c. 21

C. 3, q. 10

d. a. c. 1
c. 1
d. p. c. 1
c. 2

c. 3
d. p. c. 3

C. 3, q. 11

d. a. c. 1
c. 1
c. 3
d. p. c. 3: **1** *Hoc autem intelligendum* – **5** *auctoritatibus non prohibetur.*

C. 4

d. init.

C. 4, q. 1

d. a. c. 1
c. 1

C. 4, q. 2 & 3

d. a. c. 1
c. 1
d. p. c. 3 [i.e. *Sed obicitur illud* – *humanae actionis trahenda*, col. 541].

C. 4, q. 4

d. a. c. 1
c. 1: **1** *Nullus umquam presumat* – **4** *idoneos accusatores, defensores <atque testes>.*
c. 2

C. 4, q. 5

d. a. c. 1
c. 1

C. 4, q. 6

d. a. c. 1
c. 1
c. 2

C. 5

d. init.

C. 5, q. 1

d. a. c. 1
c. 1
c. 2

C. 5, q. 2

d. a. c. 1
c. 1
c. 2
c. 3
c. 4
d. p. c. 4

C. 5, q. 3

d. a. c. 1
c. 1: **1** *Si egrotans fuerit* – **7** *prout causa dictauerit.*
d. p. c. 1: **5** *Ecce episcopus* – **10** *se agere licet.*
c. 2
c. 3

C. 5, q. 4

d. a. c. 1
c. 1
c. 2

C. 5, q. 5

d. a. c. 1
c. 1
c. 2
d. p. c. 3
c. 4
c. 5
d. p. c. 5

C. 5, q. 6

d. a. c. 1

209

c. 1
c. 2
c. 3: **I** *Quia iuxta canoni-cas –* **II** *famae plenitudine caruisse.*
c. 4

C. 6

d. init.

C. 6, q. 1

d. a. c. 1
c. 1
c. 4
d. p. c. 6
c. 7
d. p. c. 11
c. 12
d. p. c. 16
c. 17: **I** *Infames esse eas –* **21** *gradus debent prouehi +* **24** *nec ad accusationem –* **25** *iuste recipi possunt.*
d. p. c. 19
c. 20
c. 21
d. p. c. 21: **I** *Verum hoc Augustini –* **6** *accusatione ipse repellit.*

C. 6, q. 2

d. a. c. 1
c. 1
d. p. c. 1
c. 2
c. 3

C. 6, q. 3

d. a. c. 1
c. 1
c. 2

C. 6, q. 4

d. a. c. 1
c. 1
c. 2
d. p. c. 4
c. 5
d. p. c. 5
c. 6
c. 7: **I** *Osius episcopus dixit –* **II** *Sinodus respon-dit: Placet.*

C. 6, q. 5

d. a. c. 1
c. 1
c. 2

C. 7

d. init.

C. 7, q. 1

d. a. c. 1
c. 1
c. 4: **I** *Pontifices qui aliqua –* **9** *presumptionis pullulet ambicio.*
c. 5
c. 6
c. 11
d. p. c. 11
c. 12
d. p. c. 12
c. 13
c. 14
d. p. c. 16
c. 17
d. p. c. 18
c. 19
c. 30
c. 31
d. p. c. 33
c. 34
c. 35
c. 39

d. p. c. 41
c. 42
d. p. c. 42
c. 43
d. p. c. 43
c. 44
d. p. c. 44
c. 45
d. p. c. 49

C. 7, q. 2

d. a. c. 1
c. 1

C. 8

d. init.

C. 8, q. 1

d. a. c. 1
c. 1
d. p. c. 2
c. 3
c. 4
c. 5
c. 6
d. p. c. 7
c. 8
c. 9
c. 12
c. 13
c. 14
c. 15
c. 16
c. 20
c. 21
c. 22
d. p. c. 24

C. 8, q. 2

d. a. c. 1
c. 1

tentia deciderit.
c. 38: **1** *De persona presbiteri* — **14** *executioni perfecte
contradi.*
c. 39
c. 41: **1** *Sacerdotibus autem
non* — **21** *nos iudicemus
Deus.*
c. 42
c. 43
c. 45: **1** *Si quis cum* — **13**
*litis contestatione numeran-
dum.* + **17** *Non autem
aliter* — **22** *huiusmodi causis
habentibus.* [i.e. the entire
canon is present in the
first recension, except for
what is marked as *palea*
in Friedberg's edition.]
c. 46
c. 47
d. p. c. 47
c. 48
c. 49

C. 11, q. 2
d. init.

C. 11, q. 3
d. a. c. 1
c. 1
c. 4
c. 5
c. 6
c. 9
c. 27
c. 30
c. 31
c. 32
c. 34
c. 35
c. 36
c. 37
d. p. c. 39
c. 40

d. p. c. 40: **1** *Premissis
auctoritatibus quibus* — **10**
in se exceperunt.
d. p. c. 43
c. 44
c. 46
c. 47
c. 48
c. 49
c. 50
c. 51
c. 57
c. 60
c. 61
c. 62
c. 63
c. 64
d. p. c. 64
c. 65
d. p. c. 65
c. 66: **1** *qui recte iudicat* —
3 *acceptione pecuniae
uendit.*
c. 67
c. 69
c. 70
c. 71
d. p. c. 72
d. p. c. 73
c. 74
c. 75
c. 76
d. p. c. 77
c. 78
d. p. c. 78
c. 79
c. 80
c. 81
d. p. c. 86
c. 87
c. 88
c. 89: **1** *Iniustum iudicium
et* — **3** *acta non ualeat.*
c. 90
d. p. c. 90
c. 91
c. 92
c. 93: **1** *Si dominus iubet* —

7 *quam hominibus obedire.*
c. 94
c. 95
c. 100
c. 101
d. p. c. 101
c. 102
c. 103
c. 104
c. 105

C. 12
d. init.

C. 12, q. 1
d. a. c. 1
c. 1: **1** *Omnis etas ab* — **7**
testem uitae habeant.
c. 5
c. 8
c. 9: **1** *Scimus uos non* — **7**
illis omnia communia
c. 10: **1** *Nolo ut aliquis* —
28 *quisquis cum ypocrisi* +
30 *faciat testamentum* — **33**
possit felicitatis hereditatem.
c. 14
d. p. c. 17
c. 18
d. p. c. 18
c. 19
c. 20
c. 21
c. 22
c. 23
c. 24
d. p. c. 24
c. 25
d. p. c. 25
c. 26
d. p. c. 27
c. 28
d. p. c. 28

The contents of the first recension

C. 14, q. 2

d. a. c. 1
c. 1
d. p. c. 1: **1** *Potest etiam intelligi* − **5** *pauperum testimonium dicant.*

C. 14, q. 3

d. a. c. 1
c. 1
c. 2
c. 3
d. p. c. 4

C. 14, q. 4

d. a. c. 1
c. 1
c. 2
c. 3
c. 6
c. 7
c. 8
c. 9
c. 9a: <u>*Ex concilio Cartaginensi*</u>: *Nullus clericorum amplius recipiat quam cuiquam accomodavit; si pecuniam, pecuniam; si speciem, speciem.* Aa Fd [cf. c. 6!]
c. 10
d. p. c. 11
c. 12

C. 14, q. 5

d. a. c. 1
c. 1
c. 2
c. 3
c. 6
c. 8
d. p. c. 13
c. 14
d. p. c. 14: **1** *Sed hoc*

multipliciter − **9** *bonum possunt conuerti.*

C. 14, q. 6

d. a. c. 1
c. 1: **1** *Si res aliena* − **16** *in hominem seuiat.*

C. 15

d. init.

C. 15, q. 1

d. a. c. 1
d. p. c. 2
c. 3
d. p. c. 3: **1** *Ex eo autem* − **14** *penam aut gloriam.*
d. p. c. 4.
c. 5
c. 6: **5** *Quod possumus non* − **18** *malorum sorte numerauerit.*
c. 11
d. p. c. 11: **1** *Cum itaque qui* − **6** *obicitur autem:*
d. p. c. 12: **2** *Sunt quedam que* − **7** *muneris executionem inpediunt.*
c. 13
d. p. c. 13

C. 15, q. 2

d. a. c. 1
c. 1
d. p. c. 1

C. 15, q. 3

d. a. c. 1
c. 1
c. 2
c. 3
d. p. c. 3
c. 4

d. p. c. 4: **1** *Cum autem sacris* − **4** *hoc non infertur.* <*Quecumque enim persone humanis legibus copulari prohibentur et divinis, non omnium copula a sacris canonibus admittitur, quorum conventio legibus imperatorum indulgetur* Aa> + **9** *Quamuis igitur sacris* − **27** *credi non oportet.*
c. 5
d. p. c. 5

C. 15, q. 4

d. a. c. 1
c. 1

C. 15, q. 5

d. a. c. 1
c. 1
c. 2

C. 15, q. 6

d. a. c. 1
c. 1: **1** *Si sacerdotibus uel* − **8** *successoribus sustinere permittimus.* + **11** *Confessio ergo in* − **36** *aut necessitatem fiunt.*

C. 15, q. 7

d. a. c. 1
c. 1
c. 2
c. 3
c. 4
c. 5
d. p. c. 5
c. 6

c. 13
d. p. c. 14
c. 15
d. p. c. 15: **1** *Potest etiam aliter –* **5** *obici non potest.*
d. p. c. 16: **24** *Sed sola prescriptione –* **27** *spatio prescribi possunt.*
c. 17

C. 16, q. 4

d. a. c. 1
c. 1
d. p. c. 1
c. 2
c. 3
d. p. c. 3

C. 16, q. 5

d. a. c. 1
c. 1: **1** *Consuetudo noua in –* **12** *presumpserit anathema sit.* + **13** *Is autem qui –* **16** *neglexerit anathema sit.*

C. 16, q. 6

d. a. c 1
c. 1
d. p. c. 1
c. 2
c. 6
d. p. c. 7

C. 16, q. 7

d. a. c. 1
c. 1
c. 3 [following without rubric directly upon the end of c. 1]
c. 8
c. 9
d. p. c. 9
c. 10
c. 12

c. 14
c. 15
c. 16
c. 20
c. 21
c. 22
c. 23
c. 24
d. p. c. 30
c. 31: **1** *Filiis uel nepotibus –* **6** *iudici corrigenda denun-cient.* + **9** *Ipsis tamen here-dibus –* **10** *iuris potestatem preferre.*
c. 32
c. 33
c. 34
d. p. c. 36
c. 37
d. p. c. 38

C. 17

d. init.

C. 17, q. 1

d. a. c. 1
c. 1
c. 2
d. p. c. 4

C. 17, Q. 2

c. 1
c. 2
d. p. c. 2: **1** *Ecce iste se –* **4** *et ore pronunciauit.*

C. 17, q. 3

d. init.

C. 17, q. 4

d. a. c. 1
c. 1
c. 4

c. 5: **1** *Omnes ecclesiae rap-tores –* **4** *sacrilegos esse iudicamus.*
c. 39
c. 40
d. p. c. 42
c. 43
d. p. c. 43

C. 18

d. init.

C. 18, q. 1

d. a. c. 1
c. 1

C. 18, q. 2

d. a. c. 1
c. 1
d. p. c. 1
c. 2
c. 3
c. 4
c. 5: **1** *Quam sit necessar-ium –* **20** *aliquem honorem promoueat.*
d. p. c. 8
c. 9
d. p. c. 14
c. 15
d. p. c. 18
c. 19
d. p. c. 25
c. 26
c. 27
c. 28
d. p. c. 29
c. 30
d. p. c. 31

C. 19

d. init.: **1** *Duo clerici ad –* **2** *episcopo suo petiit.* + **4** *Modo queritur si –* **9** *eis monasterii ingressus.*

The contents of the first recension

C. 19, q. 1

d. a. c. 1
c. 1

C. 19, q. 2

d. a. c. 1
c. 1
d. p. c. 1
c. 2: **1** *Duae sunt inquit –*
3 *lex est canonum.* + *Lex*
uero priuata – **11** *in corde*
scribitur. <*Si quis horum*
qui priuata lege ducitur
spiritu sancto afflatus pro-
prium, quod sub episcopo
retinet, dimittere et in mon-
asterio se saluare uoluerit,
quoniam (quo Aa*) priuata*
ducitur publica lege non
tenetur. Dignior enim est
(est enim Aa*) priuata lex*
quam publica. Quisquis
ergo hac lege ducitur etiam
episcopo suo contradicente
erit liber nostra auctoritate.>
Aa Fd

C. 19, q. 3

d. a. c. 1
c. 1
c. 2
d. p. c. 2
c. 3
d. p. c. 3
c. 4: **1** *Que semel sunt –* **4**
fieri secularia habitacula.
c. 5
d. p. c. 5
c. 6: **1** *Monasteriis omnibus*
fraternitas – **4** *modo*
audeant tonsorare?
d. p. c. 6
c. 7
d. p. c. 8

C. 20

d. init.

C. 20, q. 1

d. a. c. 1
c. 1
d. p. c. 1
c. 2
c. 3
c. 4
c. 6
d. p. c. 7
c. 8
d. p. c. 8

C. 20, q. 2

d. a. c. 1
c. 1
c. 2
d. p. c. 3
c. 4

C. 20, q. 3

d. a. c. 1
c. 1
c. 2
c. 3
d. p. c. 3
c. 4

C. 20, q. 4

d. a. c. 1
c. 1
d. p. c. 1
c. 2
d. p. c. 3

C. 21

d. init.

C. 21, q. 1

d. a. c. 1
c. 1: **1** *Clericus ab instanti*
– **13** *michi opus erat* + **14**
ministrauerunt manus istae.
d. p. c. 1
c. 2
d. p. c. 2
c. 3
c. 4
d. p. c. 6

C. 21, q. 2

d. a. c. 1
c. 1
c. 2
d. p. c. 2
c. 3
d. p. c. 3: **1** *Sed aliud est –*
3 *omnibus modis prohibetur.*

C. 21, q. 3

d. a. c. 1: *Quod autem*
clerici secularium negotiorum
procuratores esse non valeant
auctoritate Calcedonensis
synodi probatur in qua sic
statutum est (om. Aa*)*
legitur: Aa Fd
c. 1
c. 2
c. 3
c. 4
c. 5
c. 6
c. 7

C. 21, q. 4

d. a. c. 1
c. 1: **2** *Episcopos uel clericos*
– **5** *qui unguentis unguntur.*
+ **14** *Priscis enim tempori-*
bus – **22** *domibus regum*
sunt.

C. 21, q. 5

d. a. c. 1
c. 1
c. 2

C. 22

d. init.

C. 22, q. 1

d. a. c. 1
c. 1
c. 2
c. 3
c. 6
c. 8
c. 13
c. 14
d. p. c. 14
c. 15
d. p. c. 15
c. 16
d. p. c. 16: **1** *Sic etiam cum* – **28** *creatorem iurat mendaciter.*

C. 22, q. 2

d. a. c. 1
c. 1
c. 2
d. p. c. 2
c. 3
d. p. c. 3
c. 4: <*Non est iudicandus mendax*> + **12** *qui dicit falsum* – **21** *autem uoluntate mentitur.*
d. p. c. 5: **1** *Ille ergo falsum* – **2** *esse quod iurat.*
d. p. c. 7
c. 8
c. 9
c. 10
c. 13
c. 14

c. 18
d. p. c. 21
c. 22
d. p. c. 22

C. 22, q. 3

d. init.

C. 22, q. 4

d. a. c. 1
c. 1
c. 2
d. p. c. 2
c. 3
c. 4
c. 5
c. 6
c. 7
c. 8: **1** *Unusquisque simplicem sermonem* – **17** *quod amicitiae fuit.*
c. 11
c. 12
c. 13
c. 14
c. 15
c. 16
c. 17
c. 18
d. p. c. 19
c. 20
c. 21
d. p. c. 21
c. 22
d. p. c. 22
c. 23
d. p. c. 23

C. 22, q. 5

d. a. c. 1
c. 1: **1** *Qui conpulsus a* – **3** *quam animam dilexit.*
c. 4
c. 5
d. p. c. 7

c. 8
d. p. c. 8
c. 9
c. 11
d. p. c. 11
c. 12
c. 13
d. p. c. 13
c. 14
c. 15: <u>*Item*</u>. *Pueri ante xiiii annos iurare non cogantur.* Fd
d. p. c. 17
c. 18
d. p. c. 19
c. 20

C. 23

d. init.

C. 23, q. 1

d. a. c. 1
d. p. c. 1
c. 2
c. 3
c. 4
c. 5
c. 6
d. p. c. 7

C. 23, q. 2

d. a. c. 1
c. 1
c. 2
d. p. c. 2
c. 3

C. 23, q. 3

d. a. c. 1
c. 1
d. p. c. 1
c. 2
c. 3
c. 4

c. 48
d. p. c. 48
c. 49
d. p. c. 49

C. 23, q. 6

d. a. c. 1
c. 1
c. 2
c. 3
d. p. c. 4

C. 23, q. 7

d. a. c. 1
c. 1
c. 2
c. 3
c. 4: <*Idem. Divitie impi-
orum iustis thesaurizantur.
Quicquid ergo nomine ecclesiarum a parte Donati pos-
sidebant, Christiani
imperatores (impii Fd)
legibus religiosis cum ipsis
ecclesiis ad catholicam trans-
ferre iusserunt. Et post
pauca:>* **28** *Si autem consi-
deremus –* **43** *societate
catholica utantur.*
d. p. c. 4

C. 23, q. 8

d. a. c. 1
d. p. c. 6
c. 7
c. 8
c. 9
c. 11
c. 12
c. 13
c. 14
c. 16
c. 17
c. 18
d. p. c. 18

c. 19
d. p. c. 20
d. p. c. 22
c. 24
d. p. c. 25: **1** *Hinc datur
intelligi –* **8** *pontificis fieri
debet. <Unde in quodam
concilio statutum est ut episcopi non proficiscantur ad
comitatum nisi formatas ab
apostolico acceperint.>*
d. p. c. 27: **1**
*Reprehenduntur ergo
Gallicani –* **6** *orationibus
Deo conmendent.*
d. p. c. 28
c. 29
c. 30

C. 24

d. init.

C. 24, q. 1

d. a. c. 1
c. 1
d. p. c. 3
c. 4
d. p. c. 4
c. 5
c. 6
c. 7
c. 8
c. 18
c. 19
c. 20
c. 22
c. 23
c. 25
c. 26: **11** *Fides ergo –* **25**
correptionem deuita
c. 30
c. 31
c. 33
c. 34
c. 35
c. 36

d. p. c. 37
c. 38
d. p. c. 39
c. 40: **1** *si quem forte –* **11**
unitatem seruabat [one
clause missing, see ch. 2].
c. 41
c. 42

C. 24, q. 2

d. a. c. 1
c. 1
c. 2: **13** *mortuos suscitasse –* **19** *esse absoluen-
dum*
c. 3
c. 4
d. p. c. 5
c. 6

C. 24, q. 3

d. a. c. 1
c. 1
d. p. c. 1
c. 2
c. 5
c. 6
c. 7
d. p. c. 9
d. p. c. 11
c. 12
d. p. c. 25
c. 26
c. 27
d. p. c. 27
c. 28
c. 29
d. p. c. 38
c. 39

C. 25

d. init.

C. 25, q. 1

d. a. c. 1
c. 1
c. 2
c. 3
c. 4
c. 5
c. 11
c. 12
c. 13
c. 14
d. p. c. 16

C. 25, q. 2

d. a. c. 1
c. 1
c. 7
c. 8
c. 9
c. 10
c. 11
c. 12
c. 13
c. 17
c. 18
c. 19
c. 21
d. p. c. 21
c. 23
c. 24
d. p. c. 24
c. 25
d. p. c. 25

C. 26

d. init.

C. 26, q. 1

d. a. c. 1
c. 1

C. 26, q. 2

d. a. c. 1

c. 1
d. p. c. 1
c. 2
c. 3
c. 4

C. 26, q. 3 & 4

d. a. c. 1
c. 1
d. p. c. 1
c. 2
d. p. c. 2
c. 3

C. 26, q. 5

d. a. c. 1
c. 1
c. 2
c. 4: **1** *Non oportet sacris* – **3** *suarum uincula conprobantur.*
c. 5
c. 6
c. 7
c. 11
c. 12
d. p. c. 13
c. 14

C. 26, q. 6

d. a. c. 1
c. 1
d. p. c. 3
c. 4
c. 5
d. p. c. 11
c. 12
c. 13: **1** *Agnouimus penitenciam morientibus* – **5** *Dei pietate* desperet. + **8** *Quid hoc rogo* – **22** *eo promittente promeruit.*
d. p. c. 13
c. 14

C. 26, q. 7

d. a. c. 1
c. 1
c. 13
c. 14
c. 15
c. 16
c. 16a: <*Ex concilio Ancirano. Quinquennio peniteant qui divinationes expetunt.* Qui divinationes expetunt et morem (more Fd) gentilium subsecuntur aut in domos suas huiusmodi (huiuscemodi Aa) homines introducunt, exquirendi aliquid arte malefica (maleficam Fd) aut expiandi (ex add. supra lin. Fd) causa, sub regula quinquennii iaceant secundum gradum penitentie (finitos add. Fd) definitos. > Aa Fd
c. 18

C. 27

d. init.

C. 27, q. 1

d. a. c. 1
c. 1
c. 2
c. 3
c. 7
c. 9: **1** *He uero que* – **3** *etc. et infra.* + **10** *Nam si Apostolus* – **13** *fidem conatae sunt?*
c. 10
c. 11
c. 12
c. 13
c. 14
c. 16
c. 17

c. 18 [continues immedi-
ately after the end of c.
17 without inscription
and rubric]: <*et ut propositum*> **20** *ualeat custodiri
detrudere* – **31** *ualeas solli-
citudine minuere.*
c. 20
c. 21
c. 22
c. 23
c. 24
c. 25
c. 27
c. 28
c. 31
c. 38
c. 39
d. p. c. 40
c. 41
c. 43
d. p. c. 43

C. 27, q. 2

d. a. c. 1
c. 1
c. 2
d. p. c. 2
c. 3
d. p. c. 4
c. 5
c. 6
c. 9
d. p. c. 10
c. 11
c. 12
d. p. c. 15
c. 16
c. 17
d. p. c. 18
c. 19: **1** *Sunt qui dicunt* –
14 *quis audeat accusare?* +
24 *Si uero continentiam* –
29 *habet sed mulier.*
c. 21
c. 22
d. p. c. 26

c. 27
d. p. c. 28
c. 29
d. p. c. 29
c. 30
d. p. c. 30
c. 31
d. p. c. 32
c. 33
c. 34
d. p. c. 34
c. 35
d. p. c. 35
c. 36
c. 37
d. p. c. 39
c. 40
c. 41
d. p. c. 41
c. 42
c. 44
c. 45
d. p. c. 45
c. 46: **1** *Desponsatas
puellas et* – **2** *ante fuerant
desponsatae.*
d. p. c. 47
c. 48
d. p. c. 48
c. 49
d. p. c. 49
c. 50
d. p. c. 50

C. 28

d. init.

C. 28, q. 1

d. a. c. 1
c. 1
c. 2
c. 3
c. 4
c. 7
c. 8
c. 9

d. p. c. 14
d. p. c. 17

C. 28, q. 2

d. a. c. 1
c. 1
c. 2
d. p. c. 2

C. 28, q. 3

d. a. c. 1
c. 1
c. 2
d. p. c. 2

C. 29

d. init.

C. 29, q. 1

d. init.: **1** *Quod autem
coniugium* – **84** *potest eam
dimittere.* [i.e. the three
last words – *et aliam
ducere* – are missing in
the first recension.]

C. 29, q. 2

d. a. c. 1
c. 1
d. p. c. 3
c. 4
c. 5
d. p. c. 6: **1** *Cum dicitur
sciens* – **4** *fraude decepta
est.*

C. 30

d. init.

C. 30, q. 1

d. a. c. 1

c. 1
c. 2: **1** *Si quis filiastrum –* **2** *ab uxore sua.*
d. p. c. 2
c. 3
c. 4
c. 5
c. 6
c. 7
d. p. c. 10

C. 30, q. 2
d. a. c. 1
c. 1

C. 30, q. 3
d. a. c. 1
c. 1
c. 2

C. 30, q. 4
d. a. c. 1
c. 1
c. 2
d. p. c. 3
c. 4
c. 5: **1** *Post uxoris obitum –* **5** *unionem spiritus pertransitur.* <*Post susceptum vero de fonte filium vel filiam spiritualem, qui ex conpatre vel conmatre nati fuerint, matrimonio coniungi non possunt, quia leges seculi non emancipatos adoptivis prohibent copulari.*>
d. p. c. 5: **1** *Notandum uero est –* **9** *uiro suo cognoscitur.*

C. 30, q. 5
d. a. c. 1
c. 1

c. 2
c. 3: **1** *Nostrates tam mares –* **16** *uelamen celeste suscipiunt.*
c. 5
c. 6
d. p. c. 6
c. 7
d. p. c. 8
d. p. c. 9
c. 10
c. 11
d. p. c. 11

C. 31
d. init.

C. 31, q. 1
d. a. c. 1
c. 1
c. 2
d. p. c. 2
c. 3
d. p. c. 3
c. 4
c. 5
d. p. c. 7: **1** *Sed obicitur David –* **14** *quam significatione futurorum.*

C. 31, q. 2
d. a. c. 1
c. 1
c. 3
d. p. c. 4

C. 31, q. 3
d. a. c. 1
c. 1
d. p. c. 1

C. 32
d. init.

C. 32, q. 1
d. a. c. 1
c. 1
c. 2
c. 3
c. 4
c. 6
d. p. c. 10: **13** *Si ergo ut –* **17** *sed adulteri appellantur.*
c. 11
d. p. c. 13
c. 14

C. 32, q. 2
d. a. c. 1
d. p. c. 1
d. p. c. 2
d. p. c. 4
c. 5
d. p. c. 5
c. 6
d. p. c. 16

C. 32, q. 3
d. a. c. 1
c. 1
d. p. c. 1

C. 32, q. 4
d. a. c. 1
c. 1
d. p. c. 2
c. 3
c. 5
c. 6
c. 8
c. 9
c. 10
d. p. c. 10: **1** *Ecce quod nullo –* **3** *nomine iudicantur indigni.*
d. p. c. 14
c. 15

C. 32, q. 5

d. a. c. 1
c. 1
c. 3
c. 4: **10** *Idem: Lucretiam matronam* – **26** *unus adulterium admisit.*
c. 6: **1** *De pudicitia quis* – **5** *possit in corpore.* + **12** *Item Augustinus in* – **15** *prius insita castitate.*
d. p. c. 14
c. 15
c. 16
d. p. c. 16
c. 17
c. 18
c. 19
c. 20

C. 32, q. 6

d. a. c. 1
c. 1
c. 2
c. 3
d. p. c. 5

C. 32, q. 7

d. a. c. 1
c. 1
c. 2
c. 3
c. 4
c. 8
c. 9
c. 10
d. p. c. 16
c. 17
c. 18
d. p. c. 18
c. 19
c. 20
c. 21
c. 22
c. 23

d. p. c. 24
c. 25
d. p. c. 26
c. 27
c. 28

C. 32, q. 8

d. a. c. 1
c. 1

C. 33

d. init.

C. 33, q. 1

d. a. c. 1
c. 1
c. 2
d. p. c. 2
c. 3
d. p. c. 3
c. 4
d. p. c. 4

C. 33, q. 2

d. a. c. 1
c. 1
d. p. c. 4
c. 5
d. p. c. 5
c. 6
c. 8
c. 9
d. p. c. 9: **1** *In premissis auctoritatibus* – **6** *eis misericordia inpendatur.*
d. p. c. 10
c. 11
d. p. c. 11
d. p. c. 12
c. 13
c. 14
c. 19

C. 33, q. 3

TRACTATUS DE PENITENTIA

de pen. D. 1
d. a. c. 1: **1** *Utrum sola cordis* – **5** *promereri iuxta illud <Leonis pape:>*
c. 1: **2** *Lacrimas <Petri> lego, satisfactionem non lego.*
c. 2
c. 3
c. 4
c. 5
c. 30 [continues from c. 5 without inscription or rubric]: **4** *Item sicut auctoritas* – **7** *in oris confessione.*
d. p. c. 30
c. 31
c. 32
d. p. c. 32
c. 33
d. p. c. 33
c. 34
d. p. c. 34
c. 35
d. p. c. 35
c. 36
d. p. c. 36
c. 37
d. p. c. 37
c. 38
c. 39
c. 40
c. 42
c. 43
c. 44
c. 49
c. 50
c. 51 [continues from c. 50 without inscription or rubric]: **3** *Et paulo post* – **10** *Dei non habet.*
c. 52
c. 54
c. 55

c. 56: **1** *Sunt qui arbitren-*
tur – **19** *usurpatores esse*
debere. + **24** *Et infra:*
Nichil – **29** *conditionis*
intentione defluxerit.
d. p. c. 6o
c. 61
c. 62
c. 63
c. 64
c. 65
c. 66
c. 67
c. 68
c. 78
c. 79
c. 80
c. 81: **1** *Tres sunt autem –*
22 *Domino utique iudicare-*
mur.
c. 87
d. p. c. 87: **1** *His auctori-*
tatibus asseritur – **32** *iugiter*
confiteri debemus. + **41**
Similiter et illud – **203** *de*
penitencia ait.
c. 88
d. p. c. 89
c. 90

de pen. D. 2
d. a. c. 1: **3** *Alii dicunt*
penitenciam – **11** *tibi*
aliquid contingat.
d. p. c. 1
c. 2
c. 3
c. 4
c. 5
c. 6
c. 7
c. 8
c. 9
c. 10
c. 11
c. 12
d. p. c. 12
c. 13

d. p. c. 13
c. 14
d. p. c. 14
c. 15
c. 16
c. 18
c. 17
c. 19
c. 20
d. p. c. 24: **3** *Hec itaque*
karitas – **12** *redeunt et cet.*
c. 25
c. 26
c. 27
c. 28
c. 29
d. p. c. 29
c. 30
d. p. c. 30
c. 31
c. 32
c. 33
c. 34
c. 35
c. 36
c. 37
c. 38
c. 39
d. p. c. 39
c. 40
d. p. c. 40
c. 41
d. p. c. 41
c. 42
d. p. c. 42
c. 43
d. p. c. 43
c. 44
d. p. c. 44
c. 45
d. p. c. 45

de pen. D. 3
d. a. c. 1
c. 1
c. 2
c. 3
c. 4

d. p. c. 4
c. 5
c. 6: **1** *Penitenciam agere*
digne – **7** *auaritiae estibus*
anhelat?
c. 8
c. 9
c. 10
c. 11
c. 12
c. 13
c. 14
c. 15
c. 16
c. 17
d. p. c. 17
d. p. c. 21
c. 22
d. p. c. 22
c. 23
d. p. c. 23
c. 24
d. p. c. 26
c. 27
c. 28
d. p. c. 29
c. 30
c. 31
d. p. c. 31
c. 32
c. 33
d. p. c. 33
c. 34
c. 35
d. p. c. 39
c. 40
c. 41
d. p. c. 41
c. 42
d. p. c. 42
c. 43
d. p. c. 43
c. 44
d. p. c. 44
c. 45
c. 46
d. p. c. 46
c. 47

225

d. p. c. 48
c. 49
d. p. c. 49

de pen. D. 4
d. a. c. 1
c. 1
c. 2
c. 3
c. 4
c. 5
c. 6
c. 7
d. p. c. 7
c. 8
d. p. c. 8
c. 9
d. p. c. 9
c. 10
d. p. c. 10
c. 11
d. p. c. 11
c. 12
d. p. c. 12
c. 13
c. 14
d. p. c. 14
c. 15
c. 16
c. 17
c. 18
c. 19
d. p. c. 19
c. 20
d. p. c. 20
c. 21
c. 22
c. 23
d. p. c. 24

de pen. D. 5
d. a. c. 1
c. 1

de pen. D. 6
d. a. c. 1
c. 1
d. p. c. 2

de pen. D. 7
d. a. c. 1
d. p. c. 1
c. 2: **1** *Si quis positus* – **4** *bene hinc exit* + **10** *Si autem uis* – **11** *non tu illa.*
d. p. c. 4
c. 5
c. 6

C. 33, q. 4
d. a. c. 1
c. 1
c. 2
c. 6
d. p. c. 11
c. 12

C. 33, q. 5
d. a. c. 1
c. 1
c. 2
c. 3
c. 4: **1** *Quod Deo pari* – **6** *nullus defendisset annorum.*
c. 6
c. 10
c. 11
d. p. c. 11
c. 12
c. 13
c. 14
c. 15
c. 16
c. 17
c. 18
c. 19
c. 20
d. p. c. 20

C. 34
d. init.

C. 34, qq. 1 & 2
d. a. c. 1
c. 1: **1** *Cum per bellicam* – **19** *tamen culpabilis iudicetur* <*si*> **22** *in ius alienum* – **45** *merito sunt laudandae.*
c. 2

C. 35
d. init.

C. 35, q. 1
d. a. c. 1
c. 1
d. p. c. 1

C. 35, qq. 2 & 3
d. a. c. 1
c. 1
c. 3
c. 4
c. 7
c. 10: **1** *Nec eam quam* – **5** *et cunctis hominibus.*
c. 12
c. 13
c. 14
c. 16
c. 18
c. 19
d. p. c. 19
c. 20
c. 21
d. p. c. 21: **1** *Hac auctoritate dum* – **28** *ducant in uxorem.*
d. p. c. 22

C. 35, q. 4
d. a. c. 1
c. 1

BIBLIOGRAPHY

Alberigo, Giuseppe, ed., *Conciliorum oecumenicorum decreta*. 3rd edn. Bologna 1973; reprinted with facing English translation as *The Decrees of the Ecumenical Councils*, ed. Norman P. Tanner. London and Washington, D.C. 1990.

André, Jacques, *Règles et recommendations pour les éditions critiques, série latine*. Paris 1972.

Anselm of Lucca, *Anselmi episcopi Lucensis collectio canonum una cum collectione minore*, ed. by Friedrich Thaner. Innsbruck 1906–1915.

Behrends, Frederick, "Two spurious letters in the Fulbert collection." *Revue bénédictine* 80 (1970), 253–275.

Bellomo, Manlio, *The Letters and Poems of Fulbert of Chartres*. Oxford Medieval Texts. Oxford 1976.

    The Common Legal Past of Europe, 1000–1800. Studies in Medieval and Early Modern Canon Law 4. Washington, D.C. 1995.

Berardi, Carlo Sebastiano, *Gratiani canones genuini ab apocryphiis discreti*. Venice 1783.

Berger, Adolf, *Encyclopedic Dictionary of Roman Law*. Transactions of the American Philosophical Society, n.s. 43: 2. Philadelphia 1953.

Besta, Enrico, *L'opera d'Irnerio* II. Turin 1896.

Beyer, Alfred, *Lokale Abbreviationen des "Decretum Gratiani": Analyse und Vergleich der Dekretabbreviationen "Omnes leges aut divine" (Bamberg), "Humanum genus duobus regitur" (Pommersfelden) und "De his qui intra claustra monasterii consistunt" (Lichtenthal, Baden-Baden)*. Bamberger theologische Studien 6. Frankfurt am Main 1998.

Biblia latina cum glossa ordinaria. Strasburg *c.* 1480; reprinted Turnhout 1992.

Bibliotheca Casinensis seu codicum manuscriptorum qui in tabulario Casinensi asservantur series II. Montecassino 1875.

Blatt, Franz, *Novum glossarium mediae latinitatis*, M–N. Copenhagen 1959–1969.

Brasington, Bruce C., Review of *Origins of Medieval Jurisprudence*, by Charles M. Radding. In *Comitatus: A Journal of Medieval and Renaissance Studies* 20 (1989), 97–100.

Brett, Martin, "The canons of the First Lateran Council in English manuscripts." In *Proceedings of the Sixth International Congress of Medieval Canon Law*. MIC Subs. 7. Vatican City 1985, 13–28.

    "Urban II and the collections attributed to Ivo of Chartres." In *Proceedings of the Eighth International Congress of Medieval Canon Law*. MIC Subs. 9. Vatican City

1992, 27–46.

"The sources and influence of Paris, Bibliothèque de l'Arsenal MS 713." In *Proceedings of the Ninth International Congress of Medieval Canon Law.* MIC Subs. 10. Vatican City 1996, 149–167.

Brixius, Johannes Matthias, *Die Mitglieder des Kardinalkollegiums von 1130–1181.* Berlin 1912.

Brundage, James, Review of *The Origins of Medieval Jurisprudence: Pavia and Bologna 850–1150,* by Charles M. Radding. In *Journal of the History of the Behavioral Sciences* 26 (1990), 400–402.

Medieval Canon Law. London and New York 1995.

Busch, Jörg, *Der "Liber de honore ecclesiae" des Placidus von Nonantola: Eine Problemerörterung aus dem Jahre 1111: Die Arbeitsweise ihres Autors und seine Vorlagen.* Quellen und Forschungen zum Recht im Mittelalter 5. Sigmaringen 1990.

Catalunya Medieval: Del 20 de maig al 10 d'agost, Barcelona 1992. Barcelona 1992.

Cencetti, Giorgio, "Studium fuit Bononie: Note sulle storia dell'Università di Bologna nel primo mezzo secolo della sua esistenza." *Studi medievali,* ser. 3, vol. 7, fasc. 2. Spoleto 1966, 781–833.

Cetedoc Library of Christian Latin Texts: CLCLT. Turnhout 1981–. CD-ROM.

Chodorow, Stanley, *Christian Political Theory and Church Politics in the Mid-Twelfth Century.* Publications of the Center for Medieval and Renaissance Studies, UCLA 5. Berkeley 1972.

Review of *The Origins of Medieval Jurisprudence,* by Charles M. Radding. In *Speculum* 65 (1990), 743–745.

Classen, Peter, *Gerhoch von Reichersberg: Eine Biographie.* Wiesbaden 1960.

Clercq, Carolus de, ed., *Concilia Galliae, 511–695.* Corpus Christianorum: Series latina 148 A. Turnhout 1963.

Coing, Helmuth, ed., *Handbuch der Quellen und Literatur der neueren Europäischen Privatrechtsgeschichte* I. Munich 1973.

Corpus scriptorum ecclesiasticorum latinorum. Vienna 1866–.

Cortese, Ennio, *Il diritto nella storia medievale.* II, *Il basso medioevo.* Rome 1995.

Il rinascimento giuridico medievale. 2nd edn. Rome 1996.

Cushing, Kathleen G., *Papacy and Law in the Gregorian Revolution: The Canonistic Work of Anselm of Lucca.* Oxford Historical Monographs. Oxford 1998.

Deusdedit, *Die Kanonessammlung des Kardinals Deusdedit,* ed. Victor Wolf von Glanvell. Paderborn 1905.

Di Domenico, Adriana, "Codici miniati romanici nel fondo Conventi soppressi della Biblioteca Nazionale Centrale di Firenze. Camaldoli – Vallombrosa – Santa Maria Novella." Doctoral dissertation, Università degli Studi di Firenze, 1989–1990.

Dolcini, Carlo, *"Velut aurora surgente": Pepo, il vescovo Pietro e l'origine dello studium Bolognese.* Istituto storico Italiano per il medio evo: Studi storici 180. Rome 1987.

Dolezalek, Gero, Review of *Wernerius Bononiensis iudex,* by Enrico Spagnesi. In *ZRG RA* 88 (1971), 493–497.

"Tractatus de diligentia et dolo et culpa et fortuito casu: Eine Abhandlung über die Haftung für Beschädigung oder den Untergang von Sachen aus dem zwölften Jahrhundert." In *Aspekte Europäischer Rechtsgeschichte: Festgabe für Helmut Coing zum 70. Geburtstag.* Ius commune, Sonderhefte: Texte und Monographien 17. Frankfurt am Main 1982, 87–121.

Bibliography

Repertorium manuscriptorum veterum Codicis Iustiniani. Ius commune, Sonderhefte: Texte und Monographien 23: Repertorien zur Frühzeit der gelehrten Rechte. Frankfurt am Main 1985.

"The *Lectura Codicis* of Odofredus, *recensio I,* and Jacobus Balduini. In *The Two Laws: Studies in Medieval Legal History Dedicated to Stephan Kuttner,* ed. Laurent Mayali and Stephanie A. J. Tibbets. Studies in Medieval and Early Modern Canon Law 1. Washington, D.C. 1990, 97–120.

"Les gloses des manuscrits de droit: reflet des méthodes d'enseignement." In *Manuel, programmes de cours et techniques d'enseignement dans les universités médiévales.* Louvain-la-Neuve 1994, 235–255.

Dolezalek, Gero and Rudolf Weigand, "Das Geheimnis der roten Zeichen." *ZRG KA* 69 (1983), 143–199.

Donahue, Charles, "Law, civil." In *Dictionary of the Middle Ages,* ed. Joseph Strayer. New York 1982–1989.

Eheim, Fritz, "Die Handschriften des *Decretum Gratiani* in Österreich." *Studia Gratiana* 7 (1959), 125–173.

Erickson, John H., "The *Collection in Three Books* and Gratian's *Decretum.*" *BMCL* 2 (1972), 67–75.

Ewald, Paul, "Die Papstbriefe der Brittischen Sammlung." *Neues Archiv der Gesellschaft für ältere deutsche Geschichtskunde* 5 (1880), 275–414, 503–596.

Fornasari, Mario, "Collectio canonum Barberiniana." *Apollinaris* 36 (1963), 127–141, 214–297.

Initia canonum a primaevis collectionibus usque ad "Decretum Gratiani." Monumenta Italiae ecclesiastica, Subsidia 1. Florence 1972.

Fournier, Paul, "Une collection canonique italienne du commencement du XIIe siècle." *Annales de l'enseignement supérieur de Grenoble* 6 (1894), 343–438.

"Deux controverses sur les origines du *Décret* de Gratien." *Revue d'histoire et de littérature religieuses* 3 (1898), 97–116, 253–280; reprinted in Paul Fournier, *Mélanges de droit canonique,* ed. Theo Kölzer. Aalen 1983. I 751–797.

Fournier, Paul and Gabriel Le Bras, *Histoire des collections canoniques en Occident depuis les Fausses Décrétals jusqu'au "Décret" de Gratien.* Paris 1931–1932.

Fowler-Magerl, Linda, "Vier französische und spanische vorgratianische Kanonessammlungen." In *Aspekte europäischer Rechtsgeschichte: Festgabe für Helmut Coing zum 70. Geburtstag.* Ius commune, Sonderhefte: Texte und Monographien 17. Frankfurt am Main 1982, 145–146.

Ordo iudiciorum vel ordo iudiciarius: Begriff und Literaturgattung. Ius commune, Sonderhefte, Texte und Monographien 19. Frankfurt am Main 1984.

Kanones: A Selection of Canon Law Collections Compiled Outside Italy between 1000 and 1140. Piesenkofen 1998. CD-ROM.

Fransen, Gérard, "Manuscrits canoniques conservés en Espagne (Fournier, Paul)." *Revue d'histoire ecclésiastique* 49 (1954), 152–156.

"La date du *Décret* de Gratien." *Revue d'histoire ecclésiastique* 51 (1956), 521–531.

Fried, Johannes, "Die römische Kurie und die Anfänge der Prozeßliteratur." *ZRG KA* 59 (1973), 151–174.

Die Entstehung des Juristenstandes im 12. Jahrhundert. Forschungen zur neueren Privatrechtsgeschichte 21. Cologne 1974.

Friedberg, Emil, ed., *Corpus iuris canonici.* I, *Decretum magistri Gratiani.* Leipzig 1879.

ed., *Quinque compilationes antiquae nec non Collectio canonum Lipsiensis.* Leipzig 1882.

Bibliography

Fuhrmann, Horst, *Einfluß und Verbreitung der pseudo-isidorischen Fälschungen von ihrem Auftauchen bis in die neuere Zeit.* MGH Schriften 24. Munich 1972–1974.

[Fulgentius of Ruspe], *Sancti Fulgentii episcopi Ruspensis opera,* ed. J. Fraipont and C. Lambot. Corpus Christianorum: Series latina 91A. Turnhout 1968.

García, Zacharias, "Bibliotheca Patrum Latinorum Hispaniensis, 2." In *Sitzungsberichte der Kaiserlichen Akademie der Wissenschaften, philosophisch-historische Klasse* 169: 2. Vienna 1915.

García y García, Antonio, "Los manuscritos del *Decreto* de Graciano en las bibliotecas y archivos de España." *Studia Gratiana* 8 (1962), 159–193.

Iglesia, Sociedad y Derecho. Bibliotheca Salmanticensis, Estudios 74. Salamanca 1985.

Gaudemet, Jean, "Das römische Recht im *Dekret* Gratians." *Österreichisches Archiv für Kirchenrecht* 12 (1961), 177–191; reprinted in Gaudemet, *La formation du droit canonique médiéval,* no. IX.

"Les Doublets dans le *Décret* de Gratien." In *Atti del II Congresso internazionale della Società italiana di storia del diritto, Venezia 1967.* Florence 1972, 269–290; reprinted in Gaudemet, *La formation du droit canonique médiéval,* no. XI.

La formation du droit canonique médiéval. Collected Studies CS 111. London 1980.

Ghellinck, Joseph de, *Le mouvement théologique du XIIe siècle.* Museum Lessianum: Section historique 10. 2nd edn. Bruges 1948.

Gilchrist, J. T., "The *Polycarpus.*" *ZRG KA* 68 (1982), 441–452.

"Die *Epistola Widonis* oder Pseudo-Paschalis: Der erweiterte Text." *Deutsches Archiv für Erforschung des Mittelalters* 37 (1981), 576–604.

Gordley, James and Ugo A. Mattei, "Protecting possession." *The American Journal of Comparative Law* 44 (1996), 293–334.

Gossman, Francis, *Pope Urban II and Canon Law.* Washington, D.C. 1960.

Gratian, *Decretum Gratiani . . . una cum glossis Gregorii XIII pont. max. iussu editum.* Venice 1600.

The Treatise on Laws (Decretum DD. 1–20), trans. Augustine Thompson and James Gordley. Studies in Medieval and Early Modern Canon Law 2. Washington, D.C. 1993.

see also Friedberg, Emil.

Gujer, Regula, "Concordia discordantium codicum manuscriptorum? Eine Untersuchung zur D. 16 des *Decretum Gratiani* und zur Textentwicklung einiger ausgewählter Handschriften." Doctoral thesis, Universität Zürich.

"Zur Überlieferung des *Decretum Gratiani.*" In *Proceedings of the Ninth International Congress of Medieval Canon Law.* MIC Subs. 10. Vatican City 1997, 87–104.

Güterbock, Ferdinand, "Zur Edition des Geschichtswerks Otto Morenas und seiner Fortsetzer." *Neues Archiv der Gesellschaft für ältere deutsche Geschichtskunde* 48 (1930), 116–147.

Guyotjeannin, Olivier, Jacques Pycke, and Benoît-Michel Tock, *Diplomatique médiévale.* L'atelier du médiéviste 2. Turnhout 1993.

Haenel, Gustav, ed., *Lex Romana Visigothorum.* Leipzig 1848.

Heyer, Friedrich, "Der Titel der Kanonessammlung Gratians." *ZRG KA* 2 (1912), 336–342.

Hinschius, Paul, ed., *Decretales Pseudo-Isidorianae et Capitula Angilramni.* Leipzig 1863.

Hoffmann, Hartmut and Rudolf Pokorny, *Das Dekret des Bischofs Burchard von Worms: Textstufen – Frühe Verbreitung – Vorlagen.* MGH Hilfsmittel 12. Munich 1991.

Bibliography

Holtzmann, Walther, "Kanonistische Ergänzungen zur Italia pontificia." *Quellen und Forschungen aus italienischen Archiven und Bibliotheken* 38 (1958); also published separately, Tübingen 1959.

Horst, Uwe, *Die Kanonessammlung "Polycarpus" des Gregor von S. Grisogono: Quellen und Tendenzen.* MGH Hilfsmittel 5. Munich 1980.

Howlett, Richard, ed., *The Chronicles of the Reigns of Stephen, Henry II, and Richard I.* IV, *The Chronicle of Robert of Torigni.* Memorials of Great Britain and Ireland during the Middle Ages ["Roll Series"] 82. London 1889.

Hüls, Rudolf, *Kardinäle, Klerus und Kirchen Roms 1049–1130.* Bibliothek des Deutschen Historischen Instituts in Rom 48. Tübingen 1977.

Jaffé, Philipp, *Regesta pontificum Romanorum.* 2nd edn. Leipzig 1885–1888.

Jasper, Detlev, "Bernhard von Hildesheim." In *Die deutsche Literatur des Mittelalters: Verfasserlexikon* I. Berlin 1978, 766–767.

Kantorowicz, Hermann, "Die Allegationen im späteren Mittelalter." *Archiv für Urkundenforschung* 13 (1935), 15–29.

Kantorowicz, Hermann with W. W. Buckland, *Studies in the Glossators of the Roman Law: Newly Discovered Writings of the Twelfth Century.* Cambridge 1938; reprinted with "Addenda et corrigenda" by Peter Weimar, Aalen 1969.

Kantorowicz, Hermann and Beryl Smalley, "An English theologian's view of Roman law: Pepo, Irnerius, Ralph Niger." *Mediaeval and Renaissance Studies* I (1941–1943), 237–251; reprinted in Hermann Kantorowicz, *Rechtshistorische Schriften,* ed. Helmut Coing and Gerhard Immel. Freiburger Rechts- und Staatswissenschaftliche Abhandlungen 30. Karlsruhe 1970, 231–252.

Kaser, Max, *Das Römische Privatrecht.* Handbuch der Altertumswissenschaft, Abteilung 10, Teil 3, Band III. Munich 1954–1959.

Römisches Privatrecht: Ein Studienbuch. Kurzlehrbücher für das juristische Studium. 16th edn. Munich 1992. [The paragraph numbers correspond to those in other German editions as well as to those in Max Kaser, *Roman Private Law: A Translation,* trans. Rolf Dannenbring. Durban 1965 and later.]

Kehr, Paul, *Regesta pontificum Romanorum: Italia pontificia.* Berlin 1906–1975.

Krause, A., "Die Handschriften des *Decretum Gratiani* in der Admonter Stiftsbibliothek." In *Jahresbericht des Stiftsgymnasium in Admont m. Ö. R. über das Schuljahr 1950/51.* 1951.

Kretzschmar, Robert, *Alger von Lüttichs Traktat "De misericordia et iustitia": Ein Kanonistischer Konkordanzversuch aus der Zeit des Investiturstreits.* Quellen und Forschungen zum Recht im Mittelalter 2. Sigmaringen 1985.

Kuttner, Stephan, "Zur Frage der theologischen Vorlagen Gratians." *ZRG KA* 23 (1934), 243–268; reprinted in Kuttner, *Gratian and the Schools of Law,* no. III.

Repertorium der Kanonistik (1140–1234): Prodromus Corporis glossarum I. Studi e testi 71. Vatican City 1937.

"Zur neuesten Glossatorenforschung." *Studia et documenta historiae et iuris* 6 (1940), 289–294; reprinted in Kuttner, *Studies in the History of Medieval Canon Law,* no. I.

"The father of the science of canon law." *The Jurist* I (1941), 2–19.

"De Gratiani opere noviter edendo." *Apollinaris* 21 (1948), 118–128.

"New studies on the Roman law in Gratian's *Decretum.*" *Seminar* II (1953), 12–50; reprinted in Kuttner, *Gratian and the Schools of Law, 1140–1234,* no. IV.

"Additional notes on the Roman law in Gratian." *Seminar* 12 (1954), 68–74; reprinted in Kuttner, *Gratian and the Schools of Law, 1140–1234,* no. V.

Bibliography

"Annual report." *Traditio* 13 (1957), 463–466.

"Select bibliography 1959–1960." *Traditio* 16 (1960), 564–571.

"Some Gratian manuscripts with early glosses." *Traditio* 19 (1963), 532–536.

"Urban II and Gratian." *Traditio* 24 (1968), 504–505.

Gratian and the Schools of Law, 1140–1234. Collected Studies CS 185. London 1983.

"Gratien." In *Dictionnaire d'histoire et de géographie ecclésiastiques* XXI. Paris 1986, 1235–1239.

"Research on Gratian: Acta and agenda." In *Proceedings of the Seventh International Congress of Medieval Canon Law.* MIC Subs. 8. Vatican City 1988, 3–26; reprinted in Kuttner, *Studies in the History of Medieval Canon Law,* no. V.

Studies in the History of Medieval Canon Law. Collected Studies CS 325. Aldershot 1990.

Lampe, G. W. H., ed., *The Cambridge History of the Bible* II. Cambridge 1969.

Landau, Peter, *Die Entstehung des kanonischen Infamiebegriffs von Gratian bis zur Glossa ordinaria.* Forschungen zur kirchlichen Rechtsgeschichte und zum Kirchenrecht 5. Cologne 1966.

"Die Rubriken und Inskriptionen von Ivos *Panormie*: Die Ausgabe Sebastian Brants im Vergleich zur Löwener Edition des Melchior de Vosmédian und der Ausgabe von Migne." *BMCL* 12 (1982), 31–49.

"Neue Forschungen zu vorgratianischen Kanonessammlungen und den Quellen des gratianischen *Dekrets.*" *Ius commune* 11 (1984), 1–29.

"Gratian." In *Theologische Realenzyklopädie* XIV. Berlin 1985, 124–130.

"Quellen und Bedeutung des gratianischen Dekrets." *Studia et documenta historiae et iuris* 52 (1986), 218–235.

"Die Rezension C der Sammlung des Anselm von Lucca." *BMCL* 16 (1986), 17–54.

"Erweiterte Fassungen der Kanonessammlung des Anselm von Lucca aus dem 12. Jahrhundert." In *Sant'Anselmo, Mantova e la lotta per le investiture: Atti del Convegno Internazionale di Studi,* ed. Paolo Golinelli. Bologna 1987, 323–338.

"Gratian und die *Sententiae Magistri A.*" In *Aus Archiven und Bibliotheken: Festschrift für Raymund Kottje zum 65. Geburtstag.* Freiburger Beiträge zur mittelalterlichen Geschichte: Studien und Texte 3. Frankfurt am Main 1992, 311–326.

"Gratians Arbeitsplan." In *Iuri canonico promovendo: Festschrift für Heribert Schmitz zum 65. Geburtstag.* Regensburg 1994, 691–707.

"Gratian und Dionysius Exiguus: Ein Beitrag zur Kanonistischen Interpolationenkritik." In *De iure canonico Medii Aevi: Festschrift für Rudolf Weigand.* Studia Gratiana 27. Rome 1996, 271–283.

"Das *Register* Papst Gregorius I. im *Decretum Gratiani.*" In *Mittelalterliche Texte: Überlieferungen – Befunde – Deutungen,* ed. Rudolf Schieffer. MGH Schriften 42. Hanover 1996, 125–140.

"Burchard de Worms et Gratien: Pour l'étude des sources directes du *Décret* de Gratien." *RDC* 48: 2 (1998).

Landgraf, Artur Michael, *Dogmengeschichte der Frühscholastik.* Regensburg 1952–1956.

Lange, Hermann, *Römisches Recht im Mittelalter.* I, *Die Glossatoren.* Munich 1997.

Larrainzar, Carlos, "El *Decreto* de Graciano del códice Fd (= Firenze, Biblioteca Nazionale Centrale, Conventi Soppressi A.I.402): In memoriam Rudolf Weigand." *Ius Ecclesiae* 10 (1998), 421–489.

Legendre, Pierre, "Chronique de droit romain médiéval [C], I: Sur l'origine du sigle FF." *Revue d'histoire du droit* 4: 43 (1965), 309–310; reprinted in Pierre Legendre, *Ecrits juridiques du Moyen Age occidental.* Collected Studies CS 280. London 1988, no. Vc.

Lenherr, Titus, "Die Summarien zu den Texten des 2. Laterankonzils von 1139 in Gratians *Dekret.*" *AKKR* 150 (1981), 528–551.

"Arbeiten mit Gratians *Dekret.*" *AKKR* 151 (1982), 140–166.

"Fehlende 'Paleae' als Zeichen eines überlieferungsgeschichtlich jüngeren Datums von *Dekret*-Handschriften." *AKKR* 151 (1982), 495–507.

Die Exkommunikations- und Depositionsgewalt der Häretiker bei Gratian und den Dekretisten bis zur "Glossa Ordinaria" des Johannes Teutonicus. Münchener theologische Studien, III: Kanonistische Abteilung 42. Munich 1987.

Levy, Ernst, *West Roman Vulgar Law: The Law of Property.* Memoirs of the American Philosophical Society 29. Philadelphia 1951.

Lexikon des Mittelalters. Munich, 1977–.

Libelli de lite imperatorum et pontificum saeculis XI. et XII. conscripti. MGH. Munich 1891–1897.

McLaughlin, Terence, ed., *Summa Parisiensis on the "Decretum Gratiani".* Toronto 1952.

Magheri Cataluccio, M. Elena, and A. Ugo Fossa, *Biblioteca e cultura a Camaldoli: Dal medioevi all'umanesimo.* Studia Anselmiana 75. Roma 1979.

Manaresi, Cesare, ed., *I placiti del "Regnum Italiae."* Fonti per la storia d'Italia 97. Rome 1960.

Manitius, Max, *Geschichte der lateinischen Literatur des Mittelalters* III, Handbuch der Altertumswissenschaft, Abt. 9, Teil 2, Band 3. Munich 1931.

Mansi, Iohannes Domenicus, *Sacrorum conciliorum nova et amplissima collectio.* Florence and Venice 1759–1798.

Martínez Díez, Gonzalo and Felix Rodríguez, *La colección canónica Hispana.* Monumenta Hispaniae sacra, serie canonica 1. Madrid 1966–.

May, Georg, "Die Infamie im *Decretum Gratiani.*" *AKKR* 129 (1960), 389–408.

"Die Anfänge der Infamie im kanonischen Recht." *ZRG KA* 47 (1961), 77–94.

Melnikas, Anthony, *The Corpus of Miniatures in the Manuscripts of "Decretum Gratiani."* Studia Gratiana 18. Rome 1975.

Mesini, Carlo, "Postille sulla biografia del 'Magister Gratianus' padre del diritto canonico." *Apollinaris* 54 (1981), 509–537.

Metz, René, "A propos des travaux de M. Adam Vetulani." *RDC* 7 (1957), 62–85.

Migliorino, Francesco, *Fama e infamia: problemi della società medievale nel pensiero giuridico nei secoli xii e xiii.* Catania 1985.

Migne, J.-P., ed., *Patrologiae cursus completus: Series latina.* Paris 1841–1864.

Mirbt, Carl, *Die Publizistik im Zeitalter Gregors VII.* Leipzig 1894.

Mommsen, Theodor and Paul Krüger, eds., "Digesta." *Corpus iuris civilis* I. 17th edn. Berlin 1963.

Mor, Carlo Guido, "Il *Digesto* nell'età preirneriana e la formazione della 'vulgata.'" In Carlo Guido Mor, *Scritti di storia giuridica altomedievale.* Pisa 1977, 83–234.

Mordek, Hubert, "Auf der Suche nach einem verschollenen Manuskript . . .: Friedrich Maassen und der Traktat *De immunitate et sacrilegio et singulorum clericalium ordinum compositione.*" In *Aus Kirche und Reich: Studien zu Theologie, Politik und Recht im Mittelalter: Festschrift für Friedrich Kempf.* Sigmaringen 1983, 187–200.

Bibliography

Review of *The Corpus of Miniatures in the Manuscripts of "Decretum Gratiani,"* by Anthony Melnikas. In *ZRG KA* 72 (1986), 403–411.

Motta, Giuseppe, "A proposito dei testi di Origene nel *Decreto* di Graziano." *Revue bénédictine* 88 (1978), 315–320.

"Osservazioni intorno alla *Collezione Canonica in tre libri* (MSS C 135 Archivio Capitolare di Pistoia e Vat., lat. 3831)." In *Proceedings of the Fifth International Congress of Medieval Canon Law*. MIC Subs. 4. Vatican City 1980, 51–65.

Munier, Charles, ed., *Concilia Galliae, 314–506*. Corpus Christianorum: Series latina 148. Turnhout 1963, 193–194.

ed., *Concilia Africae, 345–525*. Corpus Christianorum: Series latina 149. Turnhout 1974.

Niermeyer, J. F., *Mediae latinitatis lexicon minus*. Leiden 1976.

Noonan, John T., "Who was Rolandus?" In *Law, Church, and Society: Essays in Honor of Stephan Kuttner*, ed. Kenneth Pennington and Robert Somerville. Philadelphia 1977, 21–48.

"Gratian slept here: the changing identity of the father of the systematic study of canon law." *Traditio* 35 (1979), 145–172.

Nordenfalk, Carl, Review of *The Corpus of Miniatures in the Manuscripts of "Decretum Gratiani,"* by Anthony Melnikas. In *Zeitschrift für Kunstgeschichte* 43 (1980), 403–411.

Odofredus Bononiensis, *Lectura super Digesto veteri*. Lyon 1550; reprinted as Opera iuridica rariora 2: 1. Bologna 1967–1968.

Omont, Henri, "Nouvelles acquisitions du département des manuscrits de la Bibliothèque Nationale pendant les années 1896–1897." *Bibliothèque de l'École des Chartes* 59 (1898), 81–135.

Otto Morena, *Das Geschichtswerk des Otto Morena und seiner Fortsetzer über die Taten Friedrichs I. in der Lombardei*, ed. Ferdinand Güterbock. MGH Scriptores rerum Germanicarum, Nova series, 7. Berlin 1930.

Pasqui, Ubaldo, *Documenti per la storia della città di Arezzo nel medio evo*, 1. Documenti di storia italiana 11. Florence and Arezzo 1899.

Pasztór, Edith, "Lotta per le investiture e 'ius belli': la posizione di Anselmo di Lucca." In *Sant'Anselmo, Mantova e la lotta per le investiture: Atti del Convegno Internazionale di Studi*, ed. Paolo Golinelli. Bologna 1987, 375–421.

Patrologia Latina Full Text Database. Alexandria, Va., 1992–. CD-ROM.

Paucapalea, *Summa über das "Decretum Gratiani,"* ed. Johann Friedrich von Schulte. Giessen 1890.

Pennington, Kenneth, "Learned law, droit savant, gelehrtes Recht: the tyranny of a concept." *Rivista internazionale di diritto comune* 5 (1994), 197–209; reprinted with corrections in *Syracuse Journal of International Law and Commerce* 20 (1994), 205–215.

"Medieval canonists: a bio-bibliographical listing," to appear in Pennington and Hartmann, eds., *History of Medieval Canon Law* x; provisionally available on the web at:
http://www.maxwell.syr.edu/MAXPAGES/faculty/penningk/biobibl.htm.

Pennington, Kenneth and Wilfried Hartmann, eds., *History of Medieval Canon Law*. Washington, D.C. 1999–.

Pescatore, Gustav, *Die Glossen des Irnerius*. Greifswald 1888.

"Verzeichnis legistischen Distinktionen mit Angabe des Verfassers." *ZRG RA* 33 (1912), 493–510.

Bibliography

Peter Lombard, *Magistri Petri Lombardi Sententiae in IV libris distributae.* Spicilegium Bonaventurianum, 4–5. Grottaferrata 1971–1981.

Peters, E., "Wounded names: the medieval doctrine of infamy." In *Law in Mediaeval Life and Thought*, ed. Edward B. King and Susan J. Ridyard. Sewanee Mediaeval Studies, 5. Sewanee 1990.

Pflugk-Harttung, Julius von, ed., *Acta pontificorum Romanorum inedita.* Tübingen 1880–1886.

Pinedo, Pablo, "Decretum Gratiani: dictum Gratiani." *Ius canonicum* 2 (Pamplona 1962), 149–166.

Radding, Charles M., *The Origins of Medieval Jurisprudence: Pavia and Bologna 850–1150.* New Haven 1988.

"Legal science 1000–1200: the invention of a discipline." *Rivista di storia di diritto italiano* 63 (1990), 409–432.

"Vatican Latin 1406, Mommsen's ms. S, and the reception of the *Digest* in the Middle Ages." *ZRG RA* 110 (1993), 501–551.

Rambaud-Buhot, Jacqueline, "L'étude des manuscrits du *Décret* de Gratien conservés en France." *Studia Gratiana* 1 (1950), 121–145.

"Plan et méthode de travail pour la rédaction d'un catalogue des manuscrits du *Décret* de Gratien." *Revue d'histoire ecclésiastique* 48 (1953), 215–223.

"Le legs de l'ancien droit: Gratien." In *L'âge classique 1140–1378*, by Gabriel Le Bras, Charles Lefebvre, and Jacqueline Rambaud. Histoire du droit et des institutions de l'Eglise en Occident 7. Paris 1965, 47–129.

"Les sommaires de la Panormie et l'édition de Melchior de Vosmédian." *Traditio* 23 (1967), 534–535.

Card files of notes on Gratian manuscripts, manuscript reading room, Bibliothèque Nationale de France, Paris.

Reuter, Timothy and Gabriel Silagi, eds., *Wortkonkordanz zum "Decretum Gratiani."* MGH Hilfsmittel 10. Munich 1990.

Rota, Antonio, "Il *Tractatus de equitate* come pars tertia delle *Quaestiones de iuris subtilitatibus* e il suo valore storico e politico." *Archivio giuridico* 146 (1954), 75–119.

Rybolt, John E., "The biblical hermeneutics of magister Gratian: An investigation of scripture and canon law in the twelfth century." Ph.D. dissertation, St. Louis University, 1978.

Sabatier, Petrus, *Bibliorum sacrorum latinae versiones antiquae seu Vetus Italica.* Paris 1743–1749.

Savigny, Friedrich Karl von, *Geschichte der römischen Rechts im Mittelalter.* 2nd edn. Heidelberg 1834–1851.

Schulte, Johann Friedrich von, *Die Geschichte der Quellen und Literatur des canonischen Rechts* 1. Stuttgart 1875.

Schwartz, Eduard, *Publizistische Sammlungen zum Acacianischen Schisma.* Abhandlungen der Bayerischen Akademie der Wissenschaften, philosophisch-historische Abteilung, Neue Folge 10. Munich 1934.

Schwartz, Gerhard, *Die Besetzung der Bistümer Reichsitaliens unter den sächsischen und salischen Kaisern mit den Listen der Bischöfe 951–1122.* Leipzig and Berlin 1913.

Seckel, Emil, *Heumanns Handlexikon zu den Quellen des römischen Rechts.* 9th edn. Jena 1914.

Smalley, Beryl, *The Study of the Bible in the Middle Ages.* 2nd edn. Oxford 1952.

Bibliography

Somerville, Robert, "Baluziana." *Annuarium Historiae Conciliorum* 5 (1973), 408–423; reprinted in Somerville, *Papacy, Councils, and Canon Law in the 11th–12th Centuries*, no. XIX.

"Pope Innocent II and the study of Roman law." *Revue des Etudes islamiques* 44 (1976), 105–114; reprinted in Somerville, *Papacy, Councils and Canon Law in the 11th–12th Centuries*, no. XIV.

"The councils of Pope Calixtus II: Reims 1119." In *Proceedings of the Fifth International Congress of Medieval Canon Law*. MIC Subs. 6. Vatican City 1980, 35–50; reprinted in Somerville, *Papacy, Councils, and Canon Law in the 11th–12th Centuries*, no. XII.

Papacy, Councils, and Canon Law in the 11th–12th Centuries. Collected Studies CS 312. Aldershot 1990.

"Papal excerpts in Arsenal MS 713B: Alexander II and Urban II." In *Proceedings of the Ninth International Congress of Medieval Canon Law*. MIC Subs. 10. Vatican City 1997, 169–184.

Somerville, Robert and Bruce C. Brasington, *Prefaces to Canon Law Books in Latin Christianity: Selected Translations, 500–1245*. New Haven 1998.

Somerville, Robert, with the collaboration of Stephan Kuttner, *Urban II, the "Collectio Britannica," and the Council of Melfi (1089)*. Oxford 1996.

Southern, R. W., *Scholastic Humanism and the Unification of Europe. I, Foundations*. Oxford 1995.

Spagnesi, Enrico, *Wernerius Bononiensis iudex: La figura storica d'Irnerio*. Academica Toscana di scienze e lettere "La Columbaria," Studi 16. Florence 1969.

Stelzer, Winfried, *Gelehrtes Recht in Österreich von den Anfängen bis zum frühen 14. Jahrhundert*. Mittelungen des Instituts für Österreichische Geschichtsforschung, Ergänzungsband 26. Vienna 1982.

Strayer, Joseph, ed., *Dictionary of the Middle Ages*. New York 1982–1989.

Teske, Gunnar, "Ein neuer Text des Bulgars-Briefes an den römischen Kanzler Haimerich." In *Vinculum societatis: Joachim Wollasch zum 60. Geburtstag*. Sigmaringendorf 1991.

Die Briefsammlungen des 12. Jahrhunderts in St. Viktor / Paris: Entstehung, Überlieferung und Bedeutung für die Geschichte der Abtei. Studien und Dokumente zur Gallia Pontificia/Etudes et documents pour servir à une Gallia Pontificia 2. Bonn 1993.

Theiner, Augustin, *Disquisitiones criticae in praecipuas canonum et decretalium collectiones*. Rome 1836.

Thiel, Andreas, ed., *Epistolae Romanorum pontificum genuinae et quae ad eos scriptae sunt a S. Hilaro usque ad Pelagium II*. Braunsberg 1867–1868.

Tierney, Brian, *Foundations of Conciliar Theory: The Contribution of the Medieval Canonists from Gratian to the Great Schism* (Cambridge 1955).

Torelli, Pietro, "Glosse preaccursiane alle *Istituzioni*: Nota prima: Glosse d'Irnerio." *Studi di storia e diritto in onore di Enrico Besta*. Milan 1939, 229–277; reprinted in Pietro Torelli, *Scritti di storia del diritto italiano*, Milan 1959, 43–94.

Turner, Cuthbert Hamilton, *Ecclesiae occidentalis monumenta iuris antiquissima: canonum et conciliorum Graecorum interpretationes Latinae*. Oxford 1899–1939.

Ughelli, Ferdinando, *Italia sacra sive de episcopis Italiae . . . opus singulare*. Venice 1717–1722.

Bibliography

Ullmann, Walter, "The paleae in Cambridge manuscripts of the *Decretum*." *Studia Gratiana* I (1953), 161–216; reprinted in Walter Ullmann, *Jurisprudence in the Middle Ages*. Collected Studies CS 120. London 1980, no. IV.

Van Engen, John, "Observations on *De consecratione*." In *Proceedings of the Sixth International Congress of Medieval Canon Law*. MIC Subs. 7. Vatican City 1985, 309–320.

Vetulani, Adam, "Une suite d'études pour servir à l'histoire du *Décret* de Gratien, II. Les *Nouvelles* de Justinien dans le *Décret* de Gratien." *Revue historique de droit français et étranger* 4: 16 (1937), 476–478; reprinted in Vetulani, *Sur Gratien et les décrétales*, no. II.

"Gratien et le droit romain." *Revue historique de droit français et étranger*, ser. 4, 24/25 (1946/1947), 11–48; reprinted in Vetulani, *Sur Gratien et les décrétales*, no. III.

"Encore un mot sur le droit romain dans le *Décret* de Gratien." *Apollinaris* 21 (1948), 129–134; reprinted Vetulani, *Sur Gratien et les décrétales*, no. IV.

"Nouvelles vues sur le *Décret* de Gratien." In *La Pologne au Xe Congrès international des sciences historiques à Rome*. Warsaw 1955, 83–105; reprinted in Vetulani, *Sur Gratien et les décrétales*, no. V.

"Le *Décret* de Gratien et les premiers décrétistes à la lumière d'une source nouvelle." *Studia Gratiana* 8 (1959), 275–353; reprinted in Vetulani, *Sur Gratien et les décrétales*, no. VIII.

Sur Gratien et les décrétales: Recueil d'études. Collected Studies CS 308. Aldershot 1990.

Viejo-Ximénes, J. M., "La redacción original de C. 29 del *Decreto* de Graciano." *Ius ecclesiae* 10 (1998), 149–185.

Vodola, Elisabeth, *Excommunication in the Middle Ages*. Berkeley 1986.

Wahrmund, Ludwig, *Quellen zur Geschichte des römisch-kanonischen Processes im Mittelalter* IV: 1. Innsbruck 1925.

Wattenbach, Wilhelm, "Iter Austriacum 1853." *Archiv für Kunde österreichischer Geschichts-Quellen* 14 (1855), 1–94.

Weber, Robertus, ed., *Biblia sacra iuxta vulgatam versionem*, 3rd edn. Stuttgart 1983.

Weigand, Rudolf, "Magister Rolandus und Papst Alexander III." *AKKR* 149 (1980), 3–44.

Review of *Die Exkommunikations- und Depositionsgewalt der Häretiker bei Gratian und den Dekretisten bis zur Glossa Ordinaria des Johannes Teutonicus*, by Titus Lenherr. In *AKKR* 156 (1987), 646–652.

"Fälschungen als Paleae im *Dekret* Gratians." In *Fälschungen im Mittelalter*. MGH Schriften, 33:2. Hanover 1988, 301–318.

"Frühe Kanonisten und ihre Karriere in der Kirche." *ZRG KA* 76 (1990), 135–155.

Die Glossen zum "Dekret" Gratians: Studien zu den frühen Glossen und Glossenkompositionen. Studia Gratiana 26–27. Rome 1991.

"Die Dekretabbreviatio 'Quoniam egestas' und ihre Glossen." In *Fides et ius: Festschrift für Georg May zum 65. Geburtstag*. Regensburg 1991, 249–265.

Review of *Sur Gratien et les décrétales*, by Adam Vetulani. In *ZRG KA* 78 (1992), 597–601.

Review of *The Treatise on Laws (Decretum DD. 1–20)*, by Gratian, transl. by Augustine Thompson and James Gordley. In *Theologische Revue* 92 (1996), 152–155.

Bibliography

"Zur künftigen Edition des *Dekrets* Gratians." *ZRG KA* 78 (1997), 32–51.

"Das kirchliche Wahlrecht im *Dekret* Gratians." In *Wirkungen europäischer Rechtskultur: Festschrift für Karl Kroeschell zum 70. Geburtstag*, ed. Gerhard Köbler and Hermann Niehlsen. Munich 1997.

"Chancen und Probleme einer baldigen kritischen Edition der ersten Redaktion des *Dekrets* Gratians." *BMCL* 22 (1998), 53–75.

"Versuch einer neuen, differenzierten Liste der Paleae und Dubletten im *Dekret* Gratians." In *Life, Law and Letters: Historical Studies in Honour of Antonio García y García*. Studia Gratiana 28–29. Rome 1998, 883–899.

"Mittelalterliche Texte: Gregor I., Burchard und Gratian." *ZRG KA* 84 (1998), 330–344.

Weimar, Peter, "Die Legistische Literatur und die Methode des Rechtsunterrichts der Glossatorenzeit." *Ius commune* 2 (1969), 43–83.

"Irnerius." *Lexikon des Mittelalters*. Munich, 1977–.

Werckmeister, Jean, "Les études sur le *Décret* de Gratien: Essai de bilan et perspective." *RDC* 48: 2 (1998).

West, Martin L., *Textual Criticism and Editiorial Technique*. Stuttgart 1973.

Wichner, Jacob, *Catalog of Manuscripts in Stift Admont, Austria*. Ann Arbor, Michigan: University Microfilms, 1982.

Winroth, Anders, "The making of Gratian's *Decretum*." Ph.D. dissertation, Columbia University 1996.

"The two recensions of Gratian's *Decretum*." *ZRG KA* 83 (1997), 22–31.

"Uncovering Gratian's original *Decretum* with the help of electronic resources." *Columbia Library Columns* 46: 1 (New York 1997), 26–31.

"Les deux Gratiens et le droit romain." *RDC* 48: 2 (1998).

ed., "Epistulae Alexandri papae secundi in *Collectione Britannica* asservatae." Unpublished edition.

Wojtyła, Karol, "Le traité *De penitentia* de Gratien dans l'abrégé de Gdańsk Mar. F. 75." *Studia Gratiana* 7 (1959), 355–390.

Wordsworth, Iohannes, H. I. White, and H. F. D. Sparks, *Novum testamentum Domini nostri Iesu Christi latine secundum editionem S. Hieronymi*. Oxford 1889–1954.

Zapp, Hartmut, "Paleae-Listen des 14. und 15. Jahrhunderts." *ZRG KA* 59 (1973), 83–111.

INDEX OF CITED PASSAGES IN GRATIAN'S
DECRETUM

INDEX OF PAPAL LETTERS

GENERAL INDEX

General index

General index

Pseudo-Isidorian Decretals, 15, 86, 92, 95, 148, 151, 154, 155
Pseudo-Ulric, Epistola de continentia clericorum, 91

Radding, Charles M., 171–172
Rambaud, Jacqueline, 13, 14, 28, 32, 128 n. 14, 129, 130
Ravenna, 143
reconciliation, see excommunication
Reggio Emilia, 143
restitutio in integrum, 148, 185
Richter, Emil Ludwig, 9
Ripoll, monastery, 26
Robert of Torigny, abbot of Mont St. Michel, 6
Rolandus, canonist, 141, 159, 178
Roman law, 2, 4, 12, 13, 14, 25, 26, 32, 144–145, 146–174, 191
   of barbarians, 150–151, 154
   glosses on 160, 168–170, 172–173
   Justinianic, 144, 146–147, 150–151, 154–156, 157, 159, 186, 195, 196
   pre-Justinianic, 148, 150, 154, 157
   of procedure, 161, 173–174
   vulgar, 148, 150, 151, 154
Rufinus, decretist, 141, 178

Salzburg, 23, 134, 177
Savigny, Friedrich Karl von, 157, 158, 162
scholastic methods, 2, 190, 193
Senatusconsultum Turpilianum, 155
sentence, judicial
   may be appealed, 79

corrupted, 109–110
to be feared, 78
forcing to evil, 112
unjust, 78–79, 113
unjust and iniquitous, 51–52, 99
unjust sentence harms only judge, 60, 68–70, 110
unjust sentence to be obeyed, 97
Sententiae magistri A., 17
Simplicius, pope, 103
Smaragdus, 89
Southern, R. W., 7, 170
Statuta ecclesiae antiquae, 94, 95
Stephen of Tournai, decretist, 153 n. 24, 178
Summa Parisiensis, 6, 153 n. 24, 154, 178, 189–190

Theuzo of Verona, 165

Ugo of Porta Ravennate, 158
Urban II, pope, 78, 139, 140, 189

Vetulani, Adam, 12, 13–14, 136, 142, 146–147
Vosmedian, Melchior, 16

Walfredus, 6
Walter, archbishop of Ravenna, 143
Weigand, Rudolf, 15, 23, 25, 26, 28, 32, 124, 134, 141–142, 178, 183, 186–187
Wenric of Trier, 101, 102, 103, 111, 118, 119
Wernerius, see Irnerius
Wido of Ferrara, 111
Wojtyła, Karol (Pope John Paul II), 13, 14
women as accusers, 151–153

Cambridge Studies in Medieval Life and Thought
Fourth series

Titles in series

★ *Also published as a paperback*